In this edition, a revised English translation, a new foreword, an introduction, the original Arabic text, and an expanded index of key words and concepts.

MILESTONES

ALONG THE WAY

by *Sayyid Qutb*

2nd edition

Published in the United States of America

Table of Contents

Foreword
The Relevance of Sayyid Qutb Half a Century after his Execution

Perhaps the fact that he was killed by the government, perhaps because of his ideas, or perhaps because of both, Sayyid Qutb remains a relevant figure more than 50 years after his death. His relevance is even more amplified, because he is also claimed by so many organizations within and outside the Arabic speaking world.

Born on October 9, 1906, in the town of Moshi in Asyut governorate, Sayyed Qutb took steps to claim cultural and religious authority that would prepare him to speak to power. He memorized the entire text of Qur'an before he reached the age of ten and he acquired a modern education in local public schools. At the age of 16, he moved to Cairo to complete his education and obtain a bachelor's degree from Dar al-'Ulūm College. In Cairo, he was influenced by Western ideas, socialist and otherwise, as were many Egyptian intellectuals of his generation. In 1929 he was admitted to Cairo University. After graduation, he was hired by the college, and he taught there for some time before joining the Ministry of Education as inspector of schools.

To understand his intellectual evolution, one must not underestimate Qutb's experience in the United States of America. Funded by the government of Egypt, Qutb traveled to the U.S. in 1948 to study education and curriculum development. Historical references indicate that his sending to the U.S. might have been motivated by the government's desire at the time to get rid of him so that his critical writings would stop or that he would be transformed by his experience in the powerhouse of the Western world. It did not. That journey, which only took two years, provided Qutb—the thinker and writer—with new evidence to oppose modern institutions and Western ideas.

In the U.S., he attended several institutions including Wilson Teachers' College in Washington, D.C., Colorado State College for Education in

Greeley, and Stanford University. He also traveled to other cities in the U.S. and visited Europe on his way back to Egypt. He thought that Western society was materialistic, corrupt, immoral, and filled with injustice. He was especially disturbed by what he characterized as pathological racism against Arabs and people of color in the United States and resented what he saw as prejudiced support for the state of Israel, which was founded in 1948. His book, *Social Justice in Islam*, is primarily a critique of American society and a commentary on Islamic ideals as he saw them.

Qutb's experience in the U.S. seems to have transformed him in more ways than his experience in Egypt did. He returned carrying a much anger against the West in general and the United States in particular, which he saw as the entity raising the banner of science while not possessing the spirit that is the basis of life. It is difficult to limit the emotional and material reasons that led him to the new vision that would then lead him to become an ideologue and subsequently an icon for Islamism of all its shades.

Before leaving for the U.S., his ideas were mostly of socialist bent. It was after he returned that he formally joined the Society of Muslim Brothers (*jam'iyyat al-ikhwān al-muslimūn*), the foremost Islamist movement founded in 1929 by Hassan al-Banna.

In July 1954, he was appointed editor-in-chief of the group's newspaper until it was closed by Nasser's regime two months later. Many of the leading figures of the group were subsequently arrested including Sayyid Qutb, who was sentenced to 15 years imprisonment. It was during this time that he wrote a commentary on the Quran, *In the Shadow of the Qur'ān*, which consisted of thirty parts bound in eight volumes.

Sayyid Qutb was released but arrested again few months later and charged with treason and of attempt to overthrow the Egyptian government. It was believed that the content of his book, *Milestones*, prompted the government to act. On August 19, 1966, Sayyid Qutb and two associates were handed a death sentence by a military tribunal. He was executed on August 25, 1966.

His political activism started early too, when he became a vocal supporter of al-Wafd Party, he composed many poems glorifying the party and praising its leader at the time, Saad Zaghloul. His intellect was initially influenced by Abbas al-Akkad, but it did not take him too long to develop his own social criticism and political activism. Qutb's intellectual and political evolution set the stage for many disparate entities to claim him as one of them after his death.

Communist parties claimed that he never left their camp. Others claimed that he joined the Freemasonry movement. Suspicions about Qutb's Freemasonry increased since he published many of his literary articles in the newspaper al-Taj al-Masri, the mouthpiece of the Egyptian Grand National Lodge. It was known at the time that Masonic newspapers did not allow anyone other than members of the organization to write for their publication, and an article entitled *"Why Did You Become a Freemason?"*, published April 23, 1943, was attributed to him.

However, other groups who wished to disconnect his links to this Western movement argued that Freemasonry at that time was only a social activity and was not in the form in which it was known later. Also, there were prominent figures who joined it before realizing its goals, and it is most likely that Qutb did not immerse himself or delve deeply into that experience.

Qutb's fluid evolution was anchored by one constant position—his persistent criticism of tyrannical regimes, making him a symbol of resistance to authoritarian regimes everywhere. In his clear articulation of rejecting tyranny, his rhetoric surpassed that of any of the opposition figures of the century including Hassan al-Banna, the founder of the Muslim Brotherhood. Such lucidity and courage challenging power holders made him an inspiring figure worldwide. Qutb's writings were widely spread around the world because of their special connections to discourses from disparate ideological and philosophical orientations, as his expressions were fused with literature, art, activism, and conscience.

One of the most important reasons that made his thought a threat to tyrants is that his resistance was centered around the idea of collective confrontation with an organic, dynamic organization, which constitutes a real threat to tyrants. The end of his life, too, was another factor behind the profound influence of Qutb—martyrdom, which gave his ideas and his devotion to them a garb of credibility.

A study, titled "The State among the Theoreticians of the Muslim Brotherhood," found that Qutb's strategy for change was one that coupled thought with action. The study concluded that, in Qutb's view, preaching and preaching alone is not enough. Instead, the study explained, Qutb called for the formation of a faith vanguard ready to act against the modern pre-Islamic regimes (New *Jāhiliyya*), a view that contradicted Hasan al-Banna's conciliatory views in this regard. In other words, Qutb believed that action (*Jihād*) is the primary means of getting rid of the obstacles that prevent the establishment of the Islamic state and liberate humanity from any authority other than the authority of God.

Qutb, according to those who knew him, was a determined and bright person. As a student, he ranked high among his peers. As an activist, he was a leader in student groups, and as an ideologue, he provided clarity and decisiveness.

While at Dar al-ʿUlūm, he founded the Brotherhood's branch and organized many debates during which he challenged the leadership of al-Rafi'i. One of his teachers, Muhammad Mahdi Allam, later described Qutb as "too forceful" and that "he was harsh in criticizing Ahmed Shawqi, delving into his poems until he identified faults in them." Another contemporary of his, Sheikh Ali Tantawi, who debated with him many times, described him as one who does not back down. Reflecting on Qutb's character, Tantawi said, "I did not imagine Sayyed as anything but a fighter. I only knew him to be a controversial, combative writer. Perhaps these are the traits that caused him to fall into violent clashes with his political opponents who believed that he was like other writers. Sayyed Qutb is one of the loyal guardians of the world of values, principles, and morals, which adorned his writings, especially his most famous book of all, *Milestones along the Way*." These are some of the opinions of some of his contemporaries, as expressed in interviews and lectures since his death.

Qutb is primarily a believer in the coupling of religious authority and political power. He contended that Islam is a realistic religion in the sense that it holds that prohibitions and directives alone are not sufficient, and it finds that religion does not exist without a state and without authority. He understood that religion is the system upon which people's practical lives are based, and not merely sentimental feelings that live in the conscience without authority, without legislation, and without a specific approach.

Sayyed Qutb looked at the establishment of an Islamic state wholeheartedly, and this is what he articulated during his imprisonment in his book, *Milestones along the Way*. In this work, he determined that the Western-led world order is bound to fail and collapse because of its emphasis on materialism and its rejection of spiritualism. In anticipation of this collapsing world order, he did not believe that the Islamic world will fill the empty space by default. Rather, he argued that there "must be an Islamic revival in order for it to play its expected role in leading humanity again." This perspective became foundational to other Islamist movements in the Islamic world to this day. However, none of these organizations addressed the reason why the contemporary Islamic world could fill the void by default. Why must Muslims go through a process f correction before they are able to take a leadership position? Did Islam mutate and became in need of reconfiguration, or has it not evolved yet to become in a position of leadership for all of humanity? Perhaps the lack of clarity is what made Qutb appeal to so many different Islamist trends, each projecting their own thinking in the empty spaces created by Qutb's ambiguity.

Tariq al-Zumar, the former leader of the Islamic Group, commented on Qutb's views by arguing that "Sayyed Qutb presented in his book an integrated political, social and economic vision that still maintains its credibility today."

Supporting Abdel Nasser revolution that removed the old regime, Sayyed Qutb, in the presence of Abdel Nasser and a wide audience of officers, diplomats, writers, and interested people in the Zamalek area, declared:

Revolution has truly begun, and we cannot praise it, because it has not done anything significant yet. The departure of the king is not the goal of the revolution, but rather its goal is to return the country to Islam... During the reign of the monarchy, I prepared myself for imprisonment at every moment, and I am no more secure in this era as well, or in anything other than prison, than before.

In a way, Qutb predicted that the man standing next to him, Nasser, could imprison him. Nasser did more than that—he killed him. He was jailed for ten years, then released in 1964. Only one year later, Sayyed Qutb published his book *Milestones along the Way*, after which he was hanged on August 29, 1966.

Qutb was not an outsider, an isolated figure in Egyptian society. Quite the opposite. He was one of the intellectual elites, a writer and critic, and a member of the Apollo School, connected to the writer Abbas Mahmoud al-Aqqad. Qutb had connections with the writers and notables of his time including Abbas Khadr, Abdel-Moneim Khallaf, Abdul-Hamid Gouda al-Sahar, Abdul-Qader Hamza, Ahmed Hassan al-Zayyat, Ahmed Zaki Pasha, Ali al-Tantawi, Anwar al-Maadawi, Ibrahim Abdul-Qadir al-Mazni, Mahmoud Taymour, Muhammad Mandour, Naguib Mahfouz, Taha Hussein, Tawfiq al-Hakim, and Yahya Haqqi—just to name few notables with whom he rubbed shoulders. None of that connection mattered given the uniqueness of his brand of thought and ideology. His words were not just words, they were interpreted by the political order as a plan of action for overthrowing the government. However, Qutb was more than a political activist, he was also an artist, a literary figure, and a social critic.

Ironically, political leaders' focus on his political thought masked Qutb's other contributions. The writings that threatened the ruling class did not include presenting Qutb as a critic and writer, and his Islamist audience did not care about his literary works, such as his love novel "Thorns"; his autobiography "A Child from the Village"; or his poem "The Four Specters". Similarly, the Islamist audience did not recognize Qutb's relationships with literary figures through his book "Books and Personalities," in which he reviewed works of writers of his time such as Taha Hussein, Abdel Hamid Gouda al-Sahar, and al-Zayat. Many would forget that he was the one who introduced Naguib Mahfouz to readers for the first time.

Qutb occupied a space that he created for himself. He was not a true traditionist, but he was not a true modernist either. Qutb's religious language is characterized by the simplicity of the idea. He was not a jurist who could follow the scrutiny of jurists in his writings, and he did not follow their terminology. He did not write in the language of al-Shāfiʿī, al-Ashʿarī, al-Ghazali, or Ibn Taymiyya. Similarly, in his criticism of modernity, he did not present himself as a philosopher using the language of Heidegger, Sartre, and Nietzsche, but rather a language that belonged to a new field—his own, one that flowed from him, in his tireless endeavor to redefine the role of religion in life.

This intellectual load, with its intersections, made Qutb's terminology a source of constant controversy. Writers, poets, jurists, and intellectuals will continue to dispute and contest their language, ideas and methodology. His recycled use of old terms like "believing community," "*jāhiliyya* society," "*ḥākimiyya*," "seclusion," "emotionalism," "ignorance," and "articulations" are all words that derive their power and meaning from the new framework that he proposed, the holistic one.

The new framework that Qutb introduced shattered traditional boundaries that separate Muslims along *ṭāʾifa* and *madhhab*. While doing so, his framework created a wide audience for Qutb far beyond the limits of anyone kind of Islamism, and perhaps far beyond Islam as well.

Consequently, Qutb is claimed by all, from the bottom-up social movements like the Muslim Brotherhood to the radical top-down Salafists like al-Qaeda; they all claim that Qutb was one of them, one who wrote for them, one who inspired them.

Many researchers found that Qutb has had an impact on the generation of Jihadists that emerged in the 1970s. Sharif Yunus, a historian, identifies Qutb's influence on the Jihadi groups that emerged in his time. The Jihadist historian and theorist Abu Musab al-Suri, too, concluded that "the thought of Sayyid Qutb was a "qualitative shift for the Islamic awakening" in general, and the book "*Milestones*" embodied Sayyed's thought, which is the thought of governance, differentiation, and articulation, drawing the path of Jihad." Ayman al-Zawahiri, the prominent leader of al-Qaeda, asserted that "the Jihadist movement in Egypt began its march against the regime after the mid-sixties, when the Nasserist regime launched its campaign in 1965 against the Brotherhood, and executed Sayyid Qutb."

The emergence of armed groups claiming affinity to Qutb continued, and among them was the Saleh Suriyah's group, or what was known as the "Military Technical Group," whose founder, Saleh Suriyah, built its foundations on the ideas of Sayyid Qutb.

During the same time, the Islamic Group arose in Egypt, and when it was founded by Hassan Abd al-Rahman, it adopted much of Qutb's literature, especially the ideas found in *Milestones*. It succeeded in assassinating Sadat when Khaled al-Islambouli, Tariq al-Zumar, and others in cooperation with the Egyptian Jihād organization, shot him during a military parade.

The Jihād Group was founded in Egypt, which originated entirely on Qutb's ideas, and several of its leaders were his students. Ayman al-Zawahiri, the leader of the Jihād Group before moving to Afghanistan, wrote a chapter in his book "Knights Under the Banner of the Prophet" entitled, "The Beginning," and made Sayyid Qutb's ideas the foundation for his own work. Members of this group later turned to al-Qaeda, which Osama Bin Laden relied on in the Afghanistan war, led by Ayman Al-Zawahiri, who became the organization's second-in-command after Bin Laden and inherited the group after his death.

Qutb's influence did not stop at the Egyptian Jihād movements, as many sects of Jihadists in the contemporary world were influenced by him, such as the influence of Sheikh Marwan Hadid's students in Syria and their fight against the regime in 1975.

A widespread dispute broke out among the members of the Brotherhood over the thought of Sayyid Qutb. Qutb debated Brotherhood leaders such as Salem al-Bahnasawi and Farid Abdel Khaleq, al-Banna's former secretary. Some of them reported that Sayyed Qutb announced at the time that he did not intend to describe societies in general as infidels, but the dispute between Qutb and some factions of the Brotherhood continued in prison.

Al-Hudaybi wrote a letter entitled "Preachers, Not Judges" after Qutb's death to respond to the label of "infidelity" (*takfir*) that was widespread among the Brotherhood during this period, and a number of those close to Qutb adopted it while in prison. However, al-Hudaibi did not attribute to Sayyid Qutb any of those ideas that were widespread.

It seems, then, that the attempt to interpret Qutb's words as carrying connotations beyond his original texts did not meet with consensus, despite Yusuf al-Qaradawi's reverence to Sayyid Qutb. Describing Qutb, Qaradawi stated:

> No fair scholar or just observer doubts that Sayyid Qutb is a great Muslim and a great preacher. He is a capable writer and a distinguished thinker, and he is a man who stripped his religion of all blemishes, surrendered his face to God alone, and made his prayers, rituals, life, and death belong to God, Lord of the Worlds, with no partner. There is no doubt about Sayyid Qutb's loyalty to his ideas that he believed in, and there is no doubt about his enthusiasm for it, and his death fighting for his deals, and that he placed his head on his palm, and sacrificed his soul for its sake.

The Saudi preacher Salman al-Awda wrote an article defending Qutb, and so did Ali Jarisha who said that "the scientific investigation proves that Sayyid Qutb is not responsible for the *takfir* doctrine. Because what he said is not to be taken to mean *takfir*, and this was confirmed by his brother, Muhammad Qutb, who denied this accusation." This was also the opinion of Rached Ghannouchi, head of the Ennahda movement in Tunisia.

Qutb's work will remain a case that is difficult for superficial interpretation in contemporary Islamic works, as it appears clear that Qutb's ideas carry a symbolic weight linked to his person, not just to his writings. Without doubt, Qutb as a person and as a thinker, was very controversial and that is why so many Muslims align themselves with his ideas and many others reject them. Some attribute the disparity to ambiguity. Others attribute it to evolution. Qutb, like Malcolm X of the Black Muslim movement in the U.S., evolved over time. That evolution created contradictory legacies. Whatever the case may be, Qutb is either a lesson in evolution of an Islamic thinker or a case study in incoherent thought—there is something to learn from him either way.

Qutb seems to inspire both violent Jihadist and a moderate reformist. Rafiq Habib presents an important vision in the context of Islamic currents' reading of Qutb's texts. He believes that one of the most important problems of Sayyid Qutb's thought is that he tried to combine change from below and change from above, and he tried to combine the extreme position on the current reality with the moderate position. Therefore, what Sayyid Qutb wrote became open to many interpretations, and at the same time made it inapplicable, and in his opinion, everyone who belonged to this approach either converted to the gradual reform approach or switched to the forceful, top-down change approach.

To appreciate the complexity of Qutb's ideas, one must consider Qutb's influence beyond the Sunni world. Shia founders of the modern-day Islamic republic of Iran often invoke Qutb in their political speeches and even religious lessons.

While most scholars contend that Khomeini was not influenced by Sayyid Qutb, it should be noted that such a conclusion is often justified by the lack of explicit reference to Qutb in Khomeini's writings and speeches. However, it is possible to infer that Qutb influenced Khomeini, and there are some instances that would support such a conclusion.

Khomeini's lectures, which were published in his book, *The Islamic Government*, were delivered after the execution of Sayyid Qutb and after some of his works were translated into Persian by Khomeini's students. In *The Islamic Government*, we find some similarities between some of Khomeini's ideas and the revolutionary ideas of Sayyid Qutb, if we exclude the additions related to the Shia doctrines in general and Khomeini's theroies in particular—such as his central thesis on guardianship of the jurist.

Ali Khamenei, who succeeded Khomeini, is one of the most prominent Shia leaders influenced by the ideas of Sayyid Qutb, and he described him as a "*Jihadi* thinker." Khamenei was influenced by Sayyid Qutb's thought during his youth and his involvement in secret cells opposed to the Shah's regime in Iran. He organized activist cells within the seminary in Qom in response to Khomeini's call in 1962, and Khamenei was arrested several times between 1962 and 1975.

Between the fascination on the part of his followers and the criticism and hatred on the part of his opponents, Qutb remains, fifty-fife years after his execution on August 29, 1966, a symbol, perhaps of truth from the point of view of his supporters, or terrorism according to his opponents.

This foreword is updated to account some of the commentaries and writings of more recent scholars who wrote about Qutb or who were engaged with the works of Qutb. This compilation of opinions and summary of ideas should provide more context to understanding one of Qutb's most influential writings, *Milestones along the Way*. This updated translation should be a welcomed addition to provide scholars and students of Islamic thought and events with direct access to one of the primary literatures in the field of modern Islamic thought and political activism.

The Editors

Tyler Capes, M. Al Khateeb, Abdulla Tahaoui, F. Hilmi, and Yousef Amr contributed to this edition.

January 2024.

Introduction

Today, humanity stands on the edge of the abyss, not because of the threat of annihilation hanging over its head—for this is a symptom and not the disease—but because humanity is bankrupt in terms of "values" necessary for human life to thrive truly and soundly. This is crystal clear in the Western world, which is unable to offer humanity any values. In fact, the Western world no longer possess anything that could convince its conscience that it deserves to exist now that, in it, democracy has attained what looks like bankruptcy whereby it gradually borrows from the Eastern camp especially in economic systems, namely socialism.

The Eastern camp, too, is experiencing the same conditions. The social theories, especially Marxism, which in the beginning attracted many people in the East and in the West itself, since it was a creedal ideology, it, too, lost its appeal as an "idea" and it survived as a state ideology present only within state institutions—a far cry from Marxism's foundational principles. Such theories, generally, conflict with human's nature and its corollaries. Such theories take hold in a broken environment or in one accustomed to prolonged dictatorship. However, even in these environments, these theories appear to fail in the economic and material realms— the realms for which they are supposed to excel. Russia, for instance, which exemplified the socialist order, is running out of fruit where it used to be abundant during the rule of the Tsars. Today, it imports food and wheat from abroad. Russia is forced to sell its gold reserves for food because its system of cooperative farming has failed, and its social order runs against human nature.

Humanity needs new leadership.

The Western man's leadership of humankind is nearing its end. It is coming to an end not because Western civilization is financially bankrupt or because its economic and military power has become weak. Rather, it is because the Western system has come to an end due to its depleted capital of "values" that could enable it to lead.

It is necessary for the new leadership to preserve and develop the material fruits of the creative genius of Europe, and also to provide humankind with such high ideals and values as have so far remained undiscovered by humankind, and which will also acquaint humanity with a way of life which is harmonious with human nature, which is positive and constructive, and which is practicable.

Islam is the only system which possesses these values and this way of life.

The period of the resurgence of science has also come to an end. This period, which began with the Renaissance in the sixteenth century after Christ and reached its zenith in the eighteenth and nineteenth centuries, does not possess a reviving spirit.

All nationalistic and chauvinistic ideologies which have appeared in modern times, and all the movements and theories derived from them, have also lost their vitality. In short, all man-made individual or collective theories have proved to be failures.

At this crucial and bewildering juncture, the turn of Islam and the Muslim community has arrived—the Islam that does not prohibit material inventions. Indeed, Islam counts it as an obligation on the human being from the very beginning of time, when God deputed him as His representative on earth, and regards it under certain conditions as worship of God and one of the purposes of the creation of the human species.

> And when Your Sustainer said to the angels, I am going to make My representative on earth. (Quran, 2:30).

> And I have not created *Jin* and humans except for the single purpose, which is that they worship Me. (Quran, 2:143).

The turn of the Muslim community has come to fulfill the task for humankind which God has enjoined upon it.

> You are the best community raised for the good of humankind. You enjoin what is good and forbid what is wrong, and you believe in God. (Quran, 3:110).

> We have made you a middle community, so that you be witnesses for humankind as the Messenger is a witness for you. (Quran, 2:143).

Islam cannot fulfill its role except by taking concrete form in a society and in a nation because the human being does not listen, especially in this age, to an abstract theory which did not materialize in a living society. From this point of view, we can say that the Muslim community (Umma) has been extinct for a few centuries. The Muslim community referred to here does not denote the name of a land in which Islam resides, nor is it a people whose forefathers lived under the Islamic system at some earlier time. It is the name of a group of people whose manners, ideas, concepts, rules, regulations, values, and criteria, are all derived from the Islamic source. Such a Muslim community with these characteristics vanished because the laws of God became suspended on earth.

If Islam is to play the role of the leader of humanity again, then it is necessary that the Muslim community be restored to its original form.

It is necessary to revive the Muslim community which is buried under the debris of the man-made traditions of several generations. The true Islamic community is now crushed under the weight of those false laws and customs which are not even remotely related to the Islamic teachings, a community, despite all this, calls itself the "Islamic world".

I am aware that between the attempt at revival and the attainment of leadership there is a great distance, as the Muslim community has long ago vanished from existence. The distance is broad also because the leadership of humanity has long since passed to other ideologies and other nations; other concepts and other systems have taken root. This is the era during which Europe's genius created its marvelous works in science, culture, law, and material production, due to which humanity has progressed to great heights of creativity and material comfort. It is not easy to find fault with the inventors of such marvelous things, especially since what we call the "world of Islam" is completely devoid of all this beauty.

But despite all this, it is necessary to revive Islam. The distance between the revival of Islam and the attainment of world leadership may be vast, and there may be great difficulties on the way. However, the first step must be taken for the revival of Islam.

If we are to perform our task with insight and wisdom, we must first clearly know the nature of those qualities based on which the Muslim community can fulfill its obligation as the leader of the world. This is essential so that we may not commit any blunders at the very first stage of its reconstruction and revival.

The Muslim community today is neither capable of nor required to present before humankind great genius in material inventions, which will make the world bow its head before its supremacy and re-establish once more its world leadership. Europe's creative mind is far ahead in this area and at least for a few centuries to come we cannot expect to compete with Europe and attain supremacy over it in these fields.

Therefore, we must have some other quality, the kind of quality that the modern civilization does not possess. This does not mean that we should neglect material progress. We should also give our full attention and effort in this direction, not because at this stage it is an essential requirement for attaining the leadership of humanity, but because it is an essential condition for our very existence. Islam itself, which elevates the human being to the position of representative of God on Earth, and which, under certain conditions, considers the responsibilities of this representative as the worship of God and the purpose of the human's creation, makes material progress obligatory for us.

To attain the leadership of humankind, we must have something to offer besides material progress, and this other quality can only be a faith and a way of life which, on the one hand, conserves the benefits of modern science and technology, and on the other hand, fulfills the basic human needs on the same level of excellence as technology has fulfilled them in the sphere of material comfort. Moreover, this faith and way of life must take concrete form in a human society—in a Muslim society that is.

If we look at the sources and foundations of modern ways of living, it becomes clear that the whole world is steeped in *Jāhiliyya*, (i.e., ignorance of the divine guidance) and all the marvelous material comforts and high-level inventions do not diminish this ignorance. This *Jāhiliyya* is based on rebellion against God's sovereignty on earth. *Jāhiliyya* transfers to man one of the greatest attributes of God, namely sovereignty, and makes some men lords over others. *Jāhiliyya* is now not in that simple and primitive form of the ancient *Jāhiliyya* but takes the form of claiming that the right to create values, to legislate rules of collective behavior, and to choose any way of life rests with men, without regard to what God has prescribed. The result of this rebellion against the authority of God is the oppression of His creatures. Therefore, the humiliation of the common human being under the communist systems and the exploitation of individuals and nations due to greed for wealth and imperialism under the capitalist systems are but a corollary of rebellion against God's authority and the denial of the dignity of the human being given to him by God.

In this respect, Islam's way of life is unique, for in systems other that Islam, some people worship others in some form or another. Only in the Islamic way of life do all human beings become free from the servitude of some men to others and devote themselves to the worship of God alone, deriving guidance from Him alone, and bowing before Him alone.

This is where the roads branch out. This is the new concept which we possess and can present to humanity. This and the way of life which this concept organizes for all the practical aspects of human's life. This is that vital message which humanity does not know. It is not a product of Western invention or of European genius, be it Eastern or Western.

Without doubt, we possess this new thing, which is perfect to the highest degree, a thing which humanity does not know about and is not capable of producing.

But as we have stated before, the beauty of this new system cannot be appreciated unless it takes a concrete form. Hence, it is essential that a community must arrange its affairs according to it and show it to the world. To realize this, we need to initiate the movement of Islamic revival in some Muslim country. Only such a revivalist movement will eventually attain the status of world leadership, regardless of how long it would take.

How can this process of reviving Islam be started?

It is necessary that there be a vanguard which sets out with this determination and then keeps walking on the path, marching through the vast ocean of *Jāhiliyya* which has encompassed the entire world. During its course, it should keep itself somewhat aloof from this all-encompassing *Jāhiliyya* and should also keep some ties with it.

It is necessary that this vanguard should know the landmarks and the milestones of the road toward this goal so that they may recognize the starting place, the nature, the responsibilities and the ultimate purpose of this long journey. Not only this, but they ought to be aware of their position as opposed to this *Jāhiliyya*, which has struck its stakes throughout the earth: When to cooperate with others and when to separate from them; what characteristics and qualities they should cultivate; with what characteristics and qualities the *Jāhiliyya* immediately surrounding them is armed; how to address the people of *Jāhiliyya* in the language of Islam, what topics and problems ought to be discussed; and where and how to obtain guidance in all these matters.

The milestones will necessarily be determined by the light of the first source of this faith: the Quran. It will be derived from the Quran's basic teachings, and from the concept which it created in the minds of the first group of Muslims, those whom God raised to fulfill His will, those who once changed the course of human history in the direction ordained by God.

I wrote *Milestones Along the Way* for this vanguard, which I consider to be a waiting reality about to be materialized. This work consists of four chapters: The Nature of the Quranic Method, Islamic Concept and Culture, Jihād in the Cause of God, and Revival of the Muslim Community and its characteristics. These chapters are derived from the commentary I wrote, *fī zilāl al-qur'ān* (In the Shadows of the Quran), which I have changed in some places slightly to fit the topic being discussed. I wrote the Introduction and the other chapters at various times. In writing these chapters, I provide insight into the deep truths which I came to grasp during my reflections on the way of life presented in the Noble Quran. These thoughts may appear random and disconnected. However, one thing is common among them. These thoughts are milestones along the way, and it is the nature of signs along the way to be discovered. Taken together, these writings are a first installment of a series, and with God's help, I hope to write some more collections on this topic.

CHAPTER 1
The Unique Quranic Generation

Muslims who are inviting people to Islam in every country and in every period should give more thought to one aspect of the history of Islam, and they should ponder over it deeply: The method of inviting people to Islam and how to acquire it.

At one time the message of Islam created a generation—the generation of the Companions of the Prophet, may God be pleased with them—without comparison in the history of Islam, even in the entire history of humankind. After this time, no other generation of this caliber can be found. It is true that we do find some individuals of this caliber at some point and in some place in history. However, never did a great number of such people exist in one region as was the case during the first period of Islam.

This is an obvious and open truth of history, and we ought to ponder over it deeply so that we may reach its secrets.

The Quran of this Message is still in our hands, and the Hadith of the Messenger of God, peace be on him, i.e. his guidance in practical affairs, and the history of his sacred life are also in our hands, as they were in the hands of the first Muslim community whose equal history could not produce again. The only difference is the person of the Messenger of God, peace be on him; but is this the secret?

Had the person of the Prophet, peace be on him, been absolutely essential for the establishment and fruition of this message, God would not have made Islam a universal message, ordained it as the religion for the whole of humankind, given it the status of the last divine Message for humanity, and made it to be a guide for all the inhabitants of this planet in all their affairs until the end of time.

God has taken the responsibility for preserving the Holy Quran on Himself because He knows that Islam can be established and can benefit humankind even after the time of the Prophet, peace be on him. Hence, He called His Prophet, peace be on him, back to His mercy after twenty-three years of *Risāla* and declared this religion to be valid until the end of time. Therefore, the absence of the Messenger of God, peace be on him, is not the real cause for, nor does it explain, this phenomenon.

We look, therefore, for some other reasons, and for this purpose we look at that clear spring from which the first generation of Muslims quenched their thirst. Perhaps something has been mixed with that clear spring. We should look at the way they received their training. Perhaps some changes have found their way into it.

The spring from which the Companions of the Prophet, peace be on him-drank was the Quran; only the Quran as the Hadith of the Prophet and his teachings were offspring of this fountainhead. When someone asked the Mother of the Faithful, Aisha--may God be pleased with her-- about the character of the Prophet, peace be on him, she answered, "His character was the Quran." (al-Nasa'i).

The Holy Quran was the only source from which they quenched their thirst, and this was the only mold in which they formed their lives. This was the only guidance for them, not because there was no civilization or culture or science or books or schools. Indeed, there was Roman culture, its civilization, its books, and its laws, which even today are the foundation of European culture. There was the heritage of Greek culture- its logic, its philosophy and its arts, which are still a source of inspiration for Western thought. There was the Persian civilization, its art, its poetry and its legends, and its religion and system of government. There were many other civilizations, near or far, such as the Indian and Chinese cultures, and so on. The Roman and Persian cultures were established to the north and to the south of the Arabian Peninsula, while the Jews and Christians were settled in the heart of Arabia. We believe that this generation did not place sole reliance on the Book of God for the understanding of their religion because of any ignorance of civilization and culture, but it was all according to a well thought out plan and method. An example of this purpose is found in the displeasure expressed by the Messenger of God, peace be on him -when Umar-may God be pleased with him-brought some pages from the Torah. The Messenger of God, peace be on him-said, "By God, if even Moses had been alive among you today, he would have no recourse except to follow me." (Reported by al-Hafiz Abu Ya'lā; from al-Shu`bi, from Jabir).

It is clear from this incident that the Messenger of God, peace be on him, deliberately limited the first generation of Muslims, which was undergoing the initial stages of training, to only one source of guidance, and that was the Book of God. His intention was that this group should dedicate itself purely to the Book of God and arrange its lives solely according to its teachings. That is why the Messenger of God, peace be on him-was displeased when 'Umar-may God be pleased with him-turned to a source different from the Quran.

In fact, the Messenger of God, peace be on him-intended to prepare a generation pure in heart, pure in mind, pure in understanding. Their training was to be based on the method prescribed by God Who gave the Quran, purified from the influence of all other sources.

This generation, then, drank solely from this spring and attained a unique distinction in history. In later times it happened that other sources mingled with it. Other sources used by later generations included Greek philosophy and logic, ancient Persian legends and their ideas, Jewish scriptures and traditions, Christian theology, and, in addition to these, fragments of other religions and civilizations. These mingled with the commentaries on the Quran and with scholastic theology, as they were mingled with jurisprudence and its principles. Later generations after this generation obtained their training from this mixed source, and hence the like of this generation never arose again.

We can say without any reservations that the main reason for the difference between the first unique and distinguished group of Muslims and later Muslims is that the purity of the first source of Islamic guidance was mixed with various other sources, as we have indicated.

There is another basic cause which has operated in creating this difference. That difference is in the method of learning of this unique generation.

They of the first generation did not approach the Quran for the purpose of acquiring culture and information, nor for the purpose of taste or enjoyment. None of them came to the Quran to increase his sum of knowledge for the sake of knowledge itself or to solve some scientific or legal problem, or to remove some defect in his understanding. He rather turned to the Quran to find out what the Almighty Creator had prescribed for him and for the group in which he lived, for his life and for the life of the group. He approached it to act on what he heard immediately, as a soldier on the battle- field reads "Today's Bulletin" so that he may know what is to be done. He did not read many verses of the Quran in one session, as he understood that this would lay an unbearable burden of duties and responsibilities on his shoulders. At most he would read ten verses, memorize them, and then act upon them. We know this from a tradition reported by Abdullah Ibn Mas`ud.

This understanding-the understanding that instruction is for action-opened the doors to spiritual fulfillment and to knowledge. If they had read the Quran only for the sake of discussion, learning and information, these doors would not have opened. Moreover, action became easy, the weight of responsibilities became light, and the Quran became a part of their personalities, mingling with their lives and characters so that they became living examples of faith, a faith not hidden in intellects or books, but expressing itself in a dynamic movement which changed conditions and events and the course of life.

Indeed, this Quran does not open its treasures except to him who accepts it with this spirit: the spirit of knowing with the intention of acting upon it. It did not come to be a book of intellectual content, or a book of literature, or to be considered as a book of stories or history, although it has all these facets. It came to become a way of life, a way dedicated to God. God Most High imparted it to them in a gradual manner, to be read at intervals:

> We have revealed this Quran little by little so that you may recite it to people at intervals, and We have revealed it gradually. (17:106).

The Quran did not come down all at once; rather it came down according to the needs of the Islamic society in facing new problems, according to the growth of ideas and concepts, according to the progress of general social life, and according to new challenges faced by the Muslim community in its practical life. One verse or a few verses would be revealed according to the special circumstances and events, and they would answer questions which arose in the minds of people, would explain the nature of a particular situation, and would prescribe a way of dealing with it. These verses would correct their mistakes, either of understanding or of practice, would bring them closer to God, and would explain to them the wisdom of the various aspects of the universe in the light of God's attributes. They clearly realized that every moment of their lives was under the continuous guidance and direction of the Almighty Creator and that they were traversing the path of life under the wings of God's mercy. Because of this sense of constant relationship with God, their lives were molded according to that sacred way of life which was being instructed by Him.

Instruction to be translated into action was the method of the first group of Muslims. The method of later generations was instruction for academic discussion and enjoyment. And without doubt this is the second major factor which made later generations different from the first unique generation of Islam.

A third cause is also operative in the history of Muslims; we ought to look at it also.

When a person embraced Islam during the time of the Prophet, peace be on him-he would immediately cut himself off from *Jāhiliyya*. [The state of ignorance of the guidance from God.] When he stepped into the circle of Islam, he would start a new life, separating himself completely from his past life under ignorance of the divine Law. He would look upon the deeds during his life of ignorance with mistrust and fear, with a feeling that these were impure and could not be tolerated in Islam! With this feeling, he would turn toward Islam for new guidance; and if at any time temptations overpowered him, or the old habits attracted him, or if he became lax in carrying out the injunctions of Islam, he would become restless with a sense of guilt and would feel the need to purify himself of what had happened, and would turn to the Quran to mold himself according to its guidance.

There would be a break between the Muslim's present Islam and his past *Jāhiliyya*, and this after a well thought out decision, as a result of which all his relationships with *Jāhiliyya* would be cut off and he would be joined completely to Islam, although there would be some give-and-take with the polytheists in commercial activity and daily business; yet relationships of understanding are one thing and daily business is something else.

This renunciation of the *Jāhili* environment, its customs and traditions, its ideas and concepts, proceeded from the replacement of polytheism by the concept of the Oneness of God, of the *Jāhili* view of life and the world by that of the Islamic view, and from absorption into the new Islamic community under a new leadership and dedication of all loyalties and commitments to this new society and new leadership.

This was the parting of the ways and the starting of a new journey, a journey free from the pressures of the values, concepts, and traditions of the *Jāhili* society. The Muslim encountered nothing burdensome except the torture and oppression; but he had already decided in the depths of his heart that he would face it with equanimity, and hence no pressure from the *Jāhili* society would have any effect on his continuing steadfastness.

We are also surrounded by *Jāhiliyya* today, which is of the same nature as it was during the first period of Islam, perhaps a little deeper. Our whole environment, people's beliefs and ideas, habits and art, rules and laws-is *Jāhiliyya*, even to the extent that what we consider to be Islamic culture, Islamic sources, Islamic philosophy and Islamic thought are also constructs of *Jāhiliyya*!

This is why the true Islamic values never enter our hearts, why our minds are never illuminated by Islamic concepts, and why no group of people arises among us who are of the caliber of the first generation of Islam.

It is therefore necessary-in the way of the Islamic movement-that in the early stages of our training and education we should remove ourselves from all the influences of the *Jāhiliyya* in which we live and from which we derive benefits. We must return to that pure source from which those people derived their guidance, the source which is free from any mixing or pollution. We must return to it to derive from it our concepts of the nature of the universe, the nature of human existence, and the relationship of these two with the Perfect, the Real Being, God Most High. From it we must also derive our concepts of life, our principles of government, politics, economics and all other aspects of life.

We must return to it with a sense of instruction for obedience and action, and not for academic discussion and enjoyment. We should return to it to find out what kind of person it asks us to be, and then be like that. During this process, we will also discover the artistic beauty in the Quran, the marvelous tales in the Quran, the scenes of the Day of Judgment in the Quran, the intuitive logic the Quran, and all other such benefits which are sought in the Quran by academic and literary people. We will enjoy all these other aspects, but these are not the main object of our study. Our primary purpose is to know what way of life is demanded of us by the Quran, the total view of the universe which the Quran wants us to have, what is the nature of our knowledge of God taught to us by the Quran, the kind of morals and manners which are enjoined by it, and the kind of legal and constitutional system it asks us to establish in the world.

We must also free ourselves from the clutches of *Jāhili* society, *Jāhili* concepts, *Jāhili* traditions and *Jāhili* leadership. Our mission is not to compromise with the practices of *Jāhili* society, nor can we be loyal to it. *Jāhili* society, because of its *Jāhili* characteristics, is not worthy of being compromised with. Our aim is first to change ourselves so that we may later change society.

Our foremost objective is to change the practices of this society. Our aim is to change the *Jāhili* system at its very roots -this system which is fundamentally at variance with Islam and which, with the help of force and oppression, is keeping us from living the sort of life which is demanded by our Creator.

Our first step will be to raise ourselves above the *Jāhili* society and all its values and concepts. We will not change our own values and concepts either more or less to make a bargain with this *Jāhili* society. Never! We and it are on different roads, and if we take even one step in its company, we will lose our goal entirely and lose our way as well.

We know that in this we will have difficulties and trials, and we will have to make great sacrifices. But if we are to walk in the footsteps of the first generation of Muslims, through whom God established His system and gave it victory over *Jāhiliyya*, then we will not be masters of our own wills.

It is therefore desirable that we are aware at all times of the nature of our course of action, of the nature of our position, and the nature of the road which we must travel to come out of ignorance, the same way the distinguished and unique generation of the Companions of the Prophet, peace be on him, came out of it.

CHAPTER 2
The Nature of the Quranic Method

The Meccan parts of the Noble Quran, revealed to the Prophet—peace be on him—over a period of thirteen years, dealt with only one question. The nature of this question did not change, although the manner of its presentation varied according to the style of the Quran, which refers to this question in new ways, always as though it had been raised for the first time. This was the primary question, the greatest question, the fundamental question of this new religion, a question of faith with two main aspects, the divine and the human, and the relationship between them.

This question is addressed to 'the human being' as a human being, and in this respect the Arab of one era or any other, and the non-Arab, are equal, whether he belongs to that time or to later times.

This is that human problem which does not change; this is the question of man's existence in the universe, his ultimate goal, and his position and relationship to the universe; and the question of the relationship between him and the Creator of the universe. This aspect of man's life cannot change, as it relates to his very being.

During the Meccan period, the Quran explained to man the secret of his existence and the secret of the universe surrounding him. It told him who he is, where he has come from, for what purpose and where he will go in the end, Who brought him from nonexistence into being, to Whom he will return, and what his final disposition will be. It also informed him concerning the nature of the things which he can touch and see and the things which he can sense and conceive but which he cannot see, Who created and administers this marvelous universe, Who alternates night and day, and Who renovates and varies things. It also told him how to relate to the Creator, to the physical world, and to other human beings.

This is that great question upon which man's existence depends and will continue to depend until the end of time.

The full thirteen years of the Meccan period were spent in explaining and expounding this fundamental question, that question from which all other questions and details pertaining to human life are derived.

The Quran made this question the only subject of its message during the Meccan period and never discussed other subsidiary and derived matters. These subsidiary topics were not mentioned until the All-Knowing God decided that matters pertaining to faith had been explained fully and had entered into the hearts of that select group of people who were to establish His religion and were to give it a practical form.

Those who call toward God's Religion and want to establish the way of life prescribed by this Religion should ponder at length over this significant fact, that for thirteen years the Quran exclusively expounded this faith and did not deviate from this issue to describe the details of that system which was to be established on this faith or any laws for the organization of the Muslim society.

It was God's wisdom that this fundamental question of faith and belief should be made the central theme of the initial call of the Prophet to his people. The first message which the Messenger of God, peace be on him-brought to these people was that they bear witness that "there is no deity except God" and he devoted his efforts to making known to people Who their true Sustainer is and that they should worship Him alone.

From the viewpoint of the limited understanding of man, it does not seem as though this would be the easiest way to reach the hearts of the Arabs. They knew their language well and knew the meaning of *Allah* (god), and they also knew the meaning of *lā ilāha illā allāh* (There is no deity except God). They knew that *ulūhiyya* means "sovereignty," and they also realized that ascribing sovereignty only to God meant that the authority would be taken away from the priests, the leaders of tribes, the wealthy and the rulers, and would revert to God. It meant that only God's authority would prevail in the heart and conscience, in matters pertaining to religious observances and in the affairs of life such as business, the distribution of wealth and the dispensation of justice, in short, in the souls and bodies of men. They knew very well that the proclamation, "there is no deity except Allah, was a challenge to that worldly authority which had usurped the greatest attribute of God, namely, sovereignty. It was a rebellion against all modes of behavior which have been devised under this usurpation and was a declaration of war against that authority which legislates laws not permitted by God. It was no secret to the Arabs-who knew their language very well and knew the real meaning of the message, *lā ilāha illā allāh*-what its significance was in relation to their traditions, their rule and their power. Hence, they greeted this call, this revolutionary message, with anger, and fought against it with that vigor which is known to everyone.

Why did this call begin in this manner? And why did the divine wisdom decide that this call be confronted in its initial stages with trials?

At the time of the Prophet's call to *Risāla*, the land and the wealth of the Arabs was not in the hands of the Arabs but was in the hands of other people.

In the north, Syria was under the Romans, who appointed local Arab rulers. Similarly, in the south, Yemen was under the tutelage of the Persian Empire and was ruled by Arabs under its domination. Arabs were masters only of Hijaz, Tihama and Najd, which were waterless deserts with a few oases here and there.

It is also well-known that Muhammad, peace be on him, was called *al-Amin al-Sadiq'* (The Trustworthy and Truthful) by his people. Fifteen years before his *Risāla* (mission) began the leaders of the Quraysh had made him their arbiter in the incident of the placing of the Black Stone and had been pleased with his decision. His lineage was from the Banu Hashim, which was the noblest branch of Quraysh. It can therefore be said that Muhammad, peace be on him, was capable of kindling among his compatriots the fire of Arab nationalism and would have united them. They would have responded gladly to this call, for they were weary of continual tribal warfare and blood feuds. He would then have been able to free the Arab lands from the domination of Roman and Persian imperialism and would have been able to establish a united Arab state. It can be said that if the Prophet, peace be on him, had called people in this way, instead of bearing tortures for thirteen years due to the opposition of the people in authority in the peninsula, the whole of Arabia would have accepted it.

It can be said that if Arabia had been united under his leadership and the authority had once devolved into his hands, he could have used all this to make them accept the belief in the Oneness of God, for which purpose he was sent, and to bring people to submit to their Sustainer after they had submitted to his own human authority.

But the All-Knowing and All-Wise God did not lead His Prophet- peace be on him -on this course. He led him to declare openly that there is no deity but God, and to bear patiently, with his few Companions, whatever trials came to them.

Why this? Obviously, it was not for the sake of subjecting His Prophet, peace be on him, and the Believers to oppression. Indeed, He knows that there is no other way. The way is not to free the earth from Roman and Persian tyranny to replace it with Arab tyranny. All tyranny is wicked. The Earth belongs to God and should be purified for God, and it cannot be purified for Him unless the banner, "No deity except God," is unfurled across the earth. Man is servant to God alone, and he can remain so only if he unfurls the banner, "No deity except God, *lā ilāha illā allāh*, as an Arab with the knowledge of his language understood it: No sovereignty except God's, no law except from God, and no authority of one man over another, as the authority in all respects belong to God. The bond that unites all of humanity which Islam proclaims is based on this faith alone, the faith in which all peoples of any race or color—Arabs, Romans or Persians—are equal under the banner of God.

And this is the way.

At the time of the Prophet's call to *Risāla*, Arab society was devoid of proper distribution of wealth and devoid of justice. A small group monopolized all wealth and commerce, which increased through usury. The great majority of the people were poor and hungry. The wealthy were also regarded as noble and distinguished, and the common people were not only deprived of wealth but also of dignity and honor.

It can be said that Muhammad, peace be on him, could start a social movement, declaring war against the class of nobles and the wealthy, taking away their wealth and distributing it among the poor.

It can be said that had the Prophet, peace be on him, started such a movement, Arab society would have been divided into two classes, the great majority supporting the new movement because they were sick of the tyranny of wealth, nobility and power and a small minority's possessing these things, instead of the Prophet's having to confront the society with the Message of the Oneness of God, which remained beyond the reach of all except a few noble souls.

Arguably, after the majority had joined his movement and had trusted him with leadership, and after he had gained control of the minority of the rich, Muhammad, peace be on him, could then have used his position and power to impose the belief in the Oneness of God, for which task God had appointed him as His Prophet. Therefore, first making human beings bow before his authority, he could have made them bow before the True God.

But the All-Knowing, the All-Wise God did not lead him to this course.

God knew that this was not the way. He knew that true social justice can come to a society only after all affairs have been submitted to the laws of God and the society as a whole is willing to accept the just division of wealth prescribed by Him, and every individual of the society, whether he be a giver or a taker, firmly believes that this system has been legislated by God Almighty, by obeying, the human being will not only prosper in this world but will be rewarded in the next. Society should not be in such a condition that some are driven by greed while others are burning with envy, that all the affairs of the society are decided by the sword and the gun, fear and threats, that the hearts of the population are desolate and their spirits are broken, as is the case under systems which are based on any authority other than God's.

At the time of the Prophet's call to *Risāla*, the moral level of Arabia was extremely low from every point of view. Only a few primitive tribal customs prevailed.

Oppression was the rule of the day; the poet Zuhayr Salmah described it this way:

> One who does not defend himself with weapons will perish, and one who does not oppress will be oppressed.

Another widely known saying of the *Jāhiliyya* points to this:

> Help your brother, whether he is the oppressor or being oppressed.

Drinking and gambling were traditions of society and people were proud of these habits. All the poetry of the *Jāhiliyya* time revolves around the theme of wine and gaming. Tarafa Ibn al-Abd said:

> If there had not been three things for a young man's enjoyment,
> Then I would not have cared for anything except some food.
> One of them is my excelling others in the drinking of wine
> which is so potent that if you add water to it, it bubbles.

Drinking and entertainment and spending Have been my
life, and still are.
At last, the time has come when the whole tribe has abandoned me,
As if I were a camel with a terrible itch.

Fornication was rampant in various forms and was considered something to be proud of, as is the case among all *Jāhili* societies, old or new.
'Aisha, may God be pleased with her, described the condition of society of
the *Jāhiliyya* in the following words:

There were four kinds of marriages during *Jāhiliyya*. One was as
we have it today; that is, a man would ask a person for the hand
of his daughter or his ward in marriage, would pay the marriage-
gift, and would marry her. The second type was that a man would
tell his wife, in between her menstrual periods, to call such and
such man and become pregnant by him. He would stay away from
her and would not touch her until the signs of pregnancy appeared. If he then wished, he would have intercourse with her. He
adopted this method to obtain a son of high lineage. A third form
of marriage was polyandry. A group of men, less than ten, would
come to a woman and have sexual intercourse with her. If she became pregnant and then gave birth to a child, and a few nights
passed after childbirth, she would call them. No one could refuse
this call. When they would all gather, she would tell them, 'You
know the result. I have given birth to a child.' Then she would
point to one of them and would say, 'This is his child.' The child
would then be named after that person and would be considered
his, and he could not deny this. A fourth form of marriage was that
many men would go to a woman, and she was willing to accept
any. These were prostitutes and would place a flag in front of their
doors as a sign. Anyone who wished would go to them. If such a
woman became pregnant, after the delivery many people would
gather by her and would call an expert in recognizing resemblances. To whomever he would ascribe the child's paternity, the
child would be considered his and he could not refuse it. (Bukhari,
in the Book of Marriage).

Arguably, Muhammad, peace be on him, could start a movement of moral reform for the establishment of moral standards, for the purification of the society, and for self-evaluation. As is the case with every reformer, he would have found some upright and straight people who were also unhappy about the moral degeneration of their society. These people would certainly have come to him to join his reformist movement.

Arguably, if the Prophet, peace be on him, had chosen this course, he would have easily gathered a sizeable group. Because of their moral purity and spiritual fortitude, this group of people, more than others, would have accepted the belief in the Oneness of God would have carried the responsibilities pertaining to it. The Prophet's call, "There is no deity except God," would have been spared the vigorous opposition which it encountered.

However, God Most High knew that this way is not the way. He knew that morality can only be built on faith, a faith which provides criteria, creates values, defines the authority from which these criteria and values are to be derived, and prescribes the reward of the one who accepts this authority and the punishment of those who deviate or oppose. Without this kind of belief or the concept of a higher authority, all valued remain unstable, and similarly morals based on them remain unstable, without accounting, without authority, without reward.

When, after hard work, belief became firm and the authority to which this belief refers was acknowledged, when people recognized their Sustainer and worshipped Him alone, when they became independent not only of other human beings but also of their own desires, and when "lā ilāha illā allāh" became imprinted on their hearts-then God, through this faith and through the Believers, provided everything which was needed. God's earth became free of 'Romans and Persians,' not so that the authority of 'Arabs' might prevail, but only so that God's authority might be established and that the earth might be cleared of all the rebels against Him, whether they were Roman, Persian, or Arab.

The society was freed from all oppression, and the Islamic system was established in which justice was God's justice and in which weighing was by God's balance. The banner of social justice was raised in the name of One God, and the name of the banner was Islam. No other name was added to it, and "lā ilāha illā allāh" was written on it.

Morals were elevated, hearts and souls were purified, and with the exception of a very few cases, there was no occasion even to enforce the limits and punishments which God has prescribed; for now conscience was the law-enforcer, and the pleasure of God, the hope of divine reward, and the fear of God's anger took the place of police and punishments.

Humankind was uplifted in its social order, in its morals, in all its life, to a zenith of perfection which had never been attained before and which cannot be attained afterwards except through Islam.

All this was possible because those who established this religion in the form of a state, a system and laws and regulations had first established it in their hearts and lives in the form of faith, character, worship and human relationships. They had been promised only one thing for the establishment of this religion, not victory or power, not even that this religion would be established by their hands, not related to anything of this world: one promise, that of the Garden. That was the only promise given to them for all their striving, for all the trials which they had endured, for their steadfastness in the face of the opposition of the forces of *Jāhiliyya* to that call, "There is no deity except God," which is abhorrent to those who are in power in any age and place.

When God tried them and they proved steadfast, relinquishing their own personal desires, and when God Most High knew that they were not waiting for any reward in this world, now were they desirous to see the victory of this message and the establishment of this Religion on earth by their hands, when their hearts became free of pride of lineage, of nationality, of country, of tribe, of household-in short, when God Most High saw them to be morally pure-then He granted them the great trust, the conscious assumption of being God's representative on earth. Since they were pure in faith, the requirement for which is that God's sovereignty alone extend over hearts and consciences in human relationships and morals, in lives and possessions, in modes and manners, God Most High knew that they would be true guardians of the political authority, which would be entrusted to them so that they would establish the divine law and the divine justice. He knew they would not use it to benefit their own selves or their families or tribe or nation but would dedicate this authority purely to the service of God's religion and laws, as they knew that the true source of authority is God alone and that they were only trustees.

If the call of Islam had not started in this manner, discarding all banners other than "There is no deity except God," and if it had not taken that path which apparently was difficult and trying but which in reality was easy and blessed, then it would not have been possible to establish this blessed system with this high standard.

Had this call come in its initial stages as a national call or a social movement or a reformist attempt, or had it attached other labels to the call of *"lā ilāha illā allāh,"* then this blessed system would never have been for the sake of God alone.

The Meccan period of the Quran has this glorious attribute that it imprints "There is no deity except God" on hearts and minds and teaches Muslims to adopt this method and no other-in spite of the fact that it appears difficult-and to persist in this method.

The Quran concentrated all its teaching on the question of faith alone, not mentioning the details of the system which is to be based on it or the laws which are to regulate its affairs. The people who invite others to this Religion ought to ponder over this.

Indeed, it is the nature of this Religion which requires this particular method, as this Religion stands entirely on belief in the Oneness of God, and all its institutions and laws are derived from this great principle. A simile for this Religion is a strong, tall tree whose shade spreads far and wide and whose branches reach toward the sky. Such a tree would naturally put its roots deep down into the earth and spread them over a wide area, in proportion to its size. The case of this Religion is similar. Its system extends into all aspects of life. It discusses all minor or major affairs of humankind. It orders man's life, not only in this world but also in the world to come. It gives information about the unseen as well as about the visible world. It not only deals with material things but also purifies intentions and ideas. It is like a tall, strong, wide-spreading tree; clearly its roots must go down deep and be in proportion to its size.

This aspect of the nature of Islam defines the way it is to be founded and organized: by implanting belief and strengthening it so that it seeps into the depths of the human soul. This is essential for its correct development, for only through this method can a relationship be secured between that part of the tree of religion which reaches upward and the roots which are in the depths of the earth.

When belief in *"lā ilāha illā allāh"* penetrates into the deep recesses of the heart, it also penetrates through the whole system of life, which is a practical interpretation of this faith. By this means, those who believe are already pleased with the system in which this faith uniquely determines and submit in principle to all the laws and injunctions and details even before they are declared. Indeed, the spirit of submission is the first requirement of the faith. Through this spirit of submission, the believers learn the Islamic regulations and laws with eagerness and pleasure. As soon as a command is given, the heads are bowed, and nothing more is required for its implementation except to hear it. In this manner, drinking was forbidden, usury was prohibited, and gambling was proscribed, and all the habits of the Jāhiliyya were abolished-abolished by a few verses of the Quran or by a few words from the lips of the Prophet- peace be on him. Compare this with the efforts of secular governments. At every stage they must rely on legislation, administrative institutions, police, and military power, propaganda and the press, and yet they can at most control what is done publicly, and society remains full of illegal and forbidden things. (Refer to *fī zilāl al-qur'ān* (In the Shade of the Quran), Vol. 5, pp. 78-85, to see how God forbade the drinking of alcohol. Then refer to Sayed Abul Hasan Ali Nadvi's book, The Loss to the World Due to the Decline of Muslims, quoting Abul al-A'lā Mawdūdī's *Tanqihat* to see how the United States failed in its efforts to prohibit alcohol).

Another aspect of this religion ought to be considered. This is a practical religion; it has come to order the practical affairs of life. It faces the question of practical conditions and determines whether to keep them, modify them or change them completely. Its legislation is therefore concerned only with those conditions which exist in that society which has already accepted the sovereignty of God.

Islam is not a 'theory' based on 'assumptions;' rather it is a way of life' working with 'actuality,' It is first necessary that a Muslim community come into existence which believes that "There is no deity except God," which commits itself to obey none but God, denying all other authority, and which challenges the legality of any law which is not based on this belief.

Only when such a society comes into being, faces various practical problems, and needs a system of law, then Islam initiates the constitution of law and injunctions, rules and regulations. It addresses only those people who in principle have already submitted themselves to its authority and have repudiated all other rules and regulations.

It is necessary that the believers in this faith be autonomous and have power in their own society, so that they may be able to implement this system and give currency to all its laws. Moreover, power is also needed to legislate laws according to the needs of the group as they present themselves in its day-to-day affairs.

In Mecca, the Muslims were not autonomous, nor did they have any influence in the society. Their practical life had not taken a permanent form so that they could have organized themselves according to the divine law (al-sharī'a). Hence no, regulations and laws were revealed to them by God. They were taught only belief and those moral principles which follow from this belief after it penetrates the mind. Later, when an autonomous state came into existence in *Madīna*, general laws were revealed and that system came into existence which satisfies the needs of a Muslim community, and the power of the state was behind its enforcement.

God, Be He Most High, did not desire that all laws and regulations be revealed during the Meccan period so that Muslims would have a ready-made system to be applied as soon as they reached *Madīna*; this would be out of character for this religion. Islam is more practical than this and has more foresight. It does not find a solution to hypothetical problems. It first looks at the prevailing conditions, and if it finds a viable society which, according to its form, conditions or temperament, is a Muslim society, which has submitted itself to the law of God and is weary of laws emanating from other sources, then indeed this religion provides a method for the legislation of laws according to the needs of such a society.

People who demand from Islam that it provide theories, and that it provides a completed constitution for its system, and that it provides laws, while they observe that there is not a single society on earth which has rejected man-made systems and agreed to enforce the Sharī'a, in addition to having political power for such enforcement, show that they are ignorant of the character of this religion and the way it operates in life. They are also ignorant of the purpose for which God revealed His religion.

What these people want is that Islam changes its character, its method and its history and be reduced to the level of ordinary human theories and laws. They want a short-cut solution to satisfy their immediate desires, which are simply a product of the defeatist mentality in their spirits in

---

the face of valueless, man-made laws. They want Islam to become a mere collection of abstractions and theories, the subject of whose application is non-existent conditions. However, the course prescribed by God for this religion is the same as it has been. First, belief ought to be imprinted on hearts and rule over consciences. That belief which demands that people should not bow before anyone except God or derive laws from any other source must be imprinted in the hearts and minds. Then, when such a group of people is ready and gains practical control of society, various laws will be legislated according to the practical needs of that society.

This is what God has intended for this religion. It cannot be other than what God intends, no matter what people desire.

The callers to Islam should understand that when they invite people toward the revival of religion, they should invite them to accept Islam's fundamental belief, even though these people call themselves Muslims or their birth certificates register them as Muslims. The people ought to know that Islam means accepting the creed *"lā ilāha illā allāh"* in its deepest sense, which is this: that every aspect of life should be under the sovereignty of God, and those who rebel against God's sovereignty and usurp it for themselves should be opposed; that this belief should be accepted by their hearts and minds and should be applied in their ways of living and in their practices.

When the revival of this religion starts among a people, this aspect of it must have priority. The first Islamic call was based on it. Thirteen complete years of the Meccan period of the Quran were devoted to this Message. When a group of people enters this religion in the true sense, only then can it be considered a Muslim group. Only such a group has the capability of giving a concrete form to the Islamic system in its social life, because such a group has agreed to base its life on Islam and to obey God in all aspects of life.

When such a society actually comes into existence and the basic teachings of Islam are its guide, it will proceed to formulate laws and regulations for the existing practical needs according to the general teachings of Islam. This is the correct order for bringing about a practical, realistic, and wise Islamic system.

Some sincere people who do not understand the real character of our religion are in a hurry. They have not understood that this is the way prescribed by the All-Knowing and All-Wise God. They say that if people are taught Islam's fundamentals and the Islamic laws, then the way for inviting them to Islam will become easy and people will automatically become sympathetic to Islam.

This is their wishful thinking, due to their impatience. This is akin to the idea which could have been presented to the Prophet himself, peace be on him, and which we have described in earlier pages. That is, if the Prophet, peace be on him, had started his call with nationalism, or economic revolution, or a reformist movement, his way would have become easier.

It is essential that hearts be exclusively devoted to God alone, accepting His law with full submission and rejecting all other laws, from the very beginning, even before the details are shown to attract them.

The love of the divine law, al-Shari`a, should be a consequence of pure submission to God and of freedom from servitude to anyone else, and not because it is superior to other systems in such and such details.

Without doubt the Shari`a is best since it comes from God. The laws of His creatures can hardly be compared to the laws given by the Creator. However, this point is not the basis of the Islamic call. The basis of the message is that one should accept the Shari`a without any question and reject all other laws in any shape or form. This is Islam. There is no other meaning of Islam. One who is attracted to this basic Islam has already resolved this problem; he will not require any persuasion through showing its beauty and superiority. This is one of the realities of the faith.

We ought to discuss how the Quran solved the problem of belief and faith during the thirteen years of Meccan life. The Quran did not present this in the form of a theory or a theology, nor did it present it in the style which is common to our scholastic writings on the subject of the Oneness of God.

The Quran always appeals to human nature and draws our attention to the signs of God which are within man's soul itself and are all around him. It liberates human nature from superstitions, polishes man's native intelligence to the utmost degree, and opens windows to the world and makes the human being appreciate the intricate processes of God's nature.

This is a general aspect.

A particular aspect is that the Quran, based on this belief, started a struggle in actual life against false ideas and traditions under which human nature had become helpless. To confront these special circumstances, it would not have been desirable to present Islam in the form of a theory. It took the form of a direct confrontation, with a determination to tear the curtains which had fallen on the hearts and minds of people and to break into pieces all those walls which were standing between man and the truth. Similarly, intellectual argumentation, based on verbal logic which was the hallmark of the scholastic theology of later times, was not a proper style for it. The Quran was striving against the entire human environment as it existed. It was addressing itself to the whole of humanity which was drowned under the vast ocean of corruption. The style of theology would have been useless for it because, although Islamic belief is a belief, its main program is in the practical sphere of life; it does not remain circumscribed in theoretical discussions and the speculations of theology.

The Quran, on the one hand, constructs faith in the hearts of the Muslim community and on the other attacks the surrounding *Jāhiliyya* through this community, while striving to remove all the *Jāhili* influences which are found in the ideas, practices and morals of the Muslim community. The construction of Islamic belief occurred under these stormy conditions, and not in the form of a theology or theory or scholastic argument. It was rather as an active, organic, and vital movement, the concrete representation of which was the Muslim community. The growth of the Muslim community, including its ideas, morals, education, and training, was due to its belief. The evolution of this movement was wholly the practical manifestation of the evolution of its beliefs, and this is the true method of Islam which reflects its nature and its spirit.

The bearers of the Islamic message should keep in mind this dynamic method of Islam which we have described above. They ought to know that the stage of the construction of belief, which spread over the long period of Meccan life in this fashion, was not separate from the stage of practical organization, under which an Islamic community came into existence. It was not a stage of teaching and learning the theory. It was a single stage in which, at the same time, the seed of faith was implanted and a community was organized, giving a practical structure to the Islamic teachings. Hence in the future, whenever there are attempts at the revival of Islam, this comprehensive method should be adopted.

The stage of constructing the faith should be long, and it should be gradual. Every step should be taken with firmness. This stage should not be spent in teaching the theory of beliefs but in translating the belief into a living reality. First, it should be implanted in the hearts of men. It should materialize in a dynamic social system whose internal and external growth reflects the evolution of the belief. It ought to be a dynamic movement which challenges *Jāhiliyya* both in theory and in practice, so that it becomes a living faith which grows while striving against the surrounding forces.

It is an error and what an error to think that Islam can evolve in the form of an abstract theory limited to intellectual learning and cultural knowledge. Beware of this danger, beware.

The Quran did not come down at once but took thirteen years to construct and strengthen the structure of faith. Had God wanted, He would have revealed the entire Quran at once and then left the Companions to learn it for a period of approximately thirteen years so that the Believers would master the "Islamic theory".

However, God, Most High, did not choose this method. God wanted something else. God wanted to lay the foundations of a community, a movement, and a belief simultaneously. He wanted the community and the movement to be founded on belief, while with the dynamic progress of the community the faith also grew. He wanted faith to grow with the progress of the community, while the practical life of the community was at the same time a mirror of faith. God, Most High, knew that men and societies are not founded overnight, but that it takes as much time to construct and develop a faith as it takes to organize a community, so that as the faith is completed, simultaneously a strong community also comes into existence which is the true representation and practical interpretation of the faith.

This is the character of our religion, and the Meccan period of the Quran testifies to it. We should be aware of this character and should not try to change it by being impatient or falling under the influence of a defeatist mentality in the presence of valueless, man-made theories. Through this particular quality of Islam, the first Muslim community came into existence, and in the future, whenever a Muslim community is to be created in the world, it can be created only by this method and in relation to this character.

We should be aware that any attempt to change the living faith of Islam, which is intended to penetrate into the veins and arteries of a vital society and to be a concrete organized movement, into purely theoretical teachings and academic discussions, is an attempt to show the superiority of the "Islamic theory" over the valueless and useless theories formulated by man, and is not only erroneous but also dangerous.

The requirement of Islamic belief is that it take shape in living souls, in an active organization, and in a viable community. It should take the form of a movement striving against the *Jāhili* environment while also trying to remove the influences of *Jāhili* society in its followers, because they were people of *Jāhiliyya* before the faith entered their souls, and the influence of *Jāhiliyya* might have remained in their hearts and minds as well as in their lives. Islamic belief has a much wider range of action than simply academic discussions, as it not only addresses itself to hearts and minds but also includes practices and morals.

The divine attributes, the universe, life, man, are all included in the Islamic concept, which is not only very comprehensive and perfect but also realistic and constructive. Islam, because of its very nature, abhors being reduced to pure thought-this being against its nature and also against its ultimate aim-and loves to appear personified in human beings, in a living organization and in a practical movement. Its method is to grow through the agency of living persons and through a dynamic movement and an active organization in such a way that its theory comes to fruition at the same time as its practical applications. It never remains an abstract theory but develops side-by-side with practice.

As for the idea that we should first perfect Islam as a theory, bringing it about later in the world of action, this is an error and is dangerous, being against the nature of Islam, its purpose and its structural elements.

God, Most High, says:

> We have revealed this Quran little by little so that you may recite it to people at intervals, and We have revealed it gradually. (17:106).

Gradualness and teaching at intervals are desired, so that a 'living community' based on its beliefs may come into existence, and not merely a "theory".

The message-bearers of Islam should fully understand that this is a divine religion and that its method, which is harmonious with its nature, is also based on divine guidance. It is not possible to establish this religion without following its method.

One should also understand that this religion has come to change not only the beliefs and practices of people but also the method of bringing about these changes in beliefs and practices. This religion constructs beliefs together with forming a community; it also develops its system of thought while it spends its energy in enforcing its practical aspects. The establishment of its system of thought, its beliefs and its way of living does not require different methods but is fulfilled simultaneously.

From the above explanation we know that this religion has a particular method of action. Now we ought to know that this method is eternal. It is not related to any stage or to any special conditions and environment peculiar to the first Muslim community. Indeed, this religion cannot be established-at any time-except through this method.

Islam's function is to change people's beliefs and actions as well as their outlook and way of thinking. Its method is divinely ordained and is entirely different from all the valueless methods of short-sighted human beings.

We cannot receive the divine guidance or live according to it unless we adopt the divinely ordained method, the method which God intended for reforming human thought and practice.

When we try to make Islam into a "theory" to be studied, We remove the divine method and divine outlook from its character, and we reduce it to the level of a man-made system bf thought, as if the divine method were inferior to man's methods, and as if we wanted to elevate the system of thought and action ordained by God to the level of the systems of His creatures!

This point of view is extremely dangerous, and this defeatism is ruinous.

The function of this divine system which is given to us-we, who are the callers to Islam, is to provide a certain style of thinking, purified from all those *Jāhili* styles and ways of thinking which are current in the world and which have poisoned our culture by depriving us of our own mind. If we try to change this religion in a way which is alien to its nature and which is borrowed from the ways of the predominant *Jāhiliyya*, we will deprive it of the function it has come to perform for humanity. We will deprive ourselves of the opportunity of getting rid of the yoke of the *Jāhili* ways current in our time, which dominate our minds.

This aspect of the situation is full of danger, and the resulting loss will be disastrous.

The ways of thought and action for the founding of the Islamic system are not less important or less necessary than this Islamic belief and way of life, nor are they separate from each other. Although it may seem very attractive to us to keep expounding on the beauties of the Islamic beliefs and system, we should not forget this fact: that Islam can never become a practical way of life or a dynamic movement through these means. We should also realize that this way of presenting Islam does not benefit anyone except those who are working for the Islamic movement, and even this group can benefit from it only to such an extent as corresponds with its stage of development.

I repeat that Islamic belief should at once materialize into a practical movement, and from the very instant this comes into being, the movement should become a real representation and an accurate mirror of its belief.

I will also repeat that this is the method which is natural to the divinely revealed religion of Islam, and that this method is the most superior and lasting and is extremely effective. It is closer to human nature that all those methods which present Islam to people in the form of a complete and fixed theory, before these people have engaged in a practical movement and before this has become a living reality in their hearts, growing step by step in translating this theory into actuality.

If this is the correct method for the fundamentals of Islamic belief, it is even more correct with respect to the particulars of the organizational structure and its legal details.

The *Jāhiliyya* which has surrounded us, and which weighs heavily on the minds of some sincere workers for Islam, who become impatient and want to see all the stages of the Islamic system come into existence very rapidly, has raised a very delicate question indeed. It asks them: What are the details of the system to which you are calling? How much research have you done? How many articles have you prepared and how many subjects have you written about? Have you constituted its jurisprudence on new principles?-as if nothing were lacking for the enforcement of the Islamic Law except research in jurisprudence (*Fiqh*) and its details, as if everyone had agreed upon the sovereignty of God and were willing to submit to His laws, as if the only factor remaining were the non-existence of *Mujtahidūn* (Those Muslims whose knowledge of Islamic sources of law is so deep that they can with validity exercise independent judgment in matters pertaining to legal details), who would supply a modernized version of Islamic jurisprudence. This is a vulgar joke on Islam, and every person who has any respect for this religion should raise himself above it.

By these tactics, *Jāhiliyya* wants to find an excuse to reject the divine system and to perpetuate the slavery of one man over another. It desires to turn away the power of Muslims from the work of establishing the divinely ordained way of life in order that they may not go beyond the stage of belief to the stage of a dynamic movement. It wants to distort the very nature of this method, the method in which Islamic belief matures through the struggle of its movement, in which the details of the Islamic system develop through practical striving, and in which laws are disseminated to solve practical problems and actual difficulties.

It is the duty of Muslims to expose these tactics and reduce them to dust, to reject this ridiculous proposal of the reconstruction of Islamic law for a society which is neither willing to submit to the law of God nor expresses any weariness with laws emanating from sources other than God. Such talk is a way of diverting attention from real and earnest work and is a method through which the workers for Islam can be made to waste their time in building castles in the air. It is their duty to expose these treacherous tactics.

It is their duty to adopt the method of the Islamic movement which is harmonious with this religion. This method is the source of power for this religion, as well as a source of power for them.

Islam and the method of revival of Islam are both equally important. There is no difference between Islam and the method of reviewing Islam. Any other method, however attractive it may be, cannot bring about the establishment of Islam. Other methods can work for the establishment of man-made systems, but are incapable of establishing our system. Therefore, it is as necessary to follow this method for the establishment of Islam as it is to obey the way of life it provides and to believe in its articles of faith.

Indeed, this Quran leads to a way that is straight. (17:9).

CHAPTER 3
The Characteristics of the Islamic Society and the Correct Method for Its Formation

The Messenger of God, Muhammad, peace be on him, brought the message of Islam, the last link in the long chain of invitations toward God by the noble Prophets. Throughout history, this message has remained the same: that human beings should recognize that their true sustainer and Lord is One God, that they should submit to Him alone, and that the lordship of man be eliminated. Except for a few people in history, humanity, as a whole, has never denied the existence of God and His sovereignty over the universe. Humans have rather erred in comprehending the real attributes of God, or in taking other gods besides God, associating worldly powers to God's. This association with God has been either in belief and worship, or in accepting the sovereignty of others besides God. Both of these aspects are *shirk* in the sense that they take human beings away from the religion of God, which was brought by the Prophets. After each Prophet, there was a period during which people understood this religion, but then gradually, later generations forgot it and returned to *Jāhiliyya*. They started again on the way of *shirk*, sometimes in their belief and worship and sometimes in their submission to the authority of others, and sometimes in both.

Throughout every period of human history the call toward God has had one nature. Its purpose is *islām*, which means to bring human beings into harmony with God and resigning oneself completely to God, to free them from servitude to other human beings so that they may devote themselves to the One True God, to deliver them from the clutches of human lordship and man-made laws, value systems and traditions so that they will acknowledge the sovereignty and authority of the One True God and follow His law in all spheres of life. The Islam of Muhammad-- peace be on him--came for this purpose, as well as the messages of the earlier Prophets. The entire universe is under the authority of God, and man, being a small part of it, necessarily obeys the physical laws governing the universe. It is also necessary that the same authority be acknowledged as the lawgiver for human life. Man should not cut himself off from this authority to develop a separate system and a separate scheme of life. The growth of a human being, his conditions of health and disease, and his life and death are under the scheme of those natural laws which come from God; even in the consequences of his voluntary actions he is helpless before the universal laws. Man cannot change the practice of God in the laws prevailing in the universe. It is therefore desirable that he should also follow Islam in those aspects of his life in which he is given a choice and should make the divine Law the arbiter in all matters of life so that there may be harmony between man and the rest of the universe. (See Towards Understanding Islam, by A. A. Mawdūdī).

Jāhiliyya, on the other hand, is one man's lordship over another, and in this respect it is against the system of the universe and brings the involuntary aspect of human life into conflict with its voluntary aspect. This was that *Jāhiliyya* which confronted every Prophet of God, including the last Prophet, peace be on Him-in their call toward submission to One God. This *Jāhiliyya* is not an abstract theory; in fact, under certain circumstances it has no theory at all. It always takes the form of a living movement in a society which has its own leadership, its own concepts and values, and its own traditions, habits, and feelings. It is an organized society and there is close cooperation and loyalty between its individuals, and it is always ready and alive to defend its existence consciously or unconsciously. It crushes all elements which seem to be dangerous to its personality.

When *Jāhiliyya* takes the form, not of a 'theory' but of an active movement in this fashion, then any attempt to abolish this *Jāhiliyya* and to bring people back to God which presents Islam merely as a theory will be undesirable, rather useless. *Jāhiliyya* controls the practical world, and for its support there is a living and active organization. In this situation, mere theoretical efforts to fight it cannot even be equal, much less superior to it. When the purpose is to abolish the existing system and to replace it with a new system which in its character' principles and all its general and aspects, is different from the controlling *Jāhili* system, then it stands to reason that this new system should also come into the battlefield as an organized movement and a viable group. It should come into the battlefield with a determination that its strategy, its social organization, and the relationship between its individuals should be firmer and more powerful than the existing *Jāhili* system.

The theoretical foundation of Islam, in every period of history, has been to witness "*lā ilāha illā allāh*"-"There is no deity except God", which means to bear witness that the only true deity is God, that He is the Sustainer, that He is the Ruler of the universe, and that He is the Real Sovereign; to believe in Him in one's heart, to worship Him Alone, and to put into practice His laws. Without this complete acceptance of "*lā ilāha illā allāh*", which differentiates the one who says he is a Muslim from a non-Muslim, there cannot be any practical significance to this utterance, nor will it have any weight according to Islamic law.

Theoretically, to establish it means that people should de- vote their entire lives in submission to God, should not decide any affair on their own, but must refer to God's injunctions concerning it and follow them. We know of God's guidance through only one source, that is, through the Messenger of God, peace be on him. In the second part of the Islamic creed, we bear witness '*wa ashhadu anna Muhammadan rasūlu allāh*", "And I bear witness that Muhammad is the Messenger of God."

Therefore, it is necessary that Islam's theoretical foundation-belief-materialize in the form of an organized and active group from the very beginning. It is necessary that this group separate itself from the *Jāhili* society, becoming independent and distinct from the active and organized *Jāhili* society whose aim is to block Islam. The center of this new group should be a new leadership, the leadership which first came in the person of the Prophet, peace be on him, himself, and after him was delegated to those who strove for bringing people back to God's sovereignty, His authority and His laws. A person who bears witness that there is no deity except God and that Muhammad is God's Messenger should cut off his relationship of loyalty from the *Jāhili* society, which he has forsaken, and from *Jāhili* leadership, whether it be in the guise of priests, magicians or astrologers, or in the form of political, social or economic leadership, as was the case of the Quraysh in the time of the Prophet, peace be on him. He will have to give his complete loyalty to the new Islamic movement and to the Muslim leadership.

This decisive step must be taken at the very moment a person says, "*lā ilāha illā allāh, Muhammadan rasūl allāh*" with his tongue. The Muslim society cannot come into existence without this. It cannot come into existence simply as a creed in the hearts of individual Muslims, however numerous they may be, unless they become an active, harmonious and cooperative group, distinct by itself, whose different elements, like the limbs of a human body, work together for its formation, its strengthening, its expansion, and for its defense against all those elements which attack its system, working under a leadership which is independent of the *Jāhili* leadership, which organizes its various efforts into one harmonious purpose, and which prepares for the strengthening and widening of their Islamic character and directs them to abolish the influences of their opponent, the *Jāhili* life.

Islam was founded in this manner. It was founded on a creed which, although concise, included the whole of life. This creed immediately brought into action a viable and dynamic group of people who became independent and separate from the *Jāhili* society, immediately challenging it; it never came as an abstract theory devoid of practical existence. And, in the future it can be brought about only in this manner. There is no other way for the revival of Islam in the shade of *Jāhiliyya*, in whatever age or country it appears, except to follow its natural character and to develop it into a movement and an organic system.

When Islam, according to the method described above, starts a Muslim community on this basis, forms it into an active group, and makes this faith the sole basis for the relationship between the individuals of this group, its ultimate aim is to awaken the humanity of man, to develop it, to make it powerful and strong, and to make it the most dominant factor among all the aspects found in man's being. It seeks to implement this purpose through its teachings, its rules, its laws, and injunctions.

Some human characteristics are common with those of animals, even with those of inorganic matter. This has misled the exponents of "scientific *Jāhiliyya*" to consider man to be nothing more than an animal, or even than inorganic matter. But despite the characteristics which man shares with animals and inorganic matter, man possesses certain other characteristics which distinguish him and make him a unique creation. Even the exponents of scientific ignorance were forced to admit this, the evidence of observational facts choking them; but even then, their admission of this fact is neither sincere nor unequivocal (Foremost among the modern Darwinists is Julian Huxley).

In this respect the service rendered by Islam's pure way of life has produced concrete and valuable results. Islam based the Islamic society on the association of belief alone, instead of the low associations based on race and color, language and country, regional and national interests. Instead of stressing those traits which are common to both man and animal, it promoted man's human qualities, nurtured them and made them the dominant factor. Among the concrete and brilliant results of this attitude was that the Islamic society became an open and all-inclusive community in which people of various races, nations, languages, and colors were members, there remaining no trace of these low animalistic traits. The rivers of higher talents and various abilities of all races of humankind flowed into this vast ocean and mixed in it. Their intermingling gave rise to a high level of civilization in a very short span of time, dazzling the whole world, and compounding the essences of all the human capabilities, ideas, and wisdom of that period, despite the fact in those times travel was difficult, and the means of communication were slow.

In this great Islamic society Arabs, Persians, Syrians, Egyptians, Moroccans, Turks, Chinese, Indians, Romans, Greeks, Indonesians, Africans were gathered, in short, peoples of all nations and all races. Their various characteristics were united, and with cooperation, harmony, and unity they took part in the construction of the Islamic community and Islamic culture. This marvelous civilization was not an 'Arabic civilization', even for a single day; it was purely an 'Islamic civilization'. It was never a 'nationality' but always a community of belief.

They all came together on an equal footing in the relationship of love, with their minds set upon a single goal. Therefore, they used their best abilities, developed the qualities of their race to the fullest, and brought the essence of their personal, national, and historical experiences for the development of this one community, to which they all belonged on an equal footing and in which their common bond was through their relationship to their Sustainer. In this community their 'humanity' developed without any hindrance. These are characteristics which were never achieved by any other group of people in the entire history of humankind.

The most distinguished and best-known society in ancient history is the Roman Empire. Peoples of various races, languages and temperaments came together in this society, but all this was not based on 'human relation- ship' nor was any sublime faith the uniting factor among them; rather their society was ordered on a class system, the class of 'nobles' and the class of 'slaves', throughout the Empire. Moreover, the Roman race, in general, had the leadership and the other races were considered its subjects. Hence this society could not achieve that height which was achieved by the Islamic society and did not bring those blessings which were brought by the Islamic society.

Various societies have also appeared in modern times. For example, consider the British Empire. It is like the Roman society to which it is an heir. It is based on national greed, in which the British nation has the leadership and exploits those colonies annexed by the Empire. The same is true of other European empires. The Spanish and Portuguese Empires in their times, and the French Empire, all are equal in respect to oppression and exploitation. Communism also wanted to establish a new type of society, demolishing the walls of race and color, nation and geographical region, but it is not based on 'human relationship' but on a "class system." The communist society is like the Roman society with a reversal of emphasis; there nobles had distinction, while here the proletariat has distinction. The underlying emotion of this class is hatred and envy of other classes. Such a selfish and vengeful society cannot but excite base emotions in its individuals. The very basis of it is laid down in exciting animalistic characteristics, and in developing and strengthening them. In its view, the most fundamental needs of a human being are those which are common with the animals, that is, food, shelter, and sex. From its point of view, the whole of human history is nothing but a struggle for food.

Islam, then, is the only divine way of life which brings out the noblest human characteristics, developing and using them for the construction of human society. Islam has remained unique in this respect to this day. Those who deviate from this system and want some other system, whether it be based on nationalism, color and race, class struggle, or similar corrupt theories, are truly enemies of humankind! They do not want man to develop those noble characteristics which have been given to him by his Creator nor do they wish to see a human society benefit from the harmonious blending of all those capabilities, experiences and characteristics which have been developed among the various races of humankind.

God, Most High, says about such people:

> Say: Shall We tell you who will be the greatest losers in their deeds? Those whose effort goes astray in the present life, while they think that they are doing good deeds. Those are they who disbelieve in the signs of their Lord and in the encounter with Him. Their works have failed, and on the Day of Resurrection

We shall not assign to them any value. That is their payment-Hell-for that they were unbelievers and took My signs and My Messengers in mockery. (18:103- 106).

God Almighty speaks the truth.

CHAPTER 4
Jihād in the Cause of God

Ibn Qayyim, in his book Zad al-Mi'ād, has a chapter entitled, *The Prophet's Treatment of the Unbelievers and the Hypocrites from the Beginning of His Risāla Until His Death*. In this chapter, this scholar sums up the nature of Islamic *Jihād*.

The first revelation from God which came to the Prophet, peace be on him, was *"Iqra', bismi rabbika alladhi ..."* (Read, in the name of Your Sustainer, Who created ...). This was the beginning of the Prophethood. God commanded the Prophet, peace be on him, to recite this in his heart. The commandment to preach had not yet come. Then God revealed *"ya ayyuha al-muddathir, qum fandhir"* (O you who are enwrapped in your mantle, arise and warn). The revelation of *'iqra'* was his appointment to Prophethood, while *yā ayyuha al-muddathir* was his appointment to *Risāla*. Later God commanded the Prophet, peace be on him, to warn his near relatives, then his people, then the Arabs who were around them, then all of Arabia, and finally the whole world. For thirteen years after the beginning of his *Risāla*, he called people to God through preaching, without fighting or Jizya, (A tax levied by Muslims on non-Muslim men in areas governed by Muslims, in lieu of military service), and was commanded to restrain himself and to practice patience and forbearance. Then he was commanded to migrate, and later permission was given to fight. Then he was commanded to fight those who fought him, and to restrain himself from those who did not make war with him. Later he was commanded to fight the polytheists until God's religion was fully established. After the command for *Jihād* came, the non-believers were divided into three categories: one, those with whom there was peace; two, the people with whom the Muslims were at war; and three, the Dhimmis. (Dhimmis refers to the non-Muslim peoples residing in a Muslim state for whose protection and rights the Muslim government was responsible). It was commanded that if the non-believers with whom he had a peace treaty met their obligations, he should fulfill the articles of the treaty, but if they broke this treaty, then they should be given notice of having broken it; until then, no war should be declared. If they persisted, then he should fight with them. When the chapter entitled Barā'a was revealed, the details of treatment of these three kinds of non-believers were described. It was also explained that war should be declared against those from among the People of the Book (Christians and Jews) who declare open enmity, until they agree to pay Jizya or accept Islam. Concerning the polytheists and the hypocrites, it was commanded in this chapter that *Jihād* be declared against them and that they be treated harshly. The Prophet, peace be on him, carried on *Jihād* against the polytheists by fighting and against the hypocrites by preaching and argument. In the same chapter, it was commanded that the treaties with the polytheists end at the period of their expiration. In this respect, the people with whom there were treaties were divided into three categories: The first, those who broke the treaty and did not fulfill its terms. He was ordered to fight against them. He fought with them and was victorious. The second group consisted of people with whom the treaty was made for a stated term. They had not broken this treaty nor helped anyone against the Prophet, peace be on him. Concerning them, God ordered that these treaties be completed to their full term. The third kind were those with whom there was neither a treaty nor were they fighting against the Prophet, peace be on him, or those with whom no term of expiration was stated. For this group, it was commanded that they be given four months' notice of expiration, at the end of which they should be considered open enemies and fought against. Those who broke the treaty were fought against, and those who did not have any treaty or had an indeterminate period of expiration were given four months period of grace, and terms were kept with those with whom the treaty was due to expire. All the latter people embraced Islam even before the term expired, and the non-Muslims of the state paid Jizya. After the revelation of the chapter

Bara'a, the unbelievers were of three kinds: adversaries in war, people with treaties, and Dhimmis.

The people with treaties eventually became Muslims, so there were only two kinds left: people at war and Dhimmis. The people at war were always afraid of him. Now the people of the whole world were of three kinds: One, the Muslims who believed in him; two, those with whom he had peace, and three, the opponents who kept fighting him. As far as the hypocrites were concerned, God commanded the Prophet, peace be on him, to accept their appearances and leave their intentions to God and carry on *Jihād* against them by argument and persuasion. He was commanded not to pray at their funerals nor to pray at their graves, nor should he ask forgiveness from God for them, as their affair was with God. So, this was the practice of the Prophet, peace be on him, concerning his enemies among the non-believers and the hypocrites.

In this description we find a summary of the stages of Islamic *Jihād* presented in an excellent manner. In the above summary, we find all the distinctive and far-reaching characteristics of the dynamic movement of the true religion. We should ponder over them for deep study. Here, however, we will confine ourselves to a few explanatory remarks.

First, the method of this religion is very practical. This movement treats people as they are and uses resources which are in accordance with practical conditions. Since this movement comes into conflict with the *Jāhiliyya* which prevails over ideas and beliefs, and which has a practical system of life and a political and material authority behind it, the Islamic movement had to produce parallel resources to confront this *Jāhiliyya*. This movement uses the methods of preaching and persuasion for reforming ideas and beliefs and it uses physical power and *Jihād* for abolishing the organizations and authorities of the *Jāhili* system which prevents people from reforming their ideas and beliefs but forces them to obey their erroneous ways and make them serve human lords instead of the Almighty Lord. This movement does not confine itself to mere preaching to confront physical power, as it also does not use compulsion for changing the ideas of people. These two principles are equally important in the method of this religion. Its purpose is to free those people who wish to be freed from enslavement to men so that they may serve God alone.

The second aspect of this religion is that it is a practical movement which progresses stage by stage, and at every stage it provides resources according to the practical needs of the situation and prepares the ground for the next one. It does not face practical problems with abstract theories, nor does it confront various stages with unchangeable means. Those who talk about *Jihād* in Islam and quote Quranic verses do not take into account this aspect, nor do they understand the nature of the various stages through which this movement develops, or the relationship of the verses revealed at various occasions with each stage. When they speak about *Jihād*, they speak clumsily and mix up the various stages, distorting the whole concept of *Jihād* and deriving from the Quranic verses' final principles and generalities for which there is no justification. This is because they regard every verse of the Quran as if it were the final principle of this religion. This group of thinkers, who are a product of the sorry state of the present Muslim generation, have nothing but the label of Islam and have laid down their spiritual and rational arms in defeat. They say, "Islam has prescribed only defensive war," and think that they have done some good for their religion by depriving it of its method, which is to abolish all injustice from the earth, to bring people to the worship of God alone, and to bring them out of servitude to others into the servants of the Lord. Islam does not force people to accept its belief, but it wants to provide a free environment in which they will have the choice of beliefs. What it wants is to abolish those oppressive political systems under which people are prevented from expressing their freedom to choose whatever beliefs they want, and after that it gives them complete freedom to decide whether they will accept Islam or not.

A third aspect of this religion is that the new resources or methods which it uses during its progressive movement do not take it away from its fundamental principles and aims. From the very first day, whether the Prophet, peace be on him, addressed his near relatives, or the Quraysh, or the Arabs, or the entire world, his call was one and the same. He called them to the submission to One God and rejection of the lordship of other men. On this principle there is no com- promise nor any flexibility. To attain this purpose, it proceeds according to a plan, which has a few stages, and every stage has its new resources, as we have described earlier.

A fourth aspect is that Islam provides a legal basis for the relationship of the Muslim community with other groups, as is clear from the quotation from Zād al-Mi'ād. This legal formulation is based on the principle that Islam, that is, submission to God-is a universal Message which the whole of humankind should accept or make peace with. No political system or material power should put hindrances in the way of preaching Islam. It should leave every individual free to accept or reject it, and if someone wants to accept it, it should not prevent him or fight against him. If someone does this, then it is the duty of Islam to fight him until either he is killed or until he declares his submission.

When writers with defeatist and apologetic mentalities write about "*Jihād* in Islam," trying to remove this 'blot' from Islam, then they are mixing up two things: First, that this f religion forbids the imposition of its belief by force, as is clear from the verse, "there is no compulsion in religion." (2:256), while on the other hand it tries to annihilate all those political and material powers which stand between people and Islam, which force one people to bow before another people and prevent them from accepting the sovereignty of God. These two principles have no relation to one another nor is there room to mix them. Despite this, these defeatist people try to mix the two aspects and want to confine *Jihād* to what today is called "defensive war." The Islamic *Jihād* has no relationship to modern warfare, either in its causes or in the way in which it is conducted. The causes of Islamic *Jihād* should be sought in the very nature of Islam and its role in the world, in its high principles, which have been given to it by God and for the implementation of which God appointed the Prophet, peace be on him, as His Messenger and declared him to be the last of all prophets and messengers.

This religion is a universal declaration of the freedom of man from servitude to other men and from servitude to his own desires, which is also a form of human servitude. Islam is a declaration that sovereignty belongs to God alone and that He is the Lord of all the worlds. It means a challenge to all kinds and forms of systems which are based on the concept of the sovereignty of man. In other words, where man has usurped the divine attribute. Any system in which the final decisions are referred to human beings, and in which the sources of all authority are human, deifies human beings by designating others than God as lords over men. This declaration means that the usurped authority of God be returned to Him and the usurpers be thrown out-those who by themselves devise laws for others to follow, elevating themselves to the status of lords and reducing others to the status of slaves. In short, to proclaim the authority and sovereignty of God means to eliminate all human kingship and to announce the rule of the Sustainer of the universe over the entire earth. In the words of the Quran:

He alone is God in the heavens and in the earth. (43:84).

The command belongs to God alone. He commands you not to worship anyone except Him. This is the right way of life. (12: 40).

Say: O People of the Book, come to what is common between us: that we will not worship anyone except God, and will not associate anything with Him, and will not take lords from among ourselves besides God; and if they turn away then tell them to bear witness that we are those who have submitted to God. (2: 64).

The way to establish God's rule on earth is not that some consecrated people, the priests, be given the authority to rule, as was the case with the rule of the Church, nor that some spokesmen of God become rulers, as is the case in a 'theocracy'. To establish God's rule means that His laws be enforced and that the final decision in all affairs be according to these laws.

The establishing of the dominion of God on earth, the abolishing of the dominion of man, the taking away of sovereignty from the usurper to revert it to God, and the bringing about of the enforcement of the divine Law (Sharī`a) and the abolition of man-made laws cannot be achieved only through preaching. Those who have usurped the authority of God and are oppressing God's creatures are not going to give up their power merely through preaching; if it had been so, the task of establishing God's religion in the world would have been very easy for the Prophets of God! This is contrary to the evidence from the history of the Prophets and the story of the struggle of the true religion, spread over generations.

This universal declaration of the freedom of man on the earth from every authority except that of God, and the declaration that sovereignty is God's alone and that He is the Lord of the universe, is not merely a theoretical, philosophical and passive proclamation. It is a positive, practical, and dynamic message with a view to bringing about the implementation of the Sharī'a of God and freeing people from their servitude to other men to bring them into the service of God, the One without associates. This cannot be attained unless both 'preaching' and 'the movement' are used. This is so because appropriate means are needed to meet any and every practical situation.

Because this religion proclaims the freedom of man on the earth from all authority except that of God, it is confronted in every period of human history-yesterday, today, or tomorrow, with obstacles of beliefs and concepts, physical power, and the obstacles of political, social, economic, racial and class structures. In addition, corrupt beliefs and superstitions become mixed with this religion, working side by side with it and taking root in peoples' hearts.

If through 'preaching' beliefs and ideas are confronted, through 'the movement' material obstacles are tackled. Foremost among these is that political power which rests on a complex yet interrelated ideological, racial, class, social and economic support. These two-preaching and the movement, united, confront the human situation with all the necessary methods. For the achievement of the freedom of man on earth, of all humankind throughout the earth, it is necessary that these two methods should work side by side. This is a very important point and cannot be over- emphasized.

This religion is not merely a declaration of the freedom of the Arabs, nor is its message confined to the Arabs. It addresses itself to the whole of humankind, and its sphere of work is the whole earth. God is the Sustainer not merely of the Arabs, nor is His providence limited to those who believe in the faith of Islam. God is the Sustainer of the whole world. This religion wants to bring back the whole world to its Sustainer and free it from servitude to anyone other than God. In the sight of Islam, the real servitude is following laws devised by someone, and this is that servitude which in Islam is reserved for God alone. Anyone who serves someone other than God in this sense is outside God's religion, although he may claim to profess this religion. The Prophet- peace be on him, clearly stated that, according to the Shari`a, 'to obey' is 'to worship'. Taking this meaning of worship, when the Jews and Christians 'disobeyed' God, they became like those who 'associate others with God'.

Tirmidhi has reported on the authority of 'Adi Ibn Hatim that when the Prophet's message reached him, he ran away to Syria (he had accepted Christianity before the Prophet's time), but his sister and some of the people of his tribe became prisoners of war. The Prophet, peace be on him, treated his sister kindly and gave her some gifts. She went back to her brother and invited him to Islam, and advised him to visit the Prophet, peace be on him. 'Adi agreed to this. The people were very anxious to see him come to *Madina*. When he came into the presence of the Prophet, he was wearing a silver cross. The Prophet, peace be on him-was reciting the verse. "They (the People of the Book) have taken their rabbis and priests as lords other than God". `Adi reports: "I said, 'They do not worship their priests." God's Messenger replied, "Whatever their priests and rabbis call permissible, they accept as permissible; whatever they declare as forbidden, they consider as forbidden, and they worship them."

This explanation of the above verse by the Prophet, peace be on him, makes it clear that obedience to laws and judgments is a sort of worship, and anyone who does this is considered out of this religion. It is taking some men as lords over others, while this religion has come to annihilate such practices, and it declares that all the people of the earth should become free of servitude to anyone other than God.

If the actual life of human beings is found to be different from this declaration of freedom, then it becomes incumbent upon Islam to enter the field with preaching as well as the movement, and to strike hard at all those political powers which force people to bow before them and which rule over them, unmindful of the commandments of God, and which prevent people from listening to the preaching and accepting the belief if they wish to do so. After annihilating the tyrannical force, whether it be in a political or a racial form, or in the form of class distinctions within the same race, Islam establishes a new social, economic and political system, in which the concept of the freedom of man is applied in practice.

It is not the intention of Islam to force its beliefs on people, but Islam is not merely 'belief'. As we have pointed out, Islam is a declaration of the freedom of man from servitude to other men. It strives from the beginning to abolish all those systems and governments which are based on the rule of man over men and the servitude of one human being to another. When Islam releases people from this political pressure and presents to them its spiritual message, appealing to their reason, it gives them complete freedom to accept or not to accept its beliefs. However, this freedom does not mean that they can make their desires their gods, or that they can choose to remain in the servitude of other human beings, making some men lords over others. Whatever system is to be established in the world ought to be on the authority of God, deriving its laws from Him alone. Then every individual is free, under the protection of this universal system, to adopt any belief he wishes to adopt. This is the only way in which 'the religion' can be purified for God alone. The word "religion" includes more than belief; "religion" means a way of life, and in Islam this is based on belief. But in an Islamic system there is room for all kinds of people to follow their own beliefs, while obeying the laws of the country which are themselves based on the divine authority.

Anyone who understands this character of this religion will also understand the place of *Jihād bi al-sayf* (striving through fighting), which is to clear the way for striving through preaching in the application of the Islamic movement. He will understand that Islam is not a defensive movement in the narrow sense which today is technically called a defensive war. This narrow meaning is ascribed to it by those who are under the pressure of circumstances and are defeated by the wily attacks of the orientalists, who distort the concept of Islamic *Jihād*. It was a movement to wipe out tyranny and to introduce true freedom to humankind, using resources according to the actual human situation, and it had definite stages, for each of which it utilized new methods.

If we insist on calling Islamic *Jihād* a defensive movement, then we must change the meaning of the word 'defense' and mean by it 'the defense of man' against all those elements which limit his freedom. These elements take the form of beliefs and concepts, as well as of political systems, based on economic, racial or class distinctions. When Islam first came into existence, the world was full of such systems, and the present-day *Jāhiliyya* also has various kinds of such systems.

When we take this broad meaning of the word 'defense', we understand the true character of Islam, and that it is a universal proclamation of the freedom of man from servitude to other men, the establishment of the sovereignty of God and His Lordship throughout the world, the end of man's arrogance and selfishness, and the implementation of the rule of the divine Sharī`a in human affairs.

As to persons who attempt to defend the concept of Islamic *Jihād* by interpreting it in the narrow sense of the current concept of defensive war, and who do research to prove that the battles fought in Islamic *Jihād* were all for the defense of the homeland of Islam, some of them considering the homeland of Islam to be just the Arabian peninsula-against the aggression of neighboring powers, they lack understanding of the nature of Islam and its primary aim. Such an attempt is nothing, but a product of a mind defeated by the present difficult conditions and by the attacks of the treacherous orientalists on the Islamic *Jihād*.

Can anyone say that if Abu Bakr, Umar or Uthman had been satisfied that the Roman and Persian powers were not going to attack the Arabian peninsula, they would not have striven to spread the message of Islam throughout the world? How could the message of Islam have spread when it faced such material obstacles as the political system of the state, the socio-economic system based on races and classes, and behind all these, the military power of the government?

It would be naive to assume that a call is raised to free the whole of humankind throughout the earth, and it is confined to preaching and exposition. Indeed, it strives through preaching and exposition when there is freedom of communication and when people are free from all these influences, as "there is no compulsion in religion; but when the above, mentioned obstacles and practical difficulties are put in its way, it has no recourse but to remove them by force so that when it is addressed to peoples' hearts and minds they are free to accept or reject it with an open mind.

Since the objective of the message of Islam is a decisive declaration of man's freedom, not merely on the philosophical plane but also in the actual conditions of life, it must employ *Jihād*. It is immaterial whether the homeland of Islam, in the true Islamic sense, Dar al-Islam, is in a condition of peace or whether it is threatened by its neighbors. When Islam strives for peace, its objective is not that superficial peace which requires that only that part of the earth where the followers of Islam are residing remain secure. The peace which Islam desires is that the religion (i.e. the Law of the society) be purified for God, that the obedience of all people be for God alone, and that some people should not be lords over others. After the period of the Prophet, peace be on him, only the final stages of the movement of *Jihād* are to be followed; the initial or middle stages are not applicable. They have ended, and as Ibn Qayyim states, "after the revelation of the chapter 'Barā'a, the unbelievers were of three kinds: adversaries in war, people with treaties, and Dhimmis. The people with treaties eventually became Muslims, so there were only two kinds left: People at war and Dhimmis. The people at war were always afraid of him. Now the people of the whole world were of three kinds: one, the Muslims who believed in him: two, those with whom he had peace (and from the previous sentence we understand that they were Dhimmis); and three, the opponents who kept fighting him."

These are the logical positions consonant with the character and purposes of this religion, and not what is understood by the people who are defeated by present conditions and by the attacks of the treacherous orientalists.

God held back Muslims from fighting in Mecca and in the early period of their migration to *Madīna*, and told them, "Restrain your hands, and establish regular prayers, and pay Zaka". Next, they were permitted to fight: "Permission to fight is given to those against whom war is made, because they are oppressed, and God can help them. These are the people who were expelled from their homes without cause. The next stage came when the Muslims were commanded to fight those who fight them: "Fight in the cause of God against those who fight you." And finally, war was declared against all the polytheists: "Fight against all the polytheists, as they all fight against you;" "Fight against those among the People of the Book who do not believe in God and the Last Day, who do not forbid what God and His Messenger have forbidden, and who do not consider the true religion as their religion, until they are subdued and pay Jizya." Therefore, according to the explanation by Imam Ibn Qayyim, the Muslims were first restrained from fighting; then they were permitted to fight; then they were commanded to fight against the aggressors; and finally, they were commanded to fight against all the polytheists.

With these verses from the Quran and with many Traditions of the Prophet, peace be on him, in praise of *Jihād*, and with the entire history of Islam, which is full of *Jihād*, the heart of every Muslim rejects that explanation of Jihād invented by those people whose minds have accepted defeat under unfavorable conditions and under the attacks on Islamic *Jihād* by the shrewd orientalists.

What kind of a man is it who, after listening to the commandment of God and the Traditions of the Prophet, peace be on him-and after reading about the events which occurred during the Islamic *Jihād*, still thinks that it is a temporary injunction related to transient conditions and that it is concerned only with the defense of the borders?

In the verse giving permission to fight, God has informed the Believers that the life of this world is such that checking one group of people by another is the law of God, so that the earth may be cleansed of corruption. "Permission to fight is given to those against whom war is made, because they are oppressed, and God can help them. These are the people who were expelled from their homes without cause, except that they said that our Lord is God. Had God not checked one people by another, then surely synagogues and churches and mosques would have been pulled down, where the name of God is remembered often." Therefore, this struggle is not a temporary phase but an eternal state, an eternal state, as truth and falsehood cannot co-exist on this earth. Whenever Islam stood up with the universal declaration that God's Lordship should be established over the entire earth and that men should become free from servitude to other men, the usurpers of God's authority on earth have struck out against it fiercely and have never tolerated it. It became incumbent upon Islam to strike back and release man throughout the earth from the grip of these usurpers. The eternal struggle for the freedom of man will continue until the religion is purified for God.

The command to refrain from fighting during the Meccan period was a temporary stage in a long journey. The same reason was operative during the early days of Hijrah, but after these early stages, the reason for *Jihād* was not merely to defend *Madīna*. Indeed, its defense was necessary, but this was not the aim. The aim was to protect the resources and the center of the movement, the movement for freeing humankind and demolishing the obstacles which prevented humankind from attaining this freedom.

The reasons for refraining from fighting during the Meccan period are easily understood. In Mecca preaching was permitted. The Messenger, peace be on him, was under the protection of the Banu Hashim and hence he had the opportunity to declare his message openly; he had the freedom to speak to individuals as to groups and to appeal to their hearts and minds. There was no organized political power which could prevent him from preaching and prevent people from listening. At this stage there was no need for the use of force. Besides this, there were other reasons and I have detailed these reasons in my commentary, *In the Shades of the Quran*, in explanation of the verse,

> Have you seen the people to whom it was said, restrain your hands, and establish regular prayers, and pay Zakā? (3:77).

It may be useful to reproduce 65 parts of this explanation here.

A reason for prohibiting the use of force during the Meccan period may have been that this was a stage of training and preparation in a particular environment, for a particular nation and under conditions. Under these circumstances, an important factor in training and preparation was to train the individual Arab to be patient under oppression to himself or to those he loved, to conquer his pride, and not to make personal revenge or revenge for one's dear ones the purpose of one's life. Training was also needed so that he could learn control of his nerves, not lose his temper at the first provocation as was his temperament, nor get excited at the first impulse, but so that he could develop dignity and composure in his temperament and in his action. He was to be trained to follow the discipline of a community which is under the direction of a leader, and to refer to this leader in every matter and to obey his injunctions even though they might be against his habit or taste The aim was to develop individuals of high character who would constitute the Muslim community, who would follow the directions of the leader, and who would be civilized and progressive, free of wild habits and tribalism.

Another reason for it may have been that the Quraysh were proud of their lineage and honor, and in such an environment only persuasion could be most appealing and effective. At this stage, fighting would have resulted in kindling the fires of revenge- There was already much tribal warfare based on blood feuds, such as the wars of Dahis, Gabra and Basus, which continued for years and annihilated tribe after tribe. If blood feuds were to become associated in their minds with Islam, then this impression would never have been removed. consequently, Islam, instead of being a call toward the true religion, would have become an unending sequence of tribal feuds and its basic teachings would have been forgotten at the very beginning.

Another reason may have been to avoid sowing the seed of discord and bloodshed in every household. At that time, there was no organized government which was torturing and persecuting the Believers; the Believer was persecuted, tortured and 'taught a lesson by his own patrons. Under these circumstances, permission to fight would have meant that every house would have become a battlefield. The people would have said 'So, this is Islam'! In fact, this was said about Islam, even though fighting was not permitted. During the season when the people of Arabia came to Mecca for pilgrimage and commerce, the Quraysh would have gone to them and would have said, "Muhammad is not only dividing his nation and his tribe; he is even dividing sons from fathers. What kind of a thing is this which incites the son to kill his father, the slave to kill his master, in every house and in every locality?"

Another reason may have been that God knew that a great majority of those who persecuted and tortured the early Muslims would one day become the loyal soldiers of Islam, even its great leaders. Was not 'Umar Ibn al-Khattab one of them?

Another reason may have been that the sense of honor of the Arabs, especially in a tribal framework, comes to the help of the person who is persecuted yet does not concede defeat, especially if the persecuted are honored by the people. Several such incidents can be quoted to support this thesis. When Abu Bakr, who was an honorable man, left Mecca in order to migrate to some other place, Ibn al-Daghna could not bear it and restrained him from leaving because he considered it a disgrace to the Arabs; he offered Abu Bakr his own protection. The best example of such an incident is the tearing up of the contract under which the Banu Hashim were confined to the Valley of Abu Talib when the period of their hunger and privation seemed unreasonably long. This chivalry was a peculiarity of the Arabs, while in ancient civilizations which were accustomed to seeing people humiliated, those who suffered and were persecuted were laughed at, ridiculed, and treated with contempt, and the oppressor and the tyrant were respected.

Another reason may have been that the Muslims were few and they lived only in Mecca, as the message of Islam had not reached other parts of Arabia or had reached only as hearsay. Other tribes considered it as a domestic quarrel of the Quraysh; they were watching for the outcome of this struggle. Under these circumstances, if fighting had been allowed, this limited warfare would have resulted in the complete annihilation of the Muslims; even if they had killed a great number of their opponents, they would still have been annihilated. Idolatry would have continued and the dawn of the Islamic system would never have arrived and would never have reached its zenith, while Islam is revealed to be a practical way of life for all humankind.

In the early Madīnan period fighting was also prohibited. The reason for this was that the Prophet, peace be on him, had signed a pact with the Jews of *Madīna* and with the unbelieving Arabs in and around *Madīna*, an action which was necessary at this stage.

First, there was an open opportunity for preaching and persuasion. There was no political power to circumscribe this freedom; the whole population accepted the new Muslim state and agreed upon the leadership of the Prophet, peace be on him-in all political matters. In the pact it was agreed by all parties that no one would make a treaty of peace or declare war or establish relations with any outsider without the express permission of the Prophet, peace be on him. The real power in *Madīna* was in the hands of Muslim leadership. The doors were also open for preaching Islam and there was freedom of belief.

Secondly, at this stage the Prophet, peace be on him, wanted to conserve all his efforts to combat the Quraysh, whose relentless opposition was a great obstacle in spreading Islam to other tribes which were waiting to see the final outcome of the struggle between the two groups of the Quraysh. That is why the Prophet, peace be on him, hastened to send scouting parties in various directions. The first such party was commanded by Hamzah Ibn Abdul Muttalib, and it went out during the month of Ramadan, only six months after the Immigration.

After this, there were other scouting parties, one during the ninth month after *Lā ilāha illā allāh*, the next in the thirteenth month the third sixteen months after Hijrah, and in the seventeenth month he sent a party under the leadership of Abdullah Ibn Jahsh. This party encountered some resistance, and some blood was shed. This occurred during the month of Rajab, which was considered a sacred month. The following verse of Chapter Baqara refers to it:

They ask you about fighting in the sacred months. Say: Fighting in them is a great sin, but to prevent people from the way of God, and to reject God, and to stop people from visiting the Sacred Mosque, and to expel people from their homes are a much greater sin, and oppression is worse than killing. (2:217).

During Ramadan of the same year, the Battle of Badr took place, and in Chapter Anfal this battle was reviewed.

If this stage of the Islamic movement is viewed in proper perspective, then there is no room to say that the basic aim of the Islamic movement was "defensive" in the narrow sense which some people ascribe to it today, defeated by the attacks of the treacherous orientalists.

Those who look for causes of a defensive nature in the history of the expansion of Islam are caught by the aggressive attacks of the orientalists at a time when Muslims possess neither glory nor do they possess Islam. However, by God's grace, there are those who are standing firm on the issue that Islam is a universal declaration of the freedom of man on the earth from every authority except God's authority, and that the religion ought to be purified for God; and they keep writing concerning, the Islamic *Jihād*.

But the Islamic movement does not need any arguments taken from the literature, as it stands on the clear verses of the Quran:

> They ought to fight in the way of God who have sold the life of this world for the life of the Hereafter; and whoever fights in the way of God and is killed or becomes victorious, to him shall We give a great reward. Why should not you fight in the way of God for those men, women and children who have been oppressed because they are weak and who call Our Lord. Take us out of this place whose people are oppressors, and raise for us an ally, and send for us a helper. Those who believe fight in the cause of God, while those who do not believe fight in the cause of tyranny. Then fight against the friends of Satan. Indeed, the strategy of Satan is weak. (3: 74-76).

Say to the unbelievers that if they refrain, then whatever they have done before will have forgiven them; but if they turn back, then they know what happened to earlier nations. And fight against them until there is no oppression and the religion is wholly for God. But if they refrain, then God is watching over their actions. But if they do not, then know that God is your Ally and He is your Helper. (8: 38-40).

Fight against those among the People of the Book who do not believe in God and the Last Day, who do not forbid what God and His messenger have forbidden, and who do not consider the true religion as their way of life, until they are subdued and pay Jizya. The Jews say: 'Ezra is the Son of God', and the Christians say: 'The Messiah is the Son of God'. These are mere sayings from their mouths, following those who preceded them and disbelieved. God will assail them; how they are perverted! They have taken their rabbis and priests as lords other that God, and the Messiah, son of Mary; and they were commanded to worship none but One God. There is no deity but He, glory be to Him above what they associate with Him! They desire to extinguish God's light with their mouths, and God intends to perfect His light, although the unbelievers may be in opposition. (9: 29-32).

The reasons for *Jihād* which have been described in the above verses are these: to establish God's authority in the earth; to arrange human affairs according to the true guidance provided by God; to abolish all the Satanic forces and Satanic systems of life; to end the lordship of one man over others since all men are creatures of God and no one has the authority to make them his servants or to make arbitrary laws for them. These reasons are sufficient for proclaiming *Jihād*. However, one should always keep in mind that there is no compulsion in religion; that is, once the people are free from the lordship of men, the law governing civil affairs will be purely that of God, while no one will be forced to change his beliefs and accept Islam.

The *Jihād* of Islam is to secure complete freedom for every man throughout the world by releasing him from servitude to other human beings so that he may serve his God, Who IS One and Who has no associates. This is in and of itself a sufficient reason for *Jihād*. These were the only reasons in the hearts of Muslim warriors. If they had been asked the question "why are you fighting?", none would have answered, "my country is in danger; I am fighting for its defense" or "the Persians and the Romans have come upon us," or, "we want to extend our dominion and want more spoils."

They would have answered the same as Rabat Ibn 'Amir, Hudhayfah Ibn Muhsin and Mughīra Ibn Shu`ba answered the Persian general Rustum when he asked them one by one during three successive days preceding the battle of Qādisiyya, "for what purpose have you come?" Their answer was the same: "God has sent us to bring anyone who wishes from servitude to men into the service of God alone, from the narrowness of this world into the vastness of this world and the Hereafter, and from the tyranny of religions into the justice of Islam. God raised a Messenger for this purpose to teach His creatures His way. If anyone accepts this way of life, we turn back and give his country back to him, and we fight with those who rebel until we are martyred or become victorious."

These are the reasons inherent in the very nature of this religion. Similarly, its proclamation of universal freedom, its practical way of combating actual human conditions with appropriate methods, its developing new resources at various stages, is also inherent in its message from the very beginning, and not because of any threat of aggression against Islamic lands or against the Muslims residing in them. The reason for *Jihād* exists in its message and in the actual conditions it finds in human societies, and not merely in the necessity for defense, which may be temporary and of limited extent. A Muslim person fights with his wealth and his person "in the way of God" for the sake of these values in which neither personal gain nor greed is a motive for him.

Before a Muslim steps into the battlefield, he has already fought a great battle within himself against Satan, against his own desires and ambitions, his personal interests and inclinations, the interests of his family and of his nation; against which is not from Islam; against every obstacle which comes into the way of worshipping God and the implementation of the divine authority on earth, returning this authority to God and taking it away from the rebellious usurpers.

Those who say that Islamic *Jihād* was merely for the defense of the 'homeland of Islam' diminish the greatness of the Islamic way of life and consider it less important than their 'homeland'. This is not the Islamic point of view, and their view is a creation of the modern age and is completely alien to Islamic consciousness. What is acceptable to Islamic consciousness is its belief, the way of life which this belief prescribes, and the society which lives according to this way of life. The soil of the homeland has in and of itself no value or weight. From the Islamic point of view, the only value which the soil can achieve is because on that soil God's authority is established and God's guidance is followed; and it becomes a fortress for the belief, a place for its way of life to be entitled the 'homeland of Islam', a center for the movement for the total freedom of man.

Surely, in that case the defense of the 'homeland of Islam' is the defense of the Islamic beliefs, the Islamic way of life, and the Islamic community. However, its defense is not the ultimate objective of the Islamic movement of *Jihād* but is a means of establishing the divine authority within it so that it becomes the headquarters for the movement of Islam, which is then to be carried throughout the earth to the whole of humankind, as the object of this religion is all humanity and its sphere of action is the whole Earth.

As we described above, there are many practical obstacles in establishing God's rule on earth, such as the power of the state, the social system and traditions and, in general, the whole human environment. Islam uses force only to remove these obstacles so that there may not remain any wall between Islam and individual human beings, and so that it may address their hearts and minds after releasing them from these material obstacles, and then leave them free to choose to accept or reject it.

We ought not to be deceived or embarrassed by the attacks of the Orientalists on the origin of *Jihād*, nor lose self-confidence under the pressure of present conditions and the weight of the great powers of the world to such an extent that we try to find reasons for Islamic *Jihād* outside the nature of this religion, and try to show that it was a defensive measure under temporary conditions. The need for *Jihād* remains, and will continue to remain, whether these conditions exist or not.

In pondering over historical events, we should not neglect the aspects inherent in the nature of this religion, its declaration of universal freedom, and its practical method. We ought not to confuse these with temporary needs of defense.

No doubt this religion must defend itself against aggressors. Its very existence in the form of a general declaration of the universal Lordship of God and of the freedom of man from servitude to any being other than God, and its organizing a movement under a new leadership other than the existing *Jāhili* leadership, and its creating a distinct and permanent society based on the divine authority and submission to One God, is sufficient cause for the surrounding *Jāhili* society, which is based on human authority in some form or another, to rise against it for its own preservation and for the suppression of Islam. Clearly, under these conditions, the newly organized Islamic community will have to prepare itself for defense. These conditions inevitably occur and come into existence simultaneously with the advent of Islam in any society. There is no question of Islam's liking or disliking such a situation, as the struggle is imposed upon Islam. This is a natural struggle between two systems which cannot co-exist for long. This is a fact which cannot be denied, and hence Islam has no choice but to defend itself against aggression.

But there is another fact which is much more important than this fact. It is in the very nature of Islam to take initiative for freeing the human beings throughout the earth from servitude to anyone other than God; and so it cannot be restricted within any geographic or racial limits, leaving all humankind on the whole Earth under evil control, in chaos and in servitude to powers other than God.

It may happen that the enemies of Islam may consider it expedient not to take any action against Islam, if Islam leaves them alone in their geographical boundaries to continue the lordship of some men over others and does not extend its message and its declaration of universal freedom within their domain. But Islam cannot agree to this unless they submit to its authority by paying Jizya, which will be a guarantee that they have opened their doors for the preaching of Islam and will not put any obstacle in its way through the power of the state.

This is the character of this religion and this is its function, as it is a declaration of the Lordship of God and the freedom of man from servitude to anyone other than God, for all people.

There is a great difference between this concept of Islam and the other, which considers it confined to geographical and racial limits, and does not take any action except out of fear of aggression. In the latter case, all its inherent dynamism is lost.

To understand the dynamism of Islam with clarity and depth, it is necessary to remember that Islam is a way of life for humans prescribed by God. It is not a man-made system, nor an ideology of a group of people, nor a way of life peculiar to a given race. We cannot talk about external reasons for *Jihād* unless we overlook this great truth and unless we forget that the fundamental question here is the sovereignty of God and the obedience of His creatures. It is impossible for a person to remember this great truth and still search for other reasons for Islamic *Jihād*.

The true estimate of the difference between the concept that war was forced upon Islam by *Jāhiliyya* because its very nature demanded that *Jāhili* societies would attack it, and the concept that Islam takes the initiative and enters into this struggle, cannot be made in the early stages of its movement.

In the early stages of the Islamic movement it is difficult to discriminate between these two concepts, because in either case Islam will have to do battle. However, in the final stages, when the initial battles are won, the two concepts make a great difference-a great difference in understanding the purposes and the significance of the Islamic message. And here lies the danger.

There is also a great difference in the idea that Islam is a divinely ordained way of life and in the idea that it is a geographically bounded system. According to the first idea, Islam came into this world to establish God's rule on God's earth, to invite all people toward the worship of God, and to make a concrete reality of its message in the form of a Muslim community in which individuals are free from servitude to men and have gathered together under servitude to God and follow only the Sharī`a of God. This Islam has a right to remove all those obstacles which are in its path so that it may address human reason and intuition with no interference and opposition from political systems. According to the second idea, Islam is merely a national system which has a right to take up arms only when its homeland is attacked.

In the case of either concept, Islam must strive and to struggle; but its purposes and its results are entirely different, both conceptually and practically.

Indeed, Islam has the right to take the initiative. Islam is not a heritage of any race or country; this is God's religion, and it is for the whole world. It has the right to destroy all obstacles in the form of institutions and traditions which limit man's freedom of choice. It does not attack individuals nor does it force them to accept its beliefs; it attacks institutions and traditions to release human beings from their poisonous influences, which distort human nature and which curtail human freedom.

It is the right of Islam to release humankind from servitude to human beings so that they may serve God alone, to give practical meaning to its declaration that God is the true Lord of all and that all men are free under Him. According to the Islamic concept and God's rule on earth can be established only through the Islamic system, as it is the only system ordained by God for all human beings, whether they be rulers or ruled, black or white, poor or rich, ignorant or learned. Its law is uniform for all, and all human beings are equally responsible within it. In all other systems, human beings obey other human beings and follow man-made laws. Legislation is a divine attribute; any person who concedes this right to such a claimant, whether he considers him divine or not, has accepted him as divine.

Islam is not merely a belief, so that it is enough merely to preach it. Islam, which is a way of life, takes practical steps to organize a movement for freeing man. Other societies do not give it any opportunity to organize its followers according to its own method, and hence it is the duty of Islam to annihilate all such systems, as they are obstacles in the way of universal freedom. Only in this manner can the way of life be wholly dedicated to God, so that neither any human authority nor the question of servitude remains, as is the case in all other systems which are based on man's servitude to man. Those of our contemporary Muslim scholars who are defeated by the pressure of current conditions and the attacks of treacherous orientalists do not subscribe to this characteristic of Islam. The orientalists have painted a picture of Islam as a violent movement which imposed its belief upon people by the sword. These vicious orientalists know very well that this is not true, but by this method they try to distort the true motives of Islamic *Jihād*. But our Muslim scholars, these defeated people, search for reasons of defensive with which to negate this accusation. They are ignorant of the nature of Islam and of its function, and that it has a right to take the initiative for human freedom.

These scholars, with their defeated mentality, have adopted the Western concept of 'religion', which is merely a name for 'belief' in the heart, having no relation to the practical affairs of life, and therefore they conceive of religious war as a war to impose belief on peoples' hearts.

However, this is not the case with Islam, as Islam is the way of life ordained by God for all humankind, and this way establishes the Lordship of God alone-that is, the sovereignty of God, and orders practical life in all its daily details. *Jihād* in Islam is simply a name for striving to make this system of life dominant in the world. As far as belief is concerned, it clearly depends upon opinion, under the protection of a general system in which all obstacles to freedom of personal belief have been removed. Clearly this is an entirely different matter and throws a completely new light on the Islamic *Jihād*.

Therefore, wherever an Islamic community exists which is a concrete example of the divinely-ordained system of life, it has a God-given right to step forward and take control of the political authority so that it may establish the divine system on earth, while it leaves the matter of belief to individual conscience. When God restrained Muslims from *Jihād* for a certain period, it was a question of strategy rather than of principle; this was a matter pertaining to the requirements of the movement and not to belief. Only in the light of this explanation can we understand those verses of the Holy Quran which are concerned with the various stages of this movement. In reading these verses, we should always keep in mind that one of their meanings is related to the stages of the development of Islam, while there is another general meaning which is related to the unchangeable and eternal message of Islam. We should not confuse these two aspects.

CHAPTER 5
Lā ilāha illā allāh-the Way of Life of Islam

"*lā ilāha illā allāh.*" There is no deity except Allah, is the first part the Islamic declaration of faith, meaning that there is no one to be worshipped except God; "Muhammadan Rasul Allah", "Muhammad is the Messenger of God, is the second part; meaning that this worship is to be carried out according to the teaching of the Prophet, peace be on him.

A believing Muslim is one into whose heart this declaration has penetrated completely, as the other pillars of Islam and articles of faith are derivatives of it. Therefore, belief in angels and God's Books and God's Messengers and the life hereafter and al-Qadr (the measurement of good and evil), and al-Salah (prayers), al-Sawm (fasting), al-Zaka (poor-due) and al-Hajj (pilgrimage), and the limits set by God of permissible and forbidden things, human affairs, laws, Islamic moral teachings, and so on, are all based on the foundation of worship of God, and the source of all these teachings is the person of the Prophet- peace be on him -through whom God has revealed to us.

A Muslim community is that which is a practical interpretation of the declaration of faith and all its characteristics; and the society which does not translate into practice this faith and its characteristics is not Muslim.

The declaration of faith provides the foundation for a complete system of life for the Muslim community in all its details. This way of life cannot come into being without securing this foundation first. Similarly, if the system of life is constructed on some other foundation, or if other sources are mixed with this foundation, then that community cannot be considered Islamic. God says:

> The command belongs to God alone. He commands you not to worship anyone except Him. This is the right way of life. (12:40).

> Whoever obeys the Prophet obeys God. (4:80).

This concise and decisive declaration guides us in the basic questions of our religion and in its practical movement. First, it guides us to the nature of the Muslim community; second, it shows us the method of constructing such a community; third, it tells us how to confront *Jāhili* societies; and fourth, it determines the method by which Islam changes the conditions of human life. All these problems have always been and will remain of great importance in the various stages of the Islamic movement.

The distinctive feature of a Muslim community is this: that in all its affairs it is based on worship of God alone. The declaration of faith expresses this principle and determines its character; in beliefs, in devotional acts, and in rules and regulations this declaration takes a concrete form.

A person who does not believe in the oneness of God does not worship God alone.

> Allah commands you not to take two gods. God is only One; hence fear Me. Whatever is in the heavens and the earth belongs to Him and follows His way. Will you the fear anyone other than God?" (16: 51-52).

Anyone who performs devotional acts before someone other than God, in addition to Him or exclusively, does not worship God alone.

> Say, my Salah (prayers), my acts of devotion, my life and my death, are for the Sustainer of the Worlds; He has no associate. I have been commanded this, and I am the foremost to be among the submitters. (6: 162-163).

Anyone who derives laws from a source other than God, in a way other than what He taught us through the Prophet , peace be on him-does not worship God alone.

> Are there associates of God who have made permissible for them in their religion that which God has not permitted? (42:21).

> Whatever the Prophet gives you, accept it, and whatever he prohibits you, refrain from it. (59:7).

This is the Muslim society. In this society, the beliefs and ideas of individuals, their devotional acts and religious observances, and their social system and their laws, are all based on submission to God alone. If this attitude is eliminated from any of these aspects, the whole of Islam is eliminated, as the first pillar of Islam-that is, the declaration, 'there is no deity except God, and Muhammad is the Messenger of God', becomes eliminated.

This way, and only this way, can this group become a Muslim group and the community which it organizes be Muslim. Before adopting this purity of attitude no group can be a Muslim group, and before organizing its system of life on this principle no society can be a Muslim society. The reason for this is that the first principle on which Islam is based, that is *"lā ilāha illā allāh, muhammadan rasūl allāh"* is not established in respect to both its parts.

It is necessary, therefore, before thinking of establishing the Islamic social system and organizing a Muslim community, that one should give attention to purifying the hearts of people from the worship of anyone other than God, in the way we have described above. Only those whose hearts are so purified will come together to make a group, and only such a group of people, whose beliefs and concepts, whose devotional acts and laws, are completely free of servitude to anyone other than God can start a Muslim community. Anyone who wants to live an Islamic life will automatically enter this community, and his belief, his acts of worship and the laws which he follows, will also be purified for God alone. In other words, he will be an embodiment of *"lā ilāha illā allāh, muhammadan rasūl allāh"*.

This was the way the first Muslim group was formed which eventually developed into the first Muslim community. This is the only way in which any Muslim group is started, and a Muslim community comes into being.

A Muslim community can come into existence only when individuals and groups of people reject servitude to anyone except God-in addition to Him or exclusively-and come into submission to God, Who has no associates, and decide that they will organize their scheme or life on the basis of this submission. From this a new community is born, emerging from within the old *Jāhili* society, which immediately confronts it with a new belief and a new way of life based on this belief, presenting a concrete embodiment of the creed, "There is no deity except God, and Muhammad is the Messenger of God".

The old *Jāhili* society may become submerged into the new Islamic society, or it may not, and it may make peace with the Muslim society or may fight it. However, history tells us that the *Jāhili* society chooses to fight and not to make peace, attacking the vanguard of Islam at its very inception, whether it be a few individuals or whether it be groups, and even after this vanguard has become a well-established community. From Noah to Muhammad , peace be on them-without exception, this has been the course of events at every Islamic

It is clear, then, that a Muslim community cannot be formed or continue to exist until it attains sufficient power to confront the existing *Jāhili* society. This power must be at all levels; that is to say, the power of belief and concept, the power of training and moral character, the power to organize and sustain a community, and such physical power as is necessary, if not to dominate, at least to hold itself against the onslaught of the *Jāhili* society.

But what is the *Jāhili* society, and by what method does Islam confront it?

The *Jāhili* society is any society other than the Muslim society; and if we want a more specific definition, we may say that any society is a *Jāhili* society which does not dedicate itself to submission to God alone, in its beliefs and ideas in its observances of worship, and in its legal regulations.

According to this definition, all the societies existing in the world today are *Jāhili*.

Included among these is the communist society, first because it denies the existence of God Most High and believes that the universe was created by 'matter' or by 'nature', while all man's activities and his history has been created by 'economics or 'the means of production'; second, because the way of life it adopts is based on submission to the Communist Party and not to God. A proof of this is that in all communist countries the Communist Party has full control and leadership Furthermore, the practical consequence of this ideology is that the basic needs of human beings are considered identical with those of animals, that is food and drink, clothing, shelter and sex. It deprives people of their spiritual needs, which differentiates human beings from animals. Foremost among these is belief in God and the freedom to adopt and to proclaim this faith. Similarly, it deprives people of their freedom to express individuality, which is a very special human characteristic. The individuality of a person is expressed in various ways, such as private property, the choice of work and the attainment of specialization in work, and expression in various art forms; and it distinguishes him from animals or from machines. The communist ideology and the communist system reduce the human being to the level of an animal or even to the level of a machine.

All idolatrous societies are also among the *Jāhili* societies. Such societies are found in India, Japan, the Philippines and Africa. Their *Jāhili* character consists first of the fact that they believe in other gods besides God, in addition to Him or without Him; second, they have constructed an elaborate system of devotional acts to propitiate these deities. Similarly, the laws and regulations which they follow are derived from sources other than God and His Law, whether these sources be priests or astrologers or magicians, the elders of the nation, or the secular institutions which formulate laws without regard to the Law of God, and which attain absolute authority in the name of the nation or a party or on some other basis, while absolute authority belongs to God alone, and this can be brought into action only in the way shown to us by the Prophets of God.

All Jewish and Christian societies today are also *Jāhili* societies. They have distorted the original beliefs and ascribe certain attributes of God to other beings. This association with God has taken many forms, such as the fatherhood/giving birth of God or the Trinity, sometimes it is expressed in a concept of God which is remote from the true reality of God.

> The Jews say: Ezra is the Son of God, and the Christians say: "the Messiah is the Son of God.' These are mere sayings from their mouths, following those who preceded them and disbelieved. God will assail them; how they are perverted. (9:30).

> They rejected the truth who said; God is the third of three'. Indeed, God is but One God. If they do not desist from what they say, the disbelievers among them will be met with a painful chastisement. (5:73).
> The Jews have said: God's hand is limited in what it can do. Limited are their hands, and they are cursed for what they

have said. Indeed, His hands are open; he expends how He wills. (5 :64).

"The Jews and Christians say: "We are God's children and His favorites." Say: 'Why then does He punish you for your offences? In fact, you are a person just like others. (5:18).

These societies are *Jāhili* also because their forms of worship their customs and manners are derived from their false and distorted beliefs. They are also *Jāhili* societies because their institutions and their laws are not based on submission to God alone. They neither accept the rule of God, nor do they consider God's commandments as the only valid basis of all laws; on the contrary, they have established assemblies of men which have absolute power to legislate laws, usurping the right which belongs to God alone. At the time of Revelation, the Quran classified them among those who associate others with God, as they had given their priests and rabbis the authority to devise laws in whatever way they pleased.

They have taken their rabbis and priests as lords other than God, and the Messiah, son of Mary; and they were commanded to worship none but One God. There is no god but He, glory be to Him above what they associate with Him. (5:31).

These people did not consider their priests or rabbis as divine, nor did they worship them; but they gave them the authority to make laws, obeying laws which were made by them not permitted by God. If at that time the Quran called them associators of others with God and rejectors of truth then today they are also the same, because today this authority IS not in the hands of priests and rabbis but in the hands of individuals chosen from among themselves.

Lastly, all the existing so-called "Muslim" societies are also *Jāhili* societies.

We classify them among *Jāhili* societies not because they believe in other deities besides God or because they worship anyone other than God, but because their way of life is not based on submission to God alone. Although they believe In the Unity of God, still they have relegated the legislative attribute of God to others and submit to this authority, and from this authority they derive their systems, their traditions and customs, their laws, their values and standards, and almost every practice of life. God Most High says concerning rulers:

> Those who do not judge according to what God has revealed are unbelievers." and concerning the ruled: (5:44).
> Have you not seen those who assert that they believe in what has been sent down to you and what was sent down before you, desiring to take their disputes to idols, while you were commanded to reject them? (4:65).

> But no, by your Lord, they have not believed until they make you judge regarding their disputes, and then do not find any resentment in their hearts against your verdict, but submit in full submission. (4:65).

Before this, God accused the Jews and Christians of committing Shirk, (association of other gods with God) and of unbelief, and of taking priests and rabbis as lords in addition to God, only because they had given certain rights and privileges to their priests and rabbis, which today those who call themselves 'Muslims' have given to some people among themselves. This action of the Jews and Christians was considered by God in the same category of Shirk as that of the Christians' making Jesus into the Son of God and worshipping him. The latter is a rebellion against the Oneness of God, while the former is a rebellion against His prescribed way of life and a denial of "There is no other deity except God."

Among Muslim societies, some openly declare their 'secularism' and negate all their relationships with the religion; some others pay respect to the religion only with their mouths, but in their social life they have completely abandoned it. They say that they do not believe in the 'Unseen' and want to construct their social system on the basis of 'science', as science and the Unseen are contradictory! This claim of theirs is mere ignorance, and only ignorant people can talk like this. (Refer to the discussion in Volume 7 of *fī zilāl al-qur'ān* in explanation of the verse: "He has the keys to the Unseen; no one knows it except Him".) There are some other societies which have given the authority of legislation to others besides God; they make whatever laws they please and then say, "This is the Sharī`a of God".

All these societies are the same in one respect, that none of them is based on submission to God alone.

After explaining these facts, the position of Islam in relation to all these *Jāhili* societies can be described in one sentence: it considers all these societies un-Islamic and illegal.

Islam does not look at the labels or titles which these societies have adopted; they all have one thing in common, and that is that their way of life is not based on complete submission to God alone. In this respect they share the same characteristic with a polytheistic society, the characteristic of *Jāhiliyya*.

We have now come to the last of the points mentioned in the beginning of this chapter, and that point concerns the method which Islam adopts, today, tomorrow or in the remote future-in confronting actual human conditions. This method has been described in our discussion on the nature of the Muslim society, which is, in summary, that a Muslim society bases all its decisions on submission to God alone.

After defining this nature, we can immediately answer the following question: What is the principle on which human life ought to be based:-God's religion and its system of life, or some man-made system?

Islam answers this question in a clear cut and unambiguous manner: The only principle on which the totality of human life is to be based is God's religion and its system of life. If this principle is absent, the very first pillar of Islam, that is, bearing witness to- "*lā ilāha illā allāh, muhammadan rasūl allāh*", will not be established nor its real influence felt. Unless this principle is accepted without any question and followed faithfully, the complete submission to God as taught by the Messenger of God, peace be on him, cannot be fulfilled.

> Whatever the Messenger gives you, accept it; whatever he forbids you, refrain from it. (59:7).

Furthermore, Islam asks: "Do you know better or does God?" and then answers it: "God knows and, you do not know," and "You have been given only a little of the (true) knowledge."

The One Who knows, Who has created man, and Who is his Sustainer must be the Ruler, and His religion ought to be the way of life, and man should return to Him for guidance. As far as man-made theories and religions are concerned, they become outmoded and distorted, as they are based on the knowledge of men-those who do not know, and to whom only a little of the true knowledge is given.

God's religion is not a maze nor is its way of life a fluid thing, as the second part of the declaration of faith, "Muhammad is the Messenger of God," clearly limits it. It is bounded by those principles which have come from the Messenger of God, peace be on him. If there is a clear text available from the Quran or from him, then that will be decisive and there will be no room for Ijtihad (using one's judgment). If no such clear judgment is available, then the time comes for Ijtihad, and that according to well-defined principles which are consistent with God's religion and not merely following opinions or desires.

> If you have difference of opinion concerning something, refer to God and His Messenger. (4:59).

The principles of Ijtihad and deduction are well known and there is no vagueness or looseness in them. No one is allowed to devise a law and say that it is according to the Law of God unless it is declared that God is the Legislator, and that the source of authority is God Himself and not some nation or party or individual, and a sincere attempt is made to find out the will of God through reference to His Book and the teachings of His Messenger, peace be on him. But this right cannot be delegated to a person or persons who want to establish authority by taking the name of God, as was the case in Europe under the guise of 'the Church'. There is no 'Church' in Islam; no one can speak in the name of God except His Messenger, peace be on him. There are clear injunctions which define the limits of the divine Law, the Sharī`a.

Al-dīn li-'l-wāqi` (the religion is for real world) is a statement which is quite misunderstood, and which is being used in a wrong sense. Certainly, this religion is for living, but for what kind of life? This religion is for a life which is based on its principles, which is developed according to its methods. This life is completely harmonious with human nature and satisfies all human needs, needs which are determined only by the One Who creates and Who knows His creatures:

Does He Who created not know His creatures? He is the All-Subtle, the All-Aware. (67:14).

It is not the function of religion to provide justification whatever kind of life someone is leading and to bring an authority which he can use to justify his actions. Religion is to be a criterion, to approve what is good and to discard what is evil. If the whole system of life is against the religion, then its function is to abolish this system and to construct a new one. This is the meaning, according to Islam, of the saying "religion is for living"; one ought to understand this with its correct meaning.

The question may be asked, "Is not the good of humankind the criterion for solving actual problems?" But again, we will raise the question which Islam raises itself, and which it answers, that is, "Do you know better, or God?" and, "God knows, and you do not know."

The good of humankind is inherent in the divine Laws sent down by God to the Prophet- peace be on him-which have come to us through his life. If at any time men think that their good is in going against what God has legislated, then first, they are deluded in their thinking.

They follow but speculation and their own desires, although guidance has come to them from their Sustainer. Or shall man have whatever he fancies? And to God belongs the first and the last. (53: 23-25).

Second, they are unbelievers. It is not possible for a person to declare that in his opinion good lies in going against what God has legislated, and simultaneously be a follower of this religion, or be considered its scholar, even for a single moment.

CHAPTER 6
The Universal Law

Islam constructs its foundation of faith and action (*imām/`amal*) on the principle of total submission to God alone. Its beliefs, forms of worship and rules of life are uniformly an expression of this submission and are a practical interpretation of the declaration that there is no deity except God. The details of life are derived from the practice of the Messenger of God, peace be on him-and are a practical consequence of the declaration that Muhammad is the Messenger of God.

Islam builds its entire structure in such a way that these two parts of the declaration determine its system and its characteristics. When Islam builds its structure in this manner, giving it a separate and unique position among all other systems known to man, then Islam actually becomes harmonious with the universal law, which functions not only in human existence but throughout the whole universe as well.

According to the Islamic framework, the whole universe has been created by God. The universe came into existence when God willed it, and then He ordained certain natural laws which it follows and according to which all its various parts operate harmoniously:

> When We wish to bring something into existence, We say to it, 'Be', and there it is. (16:40).

> And He created everything and measured it in due proportion. (25:2).

Behind this universe there is a Will which administers it, a Power which moves it, a Law which regulates it. This Power keeps a balance between the various parts of the universe and controls their motions. They neither collide with each other nor is there any disturbance in their system, nor do their regular motions come to a sudden stop, nor do they become disorganized. This will continue as long as the divine Will wishes it to continue. The whole universe is obedient to God's Will, His Power, and His Authority. It is not possible for it to disobey the divine Will and its ordained law for a single moment. Due to this obedience and submission, the universe continues to go on in a harmonious fashion, and no destruction or dispersion or disturbance can enter into it unless God wills it.

> Indeed, your Sustainer is God, Who created the heavens and the earth in six periods and then established Himself upon the throne of sovereignty. He causes the night to cover up the day and the day to follow the night. The sun and the moon and the stars are controlled by His command; the creation and the command are for Him alone. Glorious is God, the Sustainer of the worlds. (7:54).

The human being is a part of the universe. The laws which govern human nature are no different from the laws governing the universe. God is the Creator of the universe as well as of the human being. Human's body is made of earthly material; yet God has bestowed upon the human being certain characteristics which make him more than the earth from which he is made. God provides the human being according to a measure, a system. In his bodily functions the human being involuntarily follows the same laws of nature as other creatures. His creation is according to the will of God rather than of his father and mother. The father and mother can come together; yet they are not able to transform a sperm into a human being. The human being is born according to the method of development and the method of birth which God has prescribed for him. The human being breathes God's air in the quantity and fashion prescribed by God; he has feelings and understanding, he experiences pain, becomes hungry and thirsty, and eats and drinks. In short, the human being must live according to the laws of God and he has no choice in the matter. In this respect there is no difference between him and other inanimate or animate objects of the universe. All unconditionally submit to the Will of God and to the laws of His creation.

He Who has created the universe and humans, and Who made humans obedient to the laws which also govern the universe, has also prescribed a *shari'a* for his voluntary actions. If humans follow this law, then their life is in harmony with their own nature. From this point of view, this *shari'a* is also a part of that universal law which governs the entire universe, including the physical and biological aspects of humans.

Each word of God, whether it is an injunction or a prohibition, a promise or an admonition, a rule or guidance, is a part of the universal law and is as accurate and true as any of the laws known as the "laws of nature" the divinely ordained laws for the universe, which we find to be operative every moment according to what God has prescribed for them from the dawn of creation.

Therefore, the *shari`a* which God has given to humans to organize their life is also a universal law, as it is related to the general law of the universe and is harmonious with it. This obedience to the Sharī`a becomes a necessity for human beings so that their lives may become harmonious and in tune with the rest of the universe; not only this, but the only way in which harmony can be brought about between the physical laws which are operative in the biological life of a man and the moral laws which govern his voluntary actions is solely through obedience to the Sharī`a. Only in this way does man's personality, internal and external, become integrated.

Man cannot understand all the laws of the universe, nor can he comprehend the unity of this system; he cannot even understand the laws which govern his own person, from which he cannot deviate by a hair's breadth. Therefore, he is incapable of making laws for a system of life which can be in complete harmony with the universe, or which can even harmonize his physical needs with his external behavior. This capability belongs solely to the Creator of the universe and of men, Who not only controls the universe but also human affairs, and Who implements a uniform law according to His will.

This obedience to the Sharī`a of God is necessary for the sake of this harmony, even more necessary than the establishment of the Islamic belief, as no individual or group of individuals can be truly Muslim until they wholly submit to God alone in the manner taught by the Messenger of God- peace be on him, testifying by their actions that there is no deity except God and that Muhammad is God's Messenger.

Total harmony between human life and the law of the universe is entirely beneficial for humankind, as this is the only guarantee against any kind of discord in life. Only in this state will they be at peace with themselves and at peace with the universe, living in accord with its laws and its movements. In the same way, they will have peace of mind, as their actions will agree with their true natural demands, with no conflict between the two. Indeed, the Sharī`a of God harmonizes the external behavior of man with his internal nature in an easy way. When a man makes peace with his own nature, peace and cooperation among individuals follow automatically, as they all live together under one system, which is a part of the general system of the universe.

Therefore, blessings fall on all humankind, as this way leads in an easy manner to the knowledge of the secrets of nature, its hidden forces, and the treasures concealed in the expanses of the universe. Man uses these for the benefit of all humankind, under the guidance of the Sharī`a of God, without any conflict or competition.

In contrast to the Sharī`a of God are men's whims:

> Had the truth followed their opinions, the heavens and the earth and whosoever is in them would surely have been corrupted. (23:71).

From this, we come to know that the truth is one and not many. It is the foundation of this religion, the heavens and earth are based upon it, all the affairs of this world and of the next are settled by it, man will be accountable to God based on it, and those who deviate from the truth are punished by it, and people will be judged by God according to it. Truth is indivisible, and it is the name of that general law which God has ordained for all affairs; and everything in existence either follows it or is punished by it.

> We have sent to you a Book which speaks about you; do you not then use your reason? Many a wicked town have We destroyed and have replaced them with other people. When they felt Our Might approaching, they started to run. (It was said to them), "Do not run; return to the luxury that you gloated in and to your homes; maybe you shall be questioned.

> They said: 'Woe upon us. We have been evildoers.' So, they did not stop crying until We made them stubble, silent and still. We did not create the heavens and the earth and whatsoever is between them as a sport. Had We desired to adopt it for Us as a diversion, We would have taken it to Us from Ourselves,

had We done so. Nay, but We held the truth against falsehood, and it prevails over it, and behold. falsehood vanishes away. Then woe to you for what you ascribe (to God). To Him belongs whatsoever is in the heavens and the earth, and those who are with Him do not be- come too proud to worship Him; neither do they grow weary of glorifying Him by night and by day and never failing. (21: 10-20).

Human nature in its depths has full awareness of this truth. Man's form and body, and the organization of the vast universe around him, re- minds him that this universe is based on truth, and truth is its essence, and it is related to a central law which sustains it. There is no disturbance in it, no conflict between its parts; it does not move at random, nor does it depend on chance, nor is it devoid of an overall plan; neither is it a sport in the hands of human caprices, but runs smoothly on a precise, detailed, and prescribed course. Conflict begins when man deviates from the truth which is hidden in the depths of his own nature, under the influence of his desires, and when he follows laws based on his own opinions instead of following God's commandments. Instead of submitting to his True Master along with the rest of the universe, he rebels and revolts.

When this conflict between man and his own nature, and man and the universe, spreads to human groups, nations and races, then all the forces and resources of the universe are utilized not for the benefit of all human- kind, but for its destruction and for violence against others.

It becomes clear from the above discussion that the purpose of the es- tablishment of God's law on earth is not merely for the sake of the next world. This world and the next world are not two separate entities but are stages complementary to each other. The law given by God not only har- monizes these two stages but also harmonizes human life with the general law of the universe. Therefore, when harmony between human life and the universe ensues, its results are not postponed for the next world but are operative even in this world. However, they will reach their perfection in the Hereafter.

This, then, is the foundation of the Islamic concept of the universe and of human life as a part of this universe. By its very nature, this concept is different from all other concepts known to humankind. This is why this concept implies certain responsibilities and obligations which are not found in other concepts of life.

According to this concept, obedience to the Shari`a of God is actually a consequence of the need to harmonize human life with that law which is operative within man himself and in the rest of the universe. This need demands that the law which governs the social affairs of human beings should be in accordance with the general law of the universe; it demands that man submit to God alone, with the rest of the universe, and that no man should claim lordship over others.

A suggestion of this need for harmony which we have been talking about is found in the conversation between Abraham- peace be on him, the father of the Muslim community, and Nimrod. This man was a tyrant and claimed absolute sovereignty over his subjects; yet he did not claim sovereignty over the heavens, the planets, and stars. When the Prophet Abraham, peace be on him, put forward the argument that He Who has authority over the universe is the only One to have authority over human beings too, he became speechless:

> Have you considered the case of the man who argued with Abraham concerning his Sustainer, because God had given him rule over a country? When Abraham said: My Lord is He Who gives life and Who gives death,' he replied: 'I give life and I give death.' Abraham said: 'Indeed, God brings out the sun from the east. Then do you bring it out from the west?' Then the unbeliever became speechless. And God does not guide the evil-doing people. (2: 258).

> Do they seek a religion other than the religion of God, while whatever is in the heavens and the earth submits to Him willingly, and will return to Him? (3:83).

CHAPTER 7
Islam is the Real Civilization

Islam knows only two kinds of societies: the Islamic society and the *Jāhili* society. The Islamic society is that which follows Islam in belief and ways of worship, in law and organization, in morals and manners. The *Jāhili* society is that which does not follow Islam and in which neither the Islamic belief and concepts, nor Islamic values or standards, Islamic laws and regulations, or Islamic morals and manners are cared for.

The Islamic society is not one in which people call themselves 'Muslims' but in which the Islamic law has no status, even though prayer, fasting and Hajj are regularly observed; and the Islamic society is not one in which people invent their own version of Islam, other than what God and His Messenger, peace be on him-have prescribed and explained, and call it, for example, 'progressive Islam'.

Jāhili society appears in various forms, all of them ignorant of the divine guidance.

Sometimes it takes the form of a society in which belief in God is denied and human history is explained in terms of intellectual materialism, and 'scientific socialism' becomes its system.

Sometimes it appears in the form of a society in which God's existence is not denied, but His domain is restricted to the heavens and His rule on earth is suspended. Neither the Sharī`a nor the values prescribed by God and ordained by Him as eternal and invariable find any place in this scheme of life. In this society, people are permitted to go to mosques, churches, and synagogues; yet it does not tolerate people's demanding that the Sharī`a of God be applied in their daily affairs. Such a society denies or suspends God's sovereignty on earth, while God says plainly:

> It is He Who is Sovereign in the heavens and Sovereign in the earth. (43:84).

Because of this behavior, such a society does not follow the religion of God as defined by Him:

The command belongs to God alone. He commands you not to worship anyone except Him. This is the right way of life. (12:40).

Because of this, such a society is to be counted among *Jāhili* societies, although it may proclaim belief in God and permit people to observe their devotions in mosques, churches, and synagogues.

The Islamic society is, by its very nature, the only civilized society, and the *Jāhili* societies, in all their various forms, are backward societies. It is necessary to elucidate this great truth.

Once I announced as the title of a book of mine which was in press, *The Civilized Society of Islam*, but in my next announcement I dropped the word "civilized" from it. At this change, an Algerian author (who writes in French) commented that the reason for this change is that psychology which operates in a person's mind while defending Islam. The author expressed regret that this was an expression of immaturity which was preventing me from facing reality.

I excused this Algerian author because at one time I was of the same opinion. At that time, my thought processes were like his thought processes of today. I encountered the same difficulty which he is encountering today. That is, to understand the meaning of "civilization".

Until then, I had not gotten rid of the cultural influences which had penetrated my mind despite my Islamic attitude and inclination. The source of these influences was foreign, alien to my Islamic consciousness. Yet, these influences had clouded by intuition and concepts. The Western concept of civilization was my standard. It had prevented me from seeing with clear and penetrating vision.

However, later I saw very clearly that the Muslim society was the civilized society. Hence, the word "civilized" in the title of my book was redundant and did not add anything new. Rather, it would have obscured the thinking of the reader in the same way as my own ideas had been obscured.

Now the question is, what is the meaning of "civilization"? Let us try to explain it.

When, in a society, the sovereignty belongs to God alone, expressed in its obedience to the divine Law, only then is every person in that society free from servitude to others, and only then does he taste true freedom.

This alone is 'human civilization', as the basis of a human civilization is the complete and true freedom of every person and the full dignity of every individual of the society. On the other hand, in a society in which some people are lords who legislate, and some others are slaves who obey them, then there is no freedom in the real sense, nor dignity for every individual.

It is necessary that we clarify the point that legislation is not limited only to legal matters, as some people assign this narrow meaning to the Sharī`a. The fact is that attitudes, the way of living, the values, criteria, habits, and traditions, are all legislated and affect people. If a particular group of people forges all these chains and imprisons others in them, this will not be a free society. I n such a society some people have the position of authority, while others are subservient to them; hence this society will be backward, and in Islamic terminology is called a *Jāhili* society.

Only Islamic society is unique in this respect, in that the authority belongs to God alone; and man, cutting off his chains of servitude to other human beings, enters into the service of God and attains that real and complete freedom which is the focus of human civilization. In this society, the dignity and honor of man are respected according to what God has prescribed. He becomes the representative of God on earth, and his position becomes even higher than that of the angels.

In a society which bases its foundation on the concept, belief and way of life which all originate from the One God, man's dignity is respected to the highest degree and no one is a slave to another, as they are in societies in which the concepts, beliefs and way of life originate from human masters. In the former society, man's highest characteristics, those of the spirit and mind -are reflected, while in a society in which human relationships are based on color, race or nation, or similar criteria, these relationships become a chain for human thought and prevent man's noble characteristics from coming to the fore. A person remains human regardless of what color, race or nation he belongs to, but he cannot be called human if he is devoid of spirit and reason. Furthermore, he can change his beliefs, concepts and attitudes toward life, but he is incapable of changing his color and race, nor can he decide in what place or nation to be born. It is clear that only such a society is civilized in which human associations are based on free choice, and that society is backward in which the basis of association is something other than free choice; in Islamic terminology, it is a *Jāhili* society.

Only Islam has the distinction of basing the fundamental binding relationship in its society on belief; and on the basis of this belief, black and white and red and yellow, Arabs and Greeks, Persians and Africans, and all nations which inhabit the earth become one community. In this society God is the Lord and only He is worshipped, the most honorable is the one who is noblest in character, and all individuals are equally subject to a law which is not man-made but made by their Creator.

A society which places the highest value on the 'humanity' of man and honors the noble 'human' characteristics is truly civilized. If materialism, no matter in what form, is given the highest value, whether it be in the form of a 'theory', such as in the Marxist interpretation of history, or in the form of material production, as is the case with the United States and European countries, and all other human values are sacrificed at its altar, then such a society is a backward one, or, in Islamic terminology, is a *Jāhili* society.

The civilized society, that is, the Islamic society, does not downgrade matter, either in theory or in the form of material production, as it considers the universe in which we live, by which we are influenced, and which we influence, to be made of matter, and it considers material production to be the backbone of the vicegerency of God on earth. However, in the Islamic society material comforts are not made into the highest value at the expense of 'human' characteristics-freedom and honor, family and its obligations, morals and values, and so on, as is the case in *Jāhili* societies.

If a society is based on "human values" and "human morals" and these remain dominant in it, then that society will be civilized. Human values and human morals are not something mysterious and indefinable, nor are they "progressive" and changeable, having no roots and stability, as is claimed by the exponents of the materialistic interpretation of history or of "scientific socialism." They are the values and the morals which develop those characteristics in a human being which distinguish him from the animals and which emphasize those aspects of his personality which raise him above the animals; these are not such values and morals which develop and emphasize those characteristics in man which are common with the animals.

When the question is viewed in this manner, a fixed and well-defined line of separation is obtained which cannot be erased by the incessant attempt of the 'progressives' and the scientific societies to erase it. According to this view, moral standards are not determined by the environment and changing conditions; rather they are fixed criteria above and beyond the difference in environments. One cannot say that some moral values are agricultural and others industrial, some are capitalistic and some others socialistic, some are bourgeoisie and others proletarian. Here, the standards of morality are independent of the environment, the economic status, and the stage of development of a society; these are nothing but superficial variations. Beyond all these, we arrive at "human'" values and morals and at animalistic values and morals, this being the correct separation or, in Islamic terminology, Islamic values and morals and *Jāhili* values and morals.

Indeed, Islam establishes the values and morals which are 'human', those which develop characteristics in a human being which distinguish him from the animals. In whatever society Islam is dominant, whether it is an agricultural or industrial society, nomadic and pastoral or urban and settled, poor or rich, it implants these human values and morals, nurtures them and strengthens them; it develops human characteristics progressively and guards against degeneration toward animalism. The direction of the line which separates human values from animal-like characteristics is upward. However, if this direction is reversed, then in spite of all material progress the civilization will be backward, degenerative, and *"Jāhili"*.

If the family is the basis of the society, and the basis of the family is the division of labor between husband and wife, and the upbringing of children is the most important function of the family, then such a society is indeed civilized. In the Islamic system of life, this kind of a family provides the environment under which human values and morals develop and grow in the new generation; these values and morals cannot exist apart from the family unit. If, on the other hand, 97 free sexual relationships and illegitimate children become the basis of a society, and if the relationship between man and woman is based on lust, passion and impulse, and the division of work is not based on family responsibility and natural gifts; if woman's role is merely to be attractive, sexy and flirtatious, and if woman is freed from her basic responsibility of bringing up children; and if, on her own or under social demand, she prefers to become a hostess or a stewardess in a hotel or ship or air company, spending her ability for material productivity rather than in the training of human beings, because material production is considered to be more important, more valuable and more honorable than the development of human character, then such a civilization is "backward" from the human point of view, or "*Jāhilī*" in the Islamic terminology.

The family system and the relationship between the sexes determine the whole character of a society and whether it is backward or civilized, *Jāhili* or Islamic. Those societies which give ascendance to physical desires and animalistic morals cannot be considered civilized, no matter how much progress they may make in industry or science. This is the only measure which does not err in gauging true human progress.

In all modern *Jāhili* societies, the meaning of 'morality' is limited to such an extent that all those aspects which distinguish man from animal are considered beyond its sphere. In these Societies, illegitimate sexual relationships, even homosexuality, are not considered immoral. The meaning of ethics is limited to economic affairs or sometimes to political affairs which fall into the category of "government interests." For example, the scandal of Christine Keeler and the British minister Profumo was not considered serious to British society because of its sexual aspect; it was condemnable because Christine Keeler was also involved with a naval attaché of the Russian Embassy, and her association with a cabinet minister lied before the British Parliament! Similar scandals come to light in the American Senate. Englishmen and Americans who get involved in such spying scandals usually take refuge in Russia. These affairs are not considered immoral because of sexual deviations, but because of the danger to state secrets.

Among *Jāhili* societies, writers, journalists and editors advise both married and unmarried people that free sexual relationships are not immoral. However, it is immoral if a boy uses his partner, or a girl uses her partner, for sex, while feeling no love in his or her heart. It is bad if a wife continues to guard her chastity while her love for her husband has vanished; it is admirable if she finds another lover. Dozens of stories are written about this theme; many newspaper editorials, articles, cartoons, serious and light columns all invite this way of life.

From the point of view of 'human' progress, all such societies are not civilized but are backward.

The line of human progress goes upward from animal desires toward higher values. To control the animal desires, a progressive society lays down the foundation of a family system in which human desires find satisfaction, as well as providing for the future generation to be brought up in such a manner that it will continue the human civilization, in which human characteristics flower to their full bloom. Obviously, a society which intends to control the animal characteristics, while providing full opportunities for the development and perfection of human characteristics, requires strong safeguards for the peace and stability of the family, so that it may perform its basic task free from the influences of impulsive passions. On the other hand, if in a society immoral teachings and poisonous suggestions are rampant, and sexual activity is considered outside the sphere of morality, then in that society the humanity of man can hardly find a place to develop.

Therefore, only Islamic values and morals, Islamic teachings and safeguards, are worthy of humankind, and from this unchanging and true measure of human progress, Islam is the real civilization and Islamic society is truly civilized.

Lastly, when humankind establishes the representation of God on earth in all respects, by dedicating himself to the service of God and freeing himself from servitude to others, by establishing the system of life prescribed by God and rejecting all other systems, by arranging his life according to the Sharī`a of God and giving up all other laws, by adopting the values and standards of morality which are pleasing to God and rejecting all other standards and, after this, when he investigates the laws governing the universe and uses them for the benefit of all humankind, applies them to resources hidden in the earth in accordance with the obligation imposed on him by God as His vicegerent on earth, unearths the treasures and resources of food and raw materials for industries, and uses his technical and professional knowledge for the development of various kinds of industries, doing all these things as a God-fearing person and as a representative of God; and when his attitude toward the material and moral aspects of life is infused with this spirit, only then does man become completely civilized and the society reach the height of civilization. In Islam, mere material inventions are not considered as civilization, as a *Jāhili* society can also have material prosperity. In many places in the Quran, God has described societies of this kind, which have attained material prosperity while remaining *Jāhili*.

Hud said to his people: "What is the matter with you that you make a memorial at every high place and build palaces as if you are immortal? When you deal with others, you are tyrants. Then fear God and obey me. Fear Him Who gave you whatever you know. He gave you animals, children, gardens and rivers. I fear for you the day of a severe chastisement. (26: 128-135).

Salih said to his people: "Will you remain secure here among these things, among gardens and fountains, the farmland and palm trees with juicy fruit? You build houses skillfully out of the mountains. So, fear God and obey me, and do not obey the advice of the wasteful, those who make corruption in the earth and do not set things right. (26:146-152).

So, when they forgot what they were reminded of, We opened to them the gates of everything until, when they rejoiced in what they were given, We seized them suddenly, and behold! they were greatly confounded. So, the last remnant of the people who did evil was cut off. Praise belongs to God, the Sustainer of the Worlds." (6:43-44).

When the earth has taken on its glitter and has adorned itself fair, and its inhabitants think they have power over it, Our command comes upon it by night or by day, and We make it as stubble, as if yesterday it had not flourished. (10:24).

But as we have said earlier, Islam does not look with contempt on material progress and material inventions; in fact, it considers them when used under the divine system of life, as God's gifts. In the Quran we find that God promises His bounty to people when they are obedient to Him.

(Noah said): "I said to my people, 'Ask forgiveness from your Sustainer; indeed, He accepts repentance. He will send upon you rain from the sky continuously and will make you powerful through wealth and children, and He will raise for you gardens and make streams for you. (71:10-12).

Had the people of those towns believed and feared God, We would have opened blessings upon them from the sky and the earth, but they rejected the truth, so for their evil deeds We took them to account. (7:96).

But the important thing is that foundation on which the industrial structure is built, and those values which bind a society, and through which a society acquires the characteristics of the human civilization.

Since the basis of the Islamic society and the nature of its growth, which give rise to its community, have a unique character, one cannot apply to it those theories which can explain the establishment and growth of *Jāhili* societies. The Islamic society is born out of a movement, and this movement continues within it; it determines the places and positions of individuals in the community and then assigns them roles and responsibilities.

The origin of this movement, from which this community is born, is outside the human sphere and outside this world. Its source is a belief which has come from God to humankind, and which gives them a particular concept of the universe, of life of human history, of values and purposes, and which defines for them a way of life reflecting this concept. The initial impetus for the movement does not come from human minds, nor from the physical world, but, as we have stated before, it comes from outside the earth and outside the human sphere; and this is the first distinctive feature of the Islamic society and its organization.

Indeed, the origin of this movement is an element outside the sphere of man and outside the physical world. This element, which comes into existence from God's will, is not something expected by any human being or taken into consideration by anyone, and in the beginning, no human endeavor enters into it. This divine element sows the seed of the Islamic movement and at the same time prepares the human being for action - prepares the one who believes in the faith which reaches to him from the divine source. As soon as this single individual believes in this faith, the Islamic community comes into existence. This individual does not remain satisfied at having this faith but stands up to give its message. It is the nature of this faith that it is a virile and dynamic movement; the power which lights up this faith in this heart knows that it will not remain concealed but will come out into the open and will spread to others.

When the number of Believers reaches three, then this faith tells them; "Now you are a community, a distinct Islamic community, distinct from that *Jāhili* society which does not live according to this belief or accept its basic premise." Now the Islamic society has come into existence.

These three individuals increase to ten, the ten to a hundred, the hundred to a thousand, and the thousand increase to twelve thousand-and the Islamic society grows and becomes established.

During the progress of this movement, a struggle would already have started within the *Jāhili* society. On the one side is this newborn society, which in its belief and concepts, values and standards, existence and organization has separated itself from the *Jāhili* society, from which the Islamic society absorbs individuals. This movement, from the moment of its inception until the growth and permanent existence of its society comes about, tests every individual, and assigns him a position of responsibility according to his capacity, as measured by the Islamic balance and standards. The society automatically recognizes his capabilities, and he does not need to come forward and announce his candidacy; in fact, his belief and the values to which he and his society subscribe compel him to keep himself concealed from the eyes of those who want to give him a responsible position.

But the movement which is a natural outgrowth of the Islamic belief and which is the essence of the Islamic society does not let any individual hide himself. Every individual in this society must move. There should be a movement in his belief, a movement in his blood, a movement in his community, and in the structure of this organic society, and as the *Jāhiliyya* is all around him, and its residual influences in his mind and in the minds of those around him, the struggle goes on and the *Jihād* continues until the Day of Resurrection.

The ups and downs through which the movement passes determine the position and activity of every individual in the movement, and the organic body of this society is completed through the harmony between its individuals and their activities.

This kind of beginning and this method of organization are two of the characteristics of the Islamic society which distinguish it from other societies in respect to its existence and its structure, its nature and its form, its system and the method of regulating this system, and make it a unique and separate entity. It cannot be understood by social theories alien to it, nor can it be taught by methods foreign to its nature, nor can it be brought into existence by ways borrowed from other systems.

According to our unvarying definition of civilization, the Islamic society is not just an entity of the past, to be studied in history, but it is a demand of the present and a hope of the future. Humankind can be dignified, today or tomorrow, by striving toward this noble civilization, by pulling itself out of the abyss of *Jāhiliyya* into which it is falling. This is true not only for the industrially and economically developed nations but also for the backward nations.

The values to which we referred above as human values were never attained by humankind except in the period of Islamic civilization. We also ought to remember that by the term 'Islamic Civilization' we mean that civilization in which these values are found to the highest degree, and not a civilization which may make progress in industry, economics, and science but in which human values are suppressed.

These values are not idealistic but are practical values which can be attained through human effort, by applying the teachings of Islam correctly. These values can be attained in any environment, whatever the level of industrial and scientific progress may be, as there is no contradiction; in fact, material prosperity and scientific progress are encouraged by the teachings of Islam, as they pertain to man's role as the representative of God on earth.

Similarly, in countries which are industrially and scientifically backward, these values teach people not to remain just silent spectators but to strive for industrial and scientific progress. A civilization with these values can develop anywhere and in any environment; however, the actual form it takes is not one, but depends on the conditions and environment existing in the society in which these values develop.

The Islamic society, in its form and extent and its way of living, is not a fixed historic entity; but its existence and its civilization are based on values which are fixed historical realities. The word 'historical' used in this context only means that these values took concrete form in a particular period of human history. In fact, these values, by their nature, do not belong to any particular period; they are the truth which has come to man from the divine source-beyond the sphere of humankind and beyond the sphere of the physical universe.

The Islamic civilization can take various forms in its material and organizational structure, but the principles and values on which it is based are eternal and unchangeable. These are: the worship of God alone, the foundation of human relationships on the belief in the Oneness of God, the supremacy of the humanity of man over material things, the development of human values and the control of animalistic desires, respect for the family, the assumption of being the representative of God on earth according to His guidance and instruction, and in all affairs of this vice-regency the rule of God's law (al-Sharī`a) and the way of life prescribed by Him.

The forms of the Islamic civilization, constructed on these fixed principles, depend on actual conditions, and are influenced by and change according to the stage of industrial, economic or scientific progress. These forms are necessarily different and are a consequence of the fact that Islam possesses sufficient flexibility to enter into any system and mold that system according to its purposes; but this flexibility in the outward forms of Islamic civilization does not mean any flexibility in the Islamic belief, which is the fountainhead of this civilization, nor is it to be considered as borrowed from outside, for it is the character of this religion. However, flexibility is not to be confused with fluidity. There is a great difference between these two.

When Islam entered the central part of Africa, it clothed naked human beings, socialized them, brought them out of the deep recesses of isolation, and taught them the joy of work for exploring material resources. It brought them out of the narrow circles of tribe and clan into the vast circle of the Islamic community, and out of the worship of pagan gods into the worship of the Creator of the worlds. If this is not civilization, then what is it? This civilization was for this environment, and it used the actual resources which were available. If Islam enters some other environment, then its civilization will also take another form-but with values which are eternal, based on the existing resources of that environment.

Therefore, the development of the civilization, according to the method and manner of Islam, does not depend on any particular level of industrial, economic or scientific progress. Wherever this civilization is established, it will use all the resources, will develop them, and if in a certain place these resources are non-existent, then it will supply them and will provide the means for their growth and progress. But in all situations, it will be based on its immutable and eternal principles, and wherever such an

Islamic society comes into existence, its character and its movement will also come into existence and will make it distinguished and distinct from all *Jāhili* societies.

> The baptism of God -and who can baptize better than God? (2: 138).

CHAPTER 8
The Islamic Concept and Culture

In the sixth chapter, we have demonstrated that the first part of the first pillar of Islam is the dedication of one's life to God alone. This is the meaning of *"lā ilāha illā allāh"*. The second part means that the way of this dedication comes from the Prophet Muhammad: "Muhammadan rasūl allāh" points to this fact. Complete submission to God comes by submitting to Him through belief, practice and in law. No Muslim can believe that another being can be a 'deity', nor can he believe that one can 'worship' a creature of God or that he can be given a position of 'sovereignty'. We explained in that chapter the meaning of worship, belief, and sovereignty. In what follows we will show the true meaning of sovereignty and its relationship to culture.

In the Islamic concept, the sovereignty of God means not merely that one should derive all legal injunctions from God and judge according to these injunctions; in Islam the meaning of the 'Sharī'a' is not limited to mere legal injunctions, but includes the principles of administration, its system and its modes. This narrow meaning (i.e., that the Sharī'a is limited to legal injunctions) does not apply to the Sharī'a nor does it correspond to the Islamic concept. By 'the Sharī'a of God is meant everything legislated by God for ordering man's life; it includes the principles of belief, principles of administration and justice, principles of morality and human relationships, and principles of knowledge.

The Sharī'a includes the Islamic beliefs and concepts and their implications concerning the attributes of God, the nature of life, what is apparent and what is hidden in it, the nature of man, and the interrelationships among these. Similarly, it includes political, social and economic affairs and their principles, with the intent that they reflect complete submission to God alone. It also includes legal matters (this is what today is referred to as the Sharī'a, while the true meaning of the 'Sharī'a in Islam is entirely different). It deals with the morals, manners, values, and standards of the society, according to which persons, actions and events are measured. It also deals with all aspects of knowledge and principles of art and science. In all these guidance from God is needed, just as it is needed in legal matters.

We have discussed the sovereignty of God in relation to government and the legal system, and in relation to matters of morals, human relationships, and values and standards which prevail in a society. The point to note was that the values and standards, morals and manners, are all based on the beliefs and concepts prevalent in the society and are derived from the same divine source from which beliefs are derived.

The thing which will appear strange, not only to the common man but also to writers about Islam, is our turning to Islam and to the divine source for guidance in spheres of science and art.

A book has already been published about art in which it has been pointed out that all artistic efforts reflect a man's concepts, beliefs, and intuitions. They reflect whatever pictures of life, and the world are found in a man's intuition. All these affairs are not only governed by the Islamic concepts, but, in fact, this concept is a motivating power for a Muslim's creativity. The Islamic concept of the universe defines man's relationship to the rest of the universe and to his Creator. Its basic subject is the nature of man and his position in the universe, the purpose of his life, his function, and the true value of his life. These are all included in the Islamic concept, which is not merely an abstract idea but is a living, active motivating force which influences man's emotions and actions. (*The Principles of Islamic Art*, by Muhammad Qutb).

In short, the question of art and literary thought and its relationship to divine guidance requires a detailed discussion, and, as we have stated before, this discussion will appear strange not only to educated people but even to those Muslims who believe in the sovereignty of God in matters of law.

A Muslim cannot go to any source other than God for guidance in matters of faith, in the concept of life, acts of worship, morals and human affairs, values and standards, principles of economics and political affairs and interpretation of historical processes. It is, therefore, his duty that he should learn all these from a Muslim whose piety and character, belief and action, are beyond reproach.

However, a Muslim can go to a Muslim or to a non-Muslim to learn abstract sciences such as chemistry, physics, biology, astronomy, medicine, industry, agriculture, administration (limited to its technical aspects), technology, military arts and similar sciences and arts; although the fundamental principle is that when the Muslim community comes into existence it should provide experts in all these fields in abundance, as all these sciences and arts are a sufficient obligation (*fard al-kifāya*) on Muslims (that is to say, there ought to be a sufficient number of people who specialize in these various sciences and arts to satisfy the needs of the community).

If a proper atmosphere is not provided under which these sciences and arts develop in a Muslim society, the whole society will be considered sinful; but as long as these conditions are not attained, it is permitted for a Muslim to learn them from a Muslim or a non-Muslim and to gain experience under his direction, without any distinction of religion. These are those affairs which are included in the Hadith, "You know best the affairs of your business." These sciences are not related to the basic concepts of a Muslim about life, the universe, man, the purpose of his creation, his responsibilities, his relationship with the physical world and with the Creator; these are also not related to the principles of law, the rules and regulations which order the lives of individuals and groups, nor are they related to morals, manners, traditions, habits, values and standards which prevail in the society and which give the society its shape and form. There is no danger that a Muslim, by learning these sciences from a non-Muslim, will distort his belief or will return to *Jāhiliyya*.

But as far as the interpretation of human endeavor is concerned, whether this endeavor be individual or collective, this relates to theories of the nature of man and of the historical processes. Similarly, the explanation of the origin of the universe, the origin of the life of man, are part of metaphysics (not related to the abstract sciences such as chemistry, physics, astronomy, or medicine, etc.). Their position is like legal matters, rules and regulations which order human life. These indirectly affect man's beliefs; it is therefore not permissible for a Muslim to learn them from anyone other than a God-fearing and pious Muslim, who knows that guidance in these matters comes from God. The main purpose is, a Muslim should realize, that all these affairs are related to his faith, and that to seek guidance from God in these matters is a necessary consequence of the faith in the Oneness of God and the *Risāla* of Muhammad.

However, a Muslim can study all the opinions and thoughts of *Jāhili* writers, not from the point of view of constructing his own beliefs and concepts, but for the purpose of knowing the deviations adopted by *Jāhiliyya*, so that he may know how to correct these man-made deviations in the light of the true Islamic belief and rebut them according to the sound principles of the Islamic teachings.

Philosophy, the interpretation of history, psychology (except for those observations and experimental results which are not part of anyone's opinion) ethics, theology and comparative religion, sociology (excluding statistics and observations) all these sciences have a direction which in the past or the present has been influenced by *Jāhili* beliefs and traditions. That is why all these sciences come into conflict, explicitly or implicitly, with the fundamentals of any religion, and especially with Islam.

The situation concerning these areas of human thought and knowledge is not the same as with physics, chemistry, astronomy, biology, medicine, etc., as long as these last- mentioned sciences limit themselves to practical experiments and their results, and do not go beyond their scope into speculative philosophy. For example, Darwinist biology goes beyond the scope of its observations, without any rhyme or reason and only for the sake of expressing an opinion, in making the assumption that to explain the beginning of life and its evolution there is no need to assume a power outside the physical world.

Concerning these matters, the true guidance from his Sustainer is sufficient for a Muslim. This guidance toward belief and complete submission to God alone is so superior to all man's speculative attempts in these affairs that they appear utterly ridiculous and absurd.

The statement that "Culture is the human heritage" and that it has no country, nationality or religion is correct only in relation to science and technology-as long as we do not jump the boundary of these sciences and delve into metaphysical interpretations, and start explaining the purpose of man and his historical role in philosophical terms, even explaining away art and literature and human intuition philosophically. Beyond this limited meaning, this statement about culture is one of the tricks played by world Jewry, whose purpose is to eliminate all limitations, especially the limitations imposed by faith and religion, so that the Jews may penetrate into body politic of the whole world and then may be free to perpetuate their evil designs. At the top of the list of these activities is usury, the aim of which is that all the wealth of humankind end up in the hands of Jewish financial institutions which run on interest.

However, Islam considers that, excepting the abstract sciences and their practical applications-there are two kinds of culture. The Islamic culture, which is based on the Islamic concept, and the *Jāhili* culture, which manifests itself in various modes of living which are nevertheless all based on one thing, and that is giving human thought the status of a god so that its truth or falsity is not to be judged according to God's guidance. The Islamic culture is concerned with all theoretical and practical affairs, and it contains principles, methods and characteristics which guarantee the development and perpetuation of all cultural activities.

One ought to remember the fact that the experimental method, which is the dynamic spirit of modern Europe's industrial culture, did not originate in Europe but originated in the Islamic universities of Andalusia and of the East. The principle of the experimental method was an offshoot of the Islamic concept and its explanations of the physical world, its phenomena, its forces, and its secrets. Later, by adopting the experimental method, Europe entered the period of scientific revival, which led it step by step to great scientific heights. Meanwhile, the Muslim world gradually drifted away from Islam, because of which the scientific movement first became inert and later ended completely. Some of the causes which led to this state of inertia were internal to the Muslim society and some were external, such as the invasions of the Muslim world by the Christians and Zionists. Europe removed the foundation of Islamic belief from the methodology of the empirical sciences, and finally, when Europe rebelled against the Church, which in the name of God oppressed the common people, it deprived the empirical sciences of their Islamic method of relating them to God's guidance.

The entire basis of European thought became *Jāhili* and completely estranged from the Islamic concept, and even became contradictory and conflicting with it. It is necessary for a Muslim, therefore, to return to the guidance of God to learn the Islamic concept of life- on his own, if possible, or otherwise to seek knowledge from a God-fearing Muslim whose piety and faith are reliable.

In Islam the saying, "Seek knowledge from the one who knows," is not acceptable with respect to those sciences which relate to faith, religion, morals and values, customs and habits, and all those matters which concern human relationships.

Without doubt, Islam permits a Muslim to learn chemistry, physics, astronomy, medicine, technology and agriculture, administration, and similar technical sciences from a non-Muslim or from a Muslim who is not pious, and this under the condition that no God-fearing Muslim scientists are available to teach these sciences. This is the situation which exists now because Muslims have drifted away from their religion and their way of life and have forgotten that Islam appointed them as representatives of God and made them responsible for learning all the sciences and developing various capabilities to fulfill this high position which God has granted them. But Islam does not permit Muslims to learn the principles of their faith, the implications of their concept, the interpretation of the Quran, Hadith, the Prophet, peace be on him-the philosophy of history, the traditions of their society, the constitution of their government, the form of their politics, and similar branches of knowledge, from non-Islamic sources or from anyone other than a pious Muslim whose faith and religious knowledge is known to be reliable.

The person who is writing these lines has spent forty years of his life in reading books and in research in almost all aspects of human knowledge. He specialized in some branches of knowledge, and he studied others due to personal interest. Then he turned to the fountainhead of his faith. He came to feel that whatever he had read so far was nothing in comparison to what he found here. He does not regret spending forty years of his life in the pursuit of these sciences, because he came to know the nature of *Jāhiliyya*, its deviations, its errors and its ignorance, as well as its pomp and noise, its arrogant and boastful claims. Finally, he was convinced that a Muslim cannot combine these two sources-the source of divine guidance and the source of *Jāhiliyya*—for his education.

Even then, this is not my opinion; this is a grave matter to be decided merely by some person's opinion, and the question of depending on a Muslim's opinion does not arise when the divine standard provides us a way to judge the matter. This is the decision of God and His Messenger, peace be on him, and we refer it to them. We refer it to them in the same manner as is befitting for a Believer, as all controversial decisions ought to be referred to the judgment of God and His Prophet, peace be on him.

God Most High says in general terms concerning the ultimate aims of the Jews and Christians against Muslims:

> Many among the People of the Book wish to turn you back from
> your faith toward unbelief, due to their envy, even after the
> truth has been known to them; but forgive and excuse them

until God brings about His decision. Indeed, God has power over everything. (2:109).

The Jews and Christians will not be pleased with you unless you follow their way. Say: "Indeed, God's guidance is the true guidance'. And if, after this knowledge has come to you, you follow their desires, then you will find no helper or friend against God. (2:120).

O you who believe! If you follow a party of the People of the Book, they will return you to the state of unbelief after you have believed. (3:100).

As reported by Hafiz Abu Ya'lā, the Messenger of God- peace be on him, said: "Do not ask the People of the Book about anything. They will not guide you, In fact, they are themselves misguided. If you listen to them, you might end up accepting some falsehood or denying some truth. By God, If Moses had been alive among you, he would not be permitted (by God) anything except to follow me."

After this warning to the Muslims from God concerning the ultimate designs of the Jews and Christians, it would be extremely short-sighted of us to fall into the illusion that when the Jews and Christians discuss Islamic beliefs or Islamic history, or when they make proposals concerning Muslim society or Muslim politics or economics, they will be doing it with good intentions, or with the welfare of the Muslims at heart, or in order to seek guidance and light. People who, after this clear statement from God, still think this way are indeed deluded.

Similarly, the saying of God Most High: "Say: 'Indeed, God's guidance is the true guidance", determines the unique source to which every Muslim should turn for guidance in all these affairs, as whatever is beyond God's guidance is error and none other than He can guide, as is clear from the emphasis in the verse, "Say: 'Indeed, God's guidance is the true guidance". There is no ambiguity in the meaning of this verse and no other interpretation is possible.

There is also a decisive injunction to avoid a person who turns away from the remembrance of God and whose only object is this world. It is explained that such a person follows mere speculation-and a Muslim is forbidden to follow speculation, and he knows only what is apparent in the life of this world and does not possess the true knowledge.

> Avoid a person who has turned away from Our remembrance and does not desire anything beyond the life of this world, and this is the extent of his knowledge. Your Sustainer knows best who has gone astray from His path, and He knows best who is guided. (53:29-30).

> They only know what is apparent in the life of this world and are negligent of the Hereafter. (30:7).

A person who is negligent in remembering God and is completely occupied with the affairs of this life-and that is the case with all the 'scientists' of today- knows only what is apparent, and this is not the type of knowledge, for which a Muslim can rely completely on its possessor, except for what is permitted to be learned from them to the extent of technical knowledge. He should ignore their interpretations concerning psychological and conceptual matters. This is not the kind of knowledge, which is praised repeatedly in the Quran, for example in the verse, "Are they equal, those who know and those who do not know"? Those who take such verses out of context and argue are in error. The complete verse in which this rhetorical question is posed is as follows:

> Or is he who is worshipful in the watches of the night, prostrating and standing, he being afraid of the Hereafter and hoping for the mercy of His Sustainer? Say: Are they equal, those who know and those who do not know? Indeed, the thinking persons take heed. (39:9).

Only such a person who, in the darkness of the night, remains worshipping, standing or prostrating, who fears the Hereafter, and hopes for the mercy of his Sustainer, is truly knowing, and it is his knowledge to which the above verse refers; that is to say, the knowledge which guides toward God and the remembrance of Him,. and not that knowledge which distorts human nature toward denial of God.

The sphere of knowledge is not limited to articles of faith, religious obligations, or laws about what is permissible and what is forbidden; its sphere is very wide. It includes all these and the knowledge of natural laws and all matters concerning man s delegated role before God. However, any knowledge, the foundation of which is not based on faith, is outside the definition of that knowledge which is referred to in the Quran and the possessors of which are considered praiseworthy. There is a strong relationship between faith and all those sciences which deal with the universe and natural laws, such as astronomy, biology, physics, chemistry, and geology. All these sciences lead man toward God, unless they are perverted by personal opinions and speculations, and presented devoid of the concept of God. Such a regrettable situation occurred in Europe. In fact, there came a time in European history when very painful and hateful differences arose between scientists and the oppressive Church; consequently, the entire scientific movement in Europe started with Godlessness. This movement affected all aspects of life very deeply; in fact, it changed the entire character of European thought. The effect of this hostility of the scientific community toward the Church did not remain limited to the Church or to its beliefs, but was directed against all religion, so much so that all sciences turned against religion, whether they were speculative philosophy or technical or abstract sciences having nothing to do with religion (See *The Future Belongs to This Religion*).

The Western ways of thought and all the sciences started on the foundation of these poisonous influences with an enmity toward all religion, and with greater hostility toward Islam. This enmity toward Islam is especially pronounced and many times is the result of a well-thought-out scheme, the object of which is first to shake the foundations of Islamic beliefs and then gradually to demolish the structure of Muslim society.

If, despite knowing this, we rely on Western ways of thought, even in teaching the Islamic sciences, it will be an unforgiveable blindness on our part. Indeed, it becomes incumbent on us, while learning purely scientific or technological subjects for which we have no other sources except Western sources, to remain on guard and keep these sciences away from philosophical speculations, as these philosophical speculations are generally against religion and against Islam. A slight influence from them can pollute the clear spring of Islam.

CHAPTER 9
A Muslim's Nationality and His Belief

The day Islam gave a new concept of values and standards to humanity and showed the way to learn these values and standards, it also provided it with a new concept of human relationships. Islam came to return man to his Sustainer and to make His guidance the only source from which values and standards are to be obtained, as He is the Provider and Originator. All relationships ought to be based through Him, as we came into being through His will and shall return to Him.

Islam came to establish only one relationship which binds men together in the sight of God, and if this relationship is firmly established, then all other relationships based on blood or other considerations become eliminated.

> You will not find the people who believe in God and the Hereafter taking as allies the enemies of God and His Prophet, whether they be their fathers or sons or brothers or fellow tribesmen. (58:22).

In the world there is only one party of God; all others are parties of Satan and rebellion.

> Those who believe fight in the cause of God, and those who disbelieve fight in the cause of rebellion. Then fight the allies of Satan; indeed, Satan's strategy is weak. (3:78).

There is only one way to reach God; all other ways do not lead to Him.

> This is My straight path. Then follow it, and do not follow other ways which will scatter you from His path. (6:153).

For human life, there is only one true system, and that is Islam; all other systems are *Jāhiliyya*.

Do they want a judgement of the Days of Ignorance? Yet who is better in judgement than God, for a people having sure faith? (5:50).

There is only one law which ought to be followed, and that is the Shari`a from God; anything else is mere emotionalism and impulsiveness.

We have set you on a way ordained (by God); then follow it, and do not follow the desires of those who have no knowledge. (45:18).

The truth is one and indivisible; anything different from it is error. Is anything left besides error, beyond the truth? Then to which do you go? (10:32).

There is only one place on earth which can be called the home of Islam (Dar al-Islam), and it is that place where the Islamic state is established and the Shari`a is the authority and God's limits are observed, and where all the Muslims administer the affairs of the state with mutual consultation. The rest of the world is the home of hostility (Dar al-Harb). A Muslim can have only two possible relations with Dar al-Harb: peace with a contractual agreement, or war. A country with which there is a treaty will not be considered the home of Islam.

Those who believed, and migrated, and strove with their wealth and their persons in the cause of God, and those who gave them refuge and helped them, are the protectors of each other. As to those who believed but did not emigrate, you have no responsibility for their protection until they emigrate; but if they ask your help in religion, it is your duty to help them, except against a people between whom and you there is a treaty; and God sees whatever you do. Those who disbelieve are allies of each other. If you do not do this, there will be oppression on the earth and a great disturbance. Those who believe, and migrate, and fight in the cause of God, and those who give them refuge and help them, are in truth Believers. For them is forgiveness and generous provision. And those who accept faith afterwards and migrate and strive along with you, they are of you. (8:72-75).

Islam came with this total guidance and decisive teaching. It came to elevate man above, and release him from, the bonds of the earth and soil, the bonds of flesh and blood-which are also the bonds of the earth and soil. A Muslim has no country except that part of the earth where the Sharī`a of God is established and human relationships are based on the foundation of relationship with God; a Muslim has no nationality except his belief, which makes him a member of the Muslim community in Dar al-Islam; a Muslim has no relatives except those who share the belief in God, and a bond is established between him and other Believers through their relationship with God.

A Muslim has no relationship with his mother, father, brother, wife, and other family members except through their relationship with the Creator, and then they are also joined through blood.

> O humankind, remain mindful of your Sustainer, Who created you from one soul and created from its mate, and from the two of them scattered a great many men and women. Remain conscious of God, from Whose authority you make demands and reverence the wombs (from which you were born). (4:1).

However, divine relationship does not prohibit a Muslim from treating his parents with kindness and consideration in spite of differences of belief, as long as they do not join the front lines of the enemies of Islam. However, if they openly declare their alliance with the enemies of Islam, then all the filial relationships of a Muslim are cut off and he is not bound to be kind and considerate to them. Abdullah, son of Abdullah Ibn Ubayy, has presented us with a bright example in this respect.

Ibn Jarir, on the authority of Ibn Ziyad, has reported that the Prophet called Abdullah, son of Abdullah Ibn Ubayy, and said, "Do you know what your father said?" Abdullah asked. "May my parents be a ransom for you; what did my father say?" The prophet replied, "He said, 'If we return to *Madīna* (from the battle), the one with honor will throw out the one who is despised." Abdullah then said, "O Messenger of God, by God, he told the truth. You are the one with honor and he is the one who is despised. O

Messenger of God, the people of *Madīna* know that before you came to *Madīna*, no one was more obedient to his father than I was. But now, if it is the pleasure of God and His Prophet that I cut off his head, then I shall do so." The Prophet replied, "No". When the Muslims returned to *Madīna*, Abdullah stood in front of the gate with his sword drawn over his father's head, telling him, "Did you say that if we return to *Madīna* then the one with honor will throw out the one who is despised? By God, now you will know whether you have honor, or God's Messenger. By God, until God and His Messenger give permission, you cannot enter *Madīna*, nor will you have refuge from me." Ibn Ubayy cried aloud and said twice, "People of Khazraj, see how my son is preventing me from entering my home." But his son Abdullah kept repeating that unless the Prophet gave permission, he would not let him enter *Madīna*. Hearing this noise, some people gathered around and started pleading with Abdullah, but he stood his ground. Some people went to the Prophet and reported this incident. He told them, "Tell Abdullah to let his father enter." When Abdullah got this message, he then told his father, "Since the Prophet had given permission, you can enter now."

When the relationship of the belief is established, whether there by any relationship of blood or not, the Believers become like brothers. God Most High says, "Indeed, the Believers are brothers," which is a limitation as well as a prescription. He also says:

> Those who believed, and migrated, and strove with their wealth and their persons in the cause of God, and those who gave them refuge and helped them, are the protectors of each other. (8:72).

The protection which is referred to in this verse is not limited to a single generation but encompasses future generations as well, linking the future generations with the past generation in a sacred and eternal bond of love, loyalty and kindness.

> Those who lived (in *Madīna*) before the Emigrants and believed, love the Emigrants and do not find in their hearts any grudge when thou givest them something, but give them preference over themselves, even though they may be poor. Indeed,

the ones who restrain themselves from greed achieve prosperity. Those who came after them (the Emigrants) say; Our Lord, Forgive us and our brothers who entered the Faith before us and leave not in our hearts any grievance against those who believe. Our Lord. You are indeed Most Kind, Most Merciful. (59:9-10).

God Most High has related the stories of earlier Prophets in the Quran as an example for the Believers. In various periods the Prophets of God lighted the flame of faith and guided the Believers.

Noah called upon his Lord and said, 'O my Lord, surely my son is of my family, and Your promise is true, and You are the most Just of Judges'. He said, "O Noah, he is not of your family, as his conduct is unrighteous; so, do not ask of me that of which you have no knowledge. I give you the counsel not to act like the ignorant.' Noah said, O my Lord, I seek refuge with You lest I ask You for that of which I have no knowledge, and unless You forgive me and have mercy on me, I shall be lost. (11:45-47).

When his Lord tried Abraham with certain commands which he fulfilled, he said, 'I will make you a leader of people'. He said, 'And also those from among my offspring'? He answered, 'My promise does not extend to the evildoers. (1:124).

And when Abraham said, My Lord. Make this a city of peace and feed its people with fruits, such of them as believe in God and the Last Day. He said, and those who reject faith, I will grant them their pleasure for a while, but will eventually drive them to the chastisement of the Fire. What an evil destination. (2:126).

When the Prophet Abraham saw his father and his people persistent in their error, he turned away from them and said, I leave you and those upon whom you call besides God. I will only call upon my Sustainer, and hope that my Lord will not disappoint me. (19:48).

In relating the story of Abraham and his people, God has highlighted those aspects which are to be an example for the Believers.

> Indeed, Abraham and his companions are an example for you, when they told their people, 'We have nothing to do with you and with whatever you worship besides God. We reject them; and now there is perpetual enmity and anger between you and us unless you believe in One God. (60:4).

When those young and courageous friends who are known as the Companions of the Cave saw this same rejection among their family and tribe, they left them all, migrated from their country, and ran toward their Sustainer so that they could live as His servants.

> They were youths who believed in their Lord, and We advanced them in guidance. We gave strength to hearts, so that they stood up and said, 'Our Lord is the Lord of the heavens and the earth. We shall not call upon any god apart from Him. If we did, we would indeed have said an awful thing. These our people have taken for worship gods other than Him. Why do they not bring clear proof for what they do? Who can be more wrong than such as invert a falsehood against God? So, when you turn away from them and the things, they worship other than God, take refuge in the cave. Your Lord will shower mercies on you and will provide ease and comfort for your affairs. (18:13-16).

The wife of Noah and the wife of Lot were separated from their husbands only because their beliefs were different.

> God gives as an example for the unbelievers the wife of Noah and the wife of Lot. They were married to two of Our righteous servants; but they were false to their husbands, and they profited nothing before God on their account, but were told, 'Enter you both into the fire along with those who enter it. (66:10).

Then there is another kind of example in the wife of Pharaoh.

> And God gives as an example to those who believe the wife of
> Pharaoh. Behold, she said, My Lord, build for me in nearness
> to You a mansion in heaven, and save me from Pharaoh and
> his doings, and save me from those who do wrong. (66:11).

The Quran also describes examples of different kinds of relationships. In the story of Noah we have an example of the paternal relationship; in the story of Abraham, an example of the son and of the country; in the story of the Companions of the Cave a comprehensive example of relatives, tribe and home country. In the stories of Noah, Lot and Pharaoh there is an example of marital relationships.

After a description of the lives of the great Prophets and their relationships, we now turn to the Middle Community, that is, that of the early Muslims. We find similar examples and experiences in this community in great numbers. This community followed the divine path which God has chosen for the Believers. When the relationship of common belief was broken, in other words, when the very first relationship joining one man with another was broken, then persons of the same family or tribe were divided into different groups God Most High says in praise of the Believers:

> You will not find any people who believe in God and the Last
> Day loving those who fight God and His Messenger, even
> though they be their fathers, or their sons, or their brothers,
> or their kindred. These are the people on whose hearts God
> has imprinted faith and strengthened them with a spirit from
> Himself. And He will admit them to Gardens beneath which
> rivers flow, to dwell therein. God will be well-pleased with
> them and they with Him. They are the party of God; truly the
> party of God will prosper. (58:22).

We see that the blood relationships between Muhammad, peace be on him, and his uncle Abu Lahab and his cousin Abu Jahl were broken, and that the Emigrants from Mecca were fighting against their families and relatives and were in the front lines of Badr, while on the other hand their relations with the Helpers of *Madīna* became strengthened on the basis of a common faith. They became like brothers, even more than blood relatives. I his relationship established a new brotherhood of Muslims in which were included Arabs and non-Arabs. Suhayb from Rome and Bilal from Abyssinia and Selman from Persia were all brothers. There was no tribal partisanship among them. The pride of lineage was ended, the voice of nationalism was silenced, and the Messenger of God addressed them:

> Get rid of these partisanships; these are foul things, and He is not one of us who calls toward partisanship, who fights for partisanship, and who dies for partisanship.

This partisanship-the partisanship of lineage-ended; and this slogan-the slogan of race-died; and this pride- the pride of nationality- vanished; and man's spirit soared to higher horizons, freed from the bondage of flesh and blood and the pride of soil and country. From that day, the Muslim's country has not been a piece of land, but the homeland of Islam (Dar-al-Islam), the homeland where faith rules and the Sharī`a of God holds sway, the homeland in which he took refuge and which he defended, and in trying to extend it, he become martyred. This Islamic homeland is a refuge for any who accepts the Islamic Sharī`a to be the law of the state, as is the case with the Dhimmis. But any place where the Islamic Sharī`a is not enforced and where Islam is not dominant becomes the home of Hostility (Dar-al-Harb) for both the Muslim and the Dhimmi. A Muslim will remain prepared to fight against it, whether it be his birthplace or a place where his relatives reside or where his property or any other material interests are located.

Therefore, Muhammad, peace be on him, fought against the city of Mecca, although it was his birthplace, and his relatives lived there, and he and his Companions had houses and property there which they had left when they migrated; yet the soil of Mecca did not become Dar-al-Islam for him and his followers until it surrendered to Islam and the Sharī`a became operative in it.

This, and only this, is Islam. Islam is not a few words pronounced by the tongue, or birth in a country called Islamic, or an inheritance from a Muslim father.

No, by your Sustainer, they have not believed until they make you the arbiter of their disputes, and then do not find any grievance against your decision but submit with full submission. (4:65).

Only this is Islam, and only this is Dar-al-Islam- not the soil, not the race, not the lineage, not the tribe, and not the family.

Islam freed all humanity from the ties of the earth so that they might soar toward the skies and freed them from the chains of blood relationships -the biological chains, so that they might rise above the angels.

The homeland of the Muslim, in which he lives and which he defends, is not a piece of land; the nationality of the Muslim, by which he is identified, is not the nationality determined by a government; the family of the Muslim, in which he finds solace and which he defends, is not blood relationships; the flag of the Muslim, which he honors and under which he is martyred, is not the flag of a country; and the victory of the Muslim, which he celebrates and for which he is thankful to God, is not a military victory. It is what God has described:

When God's help and victory comes, and thou seest people entering into God's religion in multitudes, then celebrate the praises of thy Lord and ask His forgiveness. Indeed, He is the Acceptor of Repentance." (110:1-3).

The victory is achieved under the banner of faith, and under no other banners; the striving is purely for the sake of God, for the success of His religion and His law, for the protection of Dar-al-Islam, the particulars of which we have described above, and for no other purpose. It is not for the spoils or for fame, nor for the honor of a country or nation, nor for the mere protection of one's family except when supporting them against religious persecution.

The honor of martyrdom is achieved only when one is fighting in the cause of God, and if one is killed for any other purpose this honor will not be attained.

Any country which fights the Muslim because of his belief and prevents him from practicing his religion, and in which the Sharī'a is suspended, is Dar-al-Harb, even though his family or his relatives or his people live in it, or his capital is invested and his trade or commerce is in that country; and any country where the Islamic faith is dominant and its Shari`a is operative is Dar-al-Islam, even though the Muslim's family or relatives or his people do not live there, and he does not have any commercial relations with it.

The fatherland is that place where the Islamic faith, the Islamic way of life, and the Shari`a of God is dominant; only this meaning of 'fatherland' is worthy of the human being. Similarly, 'nationality' means belief and a way of life, and only this relationship is worthy of man's dignity.

Grouping according to family and tribe and nation, and race and color and country, are residues of the primitive state of man; these *Jāhili* groupings are from a period when man's spiritual values were at a low stage. The Prophet, peace be on him-has called them "dead things" against which man's spirit should revolt.

When the Jews claimed to be the chosen people of God based on their race and nationality, God Most High rejected their claim and declared that in every period, in every race and in every nation, there is only one criterion—that of faith.

> And they say: become Jews, or Christians; then you will be guided. Say: Not so: The way of Abraham, the pure in faith; and he was not among those who associate other gods with God. Say: We believe in God, and what has come down to us, and what has come down to Abraham, Ismail and Isaac and Jacob and the Tribes (of Israelites), and what was given to Moses and Jesus and to other Prophets by their Sustainer. We do not make any distinction among them, and we have submitted to Him. If then they believe as you have believed, they are guided; but if they turn away, then indeed they are stubborn. Then God suffices for you, and He is All-Hearing, All-Knowing. The baptism of God: and who can baptize better than God? And we worship Him alone. (2:135-138).

The people who are really chosen by God are the Muslim community which has gathered under God's banner without regard to differences of races, nations, colors and countries.

You are the best community raised for the good of humankind. You enjoin what is good and forbid what is evil, and you believe in God. (3:110).

This is that community in the first generation of which there were Abu Bakr from Arabia, Bilal from Abyssinia, Suhaib from Syria, Selman from Persia, and their brothers in faith. The generations which followed them were similar. Nationalism here is belief, homeland here is Dar-al-Islam, the ruler here is God, and the constitution here is the Quran.

This noble conception of homeland, of nationality, and of relationship should become imprinted on the hearts of those who invite others toward God. They should remove all influences of *Jāhiliyya* which make this concept impure and which may have the slightest element of hidden Shirk, such as shirk in relation to homeland, or in relation to race or nation, or in relation to lineage or material interests. All these have been mentioned by God Most High in one verse, in which He has placed them in one side of the balance and the belief and its responsibilities in the other side and invites people to choose.

Say: If your fathers and your sons and your brothers and your spouses and your relatives, and the wealth which you have acquired, and the commerce in which you fear decline, and the homes in which you take delight, are dearer to you than God and His Messenger and striving in His cause, then wait until God brings His judgment; and God does not guide the rebellious people. (9:24).

The callers to Islam should not have any superficial doubts in their hearts concerning the nature of *Jāhiliyya* and the nature of Islam, and the characteristics of Dar-al-Harb and of Dar-al-Islam, for through these doubts many are led to confusion. Indeed, there is no Islam in a land where Islam is not dominant and where its Sharī`a is not established; and that place is not Dar-al-Islam where Islam's way of life and its laws are not practiced. There is nothing beyond faith except unbelief, nothing beyond Islam except *Jāhiliyya*, nothing beyond the truth except falsehood.

CHAPTER 10
Far-Reaching Changes

When we invite people to Islam, whether they are believers or non-believers, we should keep in mind one fact, a fact which is a characteristic of Islam itself and which can be seen in its history. Islam is a comprehensive concept of life and the universe with its own unique characteristics. The concept of human life in all its aspects and relationships which are derived from it is also a complete system which has its characteristics. This concept is basically against all the new or old *Jāhili* concepts. Although there might be some details in which there are similarities between Islam and the *Jāhili* concepts, in relation to the principles from which these particulars are derived, the Islamic concept is different from all other theories with which man has been familiar.

The first function of Islam is that it molds human life according to this concept and gives it a practical form, and establishes a system in the world which has been prescribed by God; and for this very purpose God has raised this Muslim nation to be a practical example for humankind. God Most High says:

> You are the best community raised for the good of humankind. You enjoin what is good and forbid what is evil, and you believe in God. (3:110).

and He characterizes this community as follows:

> Those who, if We give them authority in the land, establish regular prayers, pay zakā, enjoin good, and forbid evil. (22:41).

It is not the function of Islam to compromise with the concepts of *Jāhiliyya* which are current in the world or to coexist in the same land together with a *Jāhili* system. This was not the case when it first appeared in the world, nor will it be today or in the future. *Jāhiliyya*, to whatever period it belongs, is *Jāhiliyya*; that is, deviation from the worship of One God and the way of life prescribed by God. It derives its system and laws and regulations and habits and standards and values from a source other

---

than God. On the other hand, Islam is submission to God, and its function is to invite people away from *Jāhiliyya* toward Islam.

Jāhiliyya is the worship of some people by others; that is to say, some people become dominant and make laws for others, regardless of whether these laws are against God's injunctions and without caring for the use or misuse of their authority.

Islam, on the other hand, is people's worshipping God alone, and deriving concepts and beliefs, laws and regulations and values from the authority of God, and freeing themselves from servitude to God's servants. This is the very nature of Islam and the nature of its role on the earth. This point should be emphasized to anyone whomsoever we invite to Islam, whether they be Muslims or non-Muslims.

Islam cannot accept any mixing with *Jāhiliyya*, either in its concept or in the modes of living which are derived from this concept. Either Islam will remain, or *Jāhiliyya*: Islam cannot accept or agree to a situation which is half-Islam and half-*Jāhiliyya*. In this respect Islam's stand is very clear. It says that the truth is one and cannot be divided; if it is not the truth, then it must be falsehood. The mixing and co-existence of the truth and falsehood is impossible. Command belongs to God, or otherwise to *Jāhiliyya*; God's Sharī`a will prevail, or else people's desires.

> And judge between them according to what God has revealed, and do not follow their opinions, and beware of them lest they confuse you in matters which God has revealed to you. (5:49).

> Then invite them to this and remain firmly committed to what you have been commanded, and do not follow their desires. (42:15).

> And if they do not respond to you, then know that they are following their own opinions; and who can be more misguided than one who follows his own opinion against the guidance from God? Indeed, God does not guide the wicked people. (28:50).

> We have set you on a way ordained (by God); then follow it, and do not follow the desires of those who have no knowledge. They

will not avail thee anything before God. Surely the evildoers are friends of one another, and God is the Friend of the God-fearing. (45:18).

Do they want a judgment from the Days of Ignorance? Yet who is better in judgment than God, for a people having sure faith? (5:50)

These verses make it clear that there are only two ways, and no third possibility exists: either to submit to God and His Messenger, peace be on him, or else to follow *Jāhiliyya*. If the law given by God is not made the arbiter, then naturally one will deviate from it. After this clear and decisive injunction from God Most High there is no room for any controversy or excuse-making.

The foremost duty of Islam in this world is to depose *Jāhiliyya* from the leadership of man, and to take the leadership into its own hands and enforce the particular way of life which is its permanent feature. The purpose of this rightly guided leadership is the good and success of humankind, the good which proceeds from returning to the Creator and the success which comes from being in harmony with the rest of the universe. The intention is to raise human beings to that high position which God has chosen for them and to free them from the slavery of desires. This purpose is explained by Raba'i Ibn 'Amir, when he replied to the commander-in-chief of the Persian army, Rustum. Rustum asked, "For what purpose have you come?" Raba'i answered, "God has sent us to bring anyone who wishes from servitude to men into the service of God alone, from the narrowness of this world into the vastness of this world and the Hereafter, from the tyranny of religions into the justice of Islam."

Islam did not come to support people's desires, which are expressed in their concepts, institutions, modes of living, and habits and traditions, whether they were prevalent at the advent of Islam or are prevalent now, both in the East and in the West. Islam does not sanction the rule of selfish desires. It has come to abolish all such concepts, laws, customs and traditions, and to replace them with a new concept of human life, to create a new world on the foundation of submission to the Creator. Sometimes it appears that some parts of Islam resemble some aspects of the life of people in *Jāhiliyya*; but these aspects are not *Jāhili* nor are they from

Jāhiliyya. This apparent resemblance in some minor respects is a mere coincidence; the roots of the two trees are entirely different. The tree of Islam has been sown and nurtured by the wisdom of God, while the tree of *Jāhiliyya* is the product of the soil of human desires.

> The fertile piece of land grows good vegetation with the permission of its Lord, while the bad land brings forth but little. (7:58).

Jāhiliyya is evil and corrupt, whether it be of the ancient or modern variety. Its outward manifestations may be different during different epochs, yet its roots are the same. Its roots are human desires, which do not let people come out of their ignorance and self-importance, desires which are used in the interests of some persons or some classes or some nations or some races, which interests prevail over the demand for justice, truth and goodness. But the pure law of God cuts through these roots and provides a system of laws which has no human interference, and it is not influenced by human ignorance or human desire or for the interests of a particular group of people.

This is the basic difference between the concept of life taught by God and man-made theories, and hence it is impossible to gather them together under one system. It is fruitless to try to construct a system of life which is half-Islam and half-*Jāhiliyya*. God does not forgive any association with His person, and He does not accept any association with His revealed way of life. Both are equally Shirk in the sight of God, as both are the product of the same mentality.

This truth ought to be firmly and clearly impressed on our minds, and when we present Islam to people our tongues should not hesitate to pronounce it, nor should we be ashamed, nor should we leave any doubt in people's minds, nor leave them until they are assured that if they follow Islam their lives will be completely changed. Islam will change their concepts of life as well as their modes of behavior completely. As it changes them, it bestows on them blessings beyond imagination by uplifting their concepts, improving their modes of behavior, and bringing them closer to the position of dignity worthy of human life. Nothing will remain of the modes of *Jāhiliyya* in which they were steeped, except some minor aspects which by accident appear like some aspects of Islam. Even these will not remain the same as they become joined to the great root of Islam, which is clearly different from the root to which they had been joined so far, the fruitless and evil root of *Jāhiliyya*. During this process it will not deprive them of any of the knowledge based on scientific observation; indeed, it gives a great impetus in this direction.

When we call people to Islam, it is our duty to make them understand that it is not one of the man-made religions or ideologies, nor is it a man-made system-with various names, banners and paraphernalia-but it is Islam, and nothing else. Islam has its own permanent personality and permanent concept and permanent modes. Islam guarantees for humankind a blessing greater than all these man-made systems. Islam is noble, pure, just, beautiful, springing from the source of the Most High, the Most Great God.

When we understand the essence of Islam in this manner, this understanding in itself creates in us confidence and power compassion and sympathy, while presenting Islam to the people: the confidence of a man who knows that he is with the truth, while what the people have is falsehood; and the compassion of a person who sees the suffering of humankind and knows how to bring them to ease; and the sympathy of a person who sees the error of the people and knows what supreme guidance is.

We need not rationalize Islam to them, need not appease their desires and distorted concepts. We will be extremely outspoken with them: "The ignorance in which you are living makes you impure, and God wants to purify you; the customs which you follow are defiling, and God wants to cleanse you; the life you are living is low, and God wants to uplift you; the condition which you are in is troublesome, depressing and base, and God wants to give you ease, mercy and goodness. Islam will change your concepts, your modes of living and your values; will raise you to another life so that you will look upon the life you are now living with disgust; will show you modes of living such that you will look upon all other modes, whether Eastern or Western, with contempt; and will introduce you to values such that you will look upon all current values in the world with disdain. And if, because of the sorry state you are in, you cannot see the true picture of the Islamic life, since your enemies-the enemies of this religion -are all united against the establishment of this way of life, against its taking a practical form, then let us show it to you; and, thank God, its picture is in our hearts, seen through the windows of our Quran, of our

---

Sharī`a, of our history, of our concept of the future, whose coming we do not doubt."

This is the way in which we ought to address people while presenting Islam. This is the truth, and this was the form in which Islam addressed people for the first time; this was the form, whether it was in the Arabian peninsula, in Persia or in the Roman provinces, or in whatever other places it went.

Islam looked at them from a height, as this is its true position, and addressed them with extreme love and kindness, as this is its true temperament, and explained everything to them with complete clarity, without any ambiguity, as this is its method. It never said to them that it would not touch their way of living, their modes, their concepts and their values except perhaps slightly; it did not propose similarities with their system or manners to please them, as some do today when they present Islam to the people under the names of 'Islamic Democracy' or 'Islamic Socialism', or sometimes by saying that the current economic or political or legal systems in the world need not be changed except a little to be acceptable Islamic-wise. The purpose of all this rationalization is to appease people's desires.

Indeed, the matter is entirely different! The change from this *Jāhiliyya*, which has encompassed the earth, to Islam is vast and far-reaching; and the Islamic life is the opposite of all modes of *Jāhili* life, whether ancient or modern. The miserable state of humankind is not alleviated by a few minor changes in current systems and modes. Humankind will never come out of it without this vast and far-reaching change-the change from the ways of the created to the way of the Creator, from the systems of men to the system of the Lord of men, and from the commands of servants to the command of the Lord of servants.

This is a fact, a fact which we proclaim, and proclaim loudly, without leaving any doubt or ambiguity in the minds of people.

In the beginning, people may dislike this method of giving the message, may run away from it, and may be afraid of it. But the people disliked it, ran away from it, and were afraid of it when Islam was presented to them for the first time. They hated it and were hurt when Muhammad, peace be on him-criticized their concepts, derided their deities, rejected their ways of behavior, turned away from their habits and customs, and adopted for himself and for the few believers who were with him modes of

---

behavior, values and customs other than the modes, values and customs of *Jāhiliyya*.

Then what happened? They loved the same truth which at first seemed so strange to them, from which they ran away "as if they were startled donkeys fleeing before a lion ..." (74:50-51), against which they fought with all their power and strategy, grievously torturing its adherents when they were weak in Mecca and fighting with them incessantly when they were strong in *Madīna*.

The conditions which the Islamic Call had to face in its first period were not more favorable or better than the conditions of today. It was an unknown thing, rejected by *Jāhiliyya*; it was confined to the valley of Mecca, hounded by the people in power and authority; and, at that time, it was a complete stranger to the whole world. It was surrounded by mighty and proud empires which were against its basic teachings and purposes. Despite all this it was a powerful Call, as it is powerful today and will remain powerful tomorrow. The source of its real power is hidden in the very nature of this belief; that is why it can operate under the worst conditions and in the face of the most severe opposition. It derives its power from the simple and clear truth on which it stands. Its balanced teachings are according to human nature-that nature which cannot tolerate any resistance for very long, and it is in its power to lead humankind over toward progress, no matter in what stage of economic, social, scientific or intellectual backwardness or development it may be. Another secret of its power is that it challenges *Jāhiliyya* and its physical power, without agreeing to change even a single letter of its principles. It does not compromise with *Jāhili* inclinations nor does it use rationalizations. It proclaims the truth boldly so that people may understand that it is good, that it is a mercy and a blessing.

It is God Who created men and Who knows their nature and the passages to their hearts. He knows how they accept the truth when it is proclaimed boldly, clearly, forcefully, and without hesitation and doubt!

Indeed, the capacity exists in human nature to change completely from one way of life to another; and this is much easier for it than many partial changes. And if the complete change were to be from one system of life to another which is higher, more perfect and purer than the former, this complete change is agreeable to human psychology. But who would be agreeable to changing from a system of *Jāhiliyya* to the system of Islam if the Islamic system were no more than a little change here and a little variation there? To continue with the former system is more logical. At least it is an established order, amenable to reform and change; then what is the need to abandon it for an order not yet established or applied, while it continues to resemble the old order in all its major characteristics?

We also find some people who, when talking about Islam, present it to the people as if it were something which is being accused and they want to defend it against the accusation. Among their defenses, one goes like this: "It is said that modern systems have done such and such, while Islam did not do anything comparable. But listen. It did all this some fourteen hundred years before modern civilization."

Woe to such a defense. Shame on such a defense.

Indeed, Islam does not take its justifications from the *Jāhili* system and its evil derivatives. And these 'civilizations', which have dazzled many and have defeated their spirits, are nothing but a *Jāhili* system at heart, and this system is erroneous, hollow and worthless in comparison with Islam. The argument that the people living under it are in a better condition than the people of a so-called Islamic country or the Islamic world has no weight. The people in these countries have reached this wretched state by abandoning Islam, and not because they are Muslims. The argument which Islam presents to people is this: Most certainly Islam is better beyond imagination. It has come to change *Jāhiliyya*, not to continue it; to elevate humankind from its depravity, and not to bless its manifestations which have taken the garb of "civilization".

We ought not to be defeated to such an extent that we start looking for similarities with Islam in the current systems or in some current religions or in some current ideas; we reject these systems in the East as well as in the West. We reject them all, as indeed they are retrogressive and in opposition to the direction toward which Islam intends to take humankind.

When we address people in this fashion and present to them the basic message of the comprehensive concept of Islam, the justification for changing from one concept to another, from one mode of living to another, will come from the very depths of their being. But we will not address them with this ineffective argument, saying: "Come from a system which is currently established to a system not yet applied; it will make only a little change in the established order. You should have no objection; you can continue to do what you have been doing. It will not bother you except to ask for a few changes in your habits, manners, and inclinations, and will preserve for you whatever pleases you and will not touch it except very slightly."

On the surface this method seems easy, but there is no attraction in it; moreover, it is not based on the truth. The truth is that Islam not only changes concepts and attitudes, but also the system and modes, laws and customs, since this change is so fundamental that no relationship can remain with the *Jāhili* way of life, the life which humankind is living. It is sufficient to say that it brings them both in general and from servitude to men into the service of God, Who is One:

"Believe if one wishes or reject if one wishes."

"And if one rejects, then God is independent of His creation,"

The question in essence is that of unbelief and belief, of associating others with God and the Oneness of God, and of *Jāhiliyya* and Islam. This ought to be made clear. Indeed, people are not Muslims, as they proclaim to be, as long as they live the life of *Jāhiliyya*. If someone wishes to deceive himself or to deceive others by believing that Islam can be brought in line with this *Jāhiliyya*, it is up to him. But whether this deception is for others, it cannot change anything of the actual reality. This is not Islam, and they are not Muslims. Today the task of the Call is to return these ignorant people to Islam and make them into Muslims all over again.

We are not inviting people to Islam to obtain some reward from them; we do not desire anything at all for ourselves, nor is our accounting and reward with the people. Indeed, we invite people to Islam because we love them and we wish them well, although they may torture us; and this is the characteristic of the caller to Islam, and this is his motivation. The people are entitled to learn from us the nature of Islam and the nature of the obligations it imposes on them, as well as the great blessing which it bestows on them. They are also entitled to know that the nature of what they are doing is nothing but *Jāhiliyya*; it is indeed *Jāhiliyya*, with nothing in it from Islam. It is mere desire as long as it is not the Sharī`a; and it is falsehood as long as it is not the truth, and what is beyond the truth but falsehood!

There is nothing in our Islam of which we are ashamed or anxious about defending; there is nothing in it to be smuggled to the people with deception, nor do we muffle the loud truth which it proclaims. This is the

defeated mentality, defeated before the West and before the East and before this and that mode of *Jāhiliyya*, which is found in some people, Muslims, who search for resemblances to Islam in man-made systems, or who
find justification for the actions of Islam and its decision concerning certain matters by means of the actions of *Jāhili* civilization.

A person who feels the need of defense, justification and apology is not
capable of presenting Islam to people. Indeed, he is a person who lives the
life of *Jāhiliyya*, hollow and full of contradictions, defects and evils, and
intends to provide justification for the *Jāhiliyya* he is in. These are the
offenders against Islam, and they distract some sincere persons. They confuse Islam's true nature by their defense, as if Islam were something accused standing at trial, anxious for its own defense.

During my stay in the United States, there were some people of this
kind who used to argue with us-with us few who were on the side of Islam.
Some of them took the position of defense and justification. I, on the other
hand, took the position of attacking the Western *Jāhiliyya*, its shaky religious beliefs, its social and economic modes, and its immoralities: "Look
at these concepts of the Trinity, Original Sin, Sacrifice and Redemption,
which are agreeable neither to reason nor to conscience. Look at this cap-
italism with its monopolies, its usury and whatever else is unjust in it; at
this individual freedom, devoid of human sympathy and responsibility for
relatives except under the force of law; at this materialistic attitude which
deadens the spirit; at this behavior, like animals, which you call 'Free mixing of the sexes; at this vulgarity which you call emancipation of women,
at these unfair and cumbersome laws of marriage and divorce, which are
contrary to the demands of practical life; and at Islam, with its logic,
beauty, humanity and happiness, which reaches the horizons to which
man strives but does not reach. It is a practical way of life, and its solu-
tions are based on the foundation of the wholesome nature of man."

These were the realities of Western life which we encountered. These
facts, when seen in the light of Islam, made the American people blush.
Yet there are people-exponents of Islam-who are defeated before this filth
in which *Jāhiliyya* is steeped, even to the extent that they search for resemblances to Islam among this rubbish heap of the West, and also among
the evil and dirty materialism of the East.

After this, there is no need for me to say: Certainly, we who present
Islam to the people are not the ones to go along with any of the concepts,

modes and traditions of *Jāhiliyya* however great its pressure on us may be.

Our first task is to replace this *Jāhiliyya* with Islamic ideas and traditions. This cannot be brought about by agreeing with *Jāhiliyya* and going along a few steps with it from the very beginning, as some of us think we ought to do, for this will simply mean that from the very beginning we have accepted defeat.

Of course, the current ideas of the society and its prevalent traditions apply great pressure, immense pressure, especially in the case of women; the Muslim woman is really under extreme and oppressive pressure, but this is the situation, and we must face it. First, we must be steadfast; next we must prevail upon it; then we must show *Jāhiliyya* the low state it is really in compared to the lofty and bright horizons of Islamic life which we wish to attain.

This cannot come about by going along a few steps with *Jāhiliyya*, nor by now severing relations with it and removing ourselves to a separate corner; never. The correct procedure is to mix with discretion, give and take with dignity, speak the truth with love, and show the superiority of the Faith with humility. After all this, we must realize the fact that we live during *Jāhiliyya*, that our way of life is straighter than that of *Jāhiliyya*, and that the change from *Jāhiliyya* to Islam is vast and far-reaching. The chasm between Islam and *Jāhiliyya* is great, and a bridge is not to be built across it so that the people on the two sides may mix with each other, but only so that the people of *Jāhiliyya* may come over to Islam, whether they reside in a so-called Islamic country and consider themselves Muslims or they are outside the Islamic country, in order that they may come out of darkness into light and may get rid of their miserable condition, and enjoy those blessings which we have tasted-we who have understood Islam and live in its atmosphere. If not, then we shall say to them what God commanded His Messenger, peace be on him, to say:

To you there is your way; and to me mine. (109:6).

CHAPTER 11
Faith Triumphant

Do not be dejected nor grieve. You shall be the uppermost if you have faith. (3: 139).

The first thought which comes to mind on reading this verse is that it relates to the form of *Jihād* which is actual fighting; but the spirit of this message and its application, with its manifold implications, is greater and wider than this aspect. Indeed, it describes that eternal state of mind which ought to inspire the Believer's consciousness, his thoughts, his estimates of things, events, values, and persons.

It describes a triumphant state which should remain fixed in the Believer's heart in the face of everything, every condition, every standard and every person; the superiority of the Faith and its value above all values which are derived from a source other than the source of the Faith.

It means to be above all the powers of the earth which have deviated from the way of the Faith, above all the values of the earth not derived from the source of the Faith, above all the customs of the earth not colored with the coloring of the Faith, above all the laws of the laws of the earth not sanctioned by the Faith, and above all traditions not originating in the Faith.

It means to feel superior to others when weak, few and poor, as well as when strong, many and rich.

It means the sense of supremacy which does not give in before any rebellious force, before any social custom and erroneous tradition, before any behavior which may be popular among people, but which has no authority in the Faith.

Steadfastness and strength on the battlefield are but one expression among many of the triumphant spirit which is included in this statement of Almighty God.

The superiority through faith is not a mere single act of will or a passing euphoria or a momentary passion but is a sense of superiority based on the permanent truth centered in the very nature of existence. This eternal truth is above the logic of force, the concept of environment, the terminology of society, and the customs of people, as indeed it is joined with the Living God Who does not die.

A society has a governing logic and a common mode, its pressure is strong and its weight heavy on anyone who is not protected by some powerful member of the society or who challenges it without a strong force. Accepted concepts and current ideas have a climate of their own, and it is difficult to get rid of them without a deep sense of truth, in the light of which all these concepts and ideas shrink to nothingness, and without the help of a source which is superior, greater and stronger than the source of these concepts and ideas.

The person who takes a stand against the direction of the society, its governing logic, its common mode, its values and standards, its ideas and concepts, its error and deviations -will find himself a stranger, as well as helpless, unless his authority comes from a source which is more powerful than the people, more permanent than the earth, and nobler than life.

Indeed, God does not leave the Believer alone in the face of oppression to whimper under its weight, to suffer dejection and grief, but relieves him of all this with the message:

> Do not be dejected nor grieve; you shall be the uppermost if you are Believers. (13:139).

This message relieves him from both dejection and grief, these two feelings being natural for a human being in this situation. It relieves him of both, not merely through patience and steadfastness, but also through a sense of superiority from whose heights the power of oppression, the dominant values, the current concepts, the standards, the rules, the customs and habits, and the people steeped in error, all seem low.

Indeed, the Believer is uppermost-uppermost based on the authority which is behind him and his source of guidance. Then, what is to be said of this earth, what of the people, what of the dominant values of the world, the standards current among people, while he is inspired by God, returns to God for guidance, and travels on His path?

The Believer is most superior in his understanding and his concept of the nature of the world, for the belief in One God, in the form which has come to him from Islam, is the most perfect form of understanding, the greatest truth. The picture of the world which this Faith presents is far above the heaps of concepts, beliefs and religions, and is not reached by any great philosophers, ancient or modern, nor attained by idolaters or the followers of distorted scriptures, nor approached by the base materialists. This picture is so bright, clear, beautiful and balanced that the glory of the Islamic belief shines forth as never before. And without doubt those who have grasped this knowledge are superior to all others. (See the chapter *tih wa-rukam* in, *Khasa'is al-tasawwar al-islami wa-muqawwimatuh*).

The Believer is most superior in his values and standards, by means of which he measures life, events, things, and people. The source of his belief is the knowledge of God and His attributes as described by Islam, and the knowledge of the realities prevalent in the universe at large, not merely on the small earth. This belief with its grandeur provides the Believer with values which are superior to and firmer than the defective standards made by men, who do not know anything except what is under their feet. They do not agree on the same standard within the same generation; even the same person changes his standard from moment to moment.

He is most superior in his conscience and understanding, in his morals and manners, as he believes in God Who has excellent names and attributes. This by itself creates in him a sense of dignity, purity and cleanliness, modesty and piety, and a desire for good deeds, and of being a righteously guided representative of God on earth. Furthermore, this belief gives him the assurance that the reward is in the Hereafter, the reward before which the troubles of the world and all its sorrows become insignificant. The heart of the Believer is content with it, although he may pass through this life without apparent success.

He is most superior in his law and system of life. When the Believer scans whatever man, ancient or modern, has known, and compares it with his own law and system, he realizes that all this is like the playthings of children or the searching of blind men in comparison with the perfect system and the complete law of Islam. And when he looks from his height at erring humankind with compassion and sympathy at its helplessness and error, he finds nothing in his heart except a sense of triumph over error and nonsense.

This was the attitude of the early Muslims toward the hollow expressions of pomp and power and the traditions which had enslaved the people of the Days of Ignorance. Ignorance is not limited to any particular age but is a condition which reappears whenever people deviate from the way of Islam, whether in the past, present or future.

This was the response of al-Mughirah Ibn Shu'ba when he encountered the forms, manners, standards, and expressions of *Jāhiliyya* in the camp of Rustum, the famous Persian general.

Abi Uthman al-Nahdi reports: When al-Mughirah crossed the bridge and reached the Persian army, they seated him and asked Rustum's permission for an audience. In spite of their defeat, they had not changed any of their show of pomp. Al-Mughirah proceeded. The people were all in their military uniforms, many wearing crowns, and clothed in gold-threaded garments. The floor was thickly carpeted (the carpet extending to three hundred or four hundred steps) and was to be traversed to reach the general. Al-Mughirah proceeded, his hair braided in four braids, and climbed on the throne and sat beside Rustum. The attendants jumped on him and pulled him down. He then said, 'We had heard that you were a sensible people, but I see that you are the most foolish nation. Among Arabs all are equal, and no one is slave to another, except when one is captured on the battlefield. I imagined that you treated each other equally as we do. It would have been better if you had informed me that some of you are lords over others rather than treating me like this. This IS not good manners, and we do not do it. I have come at your request and not on my own. I know now that your situation is weak and that you will be defeated. No kingdom can survive with this character and mentality."

A similar attitude was shown by Rabah Ibn 'Amir in front of Rustum and his courtiers before the battle of al-Qādisiyya:

> Before the battle of al-Qādisiyya, Sa'd Ibn Waqqas sent Rabah Ibn 'Amir as a messenger to Rustum, the commander of the Persian army and their ruler. He entered the tent which was all carpeted and curtained with silk and velvet. Rustum sat on a golden throne, crowned and wearing precious stones and pearls. Rabah, in tattered clothes, with a shield, sitting on a small horse, entered. He did not alight from his horse for some distance; then he alighted and tied the horse to a large pillow. He proceeded armed and helmeted. They said to him: 'Take off your arms'. He replied: 'I have not come on my own but on your request. If you do not like it, then I will go back'. Rustum said:

'Let him come'. He came forward leaning on his spear, making holes in the carpet. Rustum asked him: 'For what purpose you have come?" He replied: 'God has sent us to bring whoever wishes from servitude to men into the service of God alone, from the narrowness of this world into the vastness of this world and the Hereafter, from the tyranny of religions into the justice of Islam. (Ibn Kathir: *al-Bidāya wa-'l-nihāya*).

Conditions change, the Muslim loses his physical power and is conquered, yet the consciousness does not depart from him that he is the most superior. If he remains a Believer, he looks upon his conqueror from a superior position. He remains certain that this is a temporary condition which will pass away and that faith will turn the tide from which there is no escape. Even if death is his portion, he will never bow his head. Death comes to all, but for him there is martyrdom. He will proceed to the Garden, while his conquerors go to the Fire. What a difference! And he hears the voice of his Generous Lord:

Let it not deceive you that the unbelievers walk about in the land. A little respite and their abode is Hell, and what an evil place! But for those who fear their Lord are Gardens through which rivers flow, to abide therein -a hospitality from God; and that which is with God is best for the righteous. (3:196-198).

The society may be drowned in lusts, steeped in low passions, rolling in filth and dirt, thinking that it has enjoyment and freedom from chains and restrictions. Such a society may become devoid of any clean enjoyment and even of lawful food, and nothing may remain except a rubbish heap, or dirt and mud. The Believer from his height looks at the people drowning in dirt and mud. He may be the only one; yet he is not dejected nor grieved, nor does his heart desire that he take off his neat and immaculate garments and join the crowd. He remains the uppermost with the enjoyment of faith and the taste of belief.

The believer holds on to his religion like the holder of a precious stone in society devoid of religion, of character, of high values, of noble manners and of whatever is clean, pure and beautiful.

The others mock his tenacity, ridicule his ideas, laugh at his values, but this does not make the Believer weak of heart: and he looks from his height at those who mock, ridicule and laugh, and he says, as one of the great souls-those who preceded him on the long and bright path of faith, Noah (peace be on him), said:

You ridicule us. Yet indeed we shall ridicule you as you ridicule. (11:38).

And he sees the end of this bright path, and the end of the dark path in the words of God:

The criminals used to laugh at the Believers, wink at them in passing, and joke about them when they returned to their families. When they saw them, they used to say: "Certainly these people are astray". Yet they were not sent as watchers over them. Today the Believers laugh at the unbelievers and watch them while sitting on couches. Did the unbelievers get their reward according to what they used to do? (83:29-36).

Before this, the Holy Quran told us what the unbelievers said to the Believers:

When Our clear verses are recited to them, the unbelievers say to the Believers: 'Which of the two parties is superior in station, better in assembly? (19:73).

Which of the two parties? The great men who do not believe in Muhammad, or the poor who assemble around him? Which of the two parties? Al-Nadr Ibn al-Harith and ʿAmr Ibn Hisham and al-Walid Ibn al-Mughīra and Abu Sufyan Ibn Harb? Or Bilal and ʿAmmar and Khabbab? If the call of Muhammad had been better, would only such people have followed him who did not have any power or position among the Quraysh, who assembled in such a lowly place as the house of al-Arqam, while their opponents were the lords of al-Nadwah, the great and glorious assembly hall, and they possessed power, authority and grandeur?

This is the logic of this world, the logic of those of any age or any place who cannot see the higher horizons. It is the wisdom of God that belief remains independent of the glitter and glamour of worldly allurements, such as closeness to the ruler, favor from the government, popularity among the people or the satisfaction of desire. It is only striving, hard work, fighting and martyrdom. Let him accept it who may accept, who has the certainty in his heart that this is purely for the sake of God and not for the sake of people, or for the allurements and attractions so dear to people. Let him stay away from it who desires pleasures and benefits, and who is greedy for pomp and show, and who is after wealth and possessions, and who gives weight to the considerations of men although these may be light in the balance of God.

Indeed, the Believer does not borrow his values, concepts and standards from people so that he is dependent on the estimation of people; he takes them from the Sustainer of the people, and that is sufficient for him. He does not follow the desires of men so that he must fluctuate with their changing desires; he depends on the firm balance of the truth which does not fluctuate or lean to one side. Indeed, his inspiration does not come from this passing and finite world; the inspiration of his soul comes from the fountainheads of the universe. Then how can he find dejection in his soul or grief in his heart, while he is linked to the Sustainer of the people, the balance of truth, and the fountainheads of the universe?

Indeed, he is with the truth, and what is beyond the truth but falsehood? Let falsehood have power, let it have its drums and banners, and let it have its throngs and mobs; all this cannot change anything of the truth. Indeed, he is with the truth, and nothing is beyond the truth except error, and the Believer cannot prefer error to the truth. He is a Believer, and whatever be the conditions and the situation, he cannot exchange error for the truth.

> Our Master. Do not let our hearts waver after You have guided us, and bestow on us mercy from Yourself; indeed, You are the Bestower. Our Master. You will gather humankind on the Day about which there is no doubt; indeed, God does not fail in His promise. (3:8-9).

CHAPTER 12
This is the Road

By the heavens with constellations; by the Promised Day; by
the witness and the witnessed; doomed were the makers of the
pit, abundantly supplied with fuel, as they sat by it and
watched what they did with the Believers. They were outraged
with them only because they believed in God, the All-Powerful,
the All-Praiseworthy, He to Whom belongs the dominion of the
heaven and the earth. And God is Witness over everything.

Indeed, for those who persecute the believing men and women,
and later do not repent, is the penalty of Hell; for them is the
penalty of burning. As for those who believe and do good deeds,
there are Gardens through which rivers flow, and that is the
great triumph.

Most certainly, strong is the grip of your Lord. It is He Who
originates and repeats. And He is the Forgiving, the Loving,
the Lord of the Throne, Performer of what He desires. (85:1-
16).

The story of the Makers of the Pit as told in the chapter *al-Buruj* (The
Constellations) requires deep thought by those among the Believers, to
whatever time and place they belong, who invite people to God. The story,
with its introduction, description, comments and moral, as related in the
Quran, points out some profound truths concerning the nature of the Call
toward God, the reaction of people to this Call, and the consequences
which are possible in the vast scope of this Call-the scope whose vastness
encompasses the whole world, this life and the life beyond it. The Quran
through this story, points out to the Believers the road which lies before
them and prepares them to accept with fortitude whatever comes their
way; yet unknown to them, with the permission of the All-Wise God.

This is the story of a group of people who believed in God and openly
proclaimed their belief. They encountered tyrannical and oppressive enemies who were bent upon denying the right of a human being to believe in

the All-Mighty, the All-Praiseworthy God. They intended to deprive man of that dignity which has been bestowed upon him by God and without which he is reduced to a mere plaything in the hands of tyrants, to be tortured, burned alive, and provide entertainment to his tormentors by his cries of agony.

But the faith in the hearts of the Believers raised them above all persecution. Belief triumphed over life. The threat of torture did not shake them, they never recanted, and they burned in the fire until death.

Indeed, their hearts were liberated from the worship of this life. Neither the love of life nor the fear of an agonizing death could make them yield to accept dishonor. They freed themselves from this earth and all its attractions, triumphing over life through a sublime faith.

Against these believing, righteous, sublime, and honorable souls were pitted arrogant, mischievous, criminal and degraded people. And these criminals sat by the pit of fire, watching how the Believers suffered and writhed in pain. They sat there to enjoy the sight of how fire consumes living beings and how the bodies of these noble souls were reduced to cinders and ashes. And when some young man or woman, some child or old man from among these righteous Believers was thrown into the fire, their diabolical pleasure would reach a new height, and shouts of mad joy would escape their lips at the sight of blood and pieces of flesh.

This hair-raising incident shows that these rebellious people had sunk to those levels of depravity, seeking pleasure through torturing others, which are not even reached by any wild beast. A wild beast kills its prey for food, never to derive pleasure through tormenting it.

The same incident also shows the height to which the spirit of a Believer can soar, liberated and free, that height, the attainment of which has been the highest honor in all generations and in all periods.

By earthly reckoning, tyranny triumphed over faith, and this faith, although it reached its zenith in the hearts of this righteous, noble, steadfast, and sublime group, had no weight in the struggle between tyranny and faith.

The traditions relating to this incident, like the text of the Quran, say nothing concerning whether God punished these tyrants in this life for their crimes as He punished the people of Noah, the people of Hud, the people of Salih, the people of Shu`ayb, and the people of Lot, or as He caught Pharaoh with his army in all his splendor and power.

From the earthly point of view, the end was pitiful and tragic.

But did this matter finish here? Did the group of Believers, with all the sublimity of their faith, vanish, vanish in the pit of fire with their torments? And did the group of criminals, with all the depravity of their crime, go unpunished?

From the earthly point of view, this tragic end troubles the heart!

But the Quran teaches the Believers something else, reveals to them another reality, shows them another scale with which to weigh all matters, and enlightens them concerning the scope of the struggle.

Life's pleasures and pains, achievements, and frustrations, do not have any great weight in the scale, and do not determine the profit or loss. Triumph is not limited to immediate victory, which is but one of the many forms of triumph.

In the scale of God, the true weight is the weight of faith; in God's market the only commodity in demand is the commodity of faith. The highest form of triumph is the victory of soul over matter, the victory of belief over pain, and the victory of faith over persecution. In the incident described above, the souls of the Believers were victorious over fear and pain, over the allurements of the earth and of life, and they gained such victory over torture which is an honor for all humankind for all times-and this is the true victory.

All men die, and of various causes; but not all gain such victory, nor reach such heights, nor taste such freedom, nor soar to such limits of the horizon. It is God's choosing and honoring a group of people who share death with the rest of humankind but who are singled out from other people for honor -honor among the noblest angels, nay, even among all humankind, if we measure them by the standards of the total history of generations of men.

It was possible for these Believers to save their lives by giving up their faith; but with how much loss to themselves, and with what a great loss to all humankind? They would have lost and would have killed this great truth, that life without belief is worthless, without freedom is degrading, and if tyrants are allowed to dominate men's souls as well as their bodies, then it is entirely depraved.

This was that noble truth, the great truth, which the Believers realized while they were alive on the earth; they realized and found it while the fire was licking them and burning their mortal frames. This noble truth triumphed over the torment of the fire.

The scope of this struggle is not limited to this earth or to this life. The observers of this struggle are not merely a generation of men. The angels are also participants in the happenings on earth; they observe them and are a witness to them, and they weigh them in a scale which is other than the scale of a generation or even of all generations of men. The angels are noble souls who number many times more than the people on the earth. Without question the praise and respect of the angels is far greater in this scale than the opinion and judgment of the people on the earth.

And then there is the Hereafter. That will be the real sphere which is adjacent to the earthly sphere and is not separated from it, as well as in the believers' perception of this reality.

The struggle does not end here, and the real decision cannot be reached here. Any judgment based on that part of it which took place on earth is therefore incorrect, as this judgment will concern only a small and rather insignificant part of this struggle.

The former viewpoint, that is, that of the earthly scale, is limited and narrow, entertained by a hasty man. The latter viewpoint is comprehensive and far-sighted, and such a viewpoint is nurtured in a believer by the teachings of the Quran, as it is the mirror of reality and the basis of correct belief.

Among the rewards which God has promised to the Believers for their faith, obedience, steadfastness in the face of calamity, and victory over persecution is contentment of heart:

> Those who believe, and their hearts find satisfaction in remembrance of God. Indeed, remembrance of God brings contentment to the hearts. (13:28).

And it is the pleasure and love of the All-Merciful:

> Surely upon those who believe and do good deeds the All-Merciful shall assign love. (19:96)

And it is remembrance on High:

The Messenger of God, peace be on him-said: "When a certain person's child dies, God asks the angels: Did you take away the soul of My servant's child? They say: yes. Then He says: Did you take away the apple of his eye? They say Yes. Then He says: What did My servant say? They say: He praised You and said, 'Indeed, we belong to God and to Him shall we return'. Then He says: Build a house for My servant in the Garden and call it 'The House of Praise." (Tirmidhi's collection of Hadith).

He also said: "God Most High says: I am to My servant according to his thought concerning Me; when he remembers Me, I am with him; when he remembers Me to himself, I remember him to Myself; when he mentions Me among a group, I mention him in a better group. If he comes toward Me one span, I come toward him an arm's length; if he comes toward Me one arm's length, I come toward him one step; if he walks toward Me, I run toward him." (Hadith collections of Bukhari and Muslim).

And it is the keen interest of the angels in the affairs of the Believers on earth:

> The bearers of the Throne and those around it engage in their Lord's praise, and they believe in Him, and ask forgiveness for the Believers: 'Our Lord! Your mercy and knowledge encompass everything. Then forgive those who repent and follow Your path and save them from the torment of Hell. (40:7).

And it is life from God for the martyrs:

> Do not consider those as dead who were killed in the way of God; they are living and find sustenance from their Sustainer. They enjoy what God has given them from His bounty and are glad for those who are left behind (on earth) and have not reached there yet, that they shall have no fear, nor shall they grieve. They are jubilant at the favor from God and His bounty; indeed, God does not destroy the reward of the Believers. (3:169-171).

And as to rejectors of faith, the tyrants and the criminals, God has repeatedly promised that He will catch them in the Hereafter, while giving them a limited period of living on earth: although He has caught some of them in this world too, yet for the final punishment emphasis is on the Hereafter:

> Do not let yourself be deceived that the unbelievers walk about in the land; a limited enjoyment, and then their abode is Hell and what an evil place! (3:196-197).

> Do not think that God is unaware of the doings of the wicked people. He has deferred (judgment for) them to the Day when the eyes shall stare, and they shall run with necks outstretched and heads erect, their sight never returned to themselves, their hearts void. (14:42-43).

> Leave them to have fun and play until the Day comes which they have been promised. On that Day they will come out of the graves and run as if hastening toward a fixed goal -eyes down-cast, faces degraded. It will be the Day which they were promised. (70:42-44).

The life of humankind is adjoined with that of the angels; this life proceeds into the life Hereafter; and the field of struggle between good and evil, between the truth and falsehood, and between faith and tyranny, is not limited to this earth. This matter does not finish here, nor is the decision made in this world. This life and all its pleasures and pains, achievements, and frustrations, do not weigh much on the scale.

The field of struggle is very broad in space and in time, in measures and in scales. This realization enlarges the Believer's horizons and heightens his aspirations, so that this earth and whatever is in it, this life and its attachments, shrink in his sight. The Believer's greatness increases in proportion to what he sees and understands of the scopes and horizons. To create such a broad, comprehensive, noble and pure concept of faith, the story of the Makers of the Pit is a great example.

Light is also thrown on another aspect of the Call toward God and its situation with respect to all possibilities in the story of the Makers of the Pit and the chapter "Constellations" (al-Buruj).

The history of the Call toward God has witnessed various endings in this world in its struggle with other movements.

It has witnessed the annihilation of the people of Noah, the people of Hud, the people of Shu`ayb, and the people of Lot, and the escape-the bare escape-of a small group of believers. But the Quran does not state what these escapees did in the world and life after their escape. These examples tell us that sometimes God Most High gives the rebels and tyrants a taste of punishment in this world, while the full punishment still awaits them in the Hereafter.

This history of the Call witnessed the annihilation of Pharaoh and his army, and the escape of Moses and his people and the establishment of their authority in the land. Those people of that time were the most righteous in all their (the Israelites') history, although they did not attain complete steadfastness nor establish the religion of God on earth in its entirety; and this example is different from the previous ones.

This history of the Call witnessed the annihilation of the polytheists who turned away from the guidance and belief in Muhammad , peace be on him -and it witnessed the complete victory of the Believers, with the amazing victory of belief in their hearts. And for the first time in the history of humankind the way of God was established in such completeness as was not seen by man, either before or after.

And it witnessed, as we have seen, the example of the Makers of the Pit.

And it witnessed many other examples in earlier or later times with little mention in the history of faith. And even today it is witnessing such examples, which reach one or another of the possible endings recorded throughout history for centuries.

Among the various earlier or later examples, the example of the Makers of the Pit must not be forgotten.

The example must not be forgotten in which the Believers have no escape and the unbelievers are not punished! This is so that the Believers-the callers toward God -should remain fully aware that they can also meet this extreme end in the way of God, and they have no say in it. Their matter and the matter of belief rest with God.

Their task is to fulfill their obligation and go. Their obligation is to choose God, prefer belief over life, raise themselves above persecution through faith, and to testify to God with deed as well as intention. Then it is up to God to deal with them and with their enemies, with His Religion and His Call, as He deems proper. He may choose for them any one of the endings known in history, or some other ending which only He knows and sees.

They are workers for God. Whenever, whatever, however He wants them to do their work, they should do it and take the known reward. To decide what will be the ending of their endeavor is neither in their power nor is it their responsibility. This is the responsibility of the One in authority, not of those who are mere workers.

They receive the first part of their reward in the form of contentment of heart, height of understanding, beauty of ideas, liberation from desires and attractions, and freedom from fear and sorrow, in whatever condition they may be.

They receive the second part of their reward in praise; remembrance and honor among the angels, in addition to these among the people of this earth.

Then they receive the greater and the last part of their reward in the Hereafter: easy accounting and great favors.

With every kind of reward, they also receive the greatest of rewards: the pleasure of God. It is His bounty on them that He chose them for His purpose, an instrument for His power, so that He makes use of them on this earth as He deems proper.

The Quranic training of the first noble generation of Muslims was of this character to the highest degree. They lost their personalities and identities in this matter, acting as workers for the One in authority, and were pleased with God in every decision and in every condition.

The training by the Prophet- peace be on him, went side by side with the Quranic teachings, turning their hearts and eyes toward the Garden, and toward patiently persevering in their assigned task until God ordains what He intends in this world as well as what is pleasing to Him in the Hereafter

The Prophet, peace be on him, saw the intensity of tortures heaped upon `Ammar, his father, and his mother, may God be pleased with them- but he said nothing more than this: "Patience, family of Yasir. The Garden is promised for you."

Khabbab, may God be pleased with him, reported: "We complained to the Messenger of God, peace be upon him -while he was resting in the shadow of Ka'ba, saying, 'Why do you not ask God to help us? Why do you not pray for us? Then he said: 'Before you, there were people who would catch a man, bury him halfway in a hole dug in the ground, then saw his head until it split in two; or would comb with iron combs between his flesh and bones; yet this would not turn him away from his religion. By God! God will bring this matter to completion, and a time will come when a rider will ride alone from Santa to Hadhramaut and he will have no fear except of God, or of a wolf against his sheep; but you people are in a hurry." (Bukhari's Hadith Collections).

God's wisdom underlies every decision and every condition. He administers the entire universe, and, He is informed of its beginning and its end, controlling its events and its interrelationships. He knows the wisdom, hidden from us behind the curtains of the Unseen-the wisdom which, in conjunction with His will, unfolds the long process of history.

Sometimes, after generations and centuries, God unveils to us the wisdom of an event which was not understood by the contemporary people. They might have wondered: Why this? O Lord! Why did this happen? The question itself is due to ignorance from which the Believer saves himself. He already knows that behind every decision there is wisdom. His breath of concept and his far-seeing vision in space and time, and in values and scales, raises him above this unbelief whose beginning is in such a question. He journeys on God's ordained course with submission and contentment.

The Quran was creating hearts worthy of bearing the trust of being God's representatives on earth. It was necessary that these hearts be so solid, so strong and so pure, leaving behind everything and bearing everything patiently, as not to fix their sights on something of this earth, but looking beyond to the Hereafter, not seeking anything except the pleasure of God and being willing to traverse the path of life until death in poverty, difficulty, frustration, torment and sacrifice. They were not to seek any hasty reward on this earth, whether it was the reward of the victory of the Call, the dominance of Islam, and the glory of the Muslims, or even that this reward be the annihilation of the tyrants, as the All Mighty, the All Powerful had dealt with former generations of unbelievers. When such hearts were found which knew that during the course of this life they would have no expectations, and that the decision between the truth and falsehood would be made in the Hereafter-when such hearts were found, and God knew the sincerity of their intentions concerning which they had pledged, he gave them victory in the earth and bestowed upon them the trust. This trust was not for their benefit, but so that they might establish the divine system.

They became the bearers of this trust when no promise was made to them of worldly benefits which they could have demanded, nor were their sights fixed on acquiring such benefits. They were dedicated servants of God from the day they knew of no reward except His pleasure.

All the verses of the Quran in which victory is promised, or in which spoils are mentioned or where it is told that the polytheists will be punished in this world by the hands of the Believers, were revealed in *Madīna*. These were revealed only after all these matters were excluded from the Believer's scope of action, his expectation and his desire. God's help came on its own, when God intended that this way of life become actual in the life of humankind, so that generations of men could see it in a practical and concrete form, and not as a reward for the endeavors, the hard work, the sacrifice and the sufferings. This was indeed a decision of God, the wisdom of which we are trying to fathom today.

This intricate point requires deep thought by all callers toward God, to whatever country or period of time they belong. For this guarantees that they will be able to see the milestones along the way clearly and without ambiguity, and establishes the path for those who wish to travel it to the end, whatever end that might be. Then, what God intends to do with His call and with them is up to Him. They will not be anxious, while traveling this road ever paved with skulls and limbs and blood and sweat, to find help and victory. However, if God Himself intends to fulfill the completion of His call and His religion through their efforts, He will bring about His will- but not as a reward for their sufferings and sacrifices. Indeed, this world is not a place of reward.

Another fact to ponder here is a comment of the Quran on the story of the Makers of the Pit where God Most High says: "They were angered with the believers, only because they believed in God, the All-Powerful, the All-Praiseworthy." The callers to God, of any period or generation, ought to think over this deep truth.

The struggle between the believers and their enemies is in essence a struggle of belief, and not in any way of anything else. The enemies are angered only because of their faith, enraged only because of their belief. This was not a political or an economic or a racial struggle. Had it been any of these, its settlement would have been easy, the solution to its difficulties would have been simple. Essentially, it was a struggle between beliefs, either unbelief or faith, either *Jāhiliyya* or Islam. This is why the leaders of the polytheists of Mecca offered the Messenger of God, peace be on him, wealth, kingship and worldly things, on the condition that he drops only one thing: That he give up belief. Had he accepted, may God forgive us for saying this, what they asked of him, no difference whatsoever would have remained between them and him.

Indeed, this was a question of belief and a struggle for faith. The believers ought to be certain of this, regardless of what their enemies might say. They are their enemies only because of their belief- "only because they believe in God, the All-Powerful, the All-Praiseworthy," and because they make sincere their obedience and submission to God, and to God alone.

The enemies of the faithful may wish to change this struggle into an economic or political or racial struggle, so that the believers become confused concerning the true nature of the struggle and the flame of faith in their hearts becomes extinguished. Believers must not be deceived and must understand that this is a trick. The enemy, by changing the nature of the struggle, intends to deprive them of their weapon for a true victory, the victory which can take any form, be it the victory of the freedom of spirit as was case of the believers in the story of the Maker of the Pit, or dominance in the world, as a consequence of the freedom of spirit, as happened in the case of the first generation of Muslims.

We are witnessing an example of disguising the flag in an attempt of the global crusades today to deceive us from the truth, and to bring falsehoods into history, claiming to us that the crusades were a cover for colonialism. Not true. The colonialism that came late was the fig leaf for the crusader spirit, which was no longer capable of being revealed as it was in the Middle Ages. It was shattered on the rock of the faith, led by Muslims from various backgrounds, including Saladin al-Kurdi and Turan Shah the Mamluk, the backgrounds that enable them to forget their nationalism and remembered their faith, so they triumphed under the banner of the faith.

They were angered with the believers only because they believed in God, the All-Powerful, the All-Praiseworthy. (85:8).

God Almighty tells the truth, and the deceitful people lied.

Index

faith, 4, 6, 10, 14, 15, 17, 20, 21, 22, 23, 24,
  26, 27, 28, 29, 32, 36, 37, 46, 63, 64, 66,
  71, 87, 88, 93, 94, 95, 96, 97, 100, 102,
  105, 107, 108, 109, 110, 111, 114, 123,
  127, 128, 131, 132, 133, 134, 135, 136,
  139, 140
falsehood, 51, 77, 98, 106, 111, 113, 116,
  120, 129, 135, 138
family, 57, 82, 83, 84, 90, 103, 105, 106,
  107, 109, 110, 137
Fard al-Kifayah, 94
favorable, 118
fi dilal al-qur'an, 6, 23, 69, 71
Fiqh, 31
free, 5, 11, 12, 13, 16, 17, 20, 21, 33, 43, 44,
  46, 47, 48, 49, 51, 52, 56, 58, 60, 61, 65,
  80, 81, 83, 84, 85, 95, 114, 131
freedom, 26, 43, 44, 46, 47, 48, 49, 51, 54,
  55, 57, 58, 59, 61, 62, 66, 80, 81, 82, 121,
  127, 132, 137, 140
French Empire, 38
fundamental principles, 43
general teachings of Islam, 25
Hadith, 7, 8, 94, 97
Hamzah Ibn Abdul Muttalib, 54
harmonious, 2, 29, 32, 35, 38, 71, 73, 74, 75
Hereafter, 55, 77, 99, 101, 114, 125, 127,
  133, 134, 135, 136, 137, 138
Hijaz, 16
Hijrah, 51, 54
homeland of Islam, 49, 58
Hud, 86, 131, 136
human, 1, 2, 4, 6, 12, 14, 16, 17, 20, 21, 22,
  24, 26, 29, 30, 31, 33, 34, 35, 36, 37, 38,
  42, 44, 46, 47, 48, 49, 56, 57, 58, 59, 60,
  61, 63, 64, 66, 70, 71, 73, 74, 75, 77, 78,
  79, 81, 82, 83, 84, 85, 87, 89, 90, 92, 93,
  94, 95, 96, 97, 99, 101, 103, 110, 112,
  114, 115, 118, 121, 124, 130
human beings, 14, 17, 20, 29, 30, 33, 44, 47,
  48, 57, 58, 59, 61, 66, 75, 78, 81, 83, 90,
  114
human life, 14, 33, 34, 64, 70, 75, 77, 78,
  94, 101, 112, 114, 115
human nature, 1, 2, 26, 31, 61, 71, 74, 99,
  118

human situation, 46, 48
humanity, 2, 7, 27, 30, 36, 37, 58, 82, 85,
  90, 109, 121
humanity of man, 36, 85, 90
Ibn Qayyim, 40, 50
idolaters, 125
Ijtihad, 71
industrial, 83, 87, 89, 90, 96
Islam, 2, 3, 4, 5, 7, 11, 12, 13, 17, 20, 21, 22,
  23, 24, 25, 26, 27, 28, 29, 30, 31, 32, 33,
  34, 35, 36, 38, 41, 43, 44, 46, 47, 48, 49,
  50, 51, 52, 53, 54, 55, 56, 57, 58, 59, 60,
  61, 62, 63, 64, 65, 66, 70, 71, 72, 73, 79,
  80, 82, 83, 85, 86, 89, 90, 92, 93, 95, 96,
  100, 101, 102, 103, 108, 109, 110, 111,
  112, 113, 114, 115, 116, 117, 118, 119,
  120, 121, 122, 124, 125, 126, 127, 138,
  140
Islamic belief, 27, 29, 31, 32, 75, 79, 88, 90,
  95, 96, 125
Islamic call, 25, 26
Islamic Call, 118
Islamic community, 11, 27, 37, 58, 59, 62,
  87, 88, 90
Islamic country, 119, 122
Islamic culture, 12, 37, 96
Islamic Law, 31
Islamic laws, 26, 79
Islamic moral teachings, 63
Islamic movement, 12, 31, 32, 35, 42, 48,
  55, 58, 60, 64, 87
Islamic system, 3, 20, 25, 31, 32, 48, 54, 61,
  83, 119
Islamic values, 12, 79, 83, 85
Islamic world, 119
jahili, 11, 12, 13, 19, 27, 29, 30, 34, 35, 36,
  59, 60, 64, 65, 66, 67, 68, 70, 79, 80, 81,
  82, 83, 84, 85, 87, 88, 91, 94, 95, 96, 110,
  112, 114, 117, 118, 119, 120, 121
Jahiliyyah, 4, 5, 11, 12, 13, 19, 21, 27, 28,
  29, 30, 31, 32, 33, 34, 36, 42, 48, 60, 70,
  88, 89, 94, 97, 101, 111, 112, 113, 114,
  115, 117, 118, 119, 120, 121, 122, 126,
  140
Jihad, 40, 42, 43, 44, 48, 49, 50, 51, 55, 56,
  57, 58, 60, 61, 62, 88, 123

Jiziyah, 40, 50, 56, 59
Julian Huxley, 36
kindness, 103, 104, 117
kingship, 45, 140
knowledge, 9, 10, 12, 17, 28, 32, 70, 71, 76,
    85, 92, 95, 96, 97, 98, 99, 100, 102, 105,
    113, 116, 125, 134
la ilaha illa allah, 15, 17, 20, 22, 23, 25, 34,
    35, 65, 70, 92
label of Islam, 43
leadership, 1, 3, 4, 5, 11, 13, 16, 17, 34, 35,
    36, 37, 38, 54, 59, 66, 114
lineage, 16, 19, 21, 52, 108, 109, 111
logic, 8, 9, 12, 121, 123, 124, 129
love, 26, 37, 84, 104, 117, 120, 122, 131, 133
Madinah, 24, 47, 50, 51, 54, 103, 104, 108,
    118, 139
mankind, 1, 2, 3, 4, 5, 7, 22, 33, 37, 38, 44,
    46, 48, 51, 54, 58, 59, 61, 62, 72, 75, 76,
    77, 85, 87, 89, 95, 101, 103, 111, 112,
    114, 116, 117, 118, 119, 120, 125, 129,
    132, 135, 136, 139
man-made system, 30, 60, 70, 116
man-made systems, 24, 32, 116, 121
martyrdom, 109, 127
materialism, 79, 82, 121
Maududi, 23, 34
Mecca, 24, 50, 51, 53, 107, 108, 118, 140
mentality, 24, 28, 62, 115, 121, 126
Messenger, 2, 7, 8, 9, 15, 33, 35, 44, 47, 50,
    51, 57, 63, 65, 66, 70, 71, 73, 75, 79, 97,
    98, 103, 107, 108, 111, 114, 122, 134,
    137, 140
Messengers, 39, 63
method, 7, 8, 9, 11, 19, 22, 24, 27, 28, 29,
    30, 31, 32, 36, 42, 43, 59, 61, 64, 66, 70,
    74, 88, 90, 96, 117, 120
monopolies, 121
moral values, 83
morality, 20, 83, 84, 85, 92
morals, 13, 20, 21, 27, 29, 79, 82, 83, 84, 85,
    92, 93, 94, 96, 125
motivation, 120
Muhammad, 16, 17, 20, 33, 35, 53, 63, 65,
    66, 71, 73, 75, 92, 93, 94, 107, 108, 117,
    128, 136

Muhammadar Rasul Allah, 63, 65, 70, 92
Mujtahidun, 32
Muslim community, 2, 3, 4, 7, 10, 23, 24,
    27, 28, 30, 36, 44, 52, 60, 63, 64, 65, 66,
    78, 93, 103, 110
Muslim society, 4, 15, 24, 35, 65, 66, 70, 80,
    94, 96, 98, 100
Muslims, 6, 8, 9, 11, 13, 22, 23, 24, 25, 32,
    35, 40, 50, 53, 55, 57, 62, 69, 79, 93, 94,
    97, 98, 102, 104, 107, 108, 113, 119, 120,
    121, 122, 125, 137, 138, 140
nationalism, 16, 26, 38, 108
natural laws, 34, 73, 100
nature, 1, 3, 5, 10, 12, 13, 14, 22, 26, 27, 29,
    30, 32, 33, 40, 43, 44, 49, 55, 57, 58, 59,
    60, 62, 64, 66, 70, 74, 76, 77, 80, 87, 88,
    89, 92, 93, 94, 97, 111, 113, 118, 120,
    121, 123, 124, 130, 140
Noah, 66, 86, 105, 106, 107, 128, 131, 136
noble civilization, 89
nomadic, 83
Oneness of God, 11, 16, 17, 20, 22, 26, 69,
    90, 94, 120
orientalists, 48, 49, 50, 55, 58, 61
Original Sin, 121
pastoral, 83
People of the Book, 41, 45, 47, 50, 56, 97, 98
persuasion, 26, 42, 52, 54
power, 1, 15, 17, 21, 23, 24, 32, 42, 44, 45,
    46, 49, 51, 54, 58, 59, 66, 68, 86, 87, 93,
    95, 98, 116, 118, 124, 125, 127, 128, 129,
    131, 137
practical needs, 25, 43
Profumo, 84
progressive, 43, 52, 79, 82, 84
proletarian, 83
proletariat, 38
Prophet, 7, 8, 11, 13, 14, 15, 16, 17, 18, 20,
    23, 26, 33, 34, 35, 40, 43, 44, 46, 47, 49,
    50, 51, 54, 63, 64, 72, 78, 92, 97, 101,
    103, 105, 110, 137
psychology, 80, 95, 118
Quraysh, 16, 35, 43, 52, 53, 54, 128
racial form, 47
Redemption, 121
reformist movement, 20, 26

relationship, 11, 12, 14, 22, 34, 35, 36, 37, 38, 43, 44, 82, 83, 84, 92, 93, 94, 100, 101, 103, 104, 107, 108, 110, 111, 120

Repentance, 109

representation of God on earth, 85

responsibility, 7, 83, 88, 102, 121, 137

risalah, 7, 16, 17, 18, 40, 94

Russia, 84

Russian Embassy, 84

Sacrifice, 121

Salah, 63

Salih, 86, 131

Satan, 55, 57, 101

Sawm, 63

scientific ignorance, 36

servitude, 5, 26, 33, 43, 44, 46, 47, 48, 51, 57, 59, 60, 61, 65, 80, 81, 85, 113, 114, 120, 127

sexual activity, 85

sexual relationships, 83, 84

Shari`ah, 24, 26, 45, 46, 47, 49, 60, 69, 71, 74, 75, 76, 78, 79, 81, 85, 90, 92, 102, 103, 108, 109, 110, 111, 113, 117, 120

Shirk, 33, 69, 111, 115

Shu`ayb, 131, 136

social life, 10, 25, 69

social system, 28, 58, 65, 69

socialistic, 83

Son of God, 56, 67, 69

sovereignty, 4, 15, 17, 21, 23, 25, 31, 33, 35, 44, 45, 46, 48, 60, 62, 74, 78, 79, 80, 92, 93

submission, 23, 26, 33, 34, 35, 43, 44, 59, 65, 66, 68, 69, 70, 73, 92, 95, 109, 113, 114, 138, 140

Sustainer, 2, 15, 16, 20, 33, 35, 37, 40, 45, 46, 64, 70, 72, 74, 78, 86, 95, 99, 101, 103, 106, 109, 110, 129, 134

theology, 9, 26, 27, 95

theoretical teachings, 29

theories, 1, 2, 24, 28, 29, 38, 43, 70, 87, 88, 94, 112, 115

theory, 1, 3, 23, 26, 27, 28, 29, 30, 31, 34, 36, 82

tribal warfare, 16, 52

Trinity, 67, 121

tyrannical force, 47

tyrants, 86, 131, 132, 134, 136, 138

uluhiyah, 15

Umar, 8, 9, 49, 53

universal, 7, 34, 44, 46, 48, 51, 55, 57, 59, 61, 73, 74, 75

universal system, 48

usurpers, 45, 51, 58

verbal logic, 27

vicegerent, 85

vice-regency, 90

voluntary, 34, 74, 75

woman, 19, 83, 122, 131

worship, 2, 4, 5, 15, 21, 33, 35, 43, 45, 47, 56, 60, 63, 64, 65, 66, 68, 73, 77, 79, 80, 90, 92, 93, 106, 110, 112, 113, 131

ya ayyuha al-muddathir, 40

Zakah, 50, 52, 63, 112

الفهرس

مقدمة:

تقف البشرية اليوم على حافة الهاوية. لا بسبب التهديد بالفناء المعلق على رأسها. فهذا عرضٌ للمرض وليس هو المرض. ولكن بسبب إفلاسها في عالم "القيم" التي يمكن أن تنمو الحياة الإنسانية في ظلالها نموا سليما وترقى ترقيا صحيحا. وهذا واضح كل الوضوح في العالم الغربي، الذي لم يعد لديه ما يعطيه للبشرية من "القيم "، بل الذي لم يعد لديه ما يُقنع ضميره باستحقاقه للوجود، بعدما انتهت "الديمقراطية "فيه إلى ما يشبه الإفلاس، حيث بدأت تستعير- ببطء - وتقتبس من أنظمة المعسكر الشرقي وبخاصة في الأنظمة الاقتصادية. تحت اسم الاشتراكية.

كذلك الحال في المعسكر الشرقي نفسه. فالنظريات الجماعية وفي مقدمتها الماركسية التي اجتذبت في أول عهدها عددا كبيرا في الشرق - وفي الغرب نفسه - باعتبارها مذهبا يحمل طابع العقيدة، قد تراجعت هي الأخرى تراجعا واضحا من ناحية "الفكرة "حتى لتكاد تنحصر الآن في "الدولة "وأنظمتها، التي تبعد بعدا كبيرا عن أصول المذهب. وهي على العموم تناهض طبيعة الفطرة البشرية ومقتضياتها، ولا تنمو إلا في بيئة محطمة. أو بيئة قد ألفت النظام الدكتاتوري فترات طويلة. وحتى في مثل هذه البيئات قد بدأ يظهر فشلها المادي الاقتصادي - وهو الجانب الذي تقوم عليه وتتبجح به - فروسيا - التي تمثل قمة الأنظمة الجماعية - تتناقص غلاتها بعد أن كانت فائضة حتى في عهود القياصرة، وتستورد القمح والمواد الغذائية، وتبيع ما لديها من الذهب لتحصل على الطعام بسبب فشل المزارع الجماعية وفشل النظام الذي يصادم الفطرة البشرية.

لابد من قيادة جديدة للبشرية.

إن قيادة الرجل الغربي للبشرية قد أوشكت على الزوال. لا لأن الحضارة الغربية قد أفلست ماديا أو ضعفت من ناحية القوة الاقتصادية والعسكرية. ولكن لأن النظام الغربي قد انتهى دوره لأنه لم يعد يملك رصيدا من "القيم "يسمح له بالقيادة.

لابد من قيادة تملك إبقاء وتنمية الحضارة المادية التي وصلت إليها البشرية، عن طريق العبقرية الأوروبية في الإبداع المادي، وتزود البشرية بقيم جديدة كاملة - بالقياس إلى ما عرفته البشرية – وبمنهج أصيل وإيجابي وواقعي في الوقت ذاته.

والإسلام - وحده - هو الذي يملك تلك القيم، وهذا المنهج.

لقد أدت النهضة العلمية دورها. هذا الدور الذي بدأت مطالعه مع عصر النهضة في القرن السادس عشر الميلادي، ووصلت إلى ذروتها خلال القرنين الثامن عشر والتاسع عشر. ولم تعد تملك رصيدا جديدا.

كذلك أدت "الوطنية "و" القومية "التي برزت في تلك الفترة، والتجمعات الإقليمية عامة دورها خلال هذه القرون. ولم تعد هي الأخرى تملك رصيدا جديدا.

ثم فشلت الأنظمة الفردية والأنظمة الجماعية في نهاية المطاف.

ولقد جاء دور "الإسلام "ودور "الأمة "في أشد الساعات حرجا وحيرة واضطرابا. جاء دور الإسلام الذي لا يتنكر للإبداع المادي في الأرض، لأنه يعده من وظيفة الإنسان الأولى منذ أن عهد الله إليه بالخلافة في الأرض، ويعتبره - تحت شروط خاصة - عبادة لله، وتحقيقا لغاية الوجود الإنساني.

(وإِذْ قال ربك للْملائكةِ إِني جاعِلٌ في الأَرْضِ خليفة) [البقرة: 30]

(وما خلقْتُ الجِن والإنس إلا لِيعْبُدُونِ) [الذاريات: 56]

وجاء دور "الأمة المسلمة "لتحقق ما أراده الله بإخراجها للناس:

(كنْتُمْ خيْر أُمةٍ أُخْرِجتْ للِناسِ تأْمُرُون بِالْمعْرُوفِ وتنْهوْن عنِ الْمُنكرِ وتُؤْمِنُون بِاللَّهِ).. [آل عمران: 110]

(وكذلِك جعلْناكُمْ أُمة وسطا لِتكُونُوا شُهداء على الناسِ ويكُون الرسُولُ عليْكُمْ شهِيدا).. [البقرة: 143]

ولكن الإسلام لا يملك أن يؤدي دوره إلا أن يتمثل في مجتمع، أي أن يتمثل في أمة. فالبشرية لا تستمع - وبخاصة في هذا الزمان - إلى عقيدة مجردة، لا ترى مصداقها الواقعي في حياة مشهودة. و "وجود "الأمة المسلمة "يعتبر قد انقطع منذ قرون كثيرة. فالأمة المسلمة ليست "أرضا "كان يعيش فيها الإسلام. وليست "قوما "كان أجدادهم في عصر من عصور التاريخ يعيشون بالنظام الإسلامي. إنما "الأمة المسلمة "جماعة من البشر تنبثق حياتهم وتصوراتهم وأوضاعهم وأنظمتهم وقيمهم وموازينهم كلها من المنهج الإسلامي.. وهذه الأمة - بهذه المواصفات. قد انقطع وجودها منذ انقطاع الحكم بشريعة الله من فوق ظهر الأرض جميعا.

ولا بد من "إعادة "وجود هذه "الأمة "لكي يؤدي الإسلام دوره المرتقب في قيادة البشرية مرة أخرى.

لا بد من "بعث "لتلك الأمة التي واراها ركام الأجيال وركام التصورات، وركام الأوضاع، وركام الأنظمة، التي لا صلة لها بالإسلام، ولا بالمنهج الإسلامي. وإن كانت ما تزال تزعم أنها قائمة فيما يسمى "العالم الإسلامي "..

وأنا أعرف أن المسافة بين محاولة "البعث "وبين تسلم "القيادة "مسافة شاسعة. فقد غابت الأمة المسلمة عن "الوجود "وعن "الشهود "دهرا طويلا. وقد تولت قيادة البشرية أفكار أخرى وأمم أخرى، وتصورات أخرى وأوضاع أخرى فترة طويلة. وقد أبدعت العبقرية الأوروبية في هذه الفترة رصيدا ضخما من "العلم "و "الثقافة "و "الأنظمة "و "الإنتاج المادي ". وهو رصيد ضخم تقف البشرية على قمته، ولا تفرط فيه ولا فيمن يمثله بسهولة. وبخاصة أن ما يسمى "العالم الإسلامي "يكاد يكون عاطلا من كل هذه الزينة.

ولكن لا بد - مع هذه الاعتبارات كلها - من "البعث الإسلامي" مهما تكن المسافة شاسعة بين محاولة البعث وبين تسلم القيادة. فمحاولة البعث الإسلامي هي الخطوة الأولى التي لا يمكن تخطيها.

ولكي نكون على بينة من الأمر، ينبغي أن ندرك - على وجه التحديد - مؤهلات هذه الأمة للقيادة البشرية، كي لا نخطئ عناصرها في محاولة البعث الأولى.

إن هذه الأمة لا تملك الآن - وليس مطلوبا منها - أن تقدم للبشرية تفوقا خارقا في الإبداع المادي، يحنى لها الرقاب، ويفرض قيادتها العالمية من هذه الزاوية. فالعبقرية الأوروبية قد سبقته في هذا المضمار سبقا واسعا. وليس من المنتظر - خلال عدة قرون على الأقل - التفوق المادي عليها.

فلابد إذن من مؤهل آخر. المؤهل الذي تفتقده هذه الحضارة.

إن هذا لا يعني أن نهمل الإبداع المادي. فمن واجبنا أن نحاول فيه جهدنا. ولكن لا بوصفه "المؤهل" الذي نتقدم به لقيادة البشرية في المرحلة الراهنة. إنما بوصفه ضرورة ذاتية لوجودنا. كذلك بوصفه واجبا يفرضه علينا "التصور الإسلامي" الذي ينوط بالإنسان خلافة الأرض، ويجعلها - تحت شروط خاصة - عبادة لله، وتحقيقا لغاية الوجود الإنساني.

لا بد إذن من مؤهل آخر لقيادة البشرية - غير الإبداع المادي - ولن يكون هذا المؤهل سوى "العقيدة" و "المنهج" الذي يسمح للبشرية أن تحتفظ بنتاج العبقرية المادية، تحت إشراف تصور آخر يلبي حاجة الفطرة كما يلبيها الإبداع المادي، وأن تتمثل العقيدة والمنهج في تجمع إنساني. أي في مجتمع مسلم.

إن العالم يعيش اليوم كله في "جاهلية" من ناحية الأصل الذي تنبثق منه مقومات الحياة وأنظمتها. جاهلية لا تخفف منها شيئا هذه التيسيرات المادية الهائلة، وهذا الإبداع المادي الفائق.

هذه الجاهلية تقوم على أساس الاعتداء على سلطان الله في الأرض وعلى أخص خصائص الألوهية. وهي الحاكمية. إنها تسند الحاكمية إلى البشر، فتجعل بعضهم لبعض أربابا، لا في الصورة البدائية الساذجة التي عرفتها الجاهلية الأولى، ولكن في صورة ادعاء حق وضع التصورات والقيم، والشرائع والقوانين، والأنظمة والأوضاع، بمعزل عن منهج الله للحياة، وفيما لم يأذن به الله. فينشأ عن هذا الاعتداء على سلطان الله اعتداء على عباده. وما مهانة "الإنسان" عامة في الأنظمة الجماعية، وما ظلم "الأفراد" و"الشعوب بسيطرة رأس المال والاستعمار في النظم "الرأسمالية" إلا أثرا من آثار الاعتداء على سلطان الله، وإنكار الكرامة التي قررها الله للإنسان.

وفي هذا يتفرد المنهج الإسلامي. فالناس في كل نظام غير النظام الإسلامي، يعبد بعضهم بعضا - في صورة من الصور - وفي المنهج الإسلامي وحده يتحرر الناس جميعا من عبادة بعضهم لبعض، بعبادة الله وحده، والتلقي من الله وحده، والخضوع لله وحده.

وهذا هو مفترق الطريق. وهذا كذلك هو التصور الجديد الذي نملك إعطاءه للبشرية - هو وسائر ما يترتب عليه من آثار عميقة في الحياة البشرية الواقعية - وهذا هو الرصيد الذي لا تملكه البشرية، لأنه ليس من "منتجات" الحضارة الغربية، وليس من منتجات العبقرية الأوروبية. شرقية كانت أو غربية.

إننا - دون شك - نملك شيئا جديدا جدة كاملة. شيئا لا تعرفه البشرية. ولا تملك هي أن "تنتجه ".

ولكن هذا الجديد، لا بد أن يتمثل -كما قلنا - في واقع عملي. لا بد أن تعيش به أمة. وهذا يقتضي عملية "بعث" في الرقعة الإسلامية هذا البعث الذي يتبعه - على مسافة ما بعيدة أو قريبة - تسلم قيادة البشرية.

فكيف تبدأ عملية البعث الإسلامي؟

إنه لا بد من طليعة تعزم هذه العزمة، وتمضي في الطريق. تمضي في خضم الجاهلية الضاربة الأطناب في أرجاء الأرض جميعا. تمضي وهي تزاول نوعا من العزلة من جانب، ونوعا من الاتصال من الجانب الآخر بالجاهلية المحيطة.

ولا بد لهذه الطليعة التي تعزم هذه العزمة من "معالم في الطريق "معالم تعرف منها طبيعة دورها، وحقيقة وظيفتها، وصلب غايتها. ونقطة البدء في الرحلة الطويلة. كما تعرف منها طبيعة موقفها من الجاهلية الضاربة الأطناب في الأرض جميعا. أين تلتقي مع الناس وأين تفترق؟ ما خصائصها هي وما خصائص الجاهلية من حولها؟ كيف تخاطب أهل هذه الجاهلية بلغة الإسلام وفيم تخاطبها؟ ثم تعرف من أين تتلقى - في هذا كله - وكيف تتلقى؟

هذه المعالم لا بد أن تقام من المصدر الأول لهذه العقيدة. القرآن. ومن توجيهاته الأساسية، ومن التصور الذي أنشأه في نفوس الصفوة المختارة، التي صنع الله بها في الأرض ما شاء أن يصنع، والتي حولت خط سير التاريخ مرة إلى حيث شاء الله أن يسير.

لهذه الطليعة المرجوة المرتقبة كتبت "معالم في الطريق" . منها أربعة فصول مستخرجة من كتاب "في ظلال القرآن "مع تعديلات وإضافات مناسبة لموضوع كتاب المعالم. ومنها ثمانية فصول - غير هذه التقدمة - مكتوبة في فترات حسبما أوحت به اللفتات المتوالية إلى المنهج الرباني الممثل في القرآن الكريم. وكلها يجمعها - على تفرقها - أنها معالم في الطريق، كما هو الشأن في معالم كل طريق. وهي في مجموعها تمثل المجموعة الأولى من هذه "المعالم "والتي أرجو أن تتبعها مجموعة أخرى أو مجموعات، كلما هداني الله إلى معالم هذا الطريق.

وبالله التوفيق.

سيد قطب

جيل قرآني فريد

هنالك ظاهرة تاريخية ينبغي أن يقف أمامها أصحاب الدعوة الإسلامية في كل أرض وفي كل زمان. وأن يقفوا أمامها طويلا. ذلك أنها ذات أثر حاسم في منهج الدعوة واتجاهها.

لقد خرجت هذه الدعوة جيلا من الناس - جيل الصحابة رضوان الله عليهم - جيلا مميزا في تاريخ الإسلام كله وفي تاريخ البشرية جميعه. ثم لم تعد تخرج هذا الطراز مرة أخرى. نعم وُجد أفراد من ذلك الطراز على مدار التاريخ. ولكن لم يحدث قط أن تجمع مثل ذلك العدد الضخم، في مكان واحد، كما وقع في الفترة الأولى من حياة هذه الدعوة.

هذه ظاهرة واضحة واقعة، ذات مدلول ينبغي الوقوف أمامه طويلا، لعلنا نهتدي إلى سره.

إن قرآن هذه الدعوة بين أيدينا، وحديث رسول الله - صلى الله عليه وسلم - وهديه العملي، وسيرته الكريمة، كلها بين أيدينا كذلك، كما كانت بين أيدي ذلك الجيل الأول، الذي لم يتكرر في التاريخ. ولم يغب إلا شخص رسول الله - صلى الله عليه وسلم - فهل هذا هو السر؟

لو كان وجود شخص رسول الله - صلى الله عليه وسلم - حتميا لقيام هذه الدعوة، وإيتائها ثمراتها، ما جعلها الله دعوة للناس كافة، وما جعلها آخر رسالة، وما وكل إليها أمر الناس في هذه الأرض، إلى آخر الزمان.

ولكن الله - سبحانه - تكفل بحفظ الذكر، و علم أن هذه الدعوة يمكن أن تقوم بعد رسول الله - صلى الله عليه وسلم - وبمكن أن تؤتي ثمارها. فاختاره إلى جواره بعد ثلاثة وعشرين عاما من الرسالة، وأبقى هذا الدين من بعده إلى آخر الزمان. وإذن فإن غيبة شخص رسول الله - صلى الله عليه وسلم - لا تفسر تلك الظاهرة ولا تعللها.

فلنبحث إذن وراء سبب آخر. لننظر في النبع الذي كان يستقي منه هذا الجيل الأول، فلعل شيئا قد تغير فيه. ولننظر في المنهج الذي تخرجوا عليه، فلعل شيئا قد تغير فيه كذلك.

كان النبع الأول الذي استقى منه ذلك الجيل هو نبع القرآن. القرآن وحده. فما كان حديث رسول الله - صلى الله عليه وسلم - وهديه إلا أثرا من آثار ذلك النبع. فعندما سُئلت عائشة رضي الله عنها - عن خُلق رسول الله - صلى الله عليه وسلم - قالت: "كان خُلقه القرآن"[1].

---

[1] أخرجه النسائي.

كان القرآن وحده إذن هو النبع الذي يستقون منه، ويتكيفون به، ويتخرجون عليه، ولم يكن ذلك كذلك لأنه لم يكن للبشرية يومها حضارة، ولا ثقافة، ولا علم، ولا مؤلفات، ولا دراسات. كلا. فقد كانت هناك حضارة الرومان وثقافتها وكتبها وقانونها الذي ما تزال أوروبا تعيش عليه، أو على امتداده. وكانت هناك مخلفات الحضارة الإغريقية ومنطقها وفلسفتها وفنها، وهو ما يزال ينبوع التفكير الغربي حتى اليوم. وكانت هناك حضارة الفرس وفنها وشعرها وأساطيرها وعقائدها ونظم حكمها كذلك. وحضارات أخرى قاصية ودانية: حضارة الهند وحضارة الصين إلخ. وكانت الحضارتان الرومانية والفارسية تحفان بالجزيرة العربية من شمالها ومن جنوبها، كما كانت اليهودية والنصرانية تعيشان في قلب الجزيرة. فلم يكن إذن عن فقر في الحضارات العالمية والثقافات العالمية يقصر ذلك الجيل على كتاب الله وحده. في فترة تكونه. وإنما كان ذلك عن "تصميم "مرسوم، ونهج مقصود. يدل على هذا القصد غضب رسول الله - صلى الله عليه وسلم - وقد رأى في يد عمر بن الخطاب - رضي الله عنه – صحيفة من التوراة. وقوله: "إنه والله لو كان موسى حيا بين أظهركم ما حل له إلا أن يتبعني "[2].

وإذن فقد كان هناك قصد من رسول الله - صلى الله عليه وسلم - أن يقصر النبع الذي يستقي منه ذلك الجيل. في فترة التكون الأولى. على كتاب الله وحده. لتخلص نفوسهم - له وحده. ويستقيم عودهم على منهجه وحده. ومن ثم غضب أن رأى عمر بن الخطاب - رضي الله عنه - يستقي من نبع آخر.

كان رسول الله - صلى الله عليه وسلم - يريد صنع جيل خالص القلب. خالص العقل. خالص التصور. خالص الشعور. خالص التكوين من أي مؤثر آخر غير المنهج الإلهي، الذي يتضمنه القرآن الكريم.

ذلك الجيل استقى إذن من ذلك النبع وحده. فكان له في التاريخ ذلك الشأن الفريد. ثم ما الذي حدث، اختلطت الينابيع. صبت في النبع الذي استقت منه الأجيال التالية فلسفة الإغريق ومنطقهم، وأساطير الفرس وتصوراتهم، وإسرائيليات اليهود ولاهوت النصارى، وغير ذلك من رواسب الحضارات والثقافات. واختلط هذا كله بتفسير القرآن الكريم، وعلم الكلام، كما اختلط بالفقه والأصول أيضا. وتخرج على ذلك النبع المشوب سائر الأجيال بعد ذلك الجيل، فلم يتكرر ذلك الجيل أبدا.

وما من شك أن اختلاط النبع الأول كان عاملا أساسيا من عوامل ذلك الاختلاف البين بين الأجيال كلها وذلك الجيل المميز الفريد.

هناك عامل أساسي آخر غير اختلاف طبيعة النبع. ذلك هو اختلاف منهج التلقي عما كان عليه في ذلك الجيل الفريد.

---

[2] رواه الحافظ أبو يعلى عن حماد عن الشعبي عن جابر.

إنهم - في الجيل الأول - لم يكونوا يقرءون القرآن بقصد الثقافة والاطلاع، ولا بقصد التذوق والمتاع. لم يكن أحدهم يتلقى القرآن ليستكثر به من زاد الثقافة لمجرد الثقافة، ولا ليضيف إلى حصيلته من القضايا العلمية والفقهية محصولا يملأ به جعبته. إنما كان يتلقى القرآن ليتلقى أمر الله في خاصة شأنه وشأن الجماعة التي يعيش فيها، وشأن الحياة التي يحياها هو وجماعته، يتلقى ذلك الأمر ليعمل به فور سماعه، كما يتلقى الجندي في الميدان "الأمر اليومي "ليعمل به فور تلقيه. ومن ثم لم يكن أحدهم ليستكثر منه في الجلسة الواحدة، لأنه كان يحس أنه إنما يستكثر من واجبات وتكاليف يجعلها على عاتقه، فكان يكتفي بعشر آيات حتى يحفظها ويعمل بها كما جاء في حديث ابن مسعود رضي الله عنه [3].

هذا الشعور. شعور التلقي للتنفيذ. كان يفتح لهم من القرآن آفاقا من المتاع وآفاقا من المعرفة، لم تكن لتفتح عليهم لو أنهم قصدوا إليه بشعور البحث والدراسة والاطلاع، وكان ييسر لهم العمل، ويخفف عنهم ثقل التكاليف، ويخلط القرآن بذواتهم، ويحوله في نفوسهم وفي حياتهم إلى منهج واقعي، وإلى ثقافة متحركة لا تبقى داخل الأذهان ولا في بطون الصحائف، إنما تتحول آثارا وأحداثا تحول خط سير الحياة.

إن هذا القرآن لا يمنح كنوزه إلا لمن يُقبل عليه بهذه الروح: روح المعرفة المنشئة للعمل. إنه لم يجيء ليكون كتاب متاع عقلي، ولا كتاب أدب وفن، ولا كتاب قصة وتاريخ - وإن كان هذا كله من محتوياته - إنما جاء ليكون منهاج حياة. منهاجا إلهيا خالصا. وكان الله سبحانه يأخذهم بهذا المنهج مفرقا، يتلو بعضه بعضا:

(وَقُرْآنًا فَرَقْنَاهُ لِتَقْرَأَهُ عَلَى النَّاسِ عَلَى مُكْثٍ وَنَزَّلْنَاهُ تَنْزِيلًا) [الإسراء: 106]

لم ينزل هذا القرآن جملة، إنما نزل وفق الحاجات المتجددة، ووفق النمو المطرد في الأفكار والتصورات، والنمو المُطرد في المجتمع والحياة، ووفق المشكلات العملية التي تواجهها الجماعة المسلمة في حياتها الواقعية. وكانت الآية أو الآيات تنزل في الحالة الخاصة والحادثة المعينة تحدث الناس عما في نفوسهم، وتصور لهم ما هم فيه من الأمر، وترسم لهم منهج العمل في الموقف، وتصحح لهم أخطاء الشعور والسلوك، وتربطهم في هذا كله بالله ربهم، وتعرفه لهم بصفاته المؤثرة في الكون، فيحسون حينئذ أنهم يعيشون مع الملأ الأعلى، تحت عين الله، في رحاب القدرة. ومن ثم يتكيفون في واقع حياتهم، وفق ذلك المنهج الإلهي القويم.

إن منهج التلقي للتنفيذ والعمل هو الذي صنع الجيل الأول. ومنهج التلقي للدراسة والمتاع هو الذي خرج الأجيال التي تليه. وما من شك أن هذا العامل الثاني كان عاملا أساسيا كذلك في اختلاف الأجيال كلها عن ذلك الجيل المميز الفريد.

هناك عامل ثالث جدير بالانتباه والتسجيل.

لقد كان الرجل حين يدخل في الإسلام يخلع على عتبته كل ماضيه في الجاهلية. كان يشعر في اللحظة التي يجيء فيها إلى الإسلام أنه يبدأ عهدا جديدا، منفصلا كل الانفصال عن

---

[3] ذكره ابن كثير في مقدمة التفسير.

8

حياته التي عاشها في الجاهلية. وكان يقف من كل ما عهده في جاهليته موقف المستريب الشاك الحذر المتخوف، الذي يحس أن كل هذا رجس لا يصلح للإسلام. وبهذا الإحساس كان يتلقى هدْي الإسلام الجديد، فإذا غلبته نفسه مرة، وإذا اجتذبته عاداته مرة، وإذا ضعف عن تكاليف الإسلام مرة. شعر في الحال بالإثم والخطيئة، وأدرك في قرارة نفسه أنه في حاجة إلى التطهر مما وقع فيه، وعاد يحاول من جديد أن يكون على وفق الهدْي القرآني.

كانت هناك عزلة شعورية كاملة بين ماضي المسلم في جاهليته وحاضره في إسلامه، تنشأ عنها عزلة كاملة في صلاته بالمجتمع الجاهلي من حوله وروابطه الاجتماعية، فهو قد انفصل نهائيا من بيئته الجاهلية واتصل نهائيا ببيئته الإسلامية. حتى ولوكان يأخذ من بعض المشركين ويعطي في عالم التجارة والتعامل اليومي، فالعزلة الشعورية شيء والتعامل اليومي شيء آخر.

وكان هناك انخلاع من البيئة الجاهلية، وعُزْلُها وتصوراتها، وعاداتها وروابطها، ينشأ عن الانخلاع من عقيدة الشرك إلى عقيدة التوحيد، ومن تصور الجاهلية إلى تصور الإسلام عن الحياة والوجود. وينشأ من الانضمام إلى التجمع الإسلامي الجديد، بقيادته الجديدة، ومنح هذا المجتمع وهذه القيادة كل ولائه وكل طاعته وكل تبعيته.

وكان هذا مفرق الطريق، وكان بدء السير في الطريق الجديد، السير الطليق مع التخفف من كل ضغط للتقاليد التي يتواضع عليها المجتمع الجاهلي، ومن كل التصورات والقيم السائدة فيه. ولم يكن هناك إلا ما يلقاه المسلم من أذى وفتنة، ولكنه هو في ذات نفسه قد عزم وانتهى، ولم يعد لضغط التصور الجاهلي، ولا لتقاليد المجتمع الجاهلي عليه من سبيل.

نحن اليوم في جاهلية كالجاهلية التي عاصرها الإسلام أو أظلم. كل ما حولنا جاهلية. تصورات الناس وعقائدهم، عاداتهم وتقاليدهم، موارد ثقافتهم، فنونهم وآدابهم، شرائعهم وقوانينهم. حتى الكثير مما نحسبه ثقافة إسلامية، ومراجع إسلامية، وفلسفة إسلامية، وتفكيرا إسلاميا. هو كذلك من صنع هذه الجاهلية.

لذلك لا تستقيم قيم الإسلام في نفوسنا، ولا يتضح تصور الإسلام في عقولنا، ولا ينشأ فينا جيل ضخم من الناس من ذلك الطراز الذي أنشأه الإسلام أول مرة.

فلا بد إذن - في منهج الحركة الإسلامية - أن نتجرد في فترة الحضانة والتكوين من كل مؤثرات الجاهلية التي نعيش فيها ونستمد منها. لا بد أن نرجع ابتداء إلى النبع الخالص الذي استمد منه أولئك الرجال، النبع المضمون أنه لم يختلط ولم تشبه شائبة. نرجع إليه نستمد منه تصورنا لحقيقة الوجود كله ولحقيقة الوجود الإنساني ولكافة الارتباطات بين هذين الوجودين وبين الوجود الكامل الحق، وجود الله سبحانه. ومن ثم نستمد تصوراتنا للحياة، وقيمنا وأخلاقنا، ومناهجنا للحكم والسياسة والاقتصاد وكل مقومات الحياة.

ولا بد أن نرجع إليه - حين نرجع - بشعور التلقي للتنفيذ والعمل، لا بشعور الدراسة والمتاع. نرجع إليه لنعرف ماذا يطلب منا أن نكون، لنكون. وفي الطريق سنلتقي بالجمال الفني في القرآن وبالقصص الرائع في القرآن، وبمشاهد القيامة في القرآن. وبالمنطق الوجداني في القرآن. وبسائر ما يطلبه أصحاب الدراسة والمتاع. ولكننا سنلتقي بهذا كله دون أن يكون

هو هدفنا الأول. إن هدفنا الأول أن نعرف: ماذا يريد منا القرآن أن نعمل؟ ما هو التصور الكلي الذي يريد منا أن نتصور؟ كيف يريد القرآن أن يكون شعورنا بالله؟ كيف يريد أن تكون أخلاقنا وأوضاعنا ونظامنا الواقعي في الحياة؟

ثم لا بد لنا من التخلص من ضغط المجتمع الجاهلي والتصورات الجاهلية والتقاليد الجاهلية والقيادة الجاهلية. في خاصة نفوسنا. ليست مهمتنا أن نصطلح مع واقع هذا المجتمع الجاهلي ولا أن ندين بالولاء له، فهو بهذه الصفة. صفة الجاهلية. غير قابل لأن نصطلح معه. إن مهمتنا أن نغير من أنفسنا أولا لنغير هذا المجتمع أخيرا.

إن مهمتنا الأولى هي تغيير واقع هذا المجتمع. مهمتنا هي تغيير هذا الواقع الجاهلي من أساسه. هذا الواقع الذي يصطدم اصطداما أساسيا بالمنهج الإسلامي، وبالتصور الإسلامي، والذي يحرمنا بالقهر والضغط أن نعيش كما يريد لنا المنهج الإلهي أن نعيش.

إن أولى الخطوات في طريقنا هي أن نستعلي على هذا المجتمع الجاهلي وقيمه وتصوراته، وألا نعدل نحن في قيمنا وتصوراتنا قليلا أو كثيرا لنلتقي معه في منتصف الطريق. كلا. إننا وإياه على مفرق الطريق، وحين نسايره خطوة واحدة فإننا نفقد المنهج كله ونفقد الطريق.

وسنلقى في هذا عنتا ومشقة، وستفرض علينا تضحيات باهظة، ولكننا لسنا مخيرين إذا نحن شئنا أن نسلك طريق الجيل الأول الذي أقر الله به منهجه الإلهي، ونصره على منهج الجاهلية.

وإنه لمن الخير أن ندرك دائما طبيعة منهجنا، وطبيعة موقفنا، وطبيعة الطريق الذي لا بد أن نسلكه للخروج من الجاهلية كما خرج ذلك الجيل المميز الفريد.

طبيعة المنهج القرآني

ظل القرآن المكي ينزل على رسول الله - صلى الله عليه وسلم - ثلاثة عشر عاما كاملة، يحدثه فيها عن قضية واحدة. قضية واحدة لا تتغير، ولكن طريقة عرضها لا تكاد تتكرر. ذلك الأسلوب القرآني يدعها في كل عرض جديدة، حتى لكأنما يطرقها للمرة الأولى.

لقد كان يعالج القضية الأولى، والقضية الكبرى، والقضية الأساسية، في هذا الدين الجديد. قضية العقيدة. ممثلة في قاعدتها الرئيسية. الألوهية والعبودية، وما بينهما من علاقة.

لقد كان يخاطب بهذه الحقيقة "الإنسان". الإنسان بما أنه إنسان. وفي هذا المجال يستوي الإنسان العربي في ذلك الزمان والإنسان العربي في كل زمان، كما يستوي الإنسان العربي وكل إنسان، في ذلك الزمان وفي كل زمان.

إنها قضية "الإنسان" التي لا تتغير، لأنها قضية وجوده في هذا الكون وقضية مصيره. قضية علاقته بهذا الكون وبهؤلاء الأحياء، وقضية علاقته بخالق هذا الكون وخالق هذه الأحياء. وهي قضية لا تتغير، لأنها قضية الوجود والإنسان.

لقد كان هذا القرآن المكي يفسر للإنسان سر وجوده ووجود هذا الكون من حوله. كان يقول له: من هو؟ ومن أين جاء؟ ولماذا جاء؟ وإلى أين يذهب في نهاية المطاف؟ من ذا الذي جاء به من العدم والمجهول؟ ومن ذا الذي يذهب به، وما مصيره هناك؟ وكان يقول له: ما هذا الوجود الذي يحسه ويراه، والذي يحس أن وراءه غيبا يستشرفه ولا يراه؟ من أنشأ هذا الوجود المليء بالأسرار؟ من ذا يدبره؟ ومن ذا يحوره؟ ومن ذا يجدد فيه ويغير على النحو الذي يراه؟. وكان يقول له كذلك: كيف يتعامل مع خالق هذا الكون، ومع الكون أيضا، كما يبين له: كيف يتعامل العباد مع العباد؟

وكانت هذه هي القضية الكبرى التي يقوم عليها وجود "الإنسان ". وستظل هي القضية الكبرى التي يقوم عليها وجوده على توالي الأزمان.

وهكذا انقضت ثلاثة عشر عاما كاملة في تقرير هذه القضية الكبرى، القضية التي ليس وراءها شيء في حياة الإنسان إلا ما يقوم عليها من المقتضيات والتفريعات.

ولم يتجاوز القرآن المكي هذه القضية الأساسية إلى شيء مما يقوم عليها من التفريعات المتعلقة بنظام الحياة، إلا بعد أن علم الله أنها قد استوفت ما تستحقه من البيان، وأنها استقرت استقرارا مكينا ثابتا في قلوب العصبة المختارة من بني الإنسان، التي قدر الله أن يقوم هذا الدين عليها، وأن تتولى هي إنشاء النظام الواقعي الذي يتمثل فيه هذا الدين.

وأصحاب الدعوة إلى دين الله، وإلى إقامة النظام الذي يتمثل فيه هذا الدين في واقع الحياة، خليقون أن يقفوا طويلا أمام هذه الظاهرة الكبيرة، ظاهرة تصدي القرآن المكي خلال ثلاثة عشر عاما لتقرير هذه العقيدة، ثم وقوفه عندها لا يتجاوزها إلى شيء من تفصيلات النظام الذي يقوم عليها، والتشريعات التي تحكم المجتمع المسلم الذي يعتنقها.

لقد شاءت حكمة الله أن تكون قضية العقيدة هي القضية التي تتصدى لها الدعوة منذ اليوم الأول للرسالة، وأن يبدأ رسول الله - صلى الله عليه وسلم - أولى خطواته في الدعوة بدعوة الناس أن يشهدوا: أن اله إلا الله، وأن يمضي في دعوته يعرف الناس بربهم الحق، ويُعبدهم له دون سواه.

ولم تكن هذه - في ظاهر الأمر وفي نظرة العقل البشري المحجوب - هي أيسر السبل إلى قلوب العرب. فلقد كانوا يعرفون من لغتهم معنى "إله" ومعنى: "لا إله إلا الله ". كانوا يعرفون أن الألوهية تعني الحاكمية العليا. وكانوا يعرفون أن توحيد الألوهية وإفراد الله - سبحانه - بها، معناه نزع السلطان الذي يزاوله الكهان ومشيخة القبائل والأمراء والحكام، ورده كله إلى الله. السلطان على الضمائر، والسلطان على الشعائر، والسلطان على واقعيات الحياة، والسلطان في المال، والسلطان في القضاء، والسلطان في الأرواح والأبدان. كانوا يعلمون أن "لا إله إلا الله "ثورة على السلطان الأرضي الذي يغتصب أولى خصائص الألوهية، وثورة على الأوضاع التي تقوم على قاعدة من هذا الاغتصاب، وخروج على السلطات التي تحكم بشريعة من عندها لم يأذن بها الله. ولم يكن يغيب عن العرب - وهم يعرفون لغتهم جيدا ويعرفون المدلول الحقيقي لدعوة - "لا اله إلا الله "- ماذا تعني هذه الدعوة بالنسبة لأوضاعهم ورئاساتهم وسلطانهم، ومن ثم استقبلوا هذه الدعوة - أو هذه الثورة - ذلك الاستقبال العنيف، وحاربوها هذه الحرب التي يعرفها الخاص والعام.

فلِم كانت هذه نقطة البدء في هذه الدعوة؟ ولِم اقتضت حكمة الله أن تبدأ بكل هذا العناء؟

لقد بُعث رسول الله - صلى الله عليه وسلم - بهذا الدين، وأخصب بلاد العرب وأغناها ليست في أيدي العرب، إنما هي في أيدي غيرهم من الأجناس.

بلاد الشام كلها في الشمال خاضعة للروم، يحكمها أمراء عرب من قِبل الروم، وبلاد اليمن كلها في الجنوب خاضعة للفرس، يحكمها أمراء عرب من قبل الفرس، وليست في أيدي العرب إلا الحجاز وتهامة ونجد، وما إليها من الصحاري القاحلة التي تتناثر فيها الواحات الخصبة هنا وهناك.

وربما قيل: أنه كان في استطاعة محمد - صلى الله عليه وسلم - وهو الصادق الأمين الذي حكمه أشراف قريش قبل ذلك في وضع الحجر الأسود، وارتضوا حكمه، منذ خمسة عشر عاما قبل الرسالة، والذي هو في الذؤابة من بني هاشم أعلى قريش نسبا. إنه كان في استطاعته أن يثيرها قومية عربية تستهدف تجميع قبائل العرب التي أكلتها الثارات ومزقتها النزاعات، وتوجيهها وجهة قومية لاستخلاص أرضها المغتصبة من الإمبراطوريات

المستعمرة. الرومان في الشمال والفرس في الجنوب. وإعلاء راية العربية والعروبة، وإنشاء وحدة قومية في كل أرجاء الجزيرة.

وربما قيل: أنه لو دعا رسول الله - صلى الله عليه وسلم - هذه الدعوة لاستجابت له العرب قاطبة، بدلا من أن يعاني ثلاثة عشر عاما في اتجاه معارض لأهواء أصحاب السلطان في الجزيرة.

وربما قيل: أن محمدا - صلى الله عليه وسلم - كان خليقا - بعد أن يستجيب له العرب هذه الاستجابة، وبعد أن يولوه فيهم القيادة والسيادة، وبعد استجماع السلطان في يديه، والمجد فوق مفرقيه - أن يستخدم هذا كله في إقرار عقيدة التوحيد التي بعث بها، في تعبيد الناس لسلطان ربهم بعد أن عبدهم لسلطانه البشرى.

ولكن الله - سبحانه - وهو العليم الحكيم، لم يوجه رسوله - صلى الله عليه وسلم - هذا التوجيه. إنما وجهه إلى أن يصدع بـ "لا إله إلا الله "، وأن يحتمل هو والقلة التي تستجيب له كل هذا العناء.

لماذا؟ إن الله - سبحانه - لا يريد أن يُعنت رسوله والمؤمنين معه. إنما هو - سبحانه - يعلم أن ليس هذا هو الطريق، ليس الطريق أن تخلص الأرض من يد طاغوت روماني أو طاغوت فارسي، إلى يد طاغوت عربي. فالطاغوت كله طاغوت. إن الأرض لله، ويجب أن تخلص لله. ولا تخلص لله إلا أن ترتفع عليها راية: "لا إله إلا الله ". وليس الطريق أن يتحرر الناس في هذه الأرض من طاغوت روماني أو فارسي، إلى طاغوت عربي. فالطاغوت كله طاغوت. أن الناس عبيد لله وحده، ولا يكونون عبيداً لله وحده إلا أن ترتفع راية: "لا إله إلا الله "- لا إله إلا الله كما يدركها العربي العارف بمدلولات لغته،: لا حاكمية إلا الله، ولا شريعة إلا من الله، ولا سلطان لأحد على أحد، لأن السلطان كله لله، ولأن "الجنسية "التي يريدها الإسلام للناس هي جنسية العقيدة، التي يتساوى فيها العربي والروماني والفارسي وسائر الأجناس والألوان تحت راية الله.

وهذا هو الطريق

وبعث رسول الله - صلى الله عليه وسلم - بهذا الدين، والمجتمع العربي كأسوأ ما يكون المجتمع توزيعا للثروة والعدالة. قلة قليلة تملك المال والتجارة، وتتعامل بالربا فتتضاعف تجارتها ومالها. وكثرة كثيرة لا تملك إلا الشظف والجوع. والذين يملكون الثروة يملكون معها الشرف والمكانة، وجماهير كثيرة ضائعة من المال والمجد جميعا.

وربما قيل: أنه كان في استطاعة محمد--صلى الله عليه وسلم--أن يرفعها راية اجتماعية، وأن يثيرها حربا على طبقة الأشراف، وأن يطلقها دعوة تستهدف تعديل الأوضاع، ورد أموال الأغنياء على الفقراء.

وربما قيل: أنه لو دعا يومها رسول الله - صلى الله عليه وسلم - هذه الدعوة، لانقسم المجتمع العربي صفين: الكثرة الغالبة مع الدعوة الجديدة في وجه طغيان المال والشرف

والجاه، والقلة القليلة مع هذه الموروثات، بدلا من أن يقف المجتمع كله صفا في وجه "لا اله إلا الله "التي لم يرتفع إلى أفقها في ذلك الحين إلا الأفذاذ من الناس.

وربما قيل: أن محمدا - صلى الله عليه وسلم - كان خليقا بعد أن تستجيب له الكثرة، وتوليه قيادها، ويغلب بها القلة ويسلس له مقادها، أن يستخدم مكانه يومئذ وسلطانه في إقرار عقيدة التوحيد التي بعثه بها ربه، وفي تعبيد الناس لسلطان ربهم بعد أن عبدهم لسلطانه البشرى.

ولكن الله - سبحانه - وهو العليم الحكيم، لم يوجهه هذا التوجيه.

لقد كان الله - سبحانه - يعلم أن هذا ليس هو الطريق. كان يعلم أن العدالة الاجتماعية لا بد أن تنبثق في المجتمع من تصور اعتقادي شامل، يرد الأمر كله لله، ويقبل عن رضى وعن طواعية ما يقضي به الله من عدالة التوزيع، ومن تكافل الجميع، ويستقر معه في قلب الآخذ والمأخوذ منه سواء أنه ينفذ نظاما شرعه الله، ويرجو على الطاعة فيه الخير والحسنى في الدنيا والآخرة سواء. فلا تمتلئ قلوب بالطمع، ولا تمتلئ قلوب بالحقد، ولا تسير الأمور كلها بالسيف والعصا، وبالتخويف والإرهاب. ولا تفسد القلوب كلها وتختنق الأرواح، كما يقع في الأوضاع التي تقوم على غير "لا اله إلا الله ".

وبُعث رسول الله - صلى الله عليه وسلم - والمستوى الأخلاقي في الجزيرة العربية في الدرك الأسفل في جوانب منه شتى - إلى جانب ما كان في المجتمع من فضائل الخامة البدوية.

كان التظالم فاشيا في المجتمع، تعبر عنه حكمة الشاعر "زهير بن أبي سلمى ":

و من لم يذد عن حوضه بسلاحه   يهدم، ومن لا يظلم الناس يُظلمِ

ويعبر عنه القول المتعارف في الجاهلية: "انصر أخاك ظالما أو مظلوما ".

وكانت الخمر والميسر من تقاليد المجتمع الفاشية، ومن مفاخره كذلك. يعبر عن هذه الخصلة الشعر الجاهلي بجملته. كالذي يقوله طرفة بن العبد:

فلولا ثلاث هن من عيشة الفتى   وجدك لم أحفل متى قام عودي

فمنهن سبق العاذلات بشربة   كميت متى ما تعل بالماء تزبد

وما زال تشرابي الخمور ولذتي   وبذلي وإنفاقي طريفي وتالدي

إلى أن تحامتني العشيرة كلها   وأفردت إفراد البعير المعبد

وكانت الدعارة - في صور شتى - من معالم هذا المجتمع - شأنه شأن كل مجتمع جاهلي قديم أو حديث - كالتي روته عائشة رضي الله عنها:

"إن النكاح في الجاهلية كان على أربعة أنحاء: فنكاح منها نكاح الناس اليوم. يخطب الرجل إلى الرجل وليته أو بنته، فيصدقها ثم ينكحها. والنكاح الآخر كان الرجل يقول لامرأته - إذا طهرت من طمثها -: ارسلي إلى فلان فاستبضعي منه، ويعتزلها زوجها ولا يمسها أبدا حتى يتبين حملها من ذلك الرجل الذي تستبضع منه، فإذا تبين حملها أصابها الرجل إذا أحب، وإنما يفعل ذلك رغبة في نجابة الولد. فكان هذا النكاح نكاح الاستبضاع. ونكاح آخر: يجتمع الرهط ما دون العشرة فيدخلون على المرأة، كلهم يصيبها. فإذا حملت ووضعت، ومر عليها ليال بعد أن تضع حملها، أرسلت إليهم فلم يستطع رجل منهم أن يمتنع، حتى يجتمعوا عندها، تقول لهم: قد عرفتم الذي كان من أمركم، وقد ولدت، فهو ابنك يا فلان، تسمي من أحبت باسمه فيلحق به ولدها، ولا يستطيع أن يمتنع به الرجل. والنكاح الرابع: يجتمع الناس الكثير، فيدخلون على المرأة لا تمتنع من جاءها. وهن البغايا. كن ينصبن على أبوابهن رايات تكون علما، فمن أرادهن دخل عليهن، فإذا حملت إحداهن ووضعت حملها، جمعوا لها ودعوا لهم القافة، ثم ألحقوا ولدها بالذي يرون، فالتاطه، ودعى ابنه لا يمتنع عن ذلك"(4).

وربما قيل: أنه كان في استطاعة محمد - صلى الله عليه وسلم - أن يعلنها دعوة إصلاحية، تتناول تقويم الأخلاق، وتطهير المجتمع، وتزكية النفوس.

وربما قيل: أنه - صلى الله عليه وسلم - كان واجدا وقتها - كما يجد كل مصلح أخلاقي في أية بيئة - نفوسا طيبة يؤذيها هذا الدنس.

وتأخذها الأريحية والنخوة لتلبية دعوة الإصلاح والتطهر.

وربما قال قائل: أنه لو صنع رسول الله - صلى الله عليه وسلم - ذلك لاستجابت له - في أول الأمر - جمهرة صالحة، تتطهر أخلاقها، وتزكوا أرواحها، فتصبح أقرب إلى قبول العقيدة وحملها، بدلا من أن تثير دعوة "لا إله إلا الله" المعارضة القوية منذ أول الطريق.

ولكن الله - سبحانه - كان يعلم أن ليس هذا هو الطريق. كان يعلم أن الأخلاق لا تقوم إلا على أساس من عقيدة، تضع الموازين، وتقرر القيم، كما تقرر السلطة التي تستند إليها هذه الموازين والقيم، والجزاء الذي تملكه هذه السلطة، وتوقعه على الملتزمين والمخالفين. وإنه قبل تقرير هذه العقيدة، وتحديد هذه السلطة تظل القيم كلها متأرجحة وتظل الأخلاق التي تقوم عليها متأرجحة كذلك، بلا ضابط، وبلا سلطان، وبلا جزاء.

فلما تقررت العقيدة - بعد الجهد الشاق - وتقررت السلطة التي ترتكن إليها هذه العقيدة. لما عرف الناس ربهم وعبدوه وحده. لما تحرر الناس من سلطان العبيد ومن سلطان الشهوات سواء. لما تقررت في القلوب "لا إله إلا الله". صنع الله بها وبأهلها كل شيء مما يقترحه المقترحون. تطهرت الأرض من "الرومان والفرس". لا ليتقرر فيها سلطان

---

(4) أخرجه البخاري في كتاب النكاح.

"العرب". ولكن ليتقرر فيها سلطان "الله". لقد تطهرت من سلطان "الطاغوت" كله. رومانيا، وفارسيا، وعربيا، على السواء.

وتطهر المجتمع من الظلم الاجتماعي بجملته. وقام "النظام الإسلامي"، يعدل بعدل الله، ويزن بميزان الله، ويرفع راية العدالة الاجتماعية باسم الله وحده، ويسميها راية "الإسلام". لا يقرن إليها اسما آخر، ويكتب عليها: "لا اله إلا الله".

وتطهرت النفوس والأخلاق، وزكت القلوب والأرواح، دون أن يحتاج الأمر حتى للحدود والتعازير التي شرعها الله - إلا في الندرة النادرة - لأن الرقابة قامت هناك في الضمائر، ولأن الطمع في رضى الله وثوابه، والحياء والخوف من غضبه وعقابه، قد قاما مقام الرقابة ومكان العقوبات.

وارتفعت البشرية في نظامها، وفي أخلاقها، وفي حياتها كلها، إلى القمة السامقة التي لم ترتفع إليها من قبل قط، والتي لم ترتفع إليها من بعد إلا في ظل الإسلام.

ولقد تم هذا كله لأن الذين أقاموا هذا الدين في صورة دولة ونظام وشرائع وأحكام، كانوا قد أقاموا هذا الدين من قبل في ضمائرهم وفي حياتهم، في صورة عقيدة وخلق وعبادة وسلوك. وكانوا قد وعـ۪دوا على إقامة هذا الدين وعدا واحدا، لا يدخل فيه الغلب والسلطان. ولا حتى لهذا الدين على أيديهم. وعدا واحدا لا يتعلق بشيء في هذه الدنيا. وعدا واحدا هو الجنة. هذا كل وعدوه على الجهاد المضني، والابتلاء الشاق، والمضي في الدعوة، ومواجهة الجاهلية بالأمر الذي يكرهه أصحاب السلطان في كل زمان وفي كل مكان، وهو: "لا إله إلا الله".

فلما أن ابتلاهم الله فصبروا، ولما أن فرغت نفوسهم من حظ نفوسهم، ولما علم الله منهم أنهم لا ينتظرون جزاء في هذه الأرض - كائنا ما كان هذا الجزاء، ولو كان هو انتصار هذه الدعوة على أيديهم، وقيام هذا الدين في الأرض بجهدهم - ولما لم يعد في نفوسهم اعتزاز بجد ولا قوم، ولا اعتزاز بوطن ولا أرض، ولا اعتزاز بعشيرة ولا بيت. لما أن علم الله منهم ذلك كله، علم أنهم قد أصبحوا - إذن - أمناء على هذه الأمانة الكبرى. أمناء على العقيدة، التي يتفرد فيها الله - سبحانه - بالحاكمية في القلوب والضمائر، وفي السلوك والشعائر، وفي الأرواح والأموال، وفي الأوضاع والأحوال. وأمناء على السلطان الذي يوضع في أيديهم ليقوموا به على شريعة الله ينفذونها، وعلى عدل الله يقيمونه، دون أن يكون لهم من ذلك السلطان شيء لأنفسهم، ولا لعشيرتهم، ولا لقومهم، ولا لجنسهم. إنما يكون السلطان الذي في أيديهم لله، ولدينه وشريعته، لأنهم يعلمون أنه من الله، هو الذي آتاهم إياه.

ولم يكن شيء من هذا المنهج المبارك ليتحقق على هذا المستوى الرفيع، إلا أن تبدأ الدعوة ذلك البدء. وإلا أن ترفع الدعوة هذه الراية وحدها. راية لا إله إلا الله. ولا ترفع معها سواها. وإلا أن تسلك الدعوة هذا الطريق الوعر الشاق في ظاهره، المبارك الميسر في حقيقته.

وما كان هذا المنهج المبارك ليخلص لله، لو أن الدعوة بدأت خطواتها الأولى دعوة قومية، أو دعوة اجتماعية، أو دعوة أخلاقية. أو رفعت أي شعار إلى جانب شعارها الواحد: "لا اله إلا الله ".

ذلك شأن القرآن المكي كله في تقرير: "لا إله إلا الله "في القلوب والعقول، واختيار هذا الطريق - على مشقته في الظاهر - وعدم اختيار السبل الجانبية الأخرى، والإصرار على هذا الطريق.

فأما شأن هذا القرآن في تناول قضية الاعتقاد وحدها، دون التطرق الى تفصيلات النظام الذي يقوم عليها، والشرائع التي تنظم المعاملات فيها، فذلك كذلك مما ينبغي أن يقف أمامه أصحاب الدعوة لهذا الدين وقفة واعية.

إن طبيعة هذا الدين هي التي قضت بهذا. فهو دين كله يقوم على قاعدة الألوهية الواحدة. كل تنظيماته وكل تشريعاته تنبثق من هذا الأصل الكبير. وكما أن الشجرة الضخمة الباسقة، الوارفة المديدة الظلال، المتشابكة الأغصان، الضاربة في الهواء. لا بد لها أن تضرب بجذورها في التربة على أعماق بعيدة، وفي مساحات واسعة، تناسب ضخامتها وامتدادها في الهواء. فكذلك هذا الدين. إن نظامه يتناول الحياة كلها، ويتولى شؤون البشرية كبيرها وصغيرها، وينظم حياة الإنسان - لا في الحياة الدنيا وحدها ولكن كذلك في الدار الآخرة، ولا في عالم الشهادة وحده ولكن كذلك في عالم الغيب المكنون عنها، ولا في المعاملات المادية الظاهرة وحدها ولكن كذلك في أعماق الضمير ودنيا السرائر والنوايا - فهو مؤسسة ضخمة هائلة شاسعة مترامية، ولا بد له إذن من جذور وأعماق بهذه السعة والضخامة والعمق والانتشار أيضا.

هذا جانب من سر هذا الدين وطبيعته، يحدد منهجه في بناء نفسه وفي امتداده، ويجعل بناء العقيدة وتمكينها، وشمول هذه العقيدة واستغراقها لشعاب النفس كلها. ضرورة من ضروريات النشأة الصحيحة، وضمانا من ضمانات الاحتمال، والتناسق بين الظاهر من الشجرة في الهواء والضارب من جذورها في الأعماق.

ومتى استقرت عقيدة: "لا إله إلا الله "في أعماقها الغائرة البعيدة، استقر معها في نفس الوقت النظام الذي تتمثل فيه "لا إله إلا الله "، وتعين أنه النظام الوحيد الذي ترتضيه النفوس التي استقرت فيها العقيدة، واستسلمت هذه النفوس ابتداء لهذا النظام، حتى قبل أن تعرض عليها تفصيلاته، وقبل أن تعرض عليها تشريعاته. فالاستسلام ابتداء هو مقتضى الإيمان. وبمثل هذا الاستسلام تلقت النفوس - فيما بعد - تنظيمات الإسلام وتشريعاته بالرضى والقبول، لا تعترض على شيء منه فور صدوره إليها، ولا تتلكأ في تنفيذه بمجرد تلقيها له. وهكذا أبطلت الخمر، وأبطل الربا، وأبطل الميسر، وأبطلت العادات الجاهلية كلها. أبطلت بآيات من القرآن، أو كلمات من الرسول - صلى الله عليه وسلم - بينما الحكومات الأرضية تجهد في شيء من هذا كله بقوانينها وتشريعاتها، ونظمها وأوضاعها، وجندها

17

وسلطاتها، ودعايتها وإعلامها، فلا تبلغ إلا أن تضبط الظاهر من المخالفات، بينما المجتمع يعج بالمنهيات والمنكرات (5).

وجانب آخر من طبيعة هذا الدين يتجلى في هذا المنهج القويم. إن هذا الدين منهج عملي حركي جاد. جاء ليحكم الحياة في واقعها، ويواجه هذا الواقع ليقضى فيه بأمره. يقره، أو يعدله، أو يغيره من أساسه. ومن ثم فهو لا يشرع إلا لحالات واقعة فعلا، في مجتمع يعترف ابتداء بحاكمية الله وحده.

إنه ليس "نظرية" تتعامل مع "الفروض".. إنه "منهج"، يتعامل مع "الواقع".. فلا بد أولا أن يقوم المجتمع المسلم الذي يقر عقيدة: أن لا إله إلا الله، وأن الحاكمية ليست إلا لله ويرفض أن يقر بالحاكمية لأحد من دون الله، ويرفض شرعية أي وضع لا يقوم على هذه القاعدة.

وحين يقوم هذا المجتمع فعلا، تكون له حياة واقعية، تحتاج إلى تنظيم والى تشريع. وعندئذ فقط يبدأ هذا الدين في تقرير النظم وفي سن الشرائع لقوم مستسلمين أصلا للنظم والشرائع، رافضين أصلا لغيرها من النظم والشرائع.

ولا بد أن يكون للمؤمنين بهذه العقيدة من سلطان على أنفسهم وعلى مجتمعهم ما يكفل تنفيذ النظام والشرائع في هذا المجتمع حتى يكون للنظام هيبته، ويكون للشريعة جديتها. فوق ما يكون لحياة هذا المجتمع من واقعية تقتضي الأنظمة والشرائع من فورها.

والمسلمون في مكة لم يكن لهم سلطان على أنفسهم ولا على مجتمعهم. وما كانت لهم حياة واقعية مستقلة هم الذين ينظمونها بشريعة الله. ومن ثم لم ينزل الله لهم في هذه الفترة تنظيمات وشرائع، وإنما نزل لهم عقيدة، وخلقا منبثقا من هذه العقيدة بعد استقرارها في الأعماق البعيدة. فلما أن صارت لهم دولة في المدينة ذات سلطان، تنزلت عليهم الشرائع، وتقرر لهم النظام الذي يواجه حاجات المجتمع المسلم الواقعية، والذي تكفل له الدولة بسلطاتها الجدية النفاذ.

ولم يشأ الله أن ينزل عليهم النظام والشرائع في مكة، ليختزنوها جاهزة حتى تطبق بمجرد قيام الدولة في المدينة. إن هذه ليست طبيعة هذا الدين.. إنه أشد واقعية من هذا وأكثر جدية.. إنه لا يفترض المشكلات ليفترض لها حلولا. إنما يواجه الواقع حين يكون واقع مجتمع مسلم مستسلم لشريعة الله رافض لشريعة سواه بحجمه وشكله وملابساته وظروفه، ليشرع له، وفق حجمه وشكله وملابساته وظروفه.

والذين يريدون من الإسلام اليوم أن يصوغ نظريات وأن يصوغ قوالب نظام، وأن يصوغ تشريعات للحياة. بينما ليس على وجه الأرض مجتمع قد قرر فعلا تحكيم شريعة الله

---

(5) يراجع كيف حرم الله الخمر في الجزء الخامس من: " في ظلال القرآن " في الطبعة المشروعة التي تصدر عن دار الشروق. وكيف عجزت أميركا عن ذلك في كتاب: " ماذا خسر العالم بانحطاط المسلمين " للسيد أبي الحسن الندوي منقولا عن كتاب (تنقيحات) للسيد أبي الأعلى المودودي.

وحدها، ورفض كل شريعة سواها، مع تملكه للسلطة التي تفرض هذا وتنفذه. الذين يريدون من الإسلام هذا، لا يدركون طبيعة هذا الدين، ولا كيف يعمل في الحياة. كما يريد له الله.

إنهم يريدون منه أن يغير طبيعته ومنهجه وتاريخه ليشابه نظريات بشرية، ومناهج بشرية، ويحاولون أن يستعجلوه عن طريقه وخطواته ليلبي رغبات وقتية في نفوسهم، رغبات إنما تنشئها الهزيمة الداخلية في أرواحهم تجاه أنظمة بشرية صغيرة. يريدون منه أن يصوغ نفسه في قالب نظريات وفروض، تواجه مستقبلا غير موجود. والله يريد لهذا الدين أن يكون كما أراده. عقيدة تملأ القلب، وتفرض سلطانها على الضمير، عقيدة مقتضاها ألا يخضع الناس إلا لله، وألا يتلقوا الشرائع إلا منه دون سواه. وبعد أن يوجد الناس الذين هذه عقيدتهم، ويصبح لهم السلطان الفعلي في مجتمعهم، تبدأ التشريعات لمواجهة حاجاتهم الواقعية، وتنظيم حياتهم الواقعية كذلك.

هذا ما يريده الله لهذا الدين. ولن يكون إلا ما يريده الله، مهما كانت رغبات الناس.

كذلك ينبغي أن يكون مفهوما لأصحاب الدعوة الإسلامية أنهم حين يدعون الناس لإعادة إنشاء هذا الدين، يجب أن يدعوهم أولا إلى اعتناق العقيدة - حتى لو كانوا يدعون أنفسهم مسلمين، وتشهد لهم شهادات الميلاد بأنهم مسلمون. - يجب أن يعلموهم أن الإسلام هو "أولا" إقرار عقيدة: "لا إله إلا الله " بمدلولها الحقيقي، وهو رد الحاكمية لله في أمرهم كله، وطرد المعتدين على سلطان الله بادعاء هذا الحق لأنفسهم، إقرارها في ضمائرهم وشعائرهم، وإقرارها في أوضاعهم وواقعهم.

ولتكن هذه القضية هي أساس دعوة الناس إلى الإسلام، كانت هي أساس دعوتهم إلى الإسلام أول مرة. هذه الدعوة التي تكفل بها القرآن المكي طوال ثلاثة عشر عاما كاملة. فإذا دخل في هذا الدين - بمفهومه هذا الأصيل - عصبة من الناس. فهذه العصبة هي التي يطلق عليها إسم "المجتمع المسلم ". المجتمع الذي يصلح لمزاولة النظام الإسلامي في حياته الاجتماعية، لأنه قرر بينه وبين نفسه أن تقوم حياته كلها على هذا الأساس، وألا يحكم في حياته كلها إلا الله.

وحين يقوم هذا المجتمع بالفعل يبدأ عرض أسس النظام الإسلامي عليه، كما يأخذ هذا المجتمع نفسه في سن التشريعات التي تقتضيها حياته الواقعية، في إطار الأسس العامة للنظام الإسلامي. فهذا هو الترتيب الصحيح لخطوات المنهج الإسلامي. فهذا هو الترتيب الصحيح لخطوات المنهج الإسلامي الواقعي العملي الجاد.

ولقد يخيل لبعض المخلصين المتعجلين، ممن لا يتدبرون طبيعة هذا الدين، وطبيعة منهجه الرباني القويم، المؤسس على حكمة العليم الحكيم وعلمه بطبائع البشر وحاجات الحياة. نقول: لقد يخيل لبعض هؤلاء أن عرض أسس النظام الإسلامي - بل التشريعات الإسلامية كذلك - على الناس، مما ييسر لهم طريق الدعوة، ويحبب الناس في هذا الدين.

وهذا وهْمٌ تنشئه العجلة. وهْمٌ كالذي كان يقترحه المقترحون: أن تقوم دعوة رسول الله صلى الله عليه وسلم في أولها تحت راية قومية، أو راية اجتماعية، أو راية أخلاقية، تيسيرا للطريق.

إن القلوب يجب أن تخلص أولا لله، وتعلن عبوديتها له وحده، بقبول شرعه وحده، ورفض كل شرع آخر غيره. من ناحية المبدأ. قبل أن تخاطب بأي تفصيل عن ذلك الشرع يرغبها فيه.

إن الرغبة يجب أن تنبثق من إخلاص العبودية لله، والتحرر من سلطان سواه، لا من أن النظام المعروض عليها. في ذاته. خير مما لديها من الأنظمة في كذا وكذا على وجه التفصيل.

إن نظام الله خير في ذاته، لأنه من شرع الله. ولن يكون شرع العبيد يوما كشرع الله. ولكن هذه ليست قاعدة الدعوة. إن قاعدة الدعوة أن قبول شرع الله وحده أيا كان، ورفض كل شرع غيره أيا كان، هو ذاته الإسلام، وليس للإسلام مدلول سواه، فمن رغب في الإسلام ابتداء فقد فصل في القضية، ولم يعد بحاجة إلى ترغيبه بجمال النظام وأفضليته. فهذه إحدى بديهيات الإيمان.

وبعد، فلا بد أن نقول كيف عالج القرآن المكي قضية العقيدة في خلال الثلاثة عشر عاما. إنه لم يعرضها في صورة "نظرية "ولا في صورة "لاهوت ". ولم يعرضها في صورة جدل كلامي كالذي زاوله ما يسمى "علم التوحيد ".

كلا. لقد كان القرآن الكريم يخاطب فطرة "الإنسان "بما في وجوده هو وبما في الوجود حوله من دلائل وإيحاءات. كان يستنقذ فطرته من الركام، ويخلص أجهزة الاستقبال الفطرية مما ران عليها وعطل وظائفها، ويفتح منافذ الفطرة، لتتلقى الموحيات المؤثرة وتستجيب لها.

هذا بصفة عامة 00 وبصفة خاصة كان القرآن يخوض بهذه العقيدة معركة حية واقعية. كان يخوض بها معركة مع الركام المعطل للفطرة في نفوس آدمية حاضرة واقعة. ومن ثم لم يكن شكل "النظرية "هو الشكل الذي يناسب هذا الواقع الخاص. إنما هو شكل المواجهة الحية للعقابيل والسدود والحواجز والمعوقات النفسية والواقعية في النفوس الحاضرة الحية. ولم يكن الجدل الذهني - القائم على المنطق الشكلي - الذي سار عليه في العصور المتأخرة علم التوحيد، هو الشكل المناسب كذلك. فلقد كان القرآن يواجه "واقعا "بشريا كاملا بكل ملابساته الحية، ويخاطب الكينونة البشرية بجملتها في خضم هذا الواقع. وكذلك لم يكن "اللاهوت "هو الشكل المناسب. فإن العقيدة الإسلامية، ولو أنها عقيدة، إلا أنها تمثل منهج حياة واقعية للتطبيق العملي، ولا تقبع في الزاوية الضيقة التي تقبع فيها الأبحاث اللاهوتية النظرية.

كان القرآن، وهو يبني العقيدة في ضمائر الجماعة المسلمة، يخوض بهذه الجماعة المسلمة معركة ضخمة مع الجاهلية من حولها، كما يخوض بها معركة ضخمة مع رواسب الجاهلية في ضميرها هي وأخلاقها وواقعها. ومن هذه الملابسات ظهر بناء العقيدة لا في صورة "نظرية "ولا في صورة "لاهوت "، ولا في صورة "جدل كلامي ". ولكن في صورة تجمع عضوي حيوي وتكوين تنظيمي مباشر للحياة، ممثل في الجماعة المسلمة ذاتها، وكان نمو الجماعة المسلمة في تصوراتها الاعتقادي، وفي سلوكها الواقعي وفق هذا التصور، وفي دربتها على مواجهة الجاهلية كمنظمة محاربة لها. كان هذا النمو ذاته ممثلا تماما لنمو البناء العقيدي، وترجمة حية له. وهذا هو منهج الإسلام الذي يمثل طبيعته كذلك.

وإنه لمن الضروري لأصحاب الدعوة الإسلامية أن يدركوا طبيعة هذا الدين ومنهجه في الحركة على هذا النحو الذي يبني بناءه. ذلك ليعلموا أن مرحلة بناء العقيدة التي طالت في العهد المكي على هذا النحو، لم تكن منعزلة عن مرحلة التكوين العملي للحركة الإسلامية، والبناء الواقعي للجماعة المسلمة. لم تكن مرحلة تلقي "النظرية "ودراستها. ولكنها كانت مرحلة البناء القاعدي للعقيدة وللجماعة وللحركة وللوجود الفعلي معا. وهكذا ينبغي أن تكون كلما أريد إعادة هذا البناء مرة أخرى.

هكذا ينبغي أن تطول مرحلة بناء العقيدة، وأن تتم خطوات البناء على مهل، وفي عمق وتثبت. ثم هكذا ينبغي ألا تكون مرحلة دراسة نظرية للعقيدة، ولكن مرحلة ترجمة لهذه العقيدة - أولا بأول - في صورة حية، متمثلة في ضمائر متكيفة بهذه العقيدة ومتمثلة في بناء جماعي وتجمع حركي، يعبر نموه من داخله ومن خارجه عن نمو العقيدة ذاتها، ومتمثلة في حركة واقعية تواجه الجاهلية، وتخوض معها المعركة في الضمير وفي الواقع كذلك، لتتمثل العقيدة حية، وتنمو نموا حيا في خضم المعركة.

وخطأ أي خطأ - بالقياس إلى الإسلام - أن تتبلور العقيدة في صورة "نظرية "مجردة للدراسة الذهنية. المعرفية الثقافية. بل خطر أي خطر كذلك.

إن القرآن لم يقض ثلاثة عشر عاما كاملة في بناء العقيدة بسبب أنه كان يتنزل للمرة الأولى. كلا. فلو أراد الله لأنزل هذا القرآن جملة واحدة، ثم ترك أصحابه يدرسونه ثلاثة عشر عاما، أو أكثر أو أقل، حتى يستوعبوا "النظرية الإسلامية ".

ولكن الله - سبحانه - كان يريد أمرا آخر، كان يريد منهجا معينا متفردا. كان يريد بناء جماعة وبناء حركة وبناء عقيدة في وقت واحد. كان يريد أن يبني الجماعة والحركة بالعقيدة، وأن يبني العقيدة بالجماعة والحركة. كان يريد أن تكون العقيدة هي واقع الجماعة الحركي الفعلي، وأن يكون واقع الجماعة الحركي الفعلي هو الصورة المجسمة للعقيدة. وكان الله - سبحانه - يعلم أن بناء النفوس والجماعات لا يتم بين يوم وليلة، فلم يكن هنالك بد أن يستغرق بناء العقيدة المدى الذي يستغرقه بناء النفوس والجماعة. حتى إذا نضج التكوين العقيدي كانت الجماعة هي المظهر الواقعي لهذا النضوج.

هذه هي طبيعة هذا الدين - كما تستخلص من منهج القرآن المكي - ولا بد أن نعرف طبيعته هذه، وألا نحاول تغييرها تلبية لرغبات معجلة مهزومة أمام أشكال النظريات البشرية. فهو بهذه الطبيعة صنع الأمة المسلمة أول مرة، وبها يصنع الأمة المسلمة في كل مرة يراد فيها أن يعاد إخراج الأمة المسلمة للوجود كما أخرجها الله أول مرة.

يجب أن ندرك خطأ المحاولة وخطرها معا، في تحويل العقيدة الإسلامية الحية التي تحب أن تتمثل في واقع نام حي متحرك، وفي تجمع عضوي حركي. تحويلها عن طبيعتها هذه إلى "نظرية "للدراسة والمعرفة الثقافية، لمجرد أننا نريد أن نواجه النظريات البشرية الهزيلة بـ "نظرية إسلامية ".

إن العقيدة الإسلامية تحب أن تتمثل في نفوس حية، وفي تنظيم واقعي، وفي تجمع عضوي، وفي حركة تتفاعل مع الجاهلية من حولها، كما تتفاعل مع الجاهلية الراسبة في نفوس أصحابها - بوصفهم كانوا من أهل الجاهلية قبل أن تدخل العقيدة إلى نفوسهم، وتنتزعها من الوسط الجاهلي - وهي في صورتها هذه تشغل من القلوب والعقول - ومن الحياة أيضا - مساحة أضخم وأوسع وأشمل مما تشغله "النظرية ". وتشمل - فيما تشمل - مساحة النظرية ومادتها، ولكنها لا تقتصر عليها.

إن التصور الإسلامي للألوهية، وللوجود الكوني، وللحياة، وللإنسان. تصور شامل كامل. ولكنه كذلك تصور واقعي إيجابي. وهو يكره - بطبيعته - أن يتمثل في مجرد تصور ذهني معرفي، لأن هذا يخالف طبيعته وغايته. ويجب أن يتمثل في أناسي، وفي تنظيم حي، وفي حركة واقعية. وطريقته في التكون أن ينمو من خلال الأناسي والتنظيم الحي والحركة الواقعية، حتى يكتمل نظريا في نفس الوقت الذي يكتمل فيه واقعيا - ولا ينفصل في صورة "النظرية "بل يظل ممثلا في صورة "الواقع "الحركي.

وكل نمو نظري يسبق النمو الحركي الواقعي، ولا يتمثل من خلاله، هو خطأ وخطر كذلك، بالقياس إلى طبيعة هذا الدين وغايته، وطريقة تركيبه الذاتي.

والله - سبحانه - يقول:

(وقُرْآنا فرقْناه لِتقْرأه على الناسِ على مُكْثٍ ونزّلْناهُ تنْزِيلا). [الإسراء: 106]

فالفرق مقصود. والمكث مقصود كذلك، ليتم البناء التكويني، المؤلف من عقيدة في صورة "منظمة حية "لا في صورة "نظرية ".

يجب أن يعرف أصحاب هذا الدين جيدا أنه - كما إنه في ذاته دين رباني - فإن منهجه في العمل منهج رباني كذلك. متواف مع طبيعته، وإنه لا يمكن فصل حقيقة هذا الدين عن منهجه في العمل.

ويجب أن يعرفوا كذلك أن هذا الدين - كما إنه جاء ليغير التصور الاعتقادي، ومن ثم يغير الواقع الحيوي - فكذلك هو قد جاء ليغير المنهج الذي يبنى به التصور الاعتقادي، ويغير به الواقع الحيوي. جاء ليبني عقيدة وهو يبني أمة. ثم لينشئ منهج تفكير خاصا به،

22

بنفس الدرجة التي ينشئ بها تصورا اعتقاديا وواقعا حيويا. ولا انفصال بين منهج تفكيره الخاص، وتصوره الاعتقادي الخاص، وبنائه الحيوي الخاص. فكلها حزمة واحدة.

فإذا نحن عرفنا منهجه في العمل على النحو الذي بيناه، فلنعرف أن هذا المنهج أصيل، وليس منهج مرحلة ولا بيئة ولا ظروف خاصة بنشأة الجماعة المسلمة الأولى، إنما هو المنهج الذي لا يقوم بناء هذا الدين - في أي وقت - إلا به.

إنه لم تكن وظيفة الإسلام أن يغير عقيدة الناس وواقعهم فحسب، ولكن كانت وظيفته كذلك أن يغير منهج تفكيرهم، وتناولهم للتصور وللواقع، ذلك أنه منهج رباني مخالف في طبيعته كلها لمناهج البشر القاصرة الهزيلة.

ونحن لا نملك أن نصل إلى التصور الرباني وإلى الحياة الربانية، إلا عن طريق منهج تفكير رباني كذلك، المنهج الذي أراد الله أن يقيم منهج تفكير الناس على أساسه، ليصح تصورهم الاعتقادي وتكوينهم الحيوي.

نحن، حين نريد من الإسلام أن يجعل من نفسه "نظرية "للدراسة، نخرج به عن طبيعة منهج التكوين الرباني، وعن طبيعة منهج التفكير الرباني كذلك، ونخضع الإسلام لمناهج التفكير البشرية. كأنما المنهج الرباني أدنى من المناهج البشرية. وكأنما نريد لنرتقي بمنهج الله في التصور والحركة ليوازي مناهج العبيد.

والأمر من هذه الناحية يكون خطيرا، والهزيمة تكون قاتلة.

إن وظيفة المنهج الرباني أن يعطينا - نحن أصحاب الدعوة الإسلامية - منهجا خاصا للتفكير، نبرأ به من رواسب مناهج التفكير الجاهلية السائدة في الأرض، والتي تضغط على عقولنا، وتترسب في ثقافتنا. فإذا نحن أردنا أن نتناول هذا الدين بمنهج تفكير غريب عن طبيعته، من مناهج التفكير الجاهلية الغالبة، كنا قد أبطلنا وظيفته التي جاء ليؤديها للبشرية، وحرمنا أنفسنا فرصة الخلاص من ضغط المنهج الجاهلي السائد في عصرنا، وفرصة الخلاص من رواسبه في عقولنا وتكويننا.

والأمر من هذه الناحية يكون خطيرا كذلك، والخسارة تكون قاتلة.

إن منهج التفكير والحركة في بناء الإسلام، لا يقل قيمة ولا ضرورة عن منهج التصور الاعتقادي والنظام الحيوي، ولا ينفصل عنه كذلك. ومهما يخطر لنا أن نقدم هذا التصور وهذا النظام في صورة تعبيرية، فيجب ألا يغيب عن بالنا أن هذا لا ينشئ "الإسلام "في الأرض في صورة حركة واقعية، بل يجب ألا يغيب عن بالنا أنه لن يفيد من تقديمنا الإسلام في هذه الصورة إلا المشتغلون فعلا بحركة إسلامية واقعية، وأن قصارى ما يفيده هؤلاء أنفسهم من تقديم الإسلام لهم في هذه الصورة هو أن يتفاعلوا معها بالقدر الذي وصلوا هم إليه فعلا في أثناء الحركة.

ومرة أخرى أكرر أن التصور الاعتقادي يجب أن يتمثل من فوره في تجمع حركي، وأن يكون التجمع الحركي في الوقت ذاته تمثيلا صحيحا وترجمة حقيقية للتصور الاعتقادي.

ومرة أخرى أكرر كذلك أن هذا هو المنهج الطبيعي للإسلام الرباني، وأنه منهج أعلى وأقوم، وأشد فاعلية، وأكثر انطباقا على الفطرة البشرية من منهج صياغة النظريات كاملة مستقلة وتقديمها في الصورة الذهنية الباردة للناس، قبل أن يكون هؤلاء الناس مشتغلين فعلا بحركة واقعية، وقبل أن يكونوا هم أنفسهم ترجمة حية، تنمو خطوة خطوة لتمثيل ذلك المفهوم النظري.

وإذا صح هذا في أصل النظرية فهو أصح بطبيعة الحال فيما يختص بتقديم أسس النظام الذي يتمثل فيه التصور الإسلامي، أو تقديم التشريعات المفصلة لهذا النظام.

إن الجاهلية التي حولنا - كما أنها تضغط على أعصاب بعض المخلصين من أصحاب الدعوة الإسلامية، فتجعلهم يتعجلون خطوات المنهج الإسلامي - هي كذلك تتعمد أحيانا أن تحرجهم. فتسألهم: أين تفصيلات نظامكم الذي تدعون إليه؟ وماذا أعددتم لتنفيذه من بحوث ومن دراسات ومن فقه مقنن على الأصول الحديثة. كأن الذي ينقص الناس في هذا الزمان لإقامة شريعة الإسلام في الأرض هو مجرد الأحكام الفقهية والبحوث الفقهية الإسلامية. وكأنما هم مستسلمون لحاكمية الله راضون بأن تحكمهم شريعته، ولكنهم فقط لا يجدون من "المجتهدين" "فقها مقننا بالطريقة الحديثة.. وهي سخرية هازلة يجب أن يرتفع عليها كل ذي قلب يحس لهذا الدين بحرمة.

إن الجاهلية لا تريد بهذا الإحراج إلا أن تجد لنفسها تعلة في نبذ شريعة الله، واستبقاء عبودية البشر للبشر. وإلا أن تصرف العصبة المسلمة عن منهجها الرباني، فتجعلها تتجاوز مرحلة بناء العقيدة في صورة حركية، وأن تحول منهج أصحاب الدعوة الإسلامية عن طبيعته التي تتبلور فيها النظرية من خلال الحركة، وتتحدد ملامح النظام من خلال الممارسة، وتسن فيها التشريعات في مواجهة الحياة الإسلامية الواقعية بمشكلاتها الحقيقية.

ومن واجب أصحاب الدعوة الإسلامية ألا يستجيبوا للمناورة. من واجبهم أن يرفضوا إملاء منهج غريب على حركتهم وعلى دينهم. من واجبهم ألا يستخفهم الذين لا يوقنون.

ومن واجبهم أن يكشفوا مناورة الإحراج، وأن يستعلوا عليها، وأن يرفضوا السخرية الهازلة في ما يسمى "تطوير الفقه الإسلامي "في مجتمع لا يعلن خضوعه لشريعة الله ورفضه لكل شريعة سواها. من واجبهم أن يرفضوا هذه التلهية عن العمل الجاد. التلهية باستنبات البذور في الهواء. وأن يرفضوا هذه الخدعة الخبيثة.

ومن واجبهم أن يتحركوا وفق منهج هذا الدين في الحركة. فهذا من أسرار قوته. وهذا هو مصدر قوتهم كذلك.

إن "المنهج "في الإسلام يساوي "الحقيقة ". ولا انفصام بينهما. وكل منهج غريب لا يمكن أن يحقق الإسلام في النهاية. والمناهج الغربية يمكن أن تحقق أنظمتها البشرية.

ولكنها لا يمكن أن تحقق منهجنا. فالتزام المنهج ضروري كالتزام العقيدة وكالتزام النظام في كل حركة إسلامية.

(إِنَّ هَذَا الْقُرْآنَ يَهْدِي لِلَّتِي هِيَ أَقْوَمُ).

إن الدعوة الإسلامية--على يد محمد رسول الله صلى الله عليه وسلم--إنما تمثل الحلقة الأخيرة من سلسلة الدعوة الطويلة إلى الإسلام بقيادة موكب الرسل الكرام. وهذه الدعوة على مدار التاريخ البشري كانت تستهدف أمرا واحدا: هو تعريف الناس بإلههم الواحد وربهم الحق، وتعبيدهم لربهم وحده ونبذ ربوبية الخلق. ولم يكن الناس - فيما عدا أفرادا معدودة في فترات قصيرة - ينكرون مبدأ الألوهية ويجحدون وجود الله البتة، إنما هم كانوا يخطئون معرفة حقيقة ربهم الحق، أو يشركون مع الله آلهة أخرى: إما في صورة الاعتقاد والعبادة، وإما في صورة الحاكمية والاتباع، وكلاهما شرك كالآخر يخرج به الناس من دين الله، الذي كانوا يعرفونه على يد كل رسول، ثم ينكرونه إذا طال عليهم الأمد، ويرتدون إلى الجاهلية التي أخرجهم منها، ويعودون إلى الشرك بالله مرة أخرى. إما في الاعتقاد والعبادة، وإما في الاتباع والحاكمية. وإما فيها جميعا.

هذه طبيعة الدعوة إلى الله على مدار التاريخ البشري. إنها تستهدف "الإسلام ". إسلام العباد لرب العباد، وإخراجهم من عبادة العباد إلى عبادة الله وحده، بإخراجهم من سلطان العباد في حاكميتهم وشرائعهم وقيمهم وتقاليدهم، إلى سلطان الله وحاكميته وشريعته وحده في كل شأن من شؤون الحياة. وفي هذا جاء الإسلام على يد محمد صلى الله عليه وسلم، كما جاء على أيدي الرسل الكرام قبله. جاء ليرد الناس إلى حاكمية الله كشأن الكون كله الذي يحتوي الناس، فيجب أن تكون السلطة التي تنظم حياتهم هي السلطة التي تنظم وجوده، فلا يشذوا هم بمنهج وسلطان وتدبير غير المنهج والسلطان والتدبير الذي يصرف الكون كله. بل الذي يصرف وجودهم هم أنفسهم في غير الجانب الإرادي من حياتهم. فالناس محكومون بقوانين فطرية من صنع الله في نشأتهم ونموهم، وصحتهم ومرضهم، وحياتهم وموتهم، كما هم محكومون بهذه القوانين في اجتماعهم وعواقب ما يحل بهم نتيجة لحركتهم الاختيارية ذاتها، وهم لا يملكون تغيير سنة الله في القوانين الكونية التي تحكم هذا الكون وتصرفه. ومن ثم ينبغي أن يثوبوا إلى الإسلام في الجانب الإرادي من حياتهم، فيجعلوا شريعة الله هي الحاكمة في كل شأن من شؤون هذه الحياة، تنسيقا بين الجانب الإرادي في حياتهم والجانب الفطري، وتنسيقا بين وجودهم كله بشطريه هذين وبين الوجود الكوني.(6)

ولكن الجاهلية التي تقوم على حاكمية البشر للبشر، والشذوذ بهذا عن الوجود الكوني، والتصادم بين منهج الجانب الإرادي في حياة الإنسان والجانب الفطري. هذه الجاهلية التي واجهها كل رسول بالدعوة إلى الإسلام لله وحده، والتي واجهها رسول الله - صلى الله عليه وسلم - بدعوته. هذه الجاهلية لم تكن متمثلة في "نظرية "مجردة. بل ربما أحيانا لم تكن لها "نظرية "على الإطلاق. إنما كانت متمثلة دائما في تجمع حركي. متمثلة في

---

(6) يراجع بتوسع في هذه النقطة كتاب " مبادئ الإسلام " للسيد أبي الأعلى المودي أمير الجماعة الإسلامية في باكستان.

مجتمع، خاضع لقيادة هذا المجتمع، وخاضع لتصوراته وقيمه ومفاهيمه ومشاعره وتقاليده وعاداته. وهو مجتمع عضوي بين أفراده ذلك التفاعل والتكامل والتناسق والولاء والتعاون العضوي، الذي يجعل هذا المجتمع يتحرك - بإرادة واعية أو غير واعية - للمحافظة على وجوده، والدفاع عن كيانه والقضاء على عناصر الخطر التي تهدد ذلك الوجود وهذا الكيان في أية صورة من صور التهديد.

ومن أجل أن الجاهلية لا تتمثل في "نظرية "مجردة، ولكن تتمثل في تجمع حركي على هذا النحو، فإن محاولة إلغاء هذه الجاهلية، ورد الناس إلى الله مرة أخرى، لا يجوز - ولا يجدي شيئا - أن تتمثل في "نظرية "مجردة. فإنها حينئذ لا تكون مكافئة للجاهلية القائمة فعلا والمتمثلة في تجمع حركي عضوي، فضلا على أن تكون متفوقة عليها كما هو المطلوب في حالة محاولة إلغاء وجود قائم بالفعل لإقامة وجود آخر يخالفه مخالفة أساسية في طبيعته وفي منهجه وفي كلياته وجزئياته. بل لا بد لهذه المحاولة الجديدة أن تتمثل في تجمع عضوي حركي أقوى في قواعده النظرية والتنظيمية، وفي روابطه وعلاقاته ووشائجه من ذلك المجتمع الجاهلي القائم فعلا.

والقاعدة النظرية التي يقوم عليها الإسلام - على مدار التاريخ البشري - هي قاعدة: "شهادة أن لا إله إلا الله" أي إفراد الله - سبحانه - بالألوهية والربوبية والقوامة والسلطان والحاكمية. إفراده بها اعتقادا في الضمير، وعبادة في الشعائر، وشريعة في واقع الحياة. فشهادة أن لا إله إلا الله، لا توجد فعلا، ولا تعتبر موجودة شرعا إلا في هذه الصورة المتكاملة التي تعطيها وجودا جديا حقيقيا يقوم عليه اعتبار قائلها مسلما أو غير مسلم.

ومعنى تقرير هذه القاعدة من الناحية النظرية. أن تعود حياة البشر بجملتها إلى الله، لا يقضون هم في أي شأن من شؤونها، ولا في أي جانب من جوانبها، من عند أنفسهم، بل لا بد لهم أن يرجعوا إلى حكم الله فيها ليتبعوه. وحكم الله هذا يجب أن يعرفوه من مصدر واحد يبلغهم إياه، وهو رسول الله. وهذا يتمثل في شطر الشهادة الثاني من ركن الإسلام الأول: "شهادة أن محمدا رسول الله ".

هذه هي القاعدة النظرية التي يتمثل فيها الإسلام ويقوم عليها. وهي تنشئ منهجا كاملا للحياة حين تطبق في شؤون الحياة كلها، يواجه به المسلم كل فرع من فروع الحياة الفردية والجماعية في داخل دار الإسلام وخارجها، في علاقاته بالمجتمع المسلم وفي علاقات المجتمع المسلم بالمجتمعات الأخرى. (7)

ولكن الإسلام - كما قلنا - لم يكن أن يملك أن يتمثل في "نظرية "مجردة، يعتنقها من يعتنقها اعتقادا ويزاولها عبادة، ثم يبقى معتنقوها على هذا النحو أفرادا ضمن الكيان العضوي للتجمع الحركي الجاهلي القائم فعلا. فإن وجودهم على هذا النحو - مهما كثر عددهم - لا يمكن أن يؤدي إلى "وجود فعلي "للإسلام، لأن الأفراد "المسلمين نظريا "الداخلين في التركيب العضوي للمجتمع الجاهلي سيظلون مضطرون حتما للاستجابة لمطالب هذا المجتمع العضوية. سيتحركون - طوعا أو كرها، بوعي أو بغير وعي - لقضاء الحاجات الأساسية لحياة هذا المجتمع الضرورية لوجوده، وسيدافعون عن كيانه،

---

(7) راجع فصل " لا إله إلا الله منهج حياة ".

27

وسيدفعون العوامل التي تهدد وجوده وكيانه، لأن الكائن العضوي يقوم بهذه الوظائف بكل أعضائه سواء أرادوا أم لم يريدوا. أي أن الأفراد "المسلمين نظريا "سيظلون يقومون "فعلا "بتقوية المجتمع الجاهلي الذي يعملون "نظريا "لإزالته، وسيظلون خلايا حية في كيانه تمده بعناصر البقاء والامتداد. وسيعطونه كفاياتهم وخبراتهم ونشاطهم ليحيا بها ويقوى، وذلك بدلا من أن تكون حركتهم في اتجاه تقويض هذا المجتمع الجاهلي لإقامة المجتمع الإسلامي.

ومن ثم لم يكن بد أن تتمثل القاعدة النظرية للإسلام (أي العقيدة) في تجمع عضوي حركي منذ اللحظة الأولى. لم يكن بد أن ينشأ تجمع عضوي حركي آخر غير التجمع الجاهلي، منفصل ومستقل عن التجمع العضوي الحركي الجاهلي الذي يستهدف الإسلام إلغاءه، وأن يكون محور التجمع الجديد هو القيادة الجديدة المتمثلة في رسول الله - صلى الله عليه وسلم - ومن بعده في كل قيادة إسلامية تستهدف رد الناس إلى ألوهية الله وحده وربوبيته وقوامته وحاكميته وسلطانه وشريعته - وأن يخلع كل من يشهد أن لا إله إلا الله وأن محمدا رسول الله ولاءه من التجمع الحركي الجاهلي - أي التجمع الذي جاء منه - ومن قيادة ذلك التجمع - في أية صورة كانت، سواء كانت في صورة قيادة دينية من الكهنة والسدنة والسحرة والعرافين ومن إليهم، أو في صورة قيادة سياسية واجتماعية واقتصادية كالتي كانت لقريش - وأن يحصر ولاءه في التجمع العضوي الحركي الإسلامي الجديد، وفي قيادته المسلمة.

ولم يكن بد أن يتحقق هذا منذ اللحظة الأولى لدخول المسلم في الإسلام، ولنطقه بشهادة أن لا إله إلا الله وأن محمدا رسول الله، لأن وجود المجتمع المسلم لا يتحقق إلا بهذا. لا يتحقق بمجرد قيام القاعدة النظرية في قلوب أفراد مهما تبلغ كثرتهم، لا يتمثلون في تجمع عضوي متناسق متعاون، له وجود ذاتي مستقل، يعمل أعضاؤه عملا عضويا - كأعضاء الكائن الحي - على تأصيل وجوده وتعميقه وتوسيعه، وفي الدفاع عن كيانه ضد العوامل التي تهاجم وجوده وكيانه، ويعملون هذا تحت قيادة مستقلة عن قيادة المجتمع الجاهلي، تنظم حركتهم وتنسقها، وتوجههم لتأصيل وتعميق وتوسيع وجودهم الاسلامي، ولمكافحة ومقاومة وإزالة الوجود الآخر الجاهلي.

وهكذا وجد الإسلام. هكذا وجد متمثلا في قاعدة نظرية مجملة - ولكنها شاملة - يقوم عليها في نفس اللحظة تجمع عضوي حركي، مستقل منفصل عن المجتمع الجاهلي ومواجه لهذا المجتمع. ولم يوجد قط في صورة "نظرية "مجردة عن هذا الوجود الفعلي. وهكذا يمكن أن يوجد الإسلام مرة أخرى، ولا سبيل لإعادة إنشائه في المجتمع الجاهلي في أي زمان وفي أي مكان بغير الفقه الضروري لطبيعة نشأته العضوية الحركية.

وبعد: فإن الإسلام - وهو يبني الأمة المسلمة على هذه القاعدة وفق هذا المنهج، ويقيم وجودها على أساس التجمع العضوي الحركي، ويجعل آصرة هذا التجمع هي العقيدة - إنما كان يستهدف إبراز "إنسانية الإنسان "وتقويتها وتمكينها، وإعلاءها على جميع الجوانب الأخرى في الكائن الإنساني، وكان يمضي في هذا على منهجه المطرد في كل قواعده وتعليماته وشرائعه وأحكامه.

28

إن الكائن الإنساني يشترك مع الكائنات الحيوانية - بل الكائنات المادية - في صفات توهم أصحاب "الجهالة العلمية". "مرة بأنه حيوان كسائر الحيوان، ومرة بأنه مادة كسائر المواد. ولكن الإنسان مع اشتراكه في هذه "الصفات "مع الحيوان ومع المادة له "خصائص "تميزه وتفرده، وتجعل منه كائنا فريدا، كما اضطر أصحاب "الجهالة العلمية. "أخيرا أن يعترفوا والحقائق الواقعية تلوي أعناقهم ليا، فيضطرون لهذا الاعتراف في غير إخلاص ولا صراحة (8).

ولقد كان من النتائج الواقعية الباهرة للمنهج الإسلامي في هذه القضية، ولإقامة التجمع الإسلامي على آصرة العقيدة وحدها، دون أواصر الجنس والأرض واللون واللغة والمصالح الأرضية القريبة الحدود الإقليمية السخيفة. ولإبراز "خصائص الإنسان "في هذا التجمع وتنميتها وإعلائها، دون الصفات المشتركة بينه وبين الحيوان. كان من النتائج الواقعية الباهرة لهذا المنهج أن أصبح المجتمع المسلم مجتمعا مفتوحا لجميع الأجناس والأقوام والألوان واللغات، بلا عائق من هذه العوائق الحيوانية السخيفة. وإن صبت في بوتقة المجتمع الإسلامي خصائص الأجناس البشرية وكفاياتها، وانصهرت في هذه البوتقة وتمازجت، وأنشأت مركبا عضويا فائقا في فترة تعد نسبيا قصيرة، وصنعت هذه الكتلة العجيبة المتجانسة المتناسقة حضارة رائعة ضخمة تحوي خلاصة الطاقة البشرية في زمانها مجتمعة، على بعد المسافات وبطء طرق الاتصال في ذلك الزمان.

لقد اجتمع في المجتمع الإسلامي المتفوق: العربي والفارسي والشامي والمصري والمغربي والتركي والصيني والهندي والرومي والإغريقي والأندونيسي والأفريقي. إلى آخر الأقوام والأجناس. وتجمعت خصائصهم كلها لتعمل متمازجة متعاونة متناسقة في بناء المجتمع الإسلامي والحضارة الإسلامية. ولم تكن هذه الحضارة الضخمة يوما ما "عربية "إنما كانت دائما "إسلامية "، ولم تكن يوما "قومية "إنما كانت دائما "عقيدية ".

ولقد اجتمعوا كلهم على قدم المساواة وبآصرة الحب، وبشعور التطلع إلى وجهة واحدة. فبذلوا جميعهم أقصى كفاياتهم، وأبرزوا أعمق خصائص أجناسهم، وصبوا خلاصة تجاربهم الشخصية والقومية والتاريخية في بناء هذا المجتمع الواحد الذي ينتسبون إليه جميعا على قدم المساواة، وتجمع فيه بينهم آصرة تتعلق بربهم الواحد، وتبرز فيها إنسانيتهم وحدها بلا عائق، وهذا ما لم يجتمع قط لأي تجمع آخر على مدار التاريخ..

لقد كان أشهر تجمع بشري في التاريخ القديم هو تجمع الإمبراطورية الرومانية مثلا. فقد جمعت بالفعل أجناسا متعددة، ولغات متعددة، وألوانا متعددة، وأمزجة متعددة ولكن هذا كله لم يقم على "آصرة إنسانية "ولم يتمثل في قيمة عليا كالعقيدة، لقد كان هناك تجمع طبقي على أساس طبقة الأشراف وطبقة العبيد في الإمبراطورية كلها من ناحية، وتجمع عنصري على أساس سيادة الجنس الروماني - بصفة عامة - وعبودية سائر الأجناس الأخرى. ومن ثم لم يرتفع قط إلى أفق التجمع الإسلامي. ولم يؤت الثمار التي آتاها التجمع الإسلامي.

---

(8) في مقدمة هؤلاء جوليان هاكسلي من أصحاب " الدارونية الحديثة ".

كذلك قامت في التاريخ الحديث تجمعات أخرى. تجمع الإمبراطورية البريطانية مثلا. ولكنه كان كالتجمع الروماني الذي هو وريثه. تجمعا قوميا استغلاليا، يقوم على أساس سيادة القومية الإنجليزية، واستغلال المستعمرات التي تضمها الإمبراطورية. ومثله الإمبراطوريات الأوربية كلها: الإمبراطورية الأسبانية والبرتغالية في وقت ما، والإمبراطورية الفرنسية. كلها في ذلك المستوى الهابط البشع المقيت. وأرادت الشيوعية أن تقيم تجمعا من نوع آخر، يتخطى حواجز الجنس والقوم والأرض واللغة واللون، ولكنها لم تقمه على قاعدة "إنسانية "عامة، إنما أقامته على القاعدة "الطبقية ". فكان هذا التجمع هو الوجه الآخر للتجمع الروماني القديم. هذا تجمع على قاعدة طبقة "الأشراف "وذلك تجمع على قاعدة طبقة "الصعاليك "(البروليتريا)، والعاطفة التي تسوده هي عاطفة الحقد الأسود على سائر الطبقات الأخرى. وما كان لمثل هذا التجمع الصغير البغيض أن يثمر إلا ما أسوأ ما في الكائن الإنساني. فهو ابتداء قائم على أساس إبراز الصفات الحيوانية وحدها وتنميتها وتمكينها باعتبار أن "المطالب الأساسية "للإنسان هي "الطعام والمسكن والجنس "- وهي مطالب الحيوان الأولية - وباعتبار أن تاريخ الإنسان هو تاريخ البحث عن الطعام..

لقد تفرد الإسلام بمنهجه الرباني في إبراز أخص خصائص الإنسان وتنميتها وإعلائها في بناء المجتمع الإنساني. وما يزال متفردا. والذين يعدلون عنه إلى أي منهج آخر، يقوم على أية قاعدة أخرى من القوم أو الجنس أو الأرض أو الطبقة. إلى آخر هذا النتن السخيف هم أعداء الإنسان حقا. هم الذين لا يريدون لهذا الإنسان أن يتفرد في هذا الكون بخصائصه العليا كما فطره الله، ولا يريدون لمجتمعه أن ينتفع بأقصى كفايات أجناسه وخصائصها وتجاربها في امتزاج وتناسق. وهم الذين يقول الله سبحانه في أمثالهم:

(قُلْ هَلْ نُنَبِّئُكُمْ بِالْأَخْسَرِينَ أَعْمَالًا، الَّذِينَ ضَلَّ سَعْيُهُمْ فِي الْحَيَاةِ الدُّنْيَا وَهُمْ يَحْسَبُونَ أَنَّهُمْ يُحْسِنُونَ صُنْعًا، أُولَئِكَ الَّذِينَ كَفَرُوا بِآيَاتِ رَبِّهِمْ وَلِقَائِهِ فَحَبِطَتْ أَعْمَالُهُمْ فَلَا نُقِيمُ لَهُمْ يَوْمَ الْقِيَامَةِ وَزْنًا، ذَلِكَ جَزَاؤُهُمْ جَهَنَّمُ بِمَا كَفَرُوا وَاتَّخَذُوا آيَاتِي وَرُسُلِي هُزُوًا) [الكهف: 103 -106]

وصدق الله العظيم.

الجهادُ في سبيل الله

لخص الإمام ابن القيم سياق الجهاد في الإسلام في "زاد المعاد "في الفصل الذي عقده باسم: "فصل في ترتيب هديه مع الكفار والمنافقين من حين بعث إلى حين لقي الله عز وجل ": أول ما أوحى به تبارك وتعالى، أن يقرأ باسم ربه الذي خلق، وذلك أولى نبوته، فأمره أن يقرأ في نفسه "فأنذر "فنبأه بقوله: "اقرأ "وأرسله بـ: "يا أيها المدثر "، ثم أمره أن ينذر عشيرته الأقربين، ثم أنذر قومه، ثم أنذر من حولهم من العرب، ثم أنذر العرب قاطبة، ثم أنذر العالمين. فأقام بضع عشرة سنة بعد نبوته ينذر بالدعوة بغير قتال ولا جزية، ويؤمر بالكف والصبر والصفح. ثم أذن له في الهجرة وأذن له في القتال. ثم أمره أن يقاتل من قاتله، ويكف عمن اعتزله ولم يقاتله، ثم أمره بقتال المشركين حتى يكون الدين كله لله. ثم كان الكفار معه بعد الأمر بالجهاد ثلاثة أقسام: أهل صلح وهدنة، وأهل حرب، وأهل ذمة. فأمر بأن يتم لأهل العهد والصلح عهدهم، وأن يوفي لهم به ما استقاموا على العهد، فإن خاف منهم خيانة نبذ إليهم عهدهم ولم يقاتلهم حتى يعلمهم بنقض العهد، وأمر أن يقاتل من نقض عهده. ولما نزلت سورة براءة نزلت ببيان حكم هذه الأقسام كلها: فأمر أن يقاتل عدوه من أهل الكتاب حتى يعطوا الجزية، أو يدخلوا في الإسلام، وأمره فيها بجهاد الكفار والمنافقين والغلظة عليهم فجاهد الكفار بالسيف والسنان. والمنافقين بالحجة واللسان، وأمره فيها بالبراءة من عهود الكفار ونبذ عهودهم إليهم. وجعل أهل العهد في ذلك ثلاثة أقسام: قسما أمره بقتالهم، وهم الذين نقضوا عهده، ولم يستقيموا له، فحاربهم وظهر عليهم. وقسما لهم عهد مؤقت لم ينقضوه ولم يظاهروا عليه، فأمره أن يتم لهم عهدهم إلى مدتهم. وقسما لم يكن لهم عهد ولم يحاربوه، أوكان لهم عهد مطلق، فأمر أن يؤجلهم أربعة أشهر، فإذا انسلخت قاتلهم. فقتل الناقض لعهده، وأجل من لا عهد له أو له عهد مطلق، أربعة أشهر، وأمره أن يتم للموفي بعهده عهده إلى مدته، فأسلم هؤلاء كلهم ولم يقيموا على كفرهم إلى مدتهم. وضرب على أهل الذمة الجزية. فاستقر أمر الكفار معه بعد نزول براءة على ثلاثة أقسام: محاربين له، وأهل عهد، وأهل ذمة. ثم آلت حال أهل العهد والصلح إلى الإسلام فصاروا معه قسمين: محاربين، وأهل ذمة. والمحاربون له خائفون منه، فصار أهل الأرض معه ثلاثة أقسام: مسلم مؤمن به، ومسالم له آمن، وخائف محارب. وأما سيرته في المنافقين فإنه أمر أن يقبل منهم علانيتهم، ويكل سرائرهم إلى الله، وأن يجاهدهم بالعلم والحجة، وأمر أن يعرض عنهم، ويغلظ عليهم، وأن يبلغ بالقول البليغ إلى نفوسهم، ونهى أن يصلي عليهم، وأن يقوم على قبورهم، وأخبر أنه إن استغفر لهم فلن يغفر الله لهم. فهذه سيرته في أعدائه من الكفار والمنافقين).

ومن هذا التلخيص الجيد لمراحل الجهاد في الإسلام تتجلى سمات أصيلة وعميقة في المنهج الحركي لهذا الدين، جديرة بالوقوف أمامها طويلا، ولكننا لا نملك هنا إلا أن نشير إليها إشارات مجملة:

السمة الأولى: هي الواقعية الجدية في منهج هذا الدين. فهو حركة تواجه واقعا بشريا. وتواجهه بوسائل مكافئة لوجوده الواقعي. إنها تواجه جاهلية اعتقادية تصورية، تقوم عليها أنظمة واقعية عملية، تسندها سلطات ذات قوة مادية. ومن ثم تواجه الحركة الإسلامية

31

هذا الواقع كله بما يكافئه. تواجهه بالدعوة والبيان لتصحيح المعتقدات والتصورات، وتواجهه بالقوة والجهاد لإزالة الأنظمة والسلطات القائمة عليها، تلك التي تحول بين جمهرة الناس وبين التصحيح بالبيان للمعتقدات والتصورات، وتخضعهم بالقهر والتضليل وتعبدهم لغير ربهم الجليل. إنها حركة لا تكتفي بالبيان في وجه السلطان المادي، كما إنها لا تستخدم القهر المادي لضمائر الأفراد. وهذه كتلك سواء في منهج هذا الدين وهو يتحرك لإخراج الناس من العبودية للعباد إلى العبودية لله وحده كما سيجيء.

والسمة الثانية في منهج هذا الدين: هي الواقعية الحركية. فهو حركة ذات مراحل، كل مرحلة لها وسائل مكافئة لمقتضياتها وحاجاتها الواقعية، وكل مرحلة تسلم إلى المرحلة التي تليها. فهو لا يقابل الواقع بنظريات مجردة. كما أنه لا يقابل مراحل هذا الواقع بوسائل متجمدة. والذين يسوقون النصوص القرآنية للاستشهاد بها على منهج هذا الدين في الجهاد، ولا يراعون هذه السمة فيه، ولا يدركون طبيعة المراحل التي مر بها هذا المنهج، وعلاقة النصوص المختلفة بكل مرحلة منها. الذين يصنعون هذا يخلطون خلطا شديدا ويلبسون منهج هذا الدين لبسا مضللا، ويحملون النصوص ما لا تحتمله من المبادئ والقواعد النهائية. ذلك أنهم يعتبرون كل نص منها كما لو كان نصا نهائيا، يمثل القواعد النهائية في هذا الدين، ويقولون - وهم مهزومون روحيا وعقليا تحت ضغط الواقع اليائس لذراري المسلمين الذين لم يبق لهم من الإسلام إلا العنوان -: أن الإسلام لا يجاهد إلا للدفاع. ويحسبون أنهم يسدون إلى هذا الدين جميلا بتخليه عن منهجه وهو إزالة الطواغيت كلها من الأرض جميعا، وتعبيد الناس لله وحده، وإخراجهم من العبودية للعباد إلى العبودية لرب العباد. لا بقهرهم على اعتناق عقيدته، ولكن بالتخلية بينهم وبين هذه العقيدة. بعد تحطيم الأنظمة السياسية الحاكمة، أو قهرها حتى تدفع الجزية وتعلن استسلامها والتخلية بين جماهيرها وهذه العقيدة، تعتنقها أو لا تعتنقها بكامل حريتها.

والسمة الثالثة: هي أن هذه الحركة الدائبة، والوسائل المتجددة، لا تخرج هذا الدين عن قواعده المحددة، ولا عن أهدافه المرسومة. فهو - منذ اليوم الأول - سواء وهو يخاطب العشيرة الأقربين، أو يخاطب قريشا، أو يخاطب العرب أجمعين، أو يخاطب العالمين، إنما يخاطبهم بقاعدة واحدة، ويطلب منهم الانتهاء إلى هدف واحد هو إخلاص العبودية لله، والخروج من العبودية للعباد. لا مساومة في هذه القاعدة ولا لين. ثم يمضي إلى تحقيق هذا الهدف الواحد في خطة مرسومة، ذات مراحل محددة، لكل مرحلة وسائلها المتجددة. على نحو ما أسلفنا في الفقرة السابقة.

والسمة الرابعة: هي ذلك الضبط التشريعي للعلاقات بين المجتمع المسلم وسائر المجتمعات الأخرى - على النحو الملحوظ في ذلك التلخيص الجيد الذي نقلناه عن "زاد المعاد "- وقيام ذلك الضبط على أساس أن الإسلام لله هو الأصل العالمي الذي على البشرية كلها أن تفيء إليه، أو أن تسالمه بجملتها فلا تقف لدعوته بأي حائل من نظام سياسي، أو قوة مادية، وأن تخلي بينه وبين كل فرد، يختاره أو لا يختاره بمطلق إرادته، ولكن لا يقاومه ولا يحاربه. فإن فعل ذلك أحد كان على الإسلام أن يقاتله حتى يقتله أو حتى يعلن استسلامه.

والمهزومون روحيا وعقليا ممن يكتبون عن "الجهاد في الإسلام "ليدفعوا عن الإسلام هذا "الاتهام "يخلطون بين منهج هذا الدين في النص على استنكار الإكراه على العقيدة، وبين منهجه في تحطيم القوى السياسية المادية التي تحول بين الناس وبينه، والتي تعبد الناس للناس، وتمنعهم من العبودية لله. وهما أمران لا علاقة بينهما ولا مجال للالتباس فيهما. ومن أجل هذا التخليط، وقبل ذلك من أجل تلك الهزيمة. - يحاولون أن يحصروا الجهاد في الإسلام فيما يسمونه اليوم: "الحرب الدفاعية ". والجهاد في الإسلام أمر آخر لا علاقة له بحروب الناس اليوم، ولا بواعثها، ولا تكييفها كذلك. إن بواعث الجهاد في الإسلام ينبغي تلمسها في طبيعة "الإسلام "ذاته ودوره في هذه الأرض، وأهدافه العليا التي قررها الله، وذكر الله أنه أرسل هذا الرسول بهذه الرسالة، وجعله خاتم النبيين وجعلها خاتمة الرسالات.

إن هذا الدين إعلان عام لتحرير "الإنسان "في "الأرض "من العبودية للعباد - ومن العبودية لهواه أيضا وهي من العبودية للعباد - وذلك بإعلان ألوهية الله وحده - سبحانه - وربوبيته للعالمين.. إن إعلان ربوبية الله وحده للعالمين معناها: الثورة الشاملة على حاكمية البشر في كل صورها وأشكالها وأنظمتها وأوضاعها، والتمرد الكامل على كل وضع في أرجاء الأرض، الحكم فيه للبشر بصورة من الصور. أو بتعبير آخر مرادف: الألوهية فيه للبشر في صورة من الصور. ذلك أن الحكم الذي مرد الأمر فيه إلى البشر، ومصدر السلطات فيه هم البشر، هو تأليه للبشر، يجعل بعضهم لبعض أربابا من دون الله. إن هذا الإعلان معناه انتزاع سلطان الله المغتصب ورده إلى الله، وطرد المغتصبين له، الذين يحكمون الناس بشرائع من عند أنفسهم، فيقومون منهم مقام الأرباب ويقوم الناس منهم مكان العبيد. إن معناه تحطيم مملكة البشر لإقامة مملكة الله في الأرض، أو بالتعبير القرآني الكريم:

(وهُوَ الذي في السماءِ إلهٌ وفي الأرْضِ إلهٌ) [الزخرف: 84].

(إِنِ الْحُكْمُ إِلا لِلهِ أمرَ ألا تعبُدُوا إلا إيَّاهُ ذلكَ الدِّينُ الْقَيِّمُ) [يوسف: 40].

(قُلْ يا أهْلَ الْكِتابِ تعالَوْا إلى كلِمَةٍ سواءٍ بينَنا وبينْكُمْ ألا نعبُدَ إلا الله ولا نُشْرِكَ بِهِ شيئا ولا يتخِذَ بعْضُنا بعْضا أرْبابا مِنْ دُونِ الله فإنْ تولوْا فقُولُوا اشْهَدُوا بأنا مُسْلِمُونَ) [آل عمران: 64].

ومملكة الله في الأرض لا تقوم بأن يتولى الحاكمية في الأرض رجال بأعيانهم - هم رجال الدين - كما كان الأمر في سلطان الكنيسة، ولا رجال ينطقون باسم الآلهة، كما كان الحال فيما يعرف باسم "الثيوقراطية "أو الحكم الإلهي المقدس. - ولكنها تقوم بأن تكون شريعة الله هي الحاكمة، وأن يكون مرد الأمر إلى الله وفق ما قرره من شريعة مبينة.

وقيام مملكة الله في الأرض، وإزالة مملكة البشر، وانتزاع السلطان من أيدي مغتصبيه من العباد ورده إلى الله وحده. وسيادة الشريعة الإلهية وحدها وإلغاء القوانين البشرية. كل أولئك لا يتم بمجرد التبليغ والبيان، لأن المتسلطين على رقاب العباد، والمغتصبين لسلطان الله في الأرض، لا يسلمون في سلطانهم بمجرد التبليغ والبيان، وإلا فما كان أيسر عمل الرسل في إقرار دين الله في الأرض. وهذا عكس ما عرفه تاريخ الرسل - صلوات الله وسلامه عليهم - وتاريخ هذا الدين على ممر الأجيال.

إن هذا الإعلان العام لتحرير "الإنسان" في "الأرض" من كل سلطان غير سلطان الله، بإعلان إلهية الله وحده وربوبيته للعالمين، لم يكن إعلانا نظريا فلسفيا سلبيا. إنما كان إعلانا حركيا واقعيا إيجابيا. إعلانا يراد له التحقيق العملي في صورة نظام يحكم البشر بشريعة الله، ويخرجهم بالفعل من العبودية للعباد إلى العبودية لله وحده بلا شريك. ومن ثم لم يكن بد من أن يتخذ شكل "الحركة" إلى جانب شكل "البيان". ذلك ليواجه "الواقع" البشري بكل جوانبه بوسائل مكافئة لكل جوانبه.

والواقع الإنساني، أمس واليوم وغدا، يواجه هذا الدين - بوصفه إعلانا عاما لتحرير "الإنسان" في "الأرض" من كل سلطان غير سلطان الله - بعقبات اعتقادية تصورية، وعقبات مادية واقعية. وعقبات سياسية واجتماعية واقتصادية وعنصرية وطبقية، إلى جانب عقبات العقائد المنحرفة والتصورات الباطلة. وتختلط هذه بتلك وتتفاعل معها بصورة معقدة شديدة التعقيد.

وإذا كان "البيان" يواجه العقائد والتصورات، فإن "الحركة" تواجه العقبات المادية الأخرى - وفي مقدمتها السلطان السياسي القائم على العوامل الاعتقادية التصورية والعنصرية والطبقية والاجتماعية والاقتصادية المعقدة المتشابكة -. وهما معا - البيان والحركة - يواجهان "الواقع البشري" بجملته، بوسائل مكافئة لكل مكوناته. وهما معا لا بد منهما لانطلاق حركة التحرير للإنسان في الأرض. "الإنسان" كله في "الأرض" كلها. وهذه نقطة هامة لا بد من تقريرها مرة أخرى.

إن هذا الدين ليس إعلانا لتحرير الإنسان العربي. وليس رسالة خاصة بالعرب.. إن موضوعه هو "الإنسان". نوع "الإنسان". ومجاله هو "الأرض". كل "الأرض". إن الله - سبحانه - ليس ربا للعرب وحدهم ولا حتى لمن يعتنقون العقيدة الإسلامية وحدهم. إن الله هو "رب العالمين". وهذا الدين يريد أن يرد "العالمين" إلى ربهم، وأن ينتزعهم من العبودية لغيره. والعبودية الكبرى - في نظر الإسلام - هي خضوع البشر لأحكام يشرعها لهم ناس من البشر. وهذه هي "العبادة" التي يقرر أنها لا تكون إلا لله، وأن من يتوجه بها لغير الله يخرج من دين الله مهما ادعى أنه في هذا الدين. ولقد نص رسول الله - صلى الله عليه وسلم - على أن "الاتباع" في الشريعة والحكم هو "العبادة" التي صار بها اليهود والنصارى "مشركين" مخالفين لما أمروا به من "عبادة "الله وحده.

أخرج الترمذي - بإسناده - عن عدي بن حاتم - رضي الله عنه - أنه لما بلغته دعوة رسول الله - صلى الله عليه وسلم - فر إلى الشام، وكان قد تنصر في الجاهلية، فأسرت أخته وجماعة من قومه، ثم من رسول الله - صلى الله عليه وسلم - على أخته فأعطاها، فرجعت إلى أخيها فرغبته في الإسلام، وفي القدوم على رسول الله - صلى الله عليه وسلم - فتحدث الناس بقدومه، فدخل على رسول الله - صلى الله عليه وسلم - وفي عنقه - أي "عدي" صليب من فضة وكان النبي - صلى الله عليه وسلم - يقرأ هذه الآية. (اتخَذُوا أَحْبارهُمْ ورُهْبانهُمْ أَرْبابا مِنْ دُونِ اللهِ) (9). قال: فقلت: إنهم لم يعبدوهم، فقال: "بلى. إنهم حرموا عليهم الحلال وأحلوا لهم الحرام، فاتبعوهم، فذلك عبادتهم إياهم ".

وتفسير رسول الله - صلى الله عليه وسلم - لقول الله سبحانه، نص قاطع على أن الاتباع في الشريعة والحكم هو العبادة التي تخرج من الدين، وأنها هي اتخاذ بعض الناس أربابا لبعض. الأمر الذي جاء هذا الدين ليلغيه، ويعلن تحرير "الإنسان" في "الأرض" من العبودية لغير الله.

ومن ثم لم يكن بد للإسلام أن ينطلق في "الأرض" لإزالة "الواقع" المخالف لذلك الإعلان العام. بالبيان وبالحركة مجتمعين. وأن يوجه الضربات للقوى السياسية التي تعبد الناس لغير الله. - أي تحكمهم بغير شريعة الله وسلطانه - والتي تحول بينهم وبين الاستماع إلى "البيان" واعتناق "العقيدة" بحرية لا يتعرض لها السلطان. ثم لكي يقيم نظاما اجتماعيا واقتصاديا وسياسيا يسمح لحركة التحرر بالانطلاق الفعلي - بعد إزالة القوة المسيطرة - سواء كانت سياسية بحتة، أو متلبسة بالعنصرية، أو الطبقية داخل العنصر الواحد.

إنه لم يكن من قصد الإسلام قط أن يكره الناس على اعتناق عقيدته. ولكن الإسلام ليس مجرد "عقيدة ". إن الإسلام كما قلنا إعلان عام لتحرير الإنسان من العبودية للعباد. فهو يهدف ابتداء إلى إزالة الأنظمة والحكومات التي تقوم على أساس حاكمية البشر للبشر وعبودية الإنسان للإنسان. ثم يطلق الأفراد بعد ذلك أحرارا - بالفعل - في اختيار العقيدة التي يريدونها بمحض اختيارهم - بعد رفع الضغط السياسي عنهم، وبعد البيان المنير لأرواحهم وعقولهم - ولكن هذه التجربة ليس معناها أن يجعلوا إلاههم هواهم، أو أن يختاروا بأنفسهم أن يكونوا عبيدا للعباد. وأن يتخذ بعضهم بعضا أربابا من دون الله.. إن النظام الذي يحكم البشر في الأرض يجب أن تكون قاعدته العبودية لله وحده، وذلك بتلقي الشرائع منه وحده. ثم ليعتنق كل فرد - في ظل هذا النظام العام - ما يعتنقه من عقيدة. وبهذا يكون "الدين " كله لله. أي تكون الدينونة والخضوع والاتباع والعبودية كلها لله. إن مدلول "الدين " أشمل من مدلول "العقيدة ". إن الدين هو المنهج والنظام الذي يحكم الحياة، وهو في الإسلام يعتمد على العقيدة، ولكنه في عمومه أشمل من العقيدة. وفي الإسلام يمكن أن تخضع جماعات متنوعة لمنهجه العام الذي يقوم على أساس العبودية لله وحده ولو لم يعتنق بعض هذه الجماعات عقيدة الإسلام.

والذي يدرك طبيعة هذا الدين - على النحو المتقدم - يدرك معها حتمية الانطلاق الحركي للإسلام في صورة الجهاد بالسيف - إلى جانب الجهاد بالبيان - ويدرك أن ذلك لم يكن حركة دفاعية - بالمعنى الضيق الذي يفهم اليوم من اصطلاح "الحرب الدفاعية "كما يريد المهزومون - أمام ضغط الواقع الحاضر وأمام هجوم المستشرقين الماكر - أن يصوروا حركة الجهاد في الإسلام - إنما كان حركة اندفاع وانطلاق لتحرير "الإنسان " في "الأرض ". بوسائل مكافئة لكل جوانب الواقع البشري، وفي مراحل محددة لكل مرحلة منها وسائلها المتجددة.

وإذا لم يكن بد أن نسمي حركة الإسلام الجهادية حركة دفاعية، فلا بد أن نغير مفهوم كلمة "دفاع "، ونعتبره "دفاعا عن الإنسان " ذاته، ضد جميع العوامل التي تقيد حريته وتعوق تحرره. هذه العوامل التي تتمثل في المعتقدات والتصورات، كما تتمثل في الأنظمة السياسية، القائمة على الحواجز الاقتصادية والطبقية والعنصرية، التي كانت سائدة في

الأرض كلها يوم جاء الإسلام، والتي ما تزال أشكال منها سائدة في الجاهلية الحاضرة في هذا الزمان.

وبهذا التوسع في مفهوم كلمة "الدفاع" نستطيع أن نواجه حقيقة بواعث الانطلاق الإسلامي في "الأرض" بالجهاد، ونواجه طبيعة الإسلام ذاتها، وهي أنه إعلان عام لتحرير الإنسان من العبودية للعباد، وتقرير ألوهية الله وحده وربوبيته للعالمين، وتحطيم مملكة الهوى البشري في الأرض، وإقامة مملكة الشريعة الإلهية في عالم الإنسان.

أما محاولة إيجاد مبررات دفاعية للجهاد الإسلامي بالمعنى الضيق للمفهوم العصري للحرب الدفاعية، ومحاولة البحث عن أسانيد لإثبات أن وقائع الجهاد الإسلامي كانت لمجرد صد العدوان من القوى المجاورة على "الوطن الإسلامي" - وهو في عرف بعضهم جزيرة العرب - فهي محاولة تنم عن قلة إدراك لطبيعة هذا الدين، ولطبيعة الدور الذي جاء ليقوم به في الأرض. كما أنها تشي بالهزيمة أمام ضغط الواقع الحاضر، وأمام الهجوم الاستشراقي الماكر على الجهاد الإسلامي.

ترى لو كان أبو بكر وعمر وعثمان - رضي الله عنهم - قد أمنوا عدوان الروم والفرس على الجزيرة أكانوا يقعدون إذن عن دفع المد الإسلامي إلى أطراف الأرض؟ وكيف كانوا يدفعون هذا المد، وأمام الدعوة تلك العقبات المادية من أنظمة الدولة السياسية، وأنظمة المجتمع العنصرية والطبقية، والاقتصادية الناشئة من الاعتبارات العنصرية والطبقية، والتي تحميها القوة المادية للدولة كذلك؟

إنها سذاجة أن يتصور الإنسان دعوة تعلن تحرير "الإنسان". نوع الإنسان. في "الأرض". كل الأرض. ثم تقف أمام هذه العقبات تجاهدها باللسان والبيان.. إنها تجاهد باللسان والبيان حينما يخلى بينها وبين الأفراد، تخاطبهم بحرية، وهم مطلقو السراح من جميع تلك المؤثرات. فهنا "لا إكراه في الدين". أما حين توجد تلك العقبات والمؤثرات المادية، فلا بد من إزالتها أولا بالقوة، للتمكن من مخاطبة قلب الإنسان وعقله، وهو طليق من هذه الأغلال.

إن الجهاد ضرورة للدعوة، إذا كانت أهدافها هي إعلان تحرير الإنسان إعلانا جادا يواجه الواقع الفعلي بوسائل مكافئة له في كل جوانبه، ولا يكفي بالبيان الفلسفي النظري. سواء كان الوطن الإسلامي - وبالتعبير الإسلامي الصحيح: دار الإسلام - آمنا أم مهددا من جيرانه. فالإسلام حين يسعى إلى السلم، لا يقصد تلك السلم الرخيصة، وهي مجرد أن يؤمن الرقعة الخاصة التي يعتنق أهلها العقيدة الإسلامية. إنما هو يريد السلم التي يكون فيها الدين كله لله. أي تكون عبودية الناس كلهم فيها لله، والتي لا يتخذ فيها الناس بعضهم بعضا أربابا من دون الله. والعبرة بنهاية المراحل التي وصلت إليها الحركة الجهادية في الإسلام - بأمر من الله - لا بأوائل أيام الدعوة ولا بأواسطها. ولقد انتهت هذه المراحل كما يقول الإمام ابن القيم: "فاستقر أمر الكفار معه - بعد نزول براءة - على ثلاثة أقسام: محاربين له، وأهل عهد، وأهل ذمة. ثم آلت حال أهل العهد والصلح إلى الإسلام. فصاروا معه قسمين: محاربين، وأهل ذمة. والمحاربون له خائفون منه. فصار أهل الأرض معه ثلاثة أقسام: مسلم مؤمن به، ومسالم له آمن (وهم أهل الذمة كما يفهم من الجملة السابقة) وخائف محارب ."

36

وهذه هي المواقف المنطقية مع طبيعة هذا الدين وأهدافه، لا كما يفهم المهزومون أمام الواقع الحاضر، وأمام هجوم المستشرقين الماكر.

ولقد كف الله المسلمين عن القتال في مكة، وفي أول العهد بالهجرة إلى المدينة. وقيل للمسلمين: **(كُفُّوا أَيْدِيَكُمْ وَأَقِيمُوا الصَّلَاةَ وَآتُوا الزَّكَاةَ)** [10]. ثم أذن لهم فيه، فقيل لهم: **(أُذِنَ لِلَّذِينَ يُقَاتَلُونَ بِأَنَّهُمْ ظُلِمُوا وإن الله على نَصْرِهِمْ لَقَدِيرٌ مِنْ دِيَارِهِمْ بِغَيْرِ حقٍّ إلا أَنْ يَقُولُوا رَبُّنَا اللهُ وَلَوْلَا دَفْعُ اللهِ النَّاسَ بَعْضَهُمْ بِبَعْضٍ لَهُدِمَتْ صَوَامِعُ وَبِيَعٌ وَصَلَوَاتٌ وَمَسَاجِدُ يُذْكَرُ فِيهَا اسْمُ اللهِ كَثِيرًا إِنْ اللهُ لَقَوِيٌّ عَزِيزٌ، الذِينَ إِنْ مَكَّنَّاهُمْ فِي الْأَرْضِ أَقَامُوا الصَّلَاةَ وَآتُوا الزَّكَاةَ وَأَمَرُوا بِالْمَعْرُوفِ وَنَهَوْا عَنِ الْمُنْكَرِ وَلِلَّهِ عَاقِبَةُ الْأُمُورِ)** [11]. ثم فرض عليهم القتال بعد ذلك لمن قاتلهم دون من لم يقاتلهم فقيل لهم: **(وَقَاتِلُوا فِي سبيلِ اللهِ الذِينَ يُقَاتِلُونَكُمْ)** [12]. ثم فرض عليهم قتال المشركين كافة، فقيل لهم: **(وَقَاتِلُوا الْمُشْرِكِينَ كَافَّةً كَمَا يُقَاتِلُونَكُمْ كَافَّةً)** [13]. وقيل لهم: **(قَاتِلُوا الذِينَ لا يُؤْمِنُونَ بِاللهِ وَلا بِالْيَوْمِ الْآخِرِ وَلا يُحَرِّمُونَ ما حَرَّمَ اللهُ وَرَسُولُهُ وَلا يَدِينُونَ دِينَ الْحَقِّ مِنَ الذِينَ أُوتُوا الْكِتَابَ حَتَّى يُعْطُوا الْجِزْيَةَ عَنْ يَدٍ وَهُمْ صَاغِرُونَ)** [14]. فكان القتال - كما يقول الإمام ابن القيم - "محرما، ثم مأذونا به، ثم مأمورا به لمن بدأهم بالقتال، ثم مأمورا به لجميع المشركين ".

إن جدية النصوص القرآنية الواردة في الجهاد، وجدية الأحاديث النبوية التي تحض عليه، وجدية الوقائع الجهادية في صدر الإسلام، وعلى مدى طويل من تاريخه. إن هذه الجدية الواضحة تمنع أن يجول في النفس ذلك التفسير الذي يحاوله المهزومون أمام ضغط الواقع الحاضر وأمام الهجوم الاستشراقي الماكر على الجهاد الإسلامي.

ومن ذا الذي يسمع قول الله سبحانه في هذا الشأن وقول رسوله - صلى الله عليه وسلم - ويتابع وقائع الجهاد الإسلامي، ثم يظنه شأنا عارضا مقيدا بملابسات تذهب وتجيء، ويقف عند حدود الدفاع لتأمين الحدود؟

لقد بين الله للمؤمنين في أول ما نزل من الآيات التي أذن لهم فيها بالقتال أن الشأن الدائم الأصيل في طبيعة هذه الحياة الدنيا أن يدفع الناس بعضهم ببعض، لدفع الفساد عن الأرض:

(أُذِنَ لِلَّذِينَ يُقَاتَلُونَ بِأَنَّهُمْ ظُلِمُوا وإن الله على نَصْرِهِمْ لَقَدِيرٌ، الذِينَ أُخْرِجُوا مِنْ دِيَارِهِمْ بِغَيْرِ حقٍّ إلا أَنْ يَقُولُوا رَبُّنَا اللهُ وَلَوْلَا دَفْعُ اللهِ النَّاسَ بَعْضَهُمْ بِبَعْضٍ لَهُدِمَتْ صَوَامِعُ وَبِيَعٌ وَصَلَوَاتٌ وَمَسَاجِدُ يُذْكَرُ فِيهَا اسْمُ اللهِ كَثِيرًا) [الحج: 39 - 40]

وإذن فهو الشأن الدائم لا الحالة العارضة. الشأن الدائم أن لا يتعايش الحق والباطل في هذه الأرض. وأنه متى قام الإسلام بإعلانه العام لإقامة ربوبية الله للعالمين، وتحرير

[10] النساء: 77
[11] الحج: 39-41
[12] البقرة: 190
[13] التوبة: 36
[14] التوبة: 29

الإنسان من العبودية للعباد، رماه المغتصبون لسلطان الله في الأرض ولم يسالموه قط، وانطلق هو كذلك يدمر عليهم ليخرج الناس من سلطانهم ويدفع عن "الإنسان "في "الأرض "ذلك السلطان الغاصب. حال دائمة لا يقف معها الانطلاق الجهادي التحريري حتى يكون الدين كله لله.

إن الكف عن القتال في مكة لم يكن إلا مجرد مرحلة في خطة طويلة. كذلك كان الأمر أول العهد بالهجرة. والذي بعث الجماعة المسلمة في المدينة بعد الفترة الأولى للانطلاق لم يكن مجرد تأمين المدينة. هذا هدف أولي لا بد منه، ولكنه ليس الهدف الأخير. إنه هدف يضمن وسيلة الانطلاق، ويؤمن قاعدة الانطلاق. الانطلاق لتحرير "الإنسان "، ولإزالة العقبات التي تمنع "الإنسان "ذاته من الانطلاق.

وكف أيدي المسلمين في مكة عن الجهاد بالسيف مفهوم. لأنه كان مكفولا للدعوة في مكة حرية البلاغ. كان صاحبها - صلى الله عليه وسلم - يملك بحماية بني هاشم، أن يصدع بالدعوة، ويخاطب بها الآذان والعقول والقلوب، ويواجه بها الأفراد. لم تكن هناك سلطة سياسية منظمة تمنعه من إبلاغ الدعوة، أو تمنع الأفراد من سماعه. فلا ضرورة - في هذه المرحلة - لاستخدام القوة، وذلك إلى أسباب أخرى لعلها كانت قائمة في هذه المرحلة. وقد لخصتها في ظلال القرآن عند تفسير قوله تعالى: (**أَلَمْ تَرَ إِلَى الَّذِينَ قِيلَ لَهُمْ كُفُّوا أَيْدِيَكُمْ وَأَقِيمُوا الصَّلَاةَ وَآتُوا الزَّكَاةَ.**) [الآية 77 من سورة النساء]. ولا بأس في إثبات بعض هذا التلخيص هنا:

"ربما كان ذلك لأن الفترة المكية كانت فترة تربية وإعداد، في بيئة معينة، لقوم معينين، وسط ظروف معينة. ومن أهداف التربية والإعداد في مثل هذه البيئة بالذات، تربية نفس الفرد العربي على الصبر على ما لا يصبر عليه عادة من الضيم على شخصه أو على من يلوذون به، ليخلص من شخصه، ويتجرد من ذاته، ولا تعود ذاته ولا من يلوذون به محور الحياة في نظره ودافع الحركة في حياته. وتربيته كذلك على ضبط أعصابه، فلا يندفع لأول مؤثر - كما هي طبيعته - ولا يهتاج لأول مهيج، فيتم الاعتدال في طبيعته وحركته. وتربيته على أن يتبع مجتمعا منظما له قيادة يرجع إليها في كل أمر من أمور حياته، ولا يتصرف إلا وفق ما تأمره به - مهما يكن مخالفا لمألوفه وعادته - وقد كان هذا هو حجر الأساس في إعداد شخصية العربي، لإنشاء "المجتمع المسلم "الخاضع لقيادة موجهة، المترقي المتحضر، غير الهمجي أو القبلي.

"وربما كان ذلك أيضا. لأن الدعوة السلمية كانت أشد أثرا وأنفذ، في مثل بيئة قريش. ذات العنجهية والشرف. والتي قد يدفعها القتال معها - في مثل هذه المرحلة - إلى زيادة العناد، وإلى نشأة ثارات دموية جديدة كثارات العرب المعروفة التي أثارت حرب داحس والغبراء، وحرب البسوس، أعواما طويلة، تفانت فيها قبائل برمتها. وتكون هذه الثارات الجديدة مرتبطة في أذهانهم وذكرياتهم بالإسلام، فلا تهدأ بعد ذلك أبدا، ويتحول الإسلام من دعوة ودين إلى ثارات وذحول تنسى معها وجهته الأساسية، وهو في مبدئه، فلا تذكر أبدا.

"وربما كان ذلك أيضا، اجتنابا لإنشاء معركة ومقتلة في داخل كل بيت. فلم تكن هناك سلطة نظامية عامة، هي التي تعذب المؤمنين وتفتنهم، إنما كان ذلك موكولا إلى أولياء كل

فرد يعذبونه ويفتنونه "ويؤدبونه". ومعنى الإذن بالقتال - في مثل هذه البيئة - أن تقع معركة ومقتلة في كل بيت. ثم يقال: هذا هو الإسلام. ولقد قيلت حتى والإسلام يأمر بالكف عن القتال. فقد كانت دعاية قريش في الموسم. في أواسط العرب القادمين للحج والتجارة: إن محمدا يفرق بين الوالد وولده، فوق تفريقه لقومه وعشيرته. فكيف لو كان كذلك يأمر الولد بقتل الوالد، والمولى بقتل الولي. في كل بيت وفي كل محلة؟

"وربما كان ذلك أيضا لما يعلمه الله من أن كثيرين من المعاندين الذين يفتنون أوائل المسلمين عن دينهم، ويعذبونهم ويؤذونهم، هم بأنفسهم سيكونون جند الإسلام المخلص، بل من قادته. ألم يكن عمر بن الخطاب من بين هؤلاء؟.

"وربما كان ذلك أيضا، لأن النخوة العربية، في بيئة قبلية، من عادتها أن تثور للمظلوم الذي يحتمل الأذى، ولا يتراجع. وبخاصة إذا كان واقعا على كرام الناس فيهم. وقد وقعت ظواهر كثيرة تثبت صحة هذه النظرة - في هذه البيئة - فابن الدغنة لم يرض أن يترك أبا بكر - وهو رجل كريم - يهاجر ويخرج من مكة، ورأى في ذلك عارا على العرب. وعرض عليه جواره وحمايته. وآخر هذه الظواهر نقض صحيفة الحصار لبني هاشم في شعب أبي طالب، بعد ما طال عليهم الجوع واشتدت المحنة. بينما في بيئة أخرى من بيئات "الحضارة "القديمة التي مردت على الذل، قد يكون السكوت على الأذى مدعاة للهزء والسخرية والاحتقار من البيئة، وتعظيم المؤذي الظالم المعتدي.

"وربما كان ذلك، أيضا، لقلة عدد المسلمين حينذاك. وانحصارهم في مكة، حيث لم تبلغ الدعوة إلى بقية الجزيرة أو بلغت أخبارها متناثرة، حيث كانت القبائل تقف على الحياد من معركة داخلية بين قريش وبعض أبنائها، حتى ترى ماذا يكون مصير الموقف. ففي مثل هذه الحالة قد تنتهي المعركة المحدودة، إلى قتل المجموعة المسلمة القليلة - حتى ولو قتلوا هم أضعاف من سيقتل منهم - ويبقى الشرك، وتنمحي الجماعة المسلمة، ولم يقم في الأرض للإسلام نظام، ولا وجد له كيان واقعي. وهو دين جاء ليكون منهاج حياة، وليكون نظاما واقعيا للحياة.

فأما في المدينة - في أول العهد بالهجرة - فقد كانت المعاهدة التي عقدها رسول الله - صلى الله عليه وسلم - مع اليهود من أهلها ومن بقي على الشرك من العرب فيها وفيما حولها، ملابسة تقتضيها طبيعة المرحلة كذلك.

أولا: لأن هناك مجالا للتبليغ والبيان، لا تقف له سلطة سياسية تمنعه وتحول بين الناس وبينه، فقد اعترف الجميع بالدولة المسلمة الجديدة، وبقيادة رسول الله - صلى الله عليه وسلم - في تصريف شؤونها السياسية. فنصت المعاهدة على ألا يعقد أحد منهم صلحا ولا يثير حربا، ولا ينشئ علاقة خارجية إلا بإذن رسول الله - صلى الله عليه وسلم - وكان واضحا أن السلطة الحقيقية في المدينة في يد القيادة المسلمة. فالمجال أمام الدعوة مفتوح، والتخلية بين الناس وحرية الاعتقاد قائمة.

ثانيا: إن الرسول - صلى الله عليه وسلم - كان يريد التفرغ في، هذه المرحلة - لقريش، التي تقوم معارضتها لهذا الدين حجر عثرة في وجه القبائل الأخرى الواقعة في حالة انتظار لما ينتهي إليه الأمر بين قريش وبعض بنيها. لذلك بادر رسول الله - صلى الله عليه

وسلم - بإرسال "السرايا" وكان أول لواء عقده لحمزة بن عبد المطلب في شهر رمضان على رأس سبعة أشهر من الهجرة.

ثم توالت هذه السرايا، على رأس تسعة أشهر. ثم على رأس ثلاثة عشر شهرا. ثم على رأس ستة عشر شهرا. ثم كانت سرية عبد الله بن جحش في رجب على رأس سبعة عشر شهرا، وهي أول غزاة وقع فيها قتل وقتال، وكان ذلك في الشهر الحرام، والتي نزلت فيها آيات البقرة: (يَسْأَلُونَكَ عَنِ الشَّهْرِ الْحَرَامِ قِتَالٍ فِيهِ قُلْ قِتَالٌ فِيهِ كَبِيرٌ وَصَدٌّ عَنْ سَبِيلِ اللَّهِ وَكُفْرٌ بِهِ وَالْمَسْجِدِ الْحَرَامِ وَإِخْرَاجُ أَهْلِهِ مِنْهُ أَكْبَرُ عِنْدَ اللَّهِ وَالْفِتْنَةُ أَكْبَرُ مِنَ الْقَتْلِ وَلَا يَزَالُونَ يُقَاتِلُونَكُمْ حَتَّى يَرُدُّوكُمْ عَنْ دِينِكُمْ إِنِ اسْتَطَاعُوا). [البقرة: 217].

ثم كانت غزوة بدر الكبرى في رمضان من هذه السنة. وهي التي نزلت فيها سورة الأنفال.

ورؤية الموقف من خلال ملابسات الواقع، لا تدع مجالا للقول بأن "الدفاع" بمفهومه الضيق كان هو قاعدة الحركة الإسلامية، كما يقول المهزومون أمام الواقع الحاضر، وأمام الهجوم الاستشراقي الماكر.

إن الذين يلجؤون إلى تلمس أسباب دفاعية بحتة لحركة المد الإسلامي، إنما يؤخذون بحركة الهجوم الاستشراقية، في وقت لم يعد للمسلمين شوكة، بل لم يعد للمسلمين إسلام. - إلا من عصم الله ممن يصرون على تحقيق إعلان الإسلام العام بتحرير "الإنسان" في "الأرض" من كل سلطان إلا من سلطان الله، ليكون الدين كله لله - فيبحثون عن مبررات أدبية للجهاد في الإسلام.

والمد الإسلامي ليس في حاجة إلى مبررات أدبية له أكثر من المبررات التي حملتها النصوص القرآنية:

(فَلْيُقَاتِلْ فِي سَبِيلِ اللَّهِ الَّذِينَ يَشْرُونَ الْحَيَاةَ الدُّنْيَا بِالْآخِرَةِ وَمَنْ يُقَاتِلْ فِي سَبِيلِ اللَّهِ فَيُقْتَلْ أَوْ يَغْلِبْ فَسَوْفَ نُؤْتِيهِ أَجْرًا عَظِيمًا، وَمَا لَكُمْ لَا تُقَاتِلُونَ فِي سَبِيلِ اللَّهِ وَالْمُسْتَضْعَفِينَ مِنَ الرِّجَالِ وَالنِّسَاءِ وَالْوِلْدَانِ الَّذِينَ يَقُولُونَ رَبَّنَا أَخْرِجْنَا مِنْ هَذِهِ الْقَرْيَةِ الظَّالِمِ أَهْلُهَا وَاجْعَلْ لَنَا مِنْ لَدُنْكَ وَلِيًّا وَاجْعَلْ لَنَا مِنْ لَدُنْكَ نَصِيرًا، الَّذِينَ آمَنُوا يُقَاتِلُونَ فِي سَبِيلِ اللَّهِ وَالَّذِينَ كَفَرُوا يُقَاتِلُونَ فِي سَبِيلِ الطَّاغُوتِ فَقَاتِلُوا أَوْلِيَاءَ الشَّيْطَانِ إِنَّ كَيْدَ الشَّيْطَانِ كَانَ ضَعِيفًا). [النساء: 74 - 76]

(قُلْ لِلَّذِينَ كَفَرُوا إِنْ يَنْتَهُوا يُغْفَرْ لَهُمْ مَا قَدْ سَلَفَ وَإِنْ يَعُودُوا فَقَدْ مَضَتْ سُنَّتُ الْأَوَّلِينَ، وَقَاتِلُوهُمْ حَتَّى لَا تَكُونَ فِتْنَةٌ وَيَكُونَ الدِّينُ كُلُّهُ لِلَّهِ فَإِنِ انْتَهَوْا فَإِنَّ اللَّهَ بِمَا يَعْمَلُونَ بَصِيرٌ، وَإِنْ تَوَلَّوْا فَاعْلَمُوا أَنَّ اللَّهَ مَوْلَاكُمْ نِعْمَ الْمَوْلَى وَنِعْمَ النَّصِيرُ) [الأنفال: 38 - 40]

(قَاتِلُوا الَّذِينَ لَا يُؤْمِنُونَ بِاللَّهِ وَلَا بِالْيَوْمِ الْآخِرِ وَلَا يُحَرِّمُونَ مَا حَرَّمَ اللَّهُ وَرَسُولُهُ وَلَا يَدِينُونَ دِينَ الْحَقِّ مِنَ الَّذِينَ أُوتُوا الْكِتَابَ حَتَّى يُعْطُوا الْجِزْيَةَ عَنْ يَدٍ وَهُمْ صَاغِرُونَ، وَقَالَتِ الْيَهُودُ عُزَيْرٌ ابْنُ اللَّهِ وَقَالَتِ النَّصَارَى الْمَسِيحُ ابْنُ اللَّهِ ذَلِكَ قَوْلُهُمْ بِأَفْوَاهِهِمْ يُضَاهِئُونَ قَوْلَ الَّذِينَ كَفَرُوا مِنْ قَبْلُ قَاتَلَهُمُ اللَّهُ أَنَّى يُؤْفَكُونَ، اتَّخَذُوا أَحْبَارَهُمْ وَرُهْبَانَهُمْ أَرْبَابًا مِنْ دُونِ اللَّهِ وَالْمَسِيحَ ابْنَ مَرْيَمَ وَمَا أُمِرُوا إِلَّا لِيَعْبُدُوا إِلَهًا وَاحِدًا لَا إِلَهَ إِلَّا هُوَ سُبْحَانَهُ

عما يُشْرِكُون، يُرِيدُونَ أَنْ يُطْفِئُوا نُورَ اللهِ بِأَفْواهِهِمْ ويَأْبَى اللهُ إلا أَنْ يُتِمَّ نُورَهُ ولو كرِهَ الْكافِرُونَ).. [التوبة: 29 - 32].

إنها مبررات تقرير ألوهية الله في الأرض، وتحقيق منهجه في حياة الناس، ومطاردة الشياطين ومناهج الشياطين، وتحطيم سلطان البشر الذي يتعبد الناس، والناس عبيد لله وحده، لا يجوز أن يحكمهم أحد من عباده بسلطان من عند نفسه وبشريعة من هواه ورأيه. وهذا يكفي. مع تقرير مبدأ: "لا إكراه في الدين". أي لا إكراه على اعتناق العقيدة، بعد الخروج من سلطان العبيد، والإقرار بمبدأ أن السلطان كله لله، أو أن الدين كله لله، بهذا الاعتبار.

إنها مبررات التحرير العام للإنسان في الأرض. بإخراج الناس من العبودية للعباد إلى العبودية لله وحده بلا شريك. وهذه وحدها تكفي. لقد كانت هذه المبررات ماثلة في نفوس الغزاة من المسلمين، فلم يسأل أحد منهم عما أخرجه للجهاد فيقول: خرجنا ندافع عن وطننا المهدد. أو خرجنا نصد عدوان الفرس أو الروم علينا نحن المسلمين. أو خرجنا نوسع رقعتنا ونستكثر من الغنيمة.

لقد كانوا يقولون كما قال ربعي بن عامر. وحذيفة بن محصن والمغيرة بن شعبة جميعا لرستم قائد جيش الفرس في القادسية، وهو يسألهم واحدا بعد واحد في ثلاثة أيام متوالية، قبل المعركة: ما الذي جاء بكم؟ فيكون الجواب: "الله ابتعثنا لنخرج من شاء من عبادة العباد إلى عبادة الله وحده. ومن ضيق الدنيا إلى سعتها. ومن جور الأديان إلى عدل الإسلام. فأرسل رسوله بدينه إلى خلقه، فمن قبله منا قبلنا منه ورجعنا عنه، وتركناه وأرضه. ومن أبى قاتلناه حتى نفضي إلى الجنة أو الظفر".

إن هناك مبررا ذاتيا في طبيعة هذا الدين ذاته، وفي إعلانه العام، وفي منهجه الواقعي لمقابلة الواقع البشري بوسائل مكافئة لكل جوانبه، في مراحل محددة، بوسائل متجددة. وهذا المبرر الذاتي قائم ابتداء - ولو لم يوجد خطر الاعتداء على الأرض الإسلامية وعلى المسلمين فيها - إنه مبرر في طبيعة المنهج وواقعيته، وطبيعة المعوقات الفعلية في المجتمعات البشرية. لا من مجرد ملابسات دفاعية محدودة، وموقوتة.

وإنه ليكفي لأن يخرج المسلم مجاهدا بنفسه وماله. "في سبيل الله". في سبيل هذه القيم التي لا يناله هو من ورائها مغنم ذاتي، ولا يخرجه لها مغنم ذاتي.

إن المسلم قبل أن ينطلق للجهاد في المعركة يكون قد خاض معركة الجهاد الأكبر في نفسه مع الشيطان. مع هوى وشهواته. مع مطامعه ورغباته. مع مصالحه ومصالح عشيرته وقومه. مع كل شارة غير شارة الإسلام. ومع كل دافع إلا العبودية لله، وتحقيق سلطانه في الأرض وطرد سلطان الطواغيت المغتصبين لسلطان الله.

والذين يبحثون عن مبررات للجهاد الإسلامي في حماية "الوطن الإسلامي" يغضون من شأن "المنهج" ويعتبرونه أقل من "الموطن" وهذه ليست نظرة الإسلام إلى هذه الاعتبارات. إنها نظرة مستحدثة غريبة على الحس الإسلامي، فالعقيدة والمنهج الذي تتمثل فيه والمجتمع الذي يسود فيه هذا المنهج هي الاعتبارات الوحيدة في الحس الإسلامي. أما الأرض - بذاتها - فلا اعتبار لها ولا وزن. وكل قيمة للأرض في التصور الإسلامي إنما هي

مستمدة من سيادة منهج الله وسلطانه فيها، وبهذا تكون محضن العقيدة وحقل المنهج و "دار الإسلام "ونقطة الانطلاق لتحرير "الإنسان ".

وحقيقة إن حماية "دار الإسلام "حماية للعقيدة والمنهج والمجتمع الذي يسود فيه المنهج. ولكنها ليست الهدف النهائي، وليست حمايتها هي الغاية الأخيرة لحركة الجهاد الإسلامي، إنما حمايتها هي الوسيلة لقيام مملكة الله فيها، ثم لاتخاذها قاعدة انطلاق إلى الأرض كلها وإلى النوع الإنساني بجملته. فالنوع الإنساني هو موضوع هذا الدين والأرض هي مجاله الكبير.

وكما أسلفنا فإن الانطلاق بالمذهب الإلهي تقوم في وجهه عقبات مادية من سلطة الدولة، ونظام المجتمع، وأوضاع البيئة. وهذه كلها هي التي ينطلق الإسلام ليحطمها بالقوة، كي يخلو له وجه الأفراد من الناس، يخاطب ضمائرهم وأفكارهم، بعد أن يحررها من الأغلال المادية، ويترك لها بعد ذلك حرية الاختيار.

يجب ألا تخدعنا أو تفزعنا حملات المستشرقين على مبدأ "الجهاد "وألا يثقل على عاتقنا ضغط الواقع وثقله في ميزان القوى العالمية، فنروح نبحث للجهاد الإسلامي عن مبررات أدبية خارجة عن طبيعة هذا الدين، في ملابسات دفاعية وقتية، كان الجهاد سينطلق في طريقه سواء وجدت أم لم توجد.

ويجب ونحن نستعرض الواقع التاريخي ألا نغفل عن الاعتبارات الذاتية في طبيعة هذا الدين وإعلانه العام ومنهجه الواقعي، وألا نخلط بينها وبين المقتضيات الدفاعية الوقتية.

حقا إنه لم يكن بد لهذا الدين أن يدافع المهاجمين له، لأن مجرد وجوده في صورة إعلان عام لربوبية الله للعالمين، وتحرير الإنسان من العبودية لغير الله، وتمثل هذا الوجود في تجمع تنظيمي حركي تحت قيادة جديدة غير قيادات الجاهلية، وميلاد مجتمع مستقل متميز لا يعترف لأحد من البشر بالحاكمية، لأن الحاكمية فيه لله وحده. إن مجرد وجود هذا الدين في هذه الصورة لا بد أن يدفع المجتمعات الجاهلية من حوله - القائمة على قاعدة العبودية للعباد - أن تحاول سحقه، دفاعا عن وجودها ذاته، ولا بد أن يتحرك المجتمع الجديد للدفاع عن نفسه.

هذه ملابسة لا بد منها، تولد مع ميلاد الإسلام ذاته، وهذه معركة مفروضة على الإسلام فرضا، ولا خيار له في خوضها، وهذا صراع طبيعي بين وجودين لا يمكن التعايش بينهما طويلا..

هذا كله حق. ووفق هذه النظرة يكون لا بد للإسلام أن يدافع عن وجوده، ولا بد أن يخوض معركة دفاعية مفروضة عليه فرضا.

ولكن هناك حقيقة أخرى أشد أصالة من هذه الحقيقة. إن من طبيعة الوجود الإسلامي ذاته أن يتحرك إلى الأمام ابتداء. لإنقاذ "الإنسان "في "الأرض "من العبودية لغير الله، ولا يمكن أن يقف عند حدود جغرافية، ولا أن ينزوي داخل حدود عنصرية، تاركا "الإنسان ". نوع الإنسان. في "الأرض ". كل الأرض. للشر والفساد والعبودية لغير الله.

إن المعسكرات المعادية للإسلام قد يجيء عليها زمان تؤثر فيه ألا تهاجم الإسلام، إذا تركها الإسلام تزاول عبودية البشر للبشر داخل حدودها الإقليمية، ورضى أن يدعها وشأنها ولم يمد إليها دعوته وإعلانه التحريري العام. ولكن الإسلام لا يهادنها، إلا أن تعلن استسلامها لسلطانه في صورة أداء الجزية، ضمانا لفتح أبوابها لدعوته بلا عوائق مادية من السلطات القائمة فيها.

هذه طبيعة هذا الدين، وهذه وظيفته، بحكم أنه إعلان عام لربوبية الله للعالمين، وتحرير الإنسان من كل عبودية لغير الله في الناس أجمعين.

وفرق بين تصور الإسلام على هذه الطبيعة، وتصوره قابعا داخل حدود إقليمية أو عنصرية، لا يحركه إلا خوف الاعتداء. إنه في هذه الصورة الأخيرة يفقد مبرراته الذاتية في الانطلاق.

إن مبررات الانطلاق الإسلامي تبرز بوضوح وعمق عند تذكر أن هذا الدين هو منهج الله للحياة البشرية، وليس منهج إنسان، ولا مذهب شيعة من الناس، ولا نظام جنس من الأجناس.. ونحن لا نبحث عن مبررات خارجية إلا حين تفتر في حسنا هذه الحقيقة الهائلة. حين ننسى أن القضية هي قضية ألوهية الله وعبودية العباد. إنه لا يمكن أن يستحضر إنسان ما هذه الحقيقة الهائلة ثم يبحث عن مبرر آخر للجهاد الإسلامي.

والمسافة قد لا تبدو كبيرة عند مفرق الطريق، بين تصور أن الإسلام كان مضطرا لخوض معركة لا اختيار له فيها، بحكم وجوده الذاتي ووجود المجتمعات الجاهلية الأخرى التي لا بد أن تهاجمه، وتصور أنه هو بذاته لا بد أن يتحرك ابتداء، فيدخل في هذه المعركة.

المسافة عند مفرق الطريق قد لا تبدو كبيرة، فهو في كلتا الحالتين سيدخل المعركة حتما، ولكنها في نهاية الطريق تبدو هائلة شاسعة، تغير المشاعر والمفهومات الإسلامية تغييرا كبيرا. خطيرا.

إن هناك مسافة هائلة بين اعتبار الإسلام منهجا إلهيا، جاء ليقرر ألوهية الله في الأرض، وعبودية البشر جميعا لإله واحد، ويصب هذا التقرير في قالب واقعي، هو المجتمع الإنساني الذي يتحرر فيه الناس من العبودية للعباد، بالعبودية لرب العباد، فلا تحكمهم إلا شريعة الله، التي يتمثل فيها سلطان الله، أو بتعبير آخر تتمثل فيها ألوهيته. فمن حقه إذن أن يزيل العقبات كلها من طريقه، ليخاطب وجدان الأفراد وعقولهم دون حواجز ولا موانع مصطنعة من نظام الدولة السياسي، أو أوضاع الناس الاجتماعية. إن هناك مسافة هائلة بين اعتبار الإسلام على هذا النحو، واعتباره نظاما محليا في وطن بعينه فمن حقه فقط أن يدفع الهجوم عليه في داخل حدوده الإقليمية.

هذا تصور. وذاك تصور. ولو أن الإسلام في كلتا الحالتين سيجاهد. ولكن التصور الكلي لبواعث هذا الجهاد وأهدافه ونتائجه واتجهه، يختلف اختلافا بعيدا، يدخل في صميم الاعتقاد كما يدخل في صميم الخطة والاتجاه.

إن من حق الإسلام أن يتحرك ابتداء. فالإسلام ليس نحلة قوم، ولا نظام وطن، ولكنه منهج إله، ونظام عالم. ومن حقه أن يتحرك ليحطم الحواجز من الأنظمة والأوضاع

التي تغل من حرية "الإنسان" في الاختيار. وحسبه أنه لا يهاجم الأفراد ليكرههم على اعتناق عقيدته، إنما يهاجم الأنظمة والأوضاع ليحرر الأفراد من التأثيرات الفاسدة، المفسدة للفطرة، المقيدة لحرية الاختيار.

من حق الإسلام أن يُخرج "الناس "من عبادة العباد إلى عبادة الله وحده. ليحقق إعلانه العام بربوبية الله للعالمين، وتحرير الناس أجمعين. وعبادة الله وحده لا تتحقق - في التصور الإسلامي وفي الواقع العملي - إلا في ظل النظام الإسلامي، فهو وحده النظام الذي يشرع الله فيه للعباد كلهم، حاكمهم ومحكومهم، أسودهم وأبيضهم، قاصيهم ودانيهم، فقيرهم وغنيهم، تشريعا واحدا يخضع له الجميع على السواء. أما في سائر الأنظمة، فيعبد الناس العباد، لأنهم يتلقون التشريع لحياتهم من العباد. وهو من خصائص الألوهية، فأيما بشر ادعى لنفسه سلطان التشريع للناس من عند نفسه، فقد ادعى الألوهية اختصاصا وعملا، سواء ادعاها قولا أم لم يعلن هذا الادعاء. وأيما بشر آخر اعترف لذلك البشر بذلك الحق فقد اعترف له بحق الألوهية، سواء سماها باسمها أم لم يسمها.

والإسلام ليس مجرد عقيدة، حتى يقنع بإبلاغ عقيدته للناس بوسيلة البيان. إنما هو منهج يتمثل في تجمع تنظيمي حركي يزحف لتحرير كل الناس، والتجمعات الأخرى لا تمكنه من تنظيم حياة رعاياها وفق منهجه هو، ومن ثم يتحتم على الإسلام أن يزيل هذه الأنظمة بوصفها معوقات للتحرير العام، وهذا - كما قلنا من قبل - معنى أن يكون الدين كله لله، فلا تكون هناك دينونة ولا طاعة لعبد من العباد لذاته. كما هو الشأن في سائر الأنظمة التي تقم على عبودية العباد للعباد.

إن الباحثين الإسلاميين المعاصرين المهزومين تحت ضغط الواقع الحاضر وتحت الهجوم الاستشراقي الماكر، يتحرجون من تقرير تلك الحقيقة، لأن المستشرقين صوروا الإسلام حركة قهر بالسيف للإكراه على العقيدة. والمستشرقون الخبثاء يعرفون جيدا أن هذه ليست هي الحقيقة، ولكنهم يشوهون بواعث الجهاد الإسلامي بهذه الطريقة. ومن ثم يقوم المنافقون - المهزومون - عن سمعة الإسلام، بنفي هذا الاتهام، فيلجأون إلى تلمس المبررات الدفاعية. ويغفلون عن طبيعة الإسلام ووظيفته، وحقه في "تحرير الإنسان "ابتداء.

وقد غشى على أفكار الباحثين العصريين - المهزومين - ذلك التصور الغربي لطبيعة "الدين ". وإنه مجرد "عقيدة "في الضمير، لا شأن لها بالأنظمة الواقعية للحياة. ومن ثم يكون الجهاد للدين، جهادا لفرض العقيدة على الضمير.

ولكن الأمر ليس كذلك في الإسلام، فالإسلام منهج الله للحياة البشرية، وهو منهج يقوم على إفراد الله وحده بالألوهية - متمثلة في الحاكمية - وينظم الحياة الواقعية بكل تفصيلاتها اليومية. فالجهاد له جهاد لتقرير المنهج وإقامة النظام. أما العقيدة فأمر موكول إلى حرية الاقتناع، في ظل النظام العام، بعد رفع جميع المؤثرات. ومن ثم يختلف الأمر من أساسه، وتصبح له صورة جديدة كاملة.

وحيثما وجد التجمع الإسلامي، الذي يتمثل فيه المنهج الإلهي، فإن الله يمنحه حق الحركة والانطلاق لتسلم السلطان وتقرير النظام، مع ترك مسألة العقيدة الوجدانية لحرية

الوجدان، فإذا كف الله أيدي الجماعة المسلمة فترة عن الجهاد، فهذه مسألة خطة لا مسألة مبدأ، مسألة مقتضيات الحركة لا مسألة عقيدة. وعلى هذا الأساس الواضح يمكن أن نفهم النصوص القرآنية المتعددة، في المراحل التاريخية المتجددة، ولا نخلط بين دلالتها المرحلية، والدلالة العامة لخط الحركة الإسلامية الثابت الطويل.

لا إله إلا الله منهج حياة

العبودية لله وحده هي شطر الركن الأول في العقيدة الإسلامية المتمثل في شهادة: أن لا إله إلا الله. والتلقي عن رسول الله - صلى الله عليه وسلم - في كيفية هذه العبودية - هو شطرها الثاني، المتمثل في شهادة أن محمدا رسول الله.

والقلب المؤمن المسلم هو الذي تتمثل فيه هذه القاعدة بشطريها، لأن كل ما بعدهما من مقومات الإيمان، وأركان الإسلام، إنما هو مقتضى لها. فالإيمان بملائكة الله وكتبه ورسله واليوم الآخر والقدر خيره وشره، وكذلك الصلاة والزكاة والصيام والحج، ثم الحدود والتعازير والحل والحرمة والمعاملات والتشريعات والتوجيهات الإسلامية.. إنما تقوم كلها على قاعدة العبودية لله وحده، كما أن المرجع فيها كلها هو ما بلغه لنا رسول الله - صلى الله عليه وسلم - عن ربه.

والمجتمع المسلم هو الذي تتمثل فيه تلك القاعدة ومقتضياتها جميعا لأنه بغير تمثل تلك القاعدة ومقتضياتها فيه لا يكون مسلما.

ومن ثم تصبح شهادة أن لا إله إلا الله، وأن محمدا رسول الله، قاعدة لمنهج كامل تقوم عليه حياة الأمة المسلمة بحذافيرها، فلا تقوم هذه الحياة قبل أن تقوم هذه القاعدة، كما أنها لا تكون حياة إسلامية إذا قامت على غير هذه القاعدة، أو قامت على قاعدة أخرى معها، أو عدة قواعد أجنبية عنها:

(إِنِ الْحُكْمُ إِلَّا لِلَّهِ أَمَرَ أَلَّا تَعْبُدُوا إِلَّا إِيَّاهُ ذَلِكَ الدِّينُ الْقَيِّمُ)..   [يوسف: 40]

(مَنْ يُطِعِ الرَّسُولَ فَقَدْ أَطَاعَ اللَّهَ).   [النساء: 80]

هذا التقرير الموجز المطلق الحاسم يفيدنا في تحديد كلمة الفصل في قضايا أساسية في حقيقة هذا الدين، وفي حركته الواقعية كذلك:

إنه يفيدنا أولا في تحديد "طبيعة المجتمع المسلم ".

ويفيدنا ثانيا في تحديد "منهج نشأة المجتمع المسلم ".

ويفيدنا ثالثا في تحديد "منهج الإسلام في مواجهة المجتمعات الجاهلية ".

ويفيدنا رابعا في تحديد "منهج الإسلام في مواجهة واقع الحياة البشرية ".

وهي قضايا أساسية بالغة الخطورة في منهج الحركة الإسلامية قديما وحديثا.

إن السمة الأولى المميزة لطبيعة (المجتمع المسلم) هي أن هذا المجتمع يقوم على قاعدة العبودية لله وحده في أمره كله. هذه العبودية التي تمثلها وتكيفها شهادة أن لا إله إلا الله، وأن محمدا رسول الله.

وتتمثل هذه العبودية في التصور الاعتقادي، كما تتمثل في الشعائر التعبدية، كما تتمثل في الشرائع القانونية سواء.

فليس عبدا لله وحده من لا يعتقد بوحدانية الله سبحانه:

(وقال اللهُ لا تتخِذُوا إلهينِ اثنينِ إنما هُو إلهٌ واحدٌ فإياي فارهبُون، ولهُ ما في السماواتِ والأرْضِ ولهُ الدينُ واصِبا أفغيْر اللهِ تتقُون).. [النحل: 51 - 52]

ليس عبدا لله وحده من يتقدم بالشعائر التعبدية لأحد غير الله - معه أو من دونه:

(قُلْ إن صلاتي ونُسُكي ومحْياي وممماتي لله رب الْعالمِين، لا شريك لهُ وبِذلِك أُمِرْتُ وأنا أولُ الْمُسْلِمِين) [الأنعام: 162 - 163]

وليس عبدا لله وحده من يتلقى الشرائع القانونية من أحد سوى الله، عن الطريق الذي بلغنا الله به، وهو رسول الله صلى الله عليه وسلم:

(أمْ لهُمْ شُركاءُ شرعُوا لهُمْ مِن الدينِ ما لمْ يأْذنْ بِهِ اللهُ) [الشورى: 21]

(وما آتاكُمُ الرسُولُ فخُذُوهُ وما نهاكُمْ عنْهُ فانْتهُوا) [الحشر: 7]

هذا هو المجتمع المسلم. المجتمع الذي تتمثل العبودية لله وحده في معتقدات أفراده وتصوراتهم، كما تتمثل في شعائرهم وعبادتهم، كما تتمثل في نظامهم الجماعي وتشريعاتهم. وأيما جانب من هذه الجوانب تخلف عن الوجود فقد تخلف الإسلام نفسه عن الوجود. لتخلف ركنه الأول، وهو شهادة أن لا إله إلا الله وأن محمدا رسول الله.

ولقد قلنا: إن العبودية لله تتمثل في "التصور الاعتقادي". فيحسن أن نقول ما هو التصور الاعتقادي الإسلامي. إنه التصور الذي ينشأ في الإدراك البشري من تلقيه لحقائق العقيدة من مصدرها الرباني، والذي يتكيف به الإنسان في إدراكه لحقيقة ربه، ولحقيقة الكون الذي يعيش فيه - غيبه وشهوده - ولحقيقة الحياة التي ينتسب إليها - غيبها وشهودها - ولحقيقة نفسه. أي لحقيقة الإنسان ذاته. ثم يكيف على أساسه تعامله مع هذه الحقائق جميعا، تعامله مع ربه تعاملا تتمثل فيه عبوديته لله وحده، وتعامله مع الكون ونواميسه ومع الأحياء وعوالمها، ومع أفراد النوع البشري وتشكيلاته تعاملا يستمد أصوله من دين الله - كما بلغها رسول الله صلى الله عليه وسلم - تحقيقا لعبوديته لله وحده في هذا التعامل. وهو بهذه الصورة يشمل نشاط الحياة كله.

فإذا تقرر أن هذا هو "المجتمع المسلم"، فكيف ينشأ هذا المجتمع؟ ما منهج هذه النشأة؟

إن هذا المجتمع لا يقوم حتى تنشأ جماعة من الناس تقرر أن عبوديتها الكاملة لله وحده، وأنها لا تدين بالعبودية لغير الله. لا تدين بالعبودية لغير الله في الاعتقاد والتصور، ولا تدين لغير الله في العبادات والشعائر. ولا تدين بالعبودية لغير الله في النظام والشرائع. ثم تأخذ بالفعل في تنظيم حياتها كلها على أساس هذه العبودية الخالصة. تنقي ضمائرها من الاعتقاد في ألوهية أحد غير الله - معه أو من دونه - وتنقي شعائرها من التوجه بها لأحد غير الله - معه أو دونه - وتنقي شرائعها من التلقي عن أحد غير الله - معه أو من دونه.

47

عندئذ - وعندئذ فقط - تكون هذه الجماعة مسلمة، ويكون هذا المجتمع الذي أقامته مسلما كذلك. فأما قبل أن يقرر ناس من الناس إخلاص عبوديتهم لله - على النحو الذي تقدم - فإنهم لا يكونون مسلمين. وأما قبل أن ينظموا حياتهم على هذا الأساس فلا يكون مجتمعهم مسلما. ذلك أن القاعدة الأولى التي يقوم عليها الإسلام، والتي يقوم عليها المجتمع المسلم - هي شهادة أن لا إله إلا الله وأن محمدا رسول الله - لم تقم بشطريها.

وإذن فإنه قبل التفكير في إقامة نظام مجتمع إسلامي، وإقامة مجتمع مسلم على أساس هذا النظام. ينبغي أن يتجه الاهتمام أولا إلى تخليص ضمائر الأفراد من العبودية لغير الله - في أي صورة من صورها التي أسلفنا - وأن يتجمع الأفراد الذين تخلص ضمائرهم من العبودية لغير الله في جماعة مسلمة. وهذه الجماعة التي خلصت ضمائر أفرادها من العبودية لغير الله، اعتقادا وعبادة وشريعة، هي التي ينشأ منها المجتمع المسلم، وينظم إليها من يريد أن يعيش في هذا المجتمع بعقيدته وعبادته وشريعته التي تتمثل فيها العبودية لله وحده. أو بتعبير آخر تتمثل فيها شهادة أن لا إله إلا الله، وأن محمدا رسول الله.

هكذا كانت نشأة الجماعة المسلمة الأولى التي أقامت المجتمع المسلم الأول. وهكذا تكون نشأة كل جماعة مسلمة، وهكذا يقوم كل مجتمع مسلم.

إن المجتمع المسلم إنما ينشأ من انتقال أفراد ومجموعات من الناس من العبودية لغير الله - معه أو من دونه - إلى العبودية لله وحده بلا شريك، ثم من تقرير هذه المجموعات أن تقيم نظام حياتها على أساس هذه العبودية. وعندئذ يتم ميلاد جديد لمجتمع جديد، مشتق من المجتمع الجاهلي القديم، ومواجه له بعقيدة جديدة، ونظام للحياة جديد، يقوم على أساس هذه العقيدة، وتتمثل فيه قاعدة الإسلام الأولى بشطريه. شهادة أن لا إله إلا الله وأن محمدا رسول الله.

وقد ينضم المجتمع الجاهلي القديم بكامله إلى المجتمع الإسلامي الجديد وقد لا ينضم، كما أنه قد يهادن المجتمع المسلم الجديد أو يحاربه، وإن كانت السنة قد جرت بأن يشن المجتمع الجاهلي حربا لا هوادة فيها، سواء على طلائع هذا المجتمع في مرحلة نشوئه - وهو أفراد أو مجموعات - أو على هذا المجتمع نفسه بعد قيامه فعلا - وهو ما حدث في تاريخ الدعوة الإسلامية منذ نوح عليه السلام، إلى محمد عليه الصلاة والسلام، بغير استثناء.

وطبيعي أن المجتمع المسلم الجديد لا ينشأ، ولا يتقرر وجوده إلا إذا بلغ درجة من القوة يواجه بها ضغط المجتمع الجاهلي القديم، قوة الاعتقاد والتصور، وقوة الخلق والبناء النفسي، وقوة التنظيم والبناء الجماعي، وسائر أنواع القوة التي يواجه بها ضغط المجتمع الجاهلي ويتغلب عليه، أو على الأقل يصمد له.

ولكن ما هو "المجتمع الجاهلي" ؟ وما هو منهج الإسلام في مواجهته؟

إن المجتمع الجاهلي هو كل مجتمع غير المجتمع المسلم. وإذا أردنا التحديد الموضوعي قلنا: إنه هو كل مجتمع لا يخلص عبوديته لله وحده. متمثلة هذه العبودية في التصور الاعتقادي، وفي الشعائر التعبدية، وفي الشرائع القانونية.

وبهذا التعريف الموضوعي تدخل في إطار "المجتمع الجاهلي "جميع المجتمعات القائمة اليوم في الأرض فعلا.

تدخل فيه المجتمعات الشيوعية. أولا: بإلحادها في الله - سبحانه - وبإنكار وجوده أصلا، ورجع الفاعلية في هذا الوجود إلى "المادة "أو "الطبيعة "، ورجع الفاعلية في حياة الإنسان وتاريخه إلى "الاقتصاد "أو "أدوات الإنتاج "، ثانيا ": بإقامة نظام العبودية فيه للحزب - على فرض أن القيادة الجماعية في هذا النظام حقيقة واقعة. - لا لله سبحانه. ثم ما يترتب على ذلك التصور وهذا النظام من إهدار لخصائص "الإنسان "وذلك باعتبار أن "المطالب الأساسية "له هي فقط مطالب الحيوان، وهي: الطعام والشراب والملبس والمسكن والجنس. وحرمانه من حاجات روحه "الإنساني "المتميز عن الحيوان، وفي أولها: العقيدة في الله، وحرية اختيارها، وحرية التعبير عنها، وكذلك حرية التعبير عن "فرديته "وهي من أخص خصائص "إنسانيته ". هذه الفردية التي تتجلى في الملكية الفردية، وفي اختيار نوع العمل والتخصص، وفي التعبير الفني عن "الذات "إلى آخر ما يميز "الإنسان "عن "الحيوان "أو عن "الآلة "إذ أن التصور الشيوعي والنظام الشيوعي سواء، كثيرا ما يهبط بالإنسان عن مرتبة الحيوان إلى مرتبة الآلة.

وتدخل فيه المجتمعات الوثنية - وهي ما تزال قائمة في الهند واليابان والفلبين وأفريقية - تدخل فيه - أولا: بتصورها الاعتقادي القائم على تأليه غير الله - معه أو من دونه - وتدخل فيه ثانيا: بتقديم الشعائر التعبدية لشتى الآلهة والمعبودات التي تعتقد بألوهيتها. كذلك تدخل فيه بإقامة أنظمة وشرائع، المرجع فيها لغير الله وشريعته. سواء استمدت هذه الأنظمة والشرائع من المعابد والكهنة والسدنة والسحرة والشيوخ، أو استمدتها من هيئات مدنية "علمانية "تملك سلطة التشريع دون الرجوع إلى شريعة الله. أي أن لها الحاكمية العليا باسم (الشعب) أو باسم (الحزب) أو باسم كائن من كان. ذلك أن الحاكمية العليا لا تكون إلا لله سبحانه، ولا تزاول إلا بالطريقة التي بلغها عنه رسله.

وتدخل فيه المجتمعات اليهودية والنصرانية في أرجاء الأرض جميعا. تدخل فيه هذه المجتمعات أولا: بتصورها الاعتقادي المحرف، الذي لا يفرد الله - سبحانه - بالألوهية بل يجعل له شركاء في صورة من صور الشرك، سواء بالبنوة أو بالتثليث، أو بتصور الله سبحانه على غير حقيقته، وتصور علاقة خلقه به على غير حقيقتها:

(وقالتِ الْيَهُودُ عُزَيْرٌ ابْنُ اللهِ وقالتِ النصارى الْمَسِيحُ ابْنُ اللهِ ذلِكَ قَوْلُهُمْ بِأَفْوَاهِهِمْ يُضَاهِئُون قَوْلَ الَّذِين كفَرُوا مِنْ قَبْلُ قاتلهُمُ اللهُ أَنَّى يُؤْفَكُون) [التوبة: 30]

(لَقَدْ كَفَرَ الَّذِين قالُوا إِن الله ثالِثُ ثلاثةٍ وما مِنْ إِلهٍ إِلا إِلهٌ واحِدٌ وإِنْ لَمْ يَنْتَهُوا عما يَقُولُون لَيمسن الَّذِين كفَرُوا مِنْهُمْ عذابٌ أَلِيمٌ).. [المائدة: 63]

(وقالتِ الْيَهُودُ يَدُ اللهِ مَغْلُولَةٌ غُلَّتْ أَيْدِيهِمْ وَلُعِنُوا بِما قالُوا بَلْ يَداهُ مَبْسُوطَتانِ يُنْفِقُ كَيْفَ يَشاءُ).. [المائدة: 64]

(وقالتِ الْيَهُودُ والنصارى نَحْنُ أَبْناءُ اللهِ وأَحِبّاؤُهُ قُلْ فَلِمَ يُعذبُكُمْ بِذُنُوبِكُمْ بَلْ أَنْتُمْ بَشَرٌ مِمَّنْ خَلَقَ).. [المائدة: 18]

وتدخل فيه كذلك بشعائرها التعبدية ومراسمها وطقوسها المنبثقة من التصورات الاعتقادية المنحرفة الضالة. ثم تدخل فيه بأنظمتها وشرائعها، وهي كلها لا تقوم على العبودية لله وحده، بالإقرار له وحده بحق الحاكمية، واستمداد السلطان من شرعه، بل تقيم هيئات من البشر، لها حق الحاكمية العليا التي لا تكون إلا لله سبحانه. وقديما وصمهم الله بالشرك لأنهم جعلوا هذا الحق للأحبار والرهبان، يشرعون لهم من عند أنفسهم فيقبلون منهم ما يشرعونه:

(اتخَذُوا أَحْبارَهُمْ ورُهْبانَهُمْ أَرْبابا مِنْ دُونِ اللهِ والْمَسِيحَ ابْنَ مَرْيمَ وما أُمِرُوا إلا لِيَعْبُدُوا إلها واحِدا لا إلهَ إلا هُوَ سُبْحانَهُ عما يُشْرِكُونَ). [التوبة: 31]

وهم لم يكونوا يعتقدون في ألوهية الأحبار والرهبان. ولم يكونوا يتقدمون لهم بالشعائر التعبدية، إنما كانوا فقط يعترفون لهم بحق الحاكمية، فيقبلون منهم ما يشرعونه لهم، بما لم يأذن به الله، فأولى أن يوصموا اليوم بالشرك والكفر، وقد جعلوا ذلك لناس منهم ليسوا أحبارا ولا رهبانا. وكلهم سواء.

وأخيرا يدخل في إطار المجتمع الجاهلي تلك المجتمعات التي تزعم لنفسها أنها "مسلمة ".

وهذه المجتمعات لا تدخل في هذا الإطار لأنها تعتقد بألوهية أحد غير الله، ولا لأنها تقدم الشعائر التعبدية لغير الله أيضا، ولكنها تدخل في هذا الإطار لأنها لا تدين بالعبودية لله وحده في نظام حياتها. فهي - وإن لم تعتقد بألوهية أحد إلا الله - تعطي أخص خصائص الألوهية لغير الله، فتدين بحاكمية غير الله، فتتلقى من هذه الحاكمية نظامها، وشرائعها وقيمها، وموازينها، وعاداتها وتقاليدها. وكل مقومات حياتها تقريبا.

والله سبحانه يقول عن الحاكمين:

(ومَنْ لَمْ يَحْكُمْ بِما أَنْزَل اللهُ فَأُولئِكَ هُمُ الْكافِرُونَ). [المائدة: 44]

ويقول عن المحكومين:

(أَلَمْ تَرَ إلى الذِينَ يَزْعُمُونَ أَنَّهُمْ آمَنُوا بِما أُنْزِل إلَيْكَ وما أُنْزِل مِنْ قَبْلِكَ يُرِيدُونَ أَنْ يَتَحاكَمُوا إلى الطّاغُوتِ وقَدْ أُمِرُوا أَنْ يَكْفُرُوا بِهِ..) إلى أن يقول {.. فَلا وربِّكَ لا يُؤْمِنُونَ حتى يُحَكِّمُوكَ فِيما شَجَر بَيْنَهُمْ ثُم لا يَجِدُوا في أَنْفُسِهِمْ حرَجا مِما قَضَيْتَ ويُسَلِّمُوا تَسْلِيما). [النساء: 60 - 65]

كما إنه - سبحانه - قد وصف اليهود والنصارى من قبل بالشرك والكفر والحيدة عن عبادة الله وحده، واتخاذ الأحبار والرهبان أربابا من دونه، لمجرد أن جعلوا للأحبار والرهبان ما يجعله الذين يقولون عن أنفسهم أنهم "مسلمون "لناس منهم. واعتبر الله سبحانه ذلك

50

من اليهود والنصارى شركًا كاتخاذهم عيسى ابن مريم ربًا يؤلهونه ويعبدونه سواء. فهذه كتلك خروج من العبودية لله وحده، فهي خروج من دين الله، ومن شهادة أن لا إله إلا الله.

وهذه المجتمعات بعضها يعلن صراحة "علمانيته "وعدم علاقته بالدين أصلًا، وبعضها يعلن أنه "يحترم الدين "ولكنه يخرج الدين من نظامه الاجتماعي أصلًا، ويقول: إنه ينكر "الغيبية "ويقيم نظامه على "العلمية "باعتبار أن العلمية تناقض الغيبية. وهو زعم جاهل لا يقول به إلا الجهال (15) وبعضها يجعل الحاكمية الفعلية لغير الله ويشرع ما يشاء ثم يقول عما يشرعه من عند نفسه: هذه شريعة الله.. وكلها سواء في أنها لا تقوم على العبودية لله وحده.

وإذا تعين هذا، فإن موقف الإسلام من هذه المجتمعات الجاهلية كلها يتحدد في عبارة واحدة:

إنه يرفض الاعتراف بإسلامية هذه المجتمعات كلها وشرعيتها في اعتباره.

إن الإسلام لا ينظر إلى العنوانات واللافتات والشارات التي تحملها هذه المجتمعات على اختلافها. إنها كلها تلتقي في حقيقة واحدة. وهي أن الحياة فيها لا تقوم على العبودية الكاملة لله وحده. وهي من ثم تلتقي - مع سائر المجتمعات الأخرى - في صفة واحدة. صفة "الجاهلية ".

وهذا يقودنا إلى القضية الخطيرة وهي منهج الإسلام في مواجهة الواقع البشري كله. اليوم وغدًا وإلى آخر الزمان. وهنا ينفعنا ما قررناه في الفقرة الأولى عن "طبيعة المجتمع المسلم "، وقيامه على العبودية لله وحده في أمره كله.

إن تحديد هذه الطبيعة يجيب إجابة حاسمة عن هذا السؤال:

- ما الأصل الذي ترجع إليه الحياة البشرية وتقوم عليه؟ أهو دين الله ومنهجه للحياة؟ أم هو الواقع البشري أيًا كان؟

إن الإسلام يجيب على هذا السؤال إجابة حاسمة لا يتلعثم فيها ولا يتردد لحظة. إن الأصل الذي يجب أن ترجع إليه الحياة البشرية بجملتها هو دين الله ومنهجه للحياة. إن شهادة أن لا إله إلا الله وأن محمدًا رسول الله هي ركن الإسلام الأول، لا تقوم ولا تؤدى إلا أن يكون هذا هو الأصل. وأن العبودية لله وحده مع التلقي في كيفية هذه العبودية عن رسول الله - صلى الله عليه وسلم - لا تتحقق إلا أن يعترف بهذا الأصل، ثم يتبع اتباعًا كاملًا بلا تلعثم ولا تردد:

(وما آتاكُم الرسُولُ فخُذُوهُ وما نهاكُم عنْهُ فانْتهُوا) [الحشر: 7]

---

(15) يراجع ما جاء في تفسير قوله تعالى: { وَعِنْدَهُ مَفَاتِحُ الْغَيْبِ لَا يَعْلَمُهَا إِلَّا هُوَ } في الجزء السابع من الظلال.

ثم إن الإسلام يسأل:

(أَأَنْتُمْ أَعْلَمُ أَمِ اللهُ)

ويجيب:

(وَاللهُ يَعْلَمُ وَأَنْتُمْ لا تَعْلَمُون). (وما أُوتِيتُمْ مِن الْعِلْمِ إلا قَلِيلا).

والذي يعلم - والذي يخلق ويرزق كذلك - هو الذي يحكم. ودينه الذي هو منهجه
للحياة، هو الأصل الذي ترجع إليه الحياة. أما واقع البشر ونظرياتهم ومذاهبهم فهي تفسد
وتنحرف، وتقوم على علم البشر الذين لا يعلمون، والذين لم يؤتوا من العلم إلا قليلا.

ودين الله ليس غامضا، ومنهجه للحياة ليس مائعا. فهو محدد بشطر الشهادة الثاني:
محمد رسول الله، فهو محصور فيما بلغه رسول الله صلى الله عليه وسلم، من النصوص
في الأصول. فإن كان هناك نص فالنص هو الحكم، ولا اجتهاد مع النص. وإن لم يكن هناك
نص فهنا يجيء دور الاجتهاد - وفق أصوله المقررة في منهج الله ذاته. لا وفق الأهواء
والرغبات -:

(فإِنْ تنازَعْتُمْ في شيءٍ فرُدوهُ إلى اللهِ والرسُولِ). [النساء: 59]

والأصول المقررة للاجتهاد والاستنباط مقررة كذلك ومعروفة وليست غامضة ولا
مائعة. فليس لأحد أن يقول لشرع يشرعه: هذا شرع الله، إلا أن تكون الحاكمية العليا لله
معلنة، وأن يكون مصدر السلطات هو الله سبحانه لا (الشعب) ولا (الحزب) ولا أي من
البشر، وأن يرجع إلى كتاب الله وسنة رسوله لمعرفة ما يريده الله ولا يكون هذا لكل من يريد
أن يدعي سلطانا باسم الله. كالذي عرفته أوروبا يوم ذات باسم "الثيوقراطية "أو "الحكم
المقدس "فليس شيء من هذا في الإسلام. وما يملك أحد أن ينطق باسم الله إلا رسوله -
صلى الله عليه وسلم - وإنما هنالك نصوص معينة هي التي تحدد ما شرع الله.

إن كلمة "الدين للواقع "يساء فهمها، ويساء استخدامها كذلك. نعم إن هذا الدين
للواقع. ولكن لأي واقع.

. إنه الواقع الذي ينشئه هذا الدين نفسه، وفق منهجه، منطبقا على الفطرة البشرية
في سوائها، ومحققا للحاجات الإنسانية الحقيقية في شمولها. هذه الحاجات التي يقررها
الذي خلق، والذي يعلم من خلق:

(ألا يعْلَمُ منْ خلق وهُو اللطيفُ الخبِيرُ) [الملك: 14]

والدين لا يواجه الواقع أيا كان ليقره ويبحث له عن سند منه، وعن حكم شرعي يعلقه
عليه كاللافتة المستعارة. إنما يواجه الواقع ليزنه بميزانه، فيقر منه ما يقر، ويلغي منه ما يلغي،
وينشئ واقعا إن كان لا يرتضيه، وواقعه الذي ينشئه هو الواقع. وهذا المعنى بأن
الإسلام: "دين للواقع ". أو ما يجب أن تعنيه في مفهومها الصحيح.

ولعله يثار هنا سؤال:

"أليست مصلحة البشر هي التي يجب أن تصوغ واقعهم؟ ".

ومرة أخرى نرجع إلى السؤال الذي يطرحه الإسلام ويجيب عليه:

- **(أَأَنْتُمْ أَعْلَمُ أَمِ اللهُ)؟**

- **(واللهُ يَعْلَمُ وأَنْتُمْ لا تَعْلَمُون).**

إن مصلحة البشر متضمنة في شرع الله، كما أنزله الله، وكما بلغه عنه رسول الله. فإذا بدا للبشر ذات يوم أن مصلحتهم في مخالفة ما شرع الله لهم، فهم، أولا: "واهمون" فيما بدا لهم.

(إِنْ يَتَّبِعُونَ إِلا الظَّنَّ وما تَهْوى الأَنْفُسُ ولقدْ جاءهُمْ مِنْ ربِهِمُ الْهُدى، أَمْ لِلْإِنْسانِ ما تمنى، فلِلهِ الْآخِرَةُ والْأُولى).. [النجم:23-25]

وهم. ثانيا: "كافرون ". فما يدعي أحد أن المصلحة فيما يراه هو مخالفا لما شرع الله، ثم يبقى لحظة واحدة على هذا الدين. ومن أهل هذا الدين.

شريعةٌ كوْنِية

إن الإسلام حين يقيم بناءه الاعتقادي في الضمير والواقع على أساس العبودية الكاملة لله وحده، ويجعل هذه العبودية متمثلة في الاعتقاد والعبادة والشريعة على السواء، باعتبار أن هذه العبودية الكاملة لله وحده - في صورتها هذه - هي المدلول العملي لشهادة أن لا إله إلا الله. وأن التلقي في كيفية هذه العبودية عن رسول الله - صلى الله عليه وسلم - وحده هو المدلول العملي كذلك لشهادة أن محمدا رسول الله..

إن الإسلام حين يقيم بناءه كله على هذا الأساس، بحيث تمثل شهادة أن لا إله إلا الله وأن محمدا رسول الله منهج الحياة في الإسلام، وتصور ملامح هذا المنهج، وتقرر خصائصه. إن الإسلام حين يقيم بناءه على هذا النحو الفريد الذي يفرقه عن جميع الأنظمة الأخرى التي عرفتها البشرية. إنما يرجع إلى أصل أشمل في تقريره عن الوجود كله، لا عن الوجود الإنساني وحده. وإلى منهج للوجود كله لا منهج للحياة الإنسانية وحدها.

إن التصور الإسلامي يقوم على أساس أن هذا الوجود كله من خلق الله، اتجهت إرادة الله إلى كونه فكان، وأودعه الله - سبحانه - قوانينه التي يتحرك بها، والتي تتناسق بها حركة أجزائه فيما بينها، كما تتناسق بها حركته الكلية سواء.

(إِنما قَوْلُنا لِشيءٍ إِذا أرَدْناهُ أنْ نَقُول لهُ كُنْ فيَكُونُ) [النحل: 40].

(وخلق كُل شيءٍ فقدرهُ تقْدِيرا). [الفرقان: 2].

إن وراء هذا الوجود الكوني مشيئة تدبره، وقدرا يحركه، وناموسا ينسقه. هذا الناموس ينسق بين مفردات هذا الوجود كلها، وينظم حركاتها جميعا، فلا تصطدم، ولا تختل، ولا تتعارض، ولا تتوقف عن الحركة المنتظمة المستمرة - إلى ما شاء الله - كما إن هذا الوجود خاضع مستسلم للمشيئة التي تدبره، والقدر الذي يحركه، والناموس الذي ينسقه، بحيث لا يخطر له في لحظة واحدة أن يتمرد على المشيئة، أو أن يتنكر للقدر، أو أن يخالف الناموس وهو لهذا كله صالح لا يدركه العطب والفساد إلا أن يشاء الله:

(إن ربكُم اللهُ الذي خلق السماواتِ والأرْض في سِتةِ أيامٍ ثُم اسْتوى على الْعَرْش يُغْشِي اللَّيْل النهار يطْلُبُهُ حثِيثا والشمْس والْقمر والنجُوم مُسخراتٍ بِأمْرِهِ ألا لهُ الْخَلْقُ والْأمْرُ تبارك اللهُ رب الْعالمِين). [الأعراف: 54].

والإنسان من هذا الوجود الكوني، والقوانين التي تحكم فطرته ليست بمعزل عن ذلك الناموس الذي يحكم الوجود كله. لقد خلقه الله - كما خلق هذا الوجود - وهو في تكوينه المادي من طين هذه الأرض، وما وهبة الله من خصائص زائدة على مادة الطين جعلت منه إنسانا، إنما رزقه الله إياه مقدرا تقديرا، وهو خاضع من ناحية كيانه الجسمي للناموس الطبيعي الذي سنه الله له - رضي أم أبي - وخلقه وجوده وخلقه ابتداء بمشيئة الله لا بمشيئته هو ولا بمشيئة أبيه وأمه - فهما يلتقيان ولكنهما لا يملكان أن يعطيا جنين وجوده - وهو يُولد وفق الناموس الذي وضعه الله لمدة الحمل وظروف الولادة. وهو يتنفس هذا الهواء

الذي أوجده الله بمقاديره هذه، ويتنفسه بالقدر وبالكيفية التي أرادها الله له. وهو يحس ويتألم، ويجوع ويعطش، يأكل ويشرب، ويمثل الطعام والشراب. وبالجملة يعيش. وفق ناموس الله، عن غير إرادة منه ولا اختيار، شأنه في هذا شأن هذا الوجود الكوني وكل ما فيه وكل من فيه، في الخضوع المطلق لمشيئة الله وقدره وناموسه..

والله الذي خلق هذا الوجود الكوني وخلق الإنسان، والذي أخضع الإنسان لنواميسه التي أخضع لها الوجود الكوني. هو - سبحانه - الذي سن للإنسان "شريعة "لتنظيم حياته الإرادية تنظيما متناسقا مع حياته الطبيعية. فالشريعة - على هذا الأساس - إن هي إلا قطاع من الناموس الإلهي العام الذي يحكم فطرة الإنسان، وفطرة الوجود العام، وينسقها كلها جملة واحدة.

وما من كلمة من كلمات الله، ولا أمر ولا نهي، ولا وعد ولا وعيد، ولا تشريع ولا توجيه.. إلا هي شطر من الناموس العام، وصادقة في ذاتها صدق القوانين التي نسميها القوانين الطبيعية - أي القوانين الإلهية الكونية - التي نراها تتحقق في كل لحظة، بحكم ما في طبيعتها من حق أزلي أودعه الله فيها، وهي تتحقق بقدر الله.

و "الشريعة "التي سنها الله لتنظيم حياة البشر هي - من ثم - شريعة كونية. بمعنى أنها متصلة بناموس الكون العام، ومتناسقة معه. ومن ثم فإن الالتزام بها ناشئ من ضرورة تحقيق التناسق بين حياة الإنسان، وحركة الكون الذي يعيش فيه. بل من ضرورة تحقيق التناسق بين القوانين التي تحكم فطرة البشر المضمرة والقوانين التي تحكم حياتهم الظاهرة. وضرورة الالتئام بين الشخصية المضمرة والشخصية الظاهرة للإنسان.

ولما كان البشر لا يملكون أن يدركوا جميع السنن الكونية، ولا أن يحيطوا بأطراف الناموس العام - ولا حتى بهذا الذي يحكم فطرتهم ذاتها ويخضعهم له - رضوا أم أبوا - فإنهم - من ثم - لا يملكون أن يشرعوا لحياة البشر نظاما يتحقق به التناسق المطلق بين حياة الناس وحركة الكون، ولا حتى التناسق بين فطرتهم المضمرة وحياتهم الظاهرة. إنما يملك هذا خالق الكون وخالق البشر، ومدبر أمره وأمرهم، وفق الناموس الواحد الذي اختاره وارتضاه.

وكذلك يصبح العمل بشريعة الله واجبا لتحقيق ذلك التناسق. وذلك فوق وجوبه لتحقق الإسلام اعتقادا. فلا وجود للإسلام في حياة فرد أو حياة جماعة، إلا بإخلاص العبودية لله وحده، وبالتلقي في كيفية هذه العبودية عن رسول الله وحده، تحقيقا لمدلول ركن الإسلام الأول: شهادة أن لا إله إلا الله، وأن محمدا رسول الله.

وفي تحقيق التناسق المطلق بين حياة البشر وناموس الكون كل الخير للبشر، كما أن فيه الصيانة للحياة من الفساد. إنهم - في هذه الحالة وحدها - يعيشون في سلام من أنفسهم. فأما السلام مع الكون فينشأ من تطابق حركتهم مع حركة الكون، وتطابق اتجاههم مع اتجاهه. وأما السلام مع أنفسهم فينشأ من توافق حركتهم مع دوافع فطرتهم الصحيحة، فلا تقوم المعركة بين المرء وفطرته، لأن شريعة الله تنسق بين الحركة الظاهرة والفطرة المضمرة، في يسر وهدوء. وينشأ عن هذا التنسيق تنسيق آخر في ارتباط الناس ونشاطهم العام، لأنهم جميعا يسلكون حينئذ وفق منهج موحد، هو طرف من الناموس الكوني العام.

كذلك يتحقق الخير للبشرية عن طريق إهتدائها وتعرفها في يسر إلى أسرار هذا الكون، والطاقات المكنونة فيه والكنوز المذخورة في أطوائه . واستخدام هذا كله وفق شريعة الله، لتحقيق الخير البشري العام، بلا تعارض ولا اصطدام.

ومقابل شريعة الله هو أهواء البشر:

(ولو اتبع الْحق أهواءهُم لفسدتِ السماواتُ والأرْضُ ومنْ فيهن).. [المؤمنون: 71].

ومن ثم توحد النظرة الإسلامية بين الحق الذي يقوم عليه هذا الدين، والحق الذي تقوم عليه السموات والأرض. ويصلح عليه أمر الدنيا والآخرة، ويحاسب الله به ويجازي من يتعدونه. فهو حق واحد لا يتعدد، وهو الناموس الكوني العام الذي أراده الله لهذا الوجود في جميع الأحوال، والذي يخضع له ويؤخذ به كل ما في الوجود من عوالم وأشياء وأحياء.

(لقدْ أنْزلْنا إليْكُمْ كِتابا فيهِ ذكْرُكُمْ أفلا تغْقِلُون، وكمْ قصمْنا مِنْ قرْية كانتْ ظالمة وأنْشأنا بعْدها قوْما آخرين، فلما أحسوا بأسنا إذا هُمْ مِنْها يركُضُون، لا تركُضُوا وارْجِعُوا إلى ما أتْرِفْتُمْ فيهِ ومساكِنِكُمْ لعلكُمْ تُسْألُون، قالُوا يا ويْلنا إنا كُنا ظالِمين، فما زالتْ تِلْك دعْواهُمْ حتى جعلْناهُمْ حصيدا خامِدين، وما خلقْنا السماء والأرْض وما بيْنهُما لاعِبين، لوْ أردْنا أنْ نتخِذ لهْوا لاتخذْناهُ مِنْ لدُنا إنْ كُنا فاعِلين، بلْ نقْذِفُ بِالْحق على الْباطِل فيدْمغُهُ فإذا هُو زاهِقٌ ولكُمُ الْويْلُ مِما تصِفُون، ولهُ منْ في السماواتِ والأرْض ومنْ عِنْدهُ لا يسْتكْبِرُون عنْ عِبادتِه ولا يسْتحْسِرُون، يُسبحُون الليْل والنهار لا يفْتُرُون).. [الأنبياء: 10 - 20].

وفطرة الإنسان تدرك هذا الحق في أعماقها، فطبيعة تكوينه وطبيعة هذا الكون كله من حوله، توحي إلى فطرته بأن هذا الوجود قائم على الحق، وأن الحق أصيل فيه، وأنه ثابت على الناموس، لا يضطرب، ولا تتفرق به السبل، ولا تختلف دورته. ولا يصطدم بعضه ببعض، ولا يسير وفق المصادفة العابرة والفلتة الشاردة، ولا وفق الهوى المتقلب والرغبة الجامحة. إنما يمضي في نظامه الدقيق المحكم المقدر تقديرا. ومن ثم يقع الشقاق - أول ما يقع - بين الإنسان وفطرته عندما يحيد عن الحق الكامن في أعماقها، تحت تأثير هواه، وذلك عندما يتخذ شريعة لحياته مستمدة من هذا الهوى لا من شريعة الله، وعندما لا يستسلم لله استسلام هذا الوجود الكوني الخاضع لمولاه.

ومثل هذا الشقاق يقع بين الأفراد والجماعات والأمم والأجيال، كما يقع بين البشر والكون من حولهم، فتنقلب قواه وذخائره وسائل تدمير وأسباب شقاء، بدلا من أن تكون وسائل عمران وأسباب سعادة لبني الإنسان.

وإذن فإن الهدف الظاهر من قيام شريعة الله في الأرض ليس مجرد العمل للآخرة. فالدنيا والآخرة معا مرحلتان متكاملتان، وشريعة الله هي التي تنسق بين المرحلتين في حياة هذا الإنسان. تنسق الحياة كلها مع الناموس الإلهي العام.

والتناسق مع الناموس لا يؤجل سعادة الناس إلى الآخرة، بل يجعلها واقعة ومتحققة في المرحلة الأولى كذلك، ثم تتم تمامها وتبلغ كمالها في الدار الآخرة.

هذا هو أساس التصور الإسلامي للوجود كله، وللوجود الإنساني في ظل ذلك الوجود العام، وهو تصور يختلف في طبيعته اختلافا جوهريا عن كل تصور آخر عرفته البشرية، ومن ثم تقوم عليه التزامات لا تقوم على أي تصور آخر في جميع الأنظمة والنظريات.

إن الالتزام بشريعة الله - في هذا التصور - هو مقتضى الإرتباط التام بين حياة البشر وحياة الكون، وبين الناموس الذي يحكم فطرة البشر ويحكم هذا الكون، ثم ضرورة المطابقة بين هذا الناموس العام والشريعة التي تنظم حياة بني الإنسان، وتتحقق بالتزامها عبودية البشر لله وحده، كما أن عبودية هذا الكون لله وحده لا يدعيها لنفسه إنسان.

وإلى ضرورة هذا التطابق والتناسق يشير الحوار الذي جرى بين إبراهيم - عليه السلام - أبي هذه الأمة المسلمة - وبين "نمرود" المتجبر المدعي بحق السلطان على العباد في الأرض، والذي لم يستطع - مع ذلك - أن يدعي بحق السلطان على الأفلاك والأجرام في الكون، وبهت أمام إبراهيم عليه السلام، وهو يقول له: إن الذي يملك السلطان في الكون هو وحده الذي ينبغي أن يكون له السلطان في حياة البشر، ولم يحر جوابا على هذا البرهان:

(أَلَمْ تَرَ إِلَى الَّذِي حَاجَّ إِبْرَاهِيمَ فِي رَبِّهِ أَنْ آتَاهُ اللهُ الْمُلْكَ إِذْ قَالَ إِبْرَاهِيمُ رَبِّي الَّذِي يُحْيِي وَيُمِيتُ قَالَ أَنَا أُحْيِي وَأُمِيتُ قَالَ إِبْرَاهِيمُ فَإِنَّ اللهَ يَأْتِي بِالشَّمْسِ مِنَ الْمَشْرِقِ فَأْتِ بِهَا مِنَ الْمَغْرِبِ فَبُهِتَ الَّذِي كَفَرَ وَاللهُ لاَ يَهْدِي الْقَوْمَ الظَّالِمِينَ). [البقرة: 258].

وصدق الله العظيم:

(أَفَغَيْرَ دِينِ اللهِ يَبْغُونَ وَلَهُ أَسْلَمَ مَنْ فِي السَّمَاوَاتِ وَالْأَرْضِ طَوْعًا وَكَرْهًا وَإِلَيْهِ يُرْجَعُونَ). [آل عمران: 83].

الإسلامُ هُو الحضارة

الإسلام لا يعرف إلا نوعين اثنين من المجتمعات.. مجتمع إسلامي، ومجتمع جاهلي.

"المجتمع الإسلامي "هو المجتمع الذي يطبق فيه الإسلام. عقيدة وعبادة، وشريعة ونظاما، وخلقا وسلوكا. و "المجتمع الجاهلي "هو المجتمع الذي لا يطبق فيه الإسلام، ولا تحكمه عقيدته وتصوراته، وقيمه وموازينه، ونظامه وشرائعه، وخلقه وسلوكه.

ليس المجتمع الإسلامي هو الذي يضم ناسا ممن يسمون أنفسهم "مسلمين "، بينما شريعة الإسلام ليست هي قانون هذا المجتمع، وإن صلى وصام وحج البيت الحرام. وليس المجتمع الإسلامي هو الذي يبتدع لنفسه إسلاما من عند نفسه - غير ما قرره الله سبحانه، وفصله رسوله صلى الله عليه وسلم، ويسميه مثلا "الإسلام المتطور ".

و "المجتمع الجاهلي "قد يتمثل في صور شتى - كلها جاهلية -:

قد يتمثل في صورة مجتمع ينكر وجود الله تعالى، ويفسر التاريخ تفسيرا ماديا جدليا، ويطبق ما يسميه "الاشتراكية العلمية "نظاما.

وقد يتمثل في مجتمع لا ينكر وجود الله تعالى، ولكن يجعل له ملكوت السماوات، ويعزله عن ملكوت الأرض، فلا يطبق شريعته في نظام الحياة، ولا يحكم قيمه التي جعلها هو قيما ثابتة في حياة البشر، ويبيح للناس أن يعبدوا الله في البيع والكنائس والمساجد، ولكنه يحرم عليهم أن يطالبوا بتحكيم شريعة الله في حياتهم، وهو بذلك ينكر أو يعطل ألوهية الله في الأرض، التي ينص عليها قوله تعالى:

(وهُو الذِي فِي السماءِ إِلهٌ وفِي الأَرْضِ إِلهٌ). [الزخرف: 84].

ومن ثم لا يكون هذا المجتمع في دين الله الذي يحدده قوله:

(إِنِ الْحُكْمُ إِلا لِلَّهِ أَمَرَ أَلَّا تَعْبُدُوا إِلَّا إِيَّاهُ ذلِكَ الدينُ الْقيمُ). [يوسف: 40].

وبذلك يكون مجتمعا جاهليا، ولو أقر بوجود الله سبحانه ولو ترك الناس يقدمون الشعائر لله، في البيع والكنائس والمساجد.

"المجتمع الإسلامي "- بصفته تلك - هو وحده "المجتمع المتحضر "، والمجتمعات الجاهلية - بكل صورها المتعددة - مجتمعات متخلفة. ولا بد من إيضاح لهذه الحقيقة الكبيرة.

لقد كنت قد أعلنتُ مرة عن كتاب لي تحت الطبع بعنوان: "نحو مجتمع إسلامي متحضر ". ثم عدت في الإعلان التالي عنه فحذفت كلمة "متحضر "مكتفيا بأن يكون عنوان البحث - كما هو موضوعه - "نحو مجتمع إسلامي ".

ولفت هذا التعديل نظر كاتب جزائري (يكتبه بالفرنسية) ففسره على أنه ناشئ من "عملية دفاع نفسية داخلية عن الإسلام "وأسف لأن هذه العملية - غير الواعية - تحرمني مواجهة "المشكلة "على حقيقتها.

أنا أعذر هذا الكاتب. لقد كنت مثله من قبل. كنت أفكر على النحو الذي يفكر هو عليه الآن. عندما فكرت في الكتابة عن هذا الموضوع لأول مرة.. وكانت المشكلة عندي - كما هي عنده اليوم - هي مشكلة: "تعريف الحضارة ".

لم أكن قد تخلصت بعد من ضغط الرواسب الثقافية في تكويني العقلي والنفسي، وهي رواسب آتية من مصادر أجنبية. غريبة على حسي الإسلامي. وعلى الرغم من اتجاهي الإسلامي الواضح في ذلك الحين، إلا أن هذه الرواسب كانت تغبش تصوري وتطمسه. كان تصور "الحضارة "- كما هو الفكر الأوروبي - يخال لي، ويغبش تصوري، ويحرمني الرؤية الواضحة الأصيلة.

ثم انجلت الصورة. "المجتمع المسلم "هو "المجتمع المتحضر ". فكلمة "المتحضر "إذن لغو، لا يضيف شيئا جديدا. على العكس تنقل هذه الكلمة إلى حس القارئ تلك الظلال الأجنبية الغربية التي كانت تغبش تصوري، وتحرمني الرؤية الواضحة الأصيلة.

الاختلاف إذن هو على "تعريف الحضارة ". ولا بد إذن من إيضاح لهذه الحقيقة.

حين تكون الحاكمية العليا في مجتمع لله وحده - متمثلة في سيادة الشريعة الإلهية - تكون هذه هي الصورة الوحيدة التي يتحرر فيها البشر تحررا كاملا وحقيقيا من العبودية للبشر. وتكون هذه هي "الحضارة الإنسانية "لأن حضارة الإنسان تقتضي قاعدة أساسية من التحرر الحقيقي الكامل للإنسان، ومن الكرامة المطلقة لكل فرد في المجتمع. ولا حرية - في الحقيقة - ولا كرامة للإنسان - ممثلا في كل فرد من أفراده - في مجتمع بعضه أرباب يشرعون وبعضه عبيد يطيعون.

ولا بد أن نبادر فنبين أن التشريع لا ينحصر فقط في الأحكام القانونية - كما هو المفهوم الضيق في الأذهان اليوم لكلمة الشريعة - فالتصورات والمناهج، والقيم والموازين، والعادات والتقاليد. كلها تشريع يخضع الأفراد لضغطه. وحين يصنع الناس - بعضهم لبعض - هذه الضغوط، ويخضع لها البعض الآخر منهم في مجتمع، لا يكون هذا المجتمع متحررا، إنما هو مجتمع بعضه أرباب وبعضه عبيد - كما أسلفنا - وهو - من ثم - مجتمع متخلف. أو بالمصطلح الإسلامي. "مجتمع جاهلي ".

والمجتمع الإسلامي هو وحده المجتمع الذي يهيمن عليه إله إله واحد، ويخرج فيه الناس من عبادة العباد إلى عبادة الله وحده. وبذلك يتحررون التحرر الحقيقي الكامل، الذي ترتكز إليه حضارة الإنسان، وتتمثل فيه كرامته كما قدرها الله له، وهو يعلن خلافته في الأرض عنه، ويعلن كذلك تكريمه في الملأ الأعلى.

وحين تكون آصرة التجمع الأساسية في مجتمع هي العقيدة والتصور والفكرة ومنهج الحياة، ويكون هذا كله صادرا من إله واحد، تتمثل فيه السيادة العليا للبشر، وليس صادرا

من أرباب أرضية تتمثل فيها عبودية البشر للبشر. يكون ذلك التجمع ممثلا لأعلى ما في "الإنسان" من خصائص. خصائص الروح والفكر. فأما حين تكون آصرة التجمع في مجتمع هي الجنس واللون والقوم والأرض.. وما إلى ذلك من الروابط، فظاهر أن الجنس واللون والقوم والأرض لا تمثل الخصائص العليا للإنسان. فالإنسان يبقى إنسانا بعد الجنس واللون والقوم والأرض، ولكنه لا يبقى إنسانا بعد الروح والفكر. ثم هو يملك - بمحض إرادته الحرة - أن يغير عقيدته وتصوره وفكره ومنهج حياته، ولكنه لا يملك أن يغير لونه ولا جنسه، كما إنه لا يملك أن يحدد مولده في قوم ولا في أرض. فالمجتمع الذي يتجمع فيه الناس على أمر يتعلق بإرادتهم الحرة واختيارهم الذاتي هو المجتمع المتحضر. اما المجتمع الذي يتجمع فيه الناس على أمر خارج عن إرادتهم الإنسانية فهو المجتمع المتخلف. أو بالمصطلح الإسلامي. هو "المجتمع الجاهلي ".

والمجتمع الإسلامي وحده هو المجتمع الذي تمثل فيه العقيدة رابطة التجمع الأساسية، والذي تعتبر فيه العقيدة هي الجنسية التي تجمع بين الأسود والأبيض والأحمر والأصفر والعربي والرومي والفارسي والحبشي وسائر أجناس الأرض في أمة واحدة، ربها الله، وعبوديتها له وحده، والكرم فيها هو الأتقى، والكل فيها أنداد يلتقون على أمر شرعه الله لهم، ولم يشرعه أحد من العباد.

وحين تكون "إنسانية "الإنسان هي القيمة العليا في مجتمع، وتكون الخصائص "الإنسانية "فيه هي موضع التكريم والاعتبار، يكون هذا المجتمع متحضرا. فأما حين تكون "المادة "- في أية صورة - هي القيمة العليا. سواء في صورة "النظرية "كما في التفسير الماركسي للتاريخ. أو في صور "الإنتاج المادي "كما في أمريكا وأوروبا وسائر المجتمعات التي تعتبر الإنتاج المادي قيمة عليا تهدر في سبيلها القيم والخصائص والإنسانية. فإن هذا المجتمع يكون مجتمعا متخلفا. أو بالمصطلح الإسلامي مجتمعا جاهليا.

إن المجتمع المتحضر. الإسلامي. لا يحتقر المادة، لا في صورة النظرية (باعتبارها هي التي يتألف منها هذا الكون الذي نعيش فيه ونتأثر فيه ونؤثر فيه أيضا) ولا في صور "الإنتاج المادي ". فالإنتاج المادي من مقومات الخلافة في الأرض عن الله - ولكنه فقط لا يعتبرها هي القيمة العليا التي تهدر في سبيلها خصائص "الإنسان "ومقوماته.. وتهدر من أجلها حرية الفرد وكرامته. وتهدر فيها قاعدة "الأسرة "ومقوماتها، وتهدر فيها أخلاق المجتمع وحرماته. إلى آخر ما تهدره المجتمعات الجاهلية من القيم العليا والفضائل والحرمات لتحقق الوفرة في الإنتاج المادي.

وحين تكون "القيم الإنسانية "و "الأخلاق الإنسانية "التي تقوم عليها، هي السائدة في مجتمع، يكون هذا المجتمع متحضرا. والقيم الإنسانية والأخلاق الإنسانية ليست مسألة غامضة مائعة وليست كذلك قيما "متطورة "متغيرة متبدلة، لا تستقر على حال ولا ترجع إلى أصل، كما يزعم التفسير المادي للتاريخ، وكا تزعم "الاشتراكية العلمية ".

إنها القيم والأخلاق التي تنمي في الإنسان خصائص الإنسان التي يتفرد بها دون الحيوان، والتي تُغلب فيه هذا الجانب الذي يميزه ويعزوه عن الحيوان، وليست هي القيم والأخلاق التي تنمي فيه وتُغلب الجوانب التي يشترك فيها مع الحيوان.

وحين توضع المسألة هذا الوضع يبرز فيها خط فاصل وحاسم "وثابت" لا يقبل عملية التمييع المستمرة التي يحاولها "التطوريون". و "الإشتراكيون العلميون".

عندئذ لا يكون اصطلاح البيئة وعرفها هو الذي يحدد القيم الأخلاقية، إنما يكون وراء اختلاف البيئة ميزان ثابت. عندئذ لا يكون هناك قيم وأخلاق "زراعية" وأخرى "صناعية". ولا قيم وأخلاق "رأسمالية" وأخرى "اشتراكية"، ولا قيم وأخلاق "برجوازية" وأخرى "صعلوكية". ولا تكون هناك أخلاق من صنع البيئة ومستوى المعيشة وطبيعة المرحلة. إلى آخر هذه التغيرات السطحية والشكلية. إنما تكون هناك - من وراء ذلك كله - قيم وأخلاق "إنسانية" وقيم وأخلاق "حيوانية" - إذا صح هذا التعبير. - أو بالمصطلح الإسلامي: قيم وأخلاق "إسلامية" وقيم وأخلاق "جاهلية".

إن الإسلام يقرر قيمه وأخلاقه هذه "الإنسانية" - أي التي تنمي في الإنسان الجوانب التي تفرقه وتميزه عن الحيوان - ويمضي غي إنشائها وتثبيتها وصيانتها في كل المجتمعات التي يهيمن عليها سواء كانت هذه المجتمعات في طور الزراعة أم في طور الصناعة، وسواء كانت مجتمعات بدوية تعيش على الرعي أو مجتمعات حضرية مستقرة، وسواء كانت هذه المجتمعات فقيرة أو غنية. إنه يرتقي صعدا بالخصائص الإنسانية، ويحرسها من النكسة إلى الحيوانية. لأن الخط الصاعد في القيم والاعتبارات يمضي من الدرك الحيواني إلى المرتفع الإنساني. فإذا انتكس هذا الخط - مع حضارة المادة - فلن يكون ذلك حضارة. إنما هو "التخلف "أو هو "الجاهلية".

وحين تكون "الأسرة " هي قاعدة المجتمع. وتقوم هذه الأسرة على أساس "التخصص "بين الزوجين في العمل. وتكون رعاية الجيل الناشئ هي أهم وظائف الأسرة. يكون هذا المجتمع متحضرا. ذلك أن الأسرة على هذا النحو - في ظل المنهج الإسلامي - تكون هي البيئة التي تنشأ وتُنمى فيها القيم والأخلاق "الإنسانية "التي أشرنا إليها في الفقرة السابقة، ممثلة في الجيل الناشئ، والتي يستحيل أن تنشأ في وحدة أخرى غير وحدة الأسرة، فأما حين تكون العلاقات الجنسية (الحرة كما يسمونها) والنسل (غير الشرعي) هي قاعدة المجتمع. حين تقوم العلاقات بين الجنسين على أساس الهوى والنزوة والانفعال، لا على أساس الواجب والتخصص الوظيفي في الأسرة. حين تصبح وظيفة المرأة هي الزينة والغواية والفتنة. وحين تتخلى المرأة عن وظيفتها الأساسية في رعاية الجيل الجديد، وتُؤثِر هي - أوُيؤْثِر لها المجتمع - أن تكون مضيفة في فندق أو سفينة أو طائرة.. حين تنفق طاقتها في "الإنتاج المادي "و "صناعة الأدوات "ولا تنفقها في "صناعة الإنسانية ". لأن الإنتاج المادي يومئذ أغلى وأعز وأكرم من "الإنتاج الإنساني "، عندئذ يكون هنا هو "التخلف الحضاري "بالقياس الإنساني. أو تكون هي "الجاهلية "بالمصطلح الإسلامي.

وقضية الأسرة والعلاقات بين الجنسين قضية حاسمة في تحديد صفة المجتمع. متخلف أم متحضر، جاهلي أم إسلامي.. والمجتمعات التي تسود فيها القيم والأخلاق والنزعات الحيوانية في هذه العلاقة لا يمكن أن تكون مجتمعات متحضرة، مهما تبلغ من التفوق الصناعي والاقتصادي والعلمي. إن هذا المقياس لا يخطئ في قياس مدى التقدم "الإنساني".

وفي المجتمعات الجاهلية الحديثة ينحسر المفهوم "الأخلاقي"؛ بحيث يتخلى عن كل ما له علاقة بالتميز "الإنساني "عن الطابع "الحيواني". ففي هذه المجتمعات لا تعتبر العلاقات الجنسية غير الشرعية - ولا حتى العلاقات الجنسية الشاذة - رذيلة أخلاقية. إن المفهوم الأخلاقي يكاد ينحصر في المعاملات الاقتصادية - والسياسية أحيانا في حدود "مصلحة الدولة "- ففضيحة كريستين كيلر وبروفيمو الوزير الإنجليزي - مثلا - لم تكن في عرف المجتمع الإنجليزي فضيحة بسبب جانبها الجنسي. إنما كانت فضيحة لأن كريستين كيلر كانت صديقة كذلك للملحق البحري الروسي. ومن هنا يكون هناك خطر على أسرار الدولة في علاقة الوزير بهذه الفتاة. وكذلك لأنه افتضح كذبه على البرلمان الإنجليزي. والفضائح المماثلة في مجلس الشيوخ الأمريكي، وفضائح الجواسيس والموظفين الإنجليز والأمريكان الذين هربوا إلى روسيا. إنها ليست فضائح بسبب شذوذهم الجنسي. ولكن بسبب الخطر على أسرار الدولة.

والكُتاب والصحفيون والروائيون في المجتمعات الجاهلية هنا وهناك يقولونها صريحة للفتيات والزوجات: إن الاتصالات (الحرة) ليست رذائل أخلاقية. الرذيلة الأخلاقية أن يخدع الفتى رفيقته أو تخدع الفتاة رفيقها ولا تخلص له الود، بل الرذيلة أن تحافظ الزوجة على عفتها إذا كانت شهوة الحب لزوجها قد خمدت. والفضيلة أن تبحث لها عن صديق تعطيه جسدها بأمانة.. عشرات من القصص هذا محورها. ومئات التوجيهات الإخبارية والرسوم الكاريكاتورية والنكت والفكاهات هذه إيحاءاتها.

مثل هذه المجتمعات مجتمعات متخلفة. غير متحضرة. من وجهة نظر "الإنسان "وبمقياس خط التقدم "الإنساني".

إن خط التقدم الإنساني يسير في اتجاه "الضبط "للنزوات الحيوانية، وحصرها في نطاق "الأسرة "على أساس "الواجب "لتؤدي بذلك "وظيفة إنسانية "ليست اللذة غايتها، وإنما هي إعداد جيل إنساني يخلف الجيل الحاضر في ميراث الحضارة "الإنسانية "التي يميزها بروز الخصائص الإنسانية. ولا يمكن إعداد جيل يرتق في خصائص الإنسان، ويبتعد عن خصائص الحيوان، إلا في محضن أسرة محوطة بضمانات الأمن والاستقرار العاطفي، وقائمة على أساس الواجب الذي لا يتأرجح مع الانفعالات الطارئة. وفي المجتمع الذي تنشئ تلك التوجيهات والإيحاءات الخبيثة المسمومة، والذي ينحسر فيه المفهوم الأخلاقي، فيتخلى عن كل آداب الجنس، لا يمكن أن يقوم ذلك المحضن الإنساني.

من أجل ذلك كله تكون القيم والأخلاق والإيحاءات والضمانات الإسلامية هي اللائقة بالإنسان. ويكون "الإسلام هو الحضارة "ويكون المجتمع الإسلامي هو المجتمع المتحضر. بذلك المقياس الثابت الذي لا يتميع أو لا "يتطور".

وأخيرا فإنه حين يقوم "الإنسان" بالخلافة عن "الله" في أرضه على وجهها الصحيح: بأن يخلص عبوديته لله ويخلص من العبودية لغيره، وأن يحقق منهج الله وحده ويرفض الاعتراف بشرعية منهج غيره، وأن يُحكم شريعة الله وحدها في حياته كلها وينكر تحكيم شريعة سواها، وأن يعيش بالقيم والأخلاق التي قررها الله له ويسقط القيم والأخلاق المدعاة. ثم بأن يتعرف بعد ذلك كله إلى النواميس الكونية التي أودعها الله في هذا الكون المادي، ويستخدمها في ترقية الحياة، وفي استنباط خامات الأرض وأرزاقها وأقواتها التي أودعها الله إياها، وجعل تلك النواميس الكونية أختامها، ومنح الإنسان القدرة على فض هذه الأختام بالقدر الذي يلزم له في الخلافة. أي حين ينهض بالخلافة في الأرض على عهد الله وشرطه، ويصبح وهو يفجر ينابيع الرزق، ويصنع المادة الخامة، ويقيم الصناعات المتنوعة، ويستخدم ما تتيحه له كل الخبرات الفنية التي حصل عليها الإنسان في تاريخه كله. حين يصبح وهو يصنع هذا كله - "ربانيا" يقوم بالخلافة عن الله على هذا النحو - عبادة الله. يومئذ يكون هذا الإنسان كامل الحضارة، ويكون هذا المجتمع قد بلغ قمة الحضارة. فأما الإبداع المادي - وحده - فلا يسمى في الإسلام حضارة. فقد يكون وتكون معه الجاهلية. وقد ذكر الله من هذا الإبداع المادي في معرض وصف الجاهلية نماذج:

(أَتَبْنُونَ بِكُلِّ رِيعٍ آيَةً تَعْبَثُونَ، وَتَتَّخِذُونَ مَصَانِعَ لَعَلَّكُمْ تَخْلُدُونَ، وَإِذَا بَطَشْتُمْ بَطَشْتُمْ جَبَّارِينَ، فَاتَّقُوا اللهَ وَأَطِيعُونِ، وَاتَّقُوا الَّذِي أَمَدَّكُمْ بِمَا تَعْلَمُونَ، أَمَدَّكُمْ بِأَنْعَامٍ وَبَنِينَ، وَجَنَّاتٍ وَعُيُونٍ، إِنِّي أَخَافُ عَلَيْكُمْ عَذَابَ يَوْمٍ عَظِيمٍ). [الشعراء: 128 - 135].

(أَتُتْرَكُونَ فِي مَا هَاهُنَا آمِنِينَ، فِي جَنَّاتٍ وَعُيُونٍ، وَزُرُوعٍ وَنَخْلٍ طَلْعُهَا هَضِيمٌ، وَتَنْحِتُونَ مِنَ الْجِبَالِ بُيُوتًا فَارِهِينَ، فَاتَّقُوا اللهَ وَأَطِيعُونِ، وَلَا تُطِيعُوا أَمْرَ الْمُسْرِفِينَ، الَّذِينَ يُفْسِدُونَ فِي الْأَرْضِ وَلَا يُصْلِحُونَ). [الشعراء: 146 - 152].

(فَلَمَّا نَسُوا مَا ذُكِّرُوا بِهِ فَتَحْنَا عَلَيْهِمْ أَبْوَابَ كُلِّ شَيْءٍ حَتَّى إِذَا فَرِحُوا بِمَا أُوتُوا أَخَذْنَاهُمْ بَغْتَةً فَإِذَا هُمْ مُبْلِسُونَ، فَقُطِعَ دَابِرُ الْقَوْمِ الَّذِينَ ظَلَمُوا وَالْحَمْدُ لِلَّهِ رَبِّ الْعَالَمِينَ).. [الأنعام: 44 - 45].

(حَتَّى إِذَا أَخَذَتِ الْأَرْضُ زُخْرُفَهَا وَازَّيَّنَتْ وَظَنَّ أَهْلُهَا أَنَّهُمْ قَادِرُونَ عَلَيْهَا أَتَاهَا أَمْرُنَا لَيْلًا أَوْ نَهَارًا فَجَعَلْنَاهَا حَصِيدًا كَأَنْ لَمْ تَغْنَ بِالْأَمْسِ). [يونس: 24].

ولكن الإسلام - كما أسلفنا - لا يحتقر المادة، ولا يحتقر الإبداع المادي، إنما هو يجعل هذا اللون من التقدم - في ظل منهج الله - نعمة من نعم الله على عباده، يبشرهم به جزاء على طاعته:

(فَقُلْتُ اسْتَغْفِرُوا رَبَّكُمْ إِنَّهُ كَانَ غَفَّارًا، يُرْسِلِ السَّمَاءَ عَلَيْكُمْ مِدْرَارًا، وَيُمْدِدْكُمْ بِأَمْوَالٍ وَبَنِينَ وَيَجْعَلْ لَكُمْ جَنَّاتٍ وَيَجْعَلْ لَكُمْ أَنْهَارًا).. [نوح: 10 - 12].

(وَلَوْ أَنَّ أَهْلَ الْقُرَى آمَنُوا وَاتَّقَوْا لَفَتَحْنَا عَلَيْهِمْ بَرَكَاتٍ مِنَ السَّمَاءِ وَالْأَرْضِ وَلَكِنْ كَذَّبُوا فَأَخَذْنَاهُمْ بِمَا كَانُوا يَكْسِبُونَ).. [الأعراف: 96].

المهم هو القاعدة التي يقوم عليها التقدم الصناعي، والقيم التي تسود المجتمع، والتي يتألف من مجموعها خصائص الحضارة "الإنسانية".

وبعد. فإن قاعدة انطلاق المجتمع الإسلامي، وطبيعة تكوينه العضوي، تجعلان منه مجتمعا فريدا لا تنطبق عليه أية من النظريات التي تفسر قيام المجتمعات الجاهلية وطبيعة تكوينها العضوي. المجتمع الإسلامي وليد الحركة، والحركة فيه مستمرة، وهي التي تعين أقدار الأشخاص فيه وقيمهم، ومن ثم تحدد وظائفهم فيه ومراكزهم.

والحركة التي يتولد عنها هذا المجتمع ابتداء حركة آتية من خارج النطاق الأرضي، ومن خارج المحيط البشري. إنها تتمثل في عقيدة آتية من الله للبشر، تنشئ لهم تصورا خاصا للوجود والحياة والتاريخ والقيم والغايات، وتحدد لهم منهجا يترجم هذا التصور. الدفعة الأولى التي تطلق الحركة ليست منبثقة من نفوس الناس ولا من مادة الكون. إنها - كما قلنا - آتية لهم من خارج النطاق الأرضي، ومن خارج المحيط البشري. وهذا هو المميز الأول لطبيعة المجتمع الإسلامي وتركيبه.

إنه ينطلق من عنصر خارج عن محيط الإنسان وعن محيط الكون المادي.

وبهذا العنصر القدري الغيبي الذي لم يكن أحد من البشر يتوقعه أو يحسب حسابه، ودون أن يكون للإنسان يد فيه - في ابتداء الأمر - تبدأ أولى خطوات الحركة في قيام المجتمع الإسلامي، ويبدأ معها عمل "الإنسان" أيضا. إنسان يؤمن بهذه العقيدة الآتية له من ذلك المصدر الغيبي، الجارية بقدر الله وحده. وحين يؤمن هذا الإنسان الواحد بهذه العقيدة يبدأ وجود المجتمع الإسلامي (حكما). إن الإنسان الواحد لن يتلقى هذه العقيدة وينطوي على نفسه. إنه سينطلق بها. هذه طبيعتها. طبيعة الحركة الحية. إن القوة العليا التي دفعت بها إلى هذا القلب تعلم أنها ستتجاوزه حتما.. إن الدفعة الحية التي وصلت بها هذه العقيدة إلى هذا القلب ستمضي في طريقها قدما.

وحين يبلغ المؤمنون بهذه العقيدة ثلاثة نفر، فإن هذه العقيدة ذاتها تقول لهم: أنتم الآن مجتمع، مجتمع إسلامي مستقل، منفصل عن المجتمع الجاهلي الذي لا يدين لهذه العقيدة، ولا تسود فيه قيمها الأساسية - القيم التي أسلفنا الإشارة إليها - وهنا يكون المجتمع الإسلامي قد وُجد (فعلا).

والثلاثة يصبحون عشرة، والعشرة يصبحون مائة، والمائة يصبحون ألفا، والألف يصبحون إثني عشر ألفا. ويبرز ويتقرر وجود المجتمع الإسلامي.

وفي الطريق تكون المعركة قد قامت بين المجتمع الوليد الذي انفصل بعقيدته وتصوره، وانفصل بقيمه واعتباراته، وانفصل بوجوده وكينونته، عن المجتمع الجاهلي - الذي أخذ منه أفراده - وتكون الحركة من نقطة الانطلاق إلى نقطة الوجود البارز المستقل قد ميزت كل فرد من أفراد هذا المجتمع، وأعطته وزنه ومكانه في هذا المجتمع - حسب الميزان والاعتبار الإسلامي - ويكون وزنه هذا متعرفا له به من المجتمع دون أن يزكي نفسه أو يعلن عنه بل إن عقيدته وقيمه السائدة في نفسه وفي مجتمعه لتضغط عليه يومئذ ليواري نفسه عن الأنظار المتطلعة إليه في البيئة.

ولكن "الحركة "التي هي طابع العقيدة الإسلامية، وطابع هذا المجتمع الذي انبثق منها، لا تدع أحدا يتوارى. إن كل فرد من أفراد هذا المجتمع لا بد أن يتحرك. الحركة في عقيدته، والحركة في دمه، والحركة في مجتمعه، وفي تكوين هذا المجتمع العضوي. إن الجاهلية من حوله، وبقية من رواسبها في نفسه وفي نفوس من حوله، والمعركة مستمرة، والجهاد ماض إلى يوم القيامة.

على إيقاعات الحركة، وفي أثناء الحركة، يتحدد وضع كل فرد في هذا المجتمع، وتتحدد وظيفته، ويتم التكوين العضوي لهذا المجتمع بالتناسق بين مجموعة أفراده ومجموعة وظائفه.

هذه النشأة، وهذا التكوين، خاصيتان من خصائص المجتمع الإسلامي تُميزانه، تُميزان وجوده وتركيبه، وتُميزان طابعه وشكله، وتُميزان نظامه والإجراءات التنفيذية لهذا النظام أيضا، وتجعلان هذه الملامح كلها مستقلة، لا تعالج بمفهومات اجتماعية أجنبية عنها، ولا تدرس وفق منهج غريب عن طبيعتها، ولا تنفذ بإجراءات مستمدة من نظام آخر.

إن المجتمع الإسلامي - كما يبدو من تعريفنا المستقل للحضارة - ليس مجرد صورة تاريخية، يبحث عنها في ذكريات الماضي، إنما هو طلبة الحاضر وأمل المستقبل. إنه هدف يمكن أن تستشرفه البشرية كلها اليوم وغذا، لترتفع به من وهدة الجاهلية التي تتردى فيها، سواء في هذه الجاهلية الأمم المتقدمة صناعيا واقتصاديا والأمم المتخلفة أيضا.

إن تلك القيم التي أشرنا إليها إجمالا هي قيم إنسانية، لم تبلغها الإنسانية إلا في فترة "الحضارة الإسلامية ". (ويجب أن ننبه إلى ما نعنيه بمصطلح "الحضارة الإسلامية ". إنها الحضارة التي توافرت فيها تلك القيم، وليست هي كل تقدم صناعي أو اقتصادي أو علمي مع تخلف القيم عنها).

وهذه القيم ليست "مثالية خيالية "إنما هي قيم واقعية عملية، يمكن تحقيقها بالجهد البشري - في ظل المفهومات الإسلامية الصحيحة -، يمكن تحقيقها في كل بيئة بغض النظر عن نوع الحياة السائدة فيها، وعن تقدمها الصناعي والاقتصادي والعلمي. فهي لا تعارض - بل تشجع بالمنطق العقيدي ذاته - التقدم في كافة حقول الخلافة، ولكنها في الوقت ذاته لا تقف مكتوفة اليدين في البلاد التي لم تتقدم في هذه الحقول بعد. إن الحضارة يمكن أن تقوم في كل مكان وفي كل بيئة. تقوم بهذه القيم. أما أشكالها المادية التي تتخذها فلا حد لها، لأنها في كل بيئة تستخدم المقدرات الموجودة بها فعلا وتنميها.

المجتمع الإسلامي إذن - من ناحية شكله وحجمه ونوع الحياة السائدة فيه - ليس صورة تاريخية ثابتة، لكن وجوده وحضارته يرتكنان إلى قيم تاريخية ثابتة. وحين نقول: "تاريخية "لا نعني إلا أن هذه القيم قد عرفت في تاريخ معين. وإلا فهي ليست من صنع التاريخ، ولا علاقة لها بالزمن في طبيعتها. إنها حقيقة جاءت إلى البشرية من مصدر رباني. من وراء الواقع البشري. ومن وراء الوجود المادي أيضا.

والحضارة الإسلامية يمكن أن تتخذ أشكالا متنوعة في تركيبها المادي والتشكيلي، ولكن الأصول والقيم التي تقوم عليها ثابتة، لأنها هي مقومات هذه الحضارة: (العبودية لله وحده. والتجمع على آصرة العقيدة فيه. واستعلاء إنسانية الإنسان على المادة. وسيادة

القيم الإنسانية التي تنمي إنسانية الإنسان لا حيوانيته. وحرمة الأسرة. والخلافة في الأرض على عهد الله وشرطه. وتحكيم منهج الله وشريعته وحدها في شؤون هذه الخلافة).

إن "أشكال "الحضارة الإسلامية التي تقوم على هذه الأسس الثابتة، تتأثر بدرجة التقدم الصناعي والاقتصادي والعلمي، لأنها تستخدم الموجود منها فعلا في كل بيئة. ومن ثم لا بد أن تختلف أشكالها. لا بد أن تتضمن المرونة الكافية لدخول كافة البيئات والمستويات في الإطار الإسلامي، والتكيف بالقيم والمقومات الإسلامية. وهذه المرونة - في الأشكال الخارجية للحضارة - ليست مفروضة على العقيدة الإسلامية التي تنبثق منها تلك الحضارة إنما هي من طبيعتها. ولكن المرونة ليست هي التميع. والفرق بينهما بعيد جدا.

لقد كان الإسلام ينشئ الحضارة في أواسط أفريقية بين العراة. لأنه بمجرد وجوده هناك تكتسي الأجسام العارية ويدخل الناس في حضارة اللباس التي يتضمنها التوجيه الإسلامي المباشر، ويبدأ الناس في الخروج كذلك من الخمول البليد إلى نشاط العمل الموجه لاستغلال كنوز الكون المادي، ويخرجون كذلك من طور القبيلة - أو العشيرة - إلى طور الأمة، وينتقلون من عبادة الطوطم المنعزلة إلى عبادة رب العالمين. فما هي الحضارة إن لم تكن هي هذا؟ إنها حضارة هذه البيئة، التي تعتمد على إمكانياتها القائمة فعلا. فأما حين يدخل الإسلام في بيئة أخرى فإنه ينشئ - بقيمه الثابتة - شكلا آخر من أشكال الحضارة يستخدم فيه موجودات هذه البيئة وإمكانياتها الفعلية وينميها.

وهكذا لا يتوقف قيام الحضارة - بطريقة الإسلام ومنهجه - على درجة معينة من التقدم الصناعي والاقتصادي والعلمي. وإنْ كانت الحضارة حين تقوم تستخدم هذا التقدم - عند وجوده - وتدفعه إلى الأمام دفعا، وترفع أهدافه. كما إنها تنشئه إنشاء حين لا يكون، وتكفل نموه واطراده. ولكنها تظل في كل حال قائمة على أصولها المستقلة. ويبقى للمجتمع الإسلامي طابعه الخاص، وتركيبه العضوي، الناشئان عن نقطة انطلاقه الأولى، التي يتميز بها من كل مجتمعات الجاهلية.

(صِبْغَةَ اللهِ ومنْ أَحْسَنُ مِن اللهِ صِبْغَةً).. [البقرة: 138].

التصور الإسلامي والثقافة

العبودية المطلقة لله وحده هي الشطر الأول لركن الإسلام الأول، فهي المدلول المطابق لشهادة أن لا إله إلا الله، والتلقي في كيفية هذه العبودية عن رسول الله صلى الله عليه وسلم هو الشطر الثاني لهذا الركن، فهو المدلول المطابق لشهادة أن محمدا رسول الله - كما جاء في فصل: "لا إله إلا الله منهج حياة".

والعبودية المطلقة لله وحده تتمثل في اتخاذ الله وحده إلها. عقيدة وعبادة وشريعة. فلا يعتقد المسلم أن "الألوهية "تكون لأحد غير الله - سبحانه - ولا يعتقد أن "العبادة "تكون لغيره من خلقه، ولا يعتقد أن "الحاكمية "تكون لأحد من عباده. كما جاء في ذلك الفصل أيضا.

ولقد أوضحنا هناك مدلول العبودية والاعتقاد والشعائر والحاكمية، وفي هذا الفصل نوضح مدلول "الحاكمية "وعلاقته "بالثقافة ".

إن مدلول "الحاكمية "في التصور الإسلامي لا ينحصر في تلقي الشرائع القانونية من الله وحده. والتحاكم إليها وحدها. والحكم بها دون سواها. أن مدلول "الشريعة "في الإسلام لا ينحصر في التشريعات القانونية، ولا حتى في أصول الحكم ونظامه وأوضاعه. إن هذا المدلول الضيق لا يمثل مدلول "الشريعة "والتصور الإسلامي.

إن "شريعة الله "تعني كل ما شرعه الله لتنظيم الحياة البشرية. وهذا يتمثل في أصول الاعتقاد، وأصول الحكم، وأصول الأخلاق، وأصول السلوك، وأصول المعرفة أيضا.

يتمثل في الاعتقاد والتصور - بكل مقومات هذا التصور - تصور حقيقة الألوهية، وحقيقة الكون، غيبه وشهوده، وحقيقة الحياة، غيبها وشهودها، وحقيقة الإنسان، والارتباطات بين هذه الحقائق كلها، وتعامل الإنسان معها.

ويتمثل في الأوضاع السياسية والاجتماعية والاقتصادية، والأصول التي تقوم عليها، لتتمثل فيها العبودية الكاملة لله وحده.

ويتمثل في التشريعات القانونية، التي تنظم هذه الأوضاع. وهو ما يطلق عليه اسم "الشريعة "غالبا بمعناها الضيق الذي لا يمثل حقيقة مدلولها في التصور الإسلامي.

ويتمثل في قواعد الأخلاق والسلوك، في القيم والموازين التي تسود المجتمع، ويقوم بها الأشخاص والأشياء والأحداث في الحياة الاجتماعية.

ثم. يتمثل في "المعرفة "بكل جوانبها، وفي أصول النشاط الفكري والفني جملة.

وفي هذا كله لا بد من التلقي عن الله، كالتلقي في الأحكام الشرعية - بمدلولها الضيق المتداول - سواء بسواء.

والأمر في "الحاكمية "- في مدلولها المختص بالحكم والقانون - قد يكون الآن مفهوما بعد الذي سقناه بشأنه من تقريرات.

والأمر في قواعد الأخلاق والسلوك، وفي القيم والموازين التي تسود المجتمع، قد يكون مفهوما كذلك إلى حد ما. إذ أن القيم والموازين وقواعد الأخلاق والسلوك التي تسود في مجتمع ما ترجع مباشرة إلى التصور الاعتقادي السائد في هذا المجتمع، وتتلقى من ذات المصدر الذي تتلقى منه حقائق العقيدة التي يتكيف بها ذلك التصور.

أما الأمر الذي قد يكون غريبا - حتى على قراء مثل هذه البحوث الإسلامية. - فهو الرجوع في شأن النشاط الفكري والفني إلى التصور الإسلامي والى مصدره الرباني.

وفي النشاط الفني صدر كتاب كامل يتضمن بيان هذه القضية باعتبار أن النشاط الفني كله، وهو تعبير إنساني عن تصورات الإنسان وانفعالاته واستجاباته، وعن صورة الوجود والحياة في نفس إنسانية. وهذه كلها يحكمها - بل ينشئها - في النفس المسلمة تصورها الإسلامي بشموله لكل جوانب الكون والنفس والحياة، وعلاقتها بباريء الكون والنفس والحياة. وبتصورها خاصة لحقيقة هذا الإنسان، ومركزه في الكون، وغاية وجوده، ووظيفته، وقيم حياته. وكلها متضمنة في التصور الاسلامي، الذي ليس هو مجرد تصور فكري. إنما هو تصور اعتقادي حي موح مؤثر فعال دافع مسيطر على كل انبعاث في الكيان الإنساني (16).

فأما قضية النشاط الفكري، وضرورة رد هذا النشاط إلى التصور الإسلامي ومصدره الرباني، تحقيقا للعبودية الكاملة لله وحده، فهذه هي القضية التي تقتضي منا بيانا كاملا لأنها قد تكون بالقياس إلى قُراء هذا البيان - حتى المسلمين منهم الذين يرون حتمية رد الحاكمية والتشريع لله وحده - غريبة أو غير مطروقة.

إن المسلم لا يملك أن يتلقى في أمر يختص بحقائق العقيدة، أو التصور العام للوجود، أو يختص بالعبادة، أو يختص بالخلق والسلوك، والقيم والموازين، أو يختص بالمبادئ والأصول في النظام السياسي، أو الاجتماعي، أو الاقتصادي، أو يختص بتفسير بواعث النشاط الإنساني وبحركة التاريخ الإنساني. إلا من ذلك المصدر الرباني، ولا يتلقى في هذا كله إلا عن مسلم يثق في دينه وتقواه، ومزاولته لعقيدته في واقع الحياة.

ولكن المسلم يملك أن يتلقى في العلوم البحتة، كالكيمياء، والطبيعة، والأحياء، والفلك، والطب، والصناعة، والزراعة، وطرق الإدارة - من الناحية الفنية الإدارية البحتة - وطرق العمل الفنية، وطرق الحرب والقتال - من الجانب الفني- إلى آخر ما يشبه هذا النشاط. يملك أن يتلقى في هذا كله عن المسلم وغير المسلم. وإن كان الأصل في المجتمع المسلم حين يقوم، أن يسعى لتوفير هذه الكفايات في هذه الحقول كلها، باعتبارها فروض كفاية، يجب أن يتخصص فيها أفراد منه. وإلا أثم المجتمع كله إذا لم يوفر هذه الكفايات، ولم يوفر لها الجو الذي تتكون فيه وتعيش وتعمل وتنتج. ولكن إلى أن يتحقق هذا فإن للفرد المسلم أن يتلقى في هذه العلوم البحتة وتطبيقاتها العملية من المسلم وغير المسلم،

---

(16) كتاب " منهج الفن الإسلامي " لمحمد قطب.

وأن ينتفع فيها بجهد المسلم وغير المسلم، وأن يشغل فيها المسلم وغير المسلم. لأنها من الأمور الداخلة في قول رسول الله صلى الله عليه وسلم: "أنتم أعلم بأمور دنياكم ". وهي لا تتعلق بتكوين تصور المسلم عن الحياة والكون والإنسان، وغاية وجوده، وحقيقة وظيفته، ونوع ارتباطاته بالوجود من حوله، بخالق الوجود كله، ولا تتعلق بالمبادئ والشرائع والأنظمة والأوضاع التي تنظم حياته أفرادا وجماعات. ولا تتعلق بالأخلاق والآداب والتقاليد والعادات والقيم والموازين التي تسود مجتمعه وتؤلف ملامح هذا المجتمع. ومن ثم فلا خطر فيها من زيغ عقيدته، أو ارتداده إلى الجاهلية.

فأما ما يتعلق بتفسير النشاط الإنساني كله أفرادا أو مجتمعات، وهو التعلق بالنظرة إلى "نفس "الإنسان وإلى "حركة تاريخه "، وما يختص بتفسير نشأة هذا الكون، ونشأة الحياة، ونشأة هذا الإنسان ذاته - من ناحية ما وراء الطبيعة - (وهو ما لا تتعلق به العلوم البحتة من كيمياء وطبيعة وفلك وطب. إلخ) فالشأن فيه، شأن الشرائع القانونية والمبادئ والأصول التي تنظم حياته ونشاطه، مرتبط بالعقيدة ارتباطا مباشرا، فلا يجوز للمسلم أن يتلقى فيه إلا عن مسلم، يثق في دينه وتقواه، ويعلم عنه أنه يتلقى في هذا كله عن الله. والمهم أن يرتبط هذا في حس المسلم بعقيدته، وأن يعلم أن هذا مقتضى عبوديته لله وحده، أو مقتضى شهادته: أن لا إله إلا الله، وأن محمدا رسول الله.

إنه قد يطلع على كل آثار النشاط الجاهلي. ولكن لا لِيُكون منه تصوره ومعرفته في هذه الشؤون كلها، إنما ليعرف كيف تنحرف الجاهلية. وليعرف كيف يصحح ويقوم هذه الانحرافات البشرية، بردها إلى أصولها الصحيحة في مقومات التصور الإسلامي، وحقائق العقيدة الإسلامية.

إن اتجاهات "الفلسفة "بجملتها، واتجاهات "تفسير التاريخ الإنساني "بجملتها، واتجاهات "علم النفس "بجملتها - عدا الملاحظات والمشاهدات دون التفسيرات العامة لها - ومباحث "الأخلاق "بجملتها، واتجاهات دراسة "الأديان المقارنة "بجملتها، واتجاهات "التفسيرات والمذاهب الاجتماعية "بجملتها - فيما عدا المشاهدات والإحصائيات والمعلومات المباشرة، لا النتائج العامة المستخلصة منها ولا التوجيهات الكلية الناشئة عنها -. إن هذه الاتجاهات كلها في الفكر الجاهلي - أي غير الإسلامي - قديما وحديثا، متأثرة تأثرا مباشرا بتصورات اعتقادية جاهلية، وقائمة على هذه التصورات، ومعظمها - إن لم يكن كلها - يتضمن في أصوله المنهجية عداء ظاهرا أو خفيا للتصور الديني جملة، وللتصور الإسلامي على وجه خاص.

والأمر في هذه الألوان من النشاط الفكري – والعلمي. - ليس كالأمر في علوم الكيمياء والطبيعة والفلك والأحياء والطب، وما إليها - ما دامت هذه في حدود التجربة الواقعية وتسجيل النتائج الواقعية، دون أن تجاوز هذه الحدود إلى التفسير الفلسفي في صورة من صوره، وذلك كتجاوز الداروينية مثلا لمجال إثبات المشاهدات وترتيبها في علم الأحياء، إلى محال القول - بغير دليل وبغير حاجة للقول كذلك إلا الرغبة والهوى - إنه لا ضرورة لافتراض وجود قوة خارجة عن العالم الطبيعي لتفسير نشأة الحياة وتطورها.

إن لدى المسلم الكفاية من بيان ربه الصادق عن تلك الشؤون، وفي المستوى الذي تبدو فيه محاولات البشر في هذه المجالات هزيلة ومضحكة. فضلا عن أن الأمر يتعلق تعلقا مباشرا بالعقيدة، وبالعبودية الكاملة لله وحده.

إن حكاية أن "الثقافة تراث إنساني "لا وطن له ولا جنس ولا دين. هي حكاية صحيحة عندما تتعلق بالعلوم البحتة وتطبيقاتها العلمية - دون أن تتجاوز هذه المنطقة إلى التفسيرات الفلسفية "الميتافيزيقية "لنتائج هذه العلوم، ولا إلى التفسيرات الفلسفية لنفس الإنسان ونشاطه وتاريخه، ولا إلى الفن والأدب والتعبيرات الشعورية جميعا. ولكنها فيما وراء ذلك إحدى مصايد اليهود العالمية، التي يهمها تمييع الحواجز كلها - بما في ذلك، بل في أول ذلك حواجز العقيدة والتصور - لكي ينفذ اليهود إلى جسم العالم كه، وهو مسترخ مخدر، يزاول اليهود فيه نشاطهم الشيطاني، وفي أوله نشاطهم الربوي، الذي ينتهي إلى جعل حصيلة كد البشرية كلها، تؤول إلى أصحاب المؤسسات المالية الربوية من اليهود.

ولكن الإسلام يعتبر أن هناك - فيما وراء العلوم البحتة وتطبيقاتها العملية - نوعين اثنين من الثقافة: الثقافة الإسلامية القائمة على قواعد التصور الإسلامي، والثقافة الجاهلية القائمة على مناهج شتى ترجع كلها إلى قاعدة واحدة. قاعدة إقامة الفكر البشري إلها لا يرجع إلى الله في ميزانه. والثقافة الإسلامية شاملة لكل حقول النشاط الفكري والواقعي الإنساني، وفيها من القواعد والمناهج والخصائص ما يكفل نمو هذا النشاط وحيويته دائما.

ويكفي أن نعلم أن الاتجاه التجريبي، الذي قامت عليه الحضارة الصناعية الأوروبية الحاضرة، لم ينشأ ابتداء في أوروبا، وإنما نشأ في الجامعات الإسلامية في الأندلس والمشرق، مستمدا أصوله من التصور الإسلامي وتوجيهاته، إلى الكون وطبيعته الواقعية، ومدخراته وأقواته. ثُم استقلت النهضة العلمية في أوروبا بهذا المنهج، واستمرت تنمية وترقيه، بينما رُكد وترك نهائيا في العالم الإسلامي بسبب بُعد هذا العالم تدريجيا عن الإسلام، بفعل عوامل بعضها كامن في تركيب المجتمع وبعضها يتمثل في الهجوم عليه من العالم الصليبي والصهيوني ... ثم قطعت أوروبا ما بين المنهج الذي اقتبسته وبين أصوله الاعتقادية الاسلامية، وشردت به نهائيا بعيدا عن الله، في أثناء شرودها عن الكنيسة، التي كانت تستطيل على الناس - بغيا وعدوا - باسم الله. [17]

وكذلك أصبح نتاج الفكر الأوروبي بجملته - شأنه شأن إنتاج الفكر الجاهلي في جميع الأزمان في جميع البقاع - شيئا آخر، ذا طبيعة مختلفة من أساسها عن مقومات التصور الإسلامي. ومعادية في الوقت ذاته عداء أصيلا للتصور الإسلامي. ووجب على المسلم أن يرجع إلى مقومات تصوره وحدها، وألا يأخذ إلا من المصدر الرباني إن استطاع بنفسه، وإلا فلا يأخذ إلا عن مسلم تقي، يعلم عن دينه وتقواه ما يطمئنه إلى الأخذ عنه.

إن حكاية فصل "العلم "عن "صاحب العلم "لا يعرفها الإسلام فيما يختص بكل العلوم المتعلقة بمفهومات العقيدة المؤثرة في نظرة الإنسان إلى الوجود والحياة والنشاط

---

[17] راجع فصل: " الفصام النكد " في كتاب: المستقبل لهذا الدين.

الإنساني، والأوضاع، والقيم، والأخلاق، والعادات، وسائر ما يتعلق بنفس الإنسان ونشاطه من هذه النواحي.

إن الإسلام يتسامح في أن يتلقى المسلم عن غير المسلم، أو عن غير التقي من المسلمين، في علم الكيمياء البحتة، أو الطبيعة، أو الفلك، أو الطب، أو الصناعة، أو الزراعة، أو الأعمال الإدارية والكتابية. وأمثالها. وذلك في الحالات التي لا يجد فيها مسلما تقيا يأخذ عنه في هذا كله، كما هو واقع من يسمون أنفسهم المسلمين اليوم، الناشئ من بُعْدِهم عن دينهم ومنهجهم وعن التصور الإسلامي لمقتضيات الخلافة في الأرض - بإذن الله - وما يلزم لهذه الخلافة من هذه العلوم والخبرات والمهارات المختلفة. ولكنه لا يتسامح في أن يتلقى أصول عقيدته، ولا مقومات تصوره، ولا تفسير قرآنه وحديثه وسيرة نبيه، ولا منهج تاريخه وتفسير نشاطه، ولا مذهب مجتمعه، ولا نظام حكمه، ولا منهج سياسته، ولا موجبات فنه وأدبه وتعبيره ... إلخ، من مصادر غير إسلامية، ولا أن يتلقى عن غير مسلم يثق في دينه وتقواه في شيء من هذا كله.

إن الذي يكتب هذا الكلام إنسان عاش يقرأ أربعين سنة كاملة. كان عمله الأول فيها هو القراءة والاطلاع في معظم حقول المعرفة الإنسانية. ما هو من تخصصه وما هو من هواياته. ثم عاد إلى مصادر عقيدته وتصوره. فإذا هو يجد كل ما قرأه ضئيلا إلى جانب ذلك الرصيد الضخم - وما كان يمكن أن يكون إلا كذلك - وما هو بنادم على ما قضى فيه أربعين سنة من عمره. فإنما عرف الجاهلية على حقيقتها، وعلى انحرافها، وعلى ضآلتها، وعلى قزامتها ... وعلى جعجعتها وانتفاشها، وعلى غرورها وادعائها كذلك.. وعلم علم اليقين أنه لا يمكن أن يجمع المسلم بين هذين المصدرين في التلقي..

ومع ذلك فليس الذي سبق في هذه الفقرة رأيا لي أبديه. إن الأمر أكبر من أن يفتى فيه بالرأي. إنه أثقل في ميزان الله من أن يعتمد المسلم فيه على رأيه، إنما هو قول الله – سبحانه - وقول نبيه صلى الله عليه وسلم. نحكمه في هذا الشأن، ونرجع فيه إلى الله والرسول، كما يرجع الذين آمنوا إلى الله والرسول فيما يختلفون فيه.

يقول الله - سبحانه - عن الهدف النهائي لليهود والنصارى في شأن المسلمين بصفة عامة:

(وَدَّ كَثِيرٌ مِنْ أَهْلِ الْكِتَابِ لَوْ يَرُدُّونَكُمْ مِنْ بَعْدِ إِيمَانِكُمْ كُفَّارًا حَسَدًا مِنْ عِنْدِ أَنْفُسِهِمْ مِنْ بَعْدِ مَا تَبَيَّنَ لَهُمُ الْحَقُّ فَاعْفُوا وَاصْفَحُوا حَتَّى يَأْتِيَ اللَّهُ بِأَمْرِهِ إِنَّ اللَّهَ عَلَى كُلِّ شَيْءٍ قَدِيرٌ) ... [البقرة: 109].

(وَلَنْ تَرْضَى عَنْكَ الْيَهُودُ وَلَا النَّصَارَى حَتَّى تَتَّبِعَ مِلَّتَهُمْ قُلْ إِنَّ هُدَى اللَّهِ هُوَ الْهُدَى وَلَئِنِ اتَّبَعْتَ أَهْوَاءَهُمْ بَعْدَ الَّذِي جَاءَكَ مِنَ الْعِلْمِ مَا لَكَ مِنَ اللَّهِ مِنْ وَلِيٍّ وَلَا نَصِيرٍ).. [البقرة: 120]

(يَا أَيُّهَا الَّذِينَ آمَنُوا إِنْ تُطِيعُوا فَرِيقًا مِنَ الَّذِينَ أُوتُوا الْكِتَابَ يَرُدُّوكُمْ بَعْدَ إِيمَانِكُمْ كَافِرِينَ).. [آل عمران: 100]

ويقول رسول الله - صلى الله عليه وسلم - فيما رواه الحافظ أبو يعلى عن حماد عن الشعبي عن جابر - رضي الله عنهم:

"لا تسألوا أهل الكتاب عن شيء، فإنهم لن يهدوكم وقد ضلوا، وإنكم إما أن تصدقوا بباطل، وإما أن تكذبوا بحق، وإنه والله لو كان موسى حيا بين أظهركم ما حل له أن يتبعني".

وحين يتحدد الهدف النهائي لليهود والنصارى في شأن المسلمين على ذلك النحو القاطع الذي يقرره الله سبحانه، يكون من البلاهة الظن لحظة بأنهم يصدرون عن نية طيبة في أي مبحث من المباحث المتعلقة بالعقيدة الإسلامية، أو التاريخ الاسلامي، أو التوجيه في نظام المجتمع المسلم، أو في سياسته أو اقتصاده، أو يقصدون إلى خير، أو إلى هدى، أو إلى نور ... والذين يظنون ذلك فيما عند هؤلاء الناس - بعد تقرير الله سبحانه - إنما هم الغافلون.

كذلك يتحدد من قول الله سبحانه: **(قُلْ إن هُدى اللهِ هُو الْهُدى)**.. المصدر الوحيد الذي يجب على المسلم الرجوع إليه في هذه الشؤون، فليس وراء هدى الله إلا الضلال، وليس في غيره هدى، كما تفيد صيغة القصر الواردة في النص: "قُل: إن هدى الله هو الهدى "... ولا سبيل إلى الشك في مدلول هذا النص، ولا إلى تأويله كذلك.

كذلك يرد الأمر القاطع بالإعراض عمن يتولى عن ذكر الله، ويقصر اهتمامه على شؤون الحياة الدنيا، وينص على أن مثل هذا لا يعلم إلا ظنا، والمسلم منهي عن اتباع الظن، وأنه لا يعلم إلا ظاهرا من الحياة الدنيا، فهو لا يعلم علما صحيحا.

(فأعْرِضْ عَن مَنْ تولى عنْ ذِكْرِنا ولَمْ يُرِدْ إلا الْحياة الدنْيا، ذلِك مبْلغُهُم مِن الْعِلْمِ إن ربك هُو أعْلمُ بِمنْ ضل عنْ سبِيلِهِ وهُو أعْلمُ بِمنِ اهْتدى). [النجم: 29 – 30]

(يعْلمُون ظاهِرا مِن الْحياةِ الدنْيا وهُم عنِ الْآخِرةِ هُمْ غافِلُون). [الروم: 7]

والذي يغفل عن ذكر الله، ولا يريد إلا الحياة الدنيا - وهو شأن جميع "العلماء. اليوم - لا يعلم إلا هذا الظاهر، وليس هذا هو "العلم "الذي يثق المسلم في صاحبه فيتلقى عنه في كل شأنه، إنما يجوز أن يتلقى عنه في حدود علمه المادي البحت، ولا يتلقى منه تفسيرا ولا تأويلا عاما للحياة، أو النفس، أو متعلقاتها التصورية. كما أنه ليس هو العلم الذي تشير إليه الآيات القرآنية وتثني عليه، كقوله تعالى: "هل يستوي الذين يعلمون والذين لا يعلمون؟ "كما يفهم الذين ينتزعون النصوص القرآنية من سياقها ليشهدوا بها في غير مواضعها؛ فهذا السؤال التقريري وارد في آية في آية هذا نصها الكامل:

(أمنْ هُو قانِتٌ آناء اللّيْلِ ساجِدا وقائِما يحْذرُ الْآخِرة ويرْجُو رحْمة ربِهِ قُلْ هلْ يسْتوِي الذِين يعْلمُون والذِين لا يعْلمُون إنما يتذكرُ أُولُو الْألْبابِ). [الزمر: 9]

فهذا القانت آناء الليل، ساجدا وقائما، يحذر الآخرة ويرجو رحمة ربه. هو هذا الذي يعلم. وهذا هو العلم. الذي تشير إليه الآية، العلم الذي يهدي إلى الله وتقواه. لا العلم الذي يفسد الفطر فتلحد في الله.

72

إن العلم ليس مقصورا على علم العقيدة والفرائض الدينية والشرائع. فالعلم يشتمل على كل شيء، ويتعلق بالقوانين الطبيعية. وتسخيرها في خلافة الأرض تعلقه بالعقيدة والفرائض والشرائع. لكن العلم الذي ينقطع عن قاعدته الإيمانية ليس هو العلم الذي يعنيه القرآن ويثني على أهله. إن هناك ارتباطا بين القاعدة الإيمانية وعلم الفلك، وعلم الأحياء، وعلم الطبيعة، وعلم الكيمياء، وعلم طبقات الأرض. وسائر العلوم المتعلقة بالنواميس الكونية، والقوانين الحيوية. إنها كلها تؤدي إلى الله، حين لا يستخدمها الهوى المنحرف للابتعاد عن الله. كما اتجه المنهج الأوروبي في النهضة العلمية - مع الأسف - بسبب تلك الملابسات النكدة التي قامت في التاريخ الأوروبي خاصة، بين المشتغلين بالعلم وبين الكنيسة الغاشمة. ثم ترك آثاره العميقة في مناهج الفكر الأوروبي كلها، وفي طبيعة التفكير الأوروبي، وترك تلك الرواسب المسممة بالعداء لأصل التصور الديني جملة - لا لأصل التصور الكنسي وحده ولا للكنيسة وحدها - في كل ما أنتجه الفكر الأوروبي، في كل حقل من حقول المعرفة، سواء كانت فلسفة ميتافيزيقية، أو كانت بحوثا علمية بحتة لا علاقة لها - في الظاهر - بالموضوع الديني. [18]

وإذا تقرر أن مناهج الفكر الغربي، ونتاج هذا الفكر في كل حقول المعرفة، يقوم ابتداء على أساس تلك الرواسب المسممة بالعداء لأصل التصور الديني جملة، فإن تلك المناهج وهذا النتاج أشد عداء للتصور الإسلامي بصفة خاصة، لأنه يتعمد هذا العداء بصفة خاصة، ويتحرى في حالات كثيرة - في خطة متعمدة - تمييع العقيدة والتصور والمفهومات الإسلامية، ثم تحطيم الأسس التي يقوم عليها تميز المجتمع المسلم في كل مقوماته.

ومن ثم يكون من الغفلة المزرية الاعتماد على مناهج الفكر الغربي، وعلى نتاجه كذلك، في الدراسات الإسلامية. ومن ثم تجب الحيطة كذلك في أثناء دراسة العلوم البحتة - التي لا بد لنا في موقفنا الحاضر من تلقيها من مصادرها الغربية - من أية ظلال فلسفية تتعلق بها، لأن هذه الظلال معادية في أساسها للتصور الديني جملة، وللتصور الإسلامي بصفة خاصة. وأي قدر منها يكفي لتسميم الينبوع الإسلامي الصافي ...

---

[18] يراجع فصل: " الفصام والنكد " في كتاب " المستقبل لهذا الدين ".

جِنْسِية المُسْلِم وعقيدتُه

جاء الإسلام إلى هذه البشرية بتصور جديد لحقيقة الروابط والوشائج، يوم جاءها بتصور جديد لحقيقة القيم والاعتبارات، ولحقيقة الجهة التي تتلقى منها هذه القيم وهذه الاعتبارات.

جاء الإسلام ليرد الإنسان إلى ربه، وليجعل هذه السلطة هي السلطة الوحيدة التي يتلقى منها موازينه وقيمه، كما منها منها وجوده وحياته، والتي يرجع إليها بروابطه ووشائجه، كما أنه من إرادتها صدر وإليها يعود.

جاء ليقرر أن هناك وشيجة واحدة تربط الناس في الله فإذا انبتت هذه الوشيجة فلا صلة ولا مودة:

(لا تَجِدُ قَوْماً يُؤْمِنُون بِاللهِ والْيَوْمِ الْآخِرِ يُوادون مِنْ حاد الله ورسُولهُ ولوْ كانُوا آباءهُمْ أوْ أبْناءهُمْ أوْ إخْوانُهُمْ أوْ عشِيرتُهُمْ).. [المجادلة: 22]

وأن هناك حزبا واحدا لله لا يتعدد، وأحزابا أخرى كلها للشيطان وللطاغوت:

(الذين آمنُوا يُقاتِلُون في سبِيلِ اللهِ والذين كفرُوا يُقاتِلُون في سبِيلِ الطاغُوتِ فقاتِلُوا أوْلِياء الشيْطانِ إن كيْد الشيْطانِ كان ضعِيفا).. [النساء: 76]

وأن هناك طريقا واحدا يصل إلى الله وكل طريق آخر لا يؤدي إليه:

(وأن هذا صِراطِي مُسْتقِيما فاتبِعُوهُ ولا تتبِعُوا السبُل فتفرق بِكُمْ عنْ سبِيلِهِ)..
[الأنعام: 153]

وأن هناك نظاما واحدا هو النظام الإسلامي وما عداه من النظم فهو جاهلية:

(أفحُكْم الْجاهِلِيةِ يبْغُون ومنْ أحْسنُ مِن اللهِ حُكْما لِقوْمٍ يُوقِنُون) [المائدة: 50]

وأن هناك شريعة واحدة هي شريعة الله وما عداها فهو هوى:

(ثُم جعلْناك على شرِيعةٍ مِن الْأمْرِ فاتبِعْها ولا تتبِعْ أهْواء الذِين لا يعْلمُون)..
[الجاثية: 18]

وأن هناك حقا واحدا لا يتعدد، وما عداه فهو الضلال:

(فماذا بعْد الْحق إلا الضلالُ فأنى تُصْرفُون). [يونس: 32]

وأن هناك دارا واحدة هي دار الإسلام، تلك التي تقوم فيها الدولة المسلمة، فتهيمن عليها شريعة الله، وتقام فيها حدوده، ويتولى المسلمون فيها بعضهم بعضا، وما عداها فهو دار حرب، علاقة المسلم بها إما القتال، وإما المهادنة على عهد أمان، ولكنها ليست دار إسلام، ولا ولاء بين أهلها وبين المسلمين:

(إِنَّ الَّذِينَ آمَنُوا وَهَاجَرُوا وَجَاهَدُوا بِأَمْوَالِهِمْ وَأَنْفُسِهِمْ فِي سَبِيلِ اللَّهِ وَالَّذِينَ آوَوْا وَنَصَرُوا أُولَئِكَ بَعْضُهُمْ أَوْلِيَاءُ بَعْضٍ وَالَّذِينَ آمَنُوا وَلَمْ يُهَاجِرُوا مَا لَكُمْ مِنْ وَلَايَتِهِمْ مِنْ شَيْءٍ حَتَّى يُهَاجِرُوا وَإِنِ اسْتَنْصَرُوكُمْ فِي الدِّينِ فَعَلَيْكُمُ النَّصْرُ إِلَّا عَلَى قَوْمٍ بَيْنَكُمْ وَبَيْنَهُمْ مِيثَاقٌ وَاللَّهُ بِمَا تَعْمَلُونَ بَصِيرٌ، وَالَّذِينَ كَفَرُوا بَعْضُهُمْ أَوْلِيَاءُ بَعْضٍ إِلَّا تَفْعَلُوهُ تَكُنْ فِتْنَةٌ فِي الْأَرْضِ وَفَسَادٌ كَبِيرٌ، وَالَّذِينَ آمَنُوا وَهَاجَرُوا وَجَاهَدُوا فِي سَبِيلِ اللَّهِ وَالَّذِينَ آوَوْا وَنَصَرُوا أُولَئِكَ هُمُ الْمُؤْمِنُونَ حَقًّا لَهُمْ مَغْفِرَةٌ وَرِزْقٌ كَرِيمٌ، وَالَّذِينَ آمَنُوا مِنْ بَعْدُ وَهَاجَرُوا وَجَاهَدُوا مَعَكُمْ فَأُولَئِكَ مِنْكُمْ..) [الأنفال: 72 – 75]

بهذه النصاعة الكاملة، وبهذا الجزم القاطع جاء الإسلام. جاء ليرفع الإنسان ويخلصه من وشائج الأرض والطين، ومن وشائج اللحم والدم - وهي من وشائج الأرض والطين - فلا وطن للمسلم إلا الذي تقام فيه شريعة الله، فتقوم الروابط بينه وبين سكانه على أساس الارتباط في الله، ولا جنسية للمسلم إلا عقيدته التي تجعله عضوا في "الأمة المسلمة "في "دار الإسلام "، ولا قرابة للمسلم إلا تلك التي تنبثق من العقيدة في الله، فتصل الوشيجة بينه وبين أهله في الله..

ليست قرابة المسلم أباه وأمه وأخاه وزوجه وعشيرته، ما لم تنعقد الآصرة الأولى في الخالق، فتتصل من ثم بالرحم:

(يَا أَيُّهَا النَّاسُ اتَّقُوا رَبَّكُمُ الَّذِي خَلَقَكُمْ مِنْ نَفْسٍ وَاحِدَةٍ وَخَلَقَ مِنْهَا زَوْجَهَا وَبَثَّ مِنْهُمَا رِجَالًا كَثِيرًا وَنِسَاءً وَاتَّقُوا اللَّهَ الَّذِي تَسَاءَلُونَ بِهِ وَالْأَرْحَامَ).. [النساء: 1]

ولا يمنع هذا من مصاحبة الوالدين بالمعروف مع اختلاف العقيدة ما لم يقفا في الصف المعادي للجبهة المسلمة، فعندئذ لا صلة ولا مصاحبة، وعبد الله بن عبد الله بن أبي يعطينا المثل في جلاء:

روى ابن جرير بسنده عن ابن زياد قال: دعا رسول الله - صلى الله عليه وسلم - عبد الله بن عبد الله بن أبي قال: ألا ترى ما يقول أبوك؟ قال: ما يقول أبي؟ - بأبي أنت وأمي - قال: يقول لئن رجعنا إلى المدينة ليخرجن الأعز منها الأذل. فقال: فقد صدق والله يا رسول الله. أنت والله الأعز وهو الأذل. أما والله لقد قدمت المدينة يا رسول الله وأن أهل يثرب ليعلمون ما بها أحد أبر بوالده مني. ولئن كان يرضي الله ورسوله أن آتيهما لآتيهما به. فقال رسول الله صلى الله عليه وسلم: "لا ". فلما قدموا المدينة قام عبد الله بن عبد الله بن أبي على بابها بالسيف لأبيه، قال: أنت القائل: لئن رجعنا إلى المدينة ليخرجن الأعز منها الأذل؟ أما والله لتعرفن العزة لك أو لرسول الله صلى الله عليه وسلم؟ والله لا يأويك ظلها ولا تأويه أبدا إلا بإذن من الله ورسوله. فقال: يا للخزرج. ابني يمنعني بيتي. يا للخزرج ابني يمنعني بيتي. فقال: والله لا يأويه أبدا إلا بإذن منه. فاجتمع إليه رجال فكلموه فقال: والله لا يدخلن إلا بإذن من الله ورسوله. فأتوا النبي - صلى الله عليه وسلم - فأخبروه فقال: "اذهبوا إليه فقولوا له: خله ومسكنه ". فأتوه فقال: أما إذ جاء أمر النبي صلى الله عليه وسلم فنعم.

فإذا انعقدت آصرة العقيدة فالمؤمنون كلهم إخوة، ولو لم يجمعهم نسب ولا صهر:
(إِنَّمَا الْمُؤْمِنُونَ إِخْوَةٌ). على سبيل القصر والتوكيد:

(إِنَّ الَّذِينَ آمَنُوا وَهَاجَرُوا وَجَاهَدُوا بِأَمْوَالِهِمْ وَأَنْفُسِهِمْ فِي سَبِيلِ اللهِ وَالَّذِينَ آوَوْا وَنَصَرُوا أُولَئِكَ بَعْضُهُمْ أَوْلِيَاءُ بَعْضٍ).. [الأنفال: 72]

وهي ولاية تتجاوز الجيل الواحد إلى الأجيال المتعاقبة، وتربط أول هذه الأمة بآخرها، وآخرها بأولها، برباط الحب والمودة والولاء والتعاطف المكين:

(وَالَّذِينَ تَبَوَّءُوا الدَّارَ وَالْإِيمَانَ مِنْ قَبْلِهِمْ يُحِبُّونَ مَنْ هَاجَرَ إِلَيْهِمْ وَلَا يَجِدُونَ فِي صُدُورِهِمْ حَاجَةً مِمَّا أُوتُوا وَيُؤْثِرُونَ عَلَى أَنْفُسِهِمْ وَلَوْ كَانَ بِهِمْ خَصَاصَةٌ وَمَنْ يُوقَ شُحَّ نَفْسِهِ فَأُولَئِكَ هُمُ الْمُفْلِحُونَ، وَالَّذِينَ جَاءُوا مِنْ بَعْدِهِمْ يَقُولُونَ رَبَّنَا اغْفِرْ لَنَا وَلِإِخْوَانِنَا الَّذِينَ سَبَقُونَا بِالْإِيمَانِ وَلَا تَجْعَلْ فِي قُلُوبِنَا غِلًّا لِلَّذِينَ آمَنُوا رَبَّنَا إِنَّكَ رَؤُوفٌ رَحِيمٌ) [الحشر: 9 - 10]

ويضرب الله الامثال للمسلمين بالرهط الكريم من الأنبياء الذين سبقوهم في موكب الإيمان الضارب في شعاب الزمان:

(وَنَادَى نُوحٌ رَبَّهُ فَقَالَ رَبِّ إِنَّ ابْنِي مِنْ أَهْلِي وَإِنَّ وَعْدَكَ الْحَقُّ وَأَنْتَ أَحْكَمُ الْحَاكِمِينَ، قَالَ يَا نُوحُ إِنَّهُ لَيْسَ مِنْ أَهْلِكَ إِنَّهُ عَمَلٌ غَيْرُ صَالِحٍ فَلَا تَسْأَلْنِ مَا لَيْسَ لَكَ بِهِ عِلْمٌ إِنِّي أَعِظُكَ أَنْ تَكُونَ مِنَ الْجَاهِلِينَ، قَالَ رَبِّ إِنِّي أَعُوذُ بِكَ أَنْ أَسْأَلَكَ مَا لَيْسَ لِي بِهِ عِلْمٌ وَإِلَّا تَغْفِرْ لِي وَتَرْحَمْنِي أَكُنْ مِنَ الْخَاسِرِينَ).. [هود: 45 - 47]

(وَإِذِ ابْتَلَى إِبْرَاهِيمَ رَبُّهُ بِكَلِمَاتٍ فَأَتَمَّهُنَّ قَالَ إِنِّي جَاعِلُكَ لِلنَّاسِ إِمَامًا قَالَ وَمِنْ ذُرِّيَتِي قَالَ لَا يَنَالُ عَهْدِي الظَّالِمِينَ).. [البقرة: 124]

(وَإِذْ قَالَ إِبْرَاهِيمُ رَبِّ اجْعَلْ هَذَا بَلَدًا آمِنًا وَارْزُقْ أَهْلَهُ مِنَ الثَّمَرَاتِ مَنْ آمَنَ مِنْهُمْ بِاللهِ وَالْيَوْمِ الْآخِرِ قَالَ وَمَنْ كَفَرَ فَأُمَتِّعُهُ قَلِيلًا ثُمَّ أَضْطَرُّهُ إِلَى عَذَابِ النَّارِ وَبِئْسَ الْمَصِيرُ).. [البقرة: 126]

ويعتزل إبراهيم أباه وأهله حين يرى منهم الإصرار على الضلال:

(وَأَعْتَزِلُكُمْ وَمَا تَدْعُونَ مِنْ دُونِ اللهِ وَأَدْعُو رَبِّي عَسَى أَلَّا أَكُونَ بِدُعَاءِ رَبِّي شَقِيًّا).. [مريم: 48]

ويحكي الله عن إبراهيم وقومه ما فيه أسوة وقدوة:

(قَدْ كَانَتْ لَكُمْ أُسْوَةٌ حَسَنَةٌ فِي إِبْرَاهِيمَ وَالَّذِينَ مَعَهُ إِذْ قَالُوا لِقَوْمِهِمْ إِنَّا بُرَآءُ مِنْكُمْ وَمِمَّا تَعْبُدُونَ مِنْ دُونِ اللهِ كَفَرْنَا بِكُمْ وَبَدَا بَيْنَنَا وَبَيْنَكُمُ الْعَدَاوَةُ وَالْبَغْضَاءُ أَبَدًا حَتَّى تُؤْمِنُوا بِاللهِ وَحْدَهُ). [الممتحنة: 4]

والفتية أصحاب الكهف يعتزلون أهلهم وقومهم وأرضهم ليخلصوا لله بدينهم، ويفروا إلى ربهم بعقيدتهم، حين عز عليهم أن يجدوا لها مكانا في الوطن والأهل والعشيرة.

(إِنَّهُمْ فِتْيَةٌ آمَنُوا بِرَبِّهِمْ وَزِدْنَاهُمْ هُدًى، وَرَبَطْنَا عَلَى قُلُوبِهِمْ إِذْ قَامُوا فَقَالُوا رَبُّنَا رَبُّ السَّمَاوَاتِ وَالْأَرْضِ لَنْ نَدْعُوَ مِنْ دُونِهِ إِلَهًا لَقَدْ قُلْنَا إِذًا شَطَطًا، هَؤُلَاءِ قَوْمُنَا اتَّخَذُوا

مِنْ دُونِهِ آلِهَةً لَوْلَا يَأْتُونَ عَلَيْهِمْ بِسُلْطَانٍ بَيِّنٍ فَمَنْ أَظْلَمُ مِمَّنِ افْتَرَى عَلَى اللَّهِ كَذِبًا، وَإِذِ اعْتَزَلْتُمُوهُمْ وَمَا يَعْبُدُونَ إِلَّا اللَّهَ فَأْوُوا إِلَى الْكَهْفِ يَنْشُرْ لَكُمْ رَبُّكُمْ مِنْ رَحْمَتِهِ وَيُهَيِّئْ لَكُمْ مِنْ أَمْرِكُمْ مِرْفَقًا).. [الكهف: 13 - 16]

وامرأة نوح وامرأة لوط يفرق بينهما وبين زوجيهما حين تفترق العقيدة:

(ضَرَبَ اللَّهُ مَثَلًا لِلَّذِينَ كَفَرُوا امْرَأَةَ نُوحٍ وَامْرَأَةَ لُوطٍ كَانَتَا تَحْتَ عَبْدَيْنِ مِنْ عِبَادِنَا صَالِحَيْنِ فَخَانَتَاهُمَا فَلَمْ يُغْنِيَا عَنْهُمَا مِنَ اللَّهِ شَيْئًا وَقِيلَ ادْخُلَا النَّارَ مَعَ الدَّاخِلِينَ). [التحريم: 10]

وامرأة فرعون على الضفة الأخرى:

(وَضَرَبَ اللَّهُ مَثَلًا لِلَّذِينَ آمَنُوا امْرَأَةَ فِرْعَوْنَ إِذْ قَالَتْ رَبِّ ابْنِ لِي عِنْدَكَ بَيْتًا فِي الْجَنَّةِ وَنَجِّنِي مِنْ فِرْعَوْنَ وَعَمَلِهِ وَنَجِّنِي مِنَ الْقَوْمِ الظَّالِمِينَ).. [التحريم: 11]

وهكذا تتعدد الأمثال في جميع الوشائج والروابط. وشيجة الأبوة في قصة نوح، ووشيجة البنوة والوطن في قصة إبراهيم، ووشيجة الأهل والعشيرة والوطن جميعا في قصة أصحاب الكهف، ورابطة الزوجية في قصص امرأتي نوح ولوط وامرأة فرعون.

وهكذا يمضي الموكب الكريم في تصوره لحقيقة الروابط والوشائج. حتى تجيء الأمة الوسط، فتجد هذا الرصيد من الأمثال والنماذج والتجارب، فتمضي على النهج الرباني للأمة المؤمنة، وتفترق العشيرة الواحدة، ويفترق البيت الواحد، حين تفترق العقيدة، وحيث تنبت الوشيجة الأولى، ويقول الله سبحانه في صفة المؤمنين قوله الكريم:

(لَا تَجِدُ قَوْمًا يُؤْمِنُونَ بِاللَّهِ وَالْيَوْمِ الْآخِرِ يُوَادُّونَ مَنْ حَادَّ اللَّهَ وَرَسُولَهُ وَلَوْ كَانُوا آبَاءَهُمْ أَوْ أَبْنَاءَهُمْ أَوْ إِخْوَانَهُمْ أَوْ عَشِيرَتَهُمْ أُولَئِكَ كَتَبَ فِي قُلُوبِهِمُ الْإِيمَانَ وَأَيَّدَهُمْ بِرُوحٍ مِنْهُ وَيُدْخِلُهُمْ جَنَّاتٍ تَجْرِي مِنْ تَحْتِهَا الْأَنْهَارُ خَالِدِينَ فِيهَا رَضِيَ اللَّهُ عَنْهُمْ وَرَضُوا عَنْهُ أُولَئِكَ حِزْبُ اللَّهِ أَلَا إِنَّ حِزْبَ اللَّهِ هُمُ الْمُفْلِحُونَ).. [المجادلة: 22]

وحين انبتت وشيجة القرابة بين محمد - صلى الله عليه وسلم - وبين عمه أبي لهب، وابن عمه عمرو بن هشام (أبو جهل) وحين قاتل المهاجرون أهلهم وأقرباءهم وقتلوهم يوم بدر. حينئذ اتصلت وشيجة العقيدة بين المهاجرين والأنصار، فإذا هم أهل وإخوة، واتصلت الوشيجة بين المسلمين العرب وإخوانهم: صهيب الرومي، وبلال الحبشي، وسلمان الفارسي. وتوارت عصبية القبيلة، وعصبية الجنس، وعصبية الأرض. وقال لهم رسول الله - صلى الله عليه وسلم -: "دعوها فإنها منتنة ". وقال لهم: "ليس منا من دعا إلى عصبية، وليس منا من قاتل على عصبية، وليس منا من مات على عصبية ". فانتهى أمر هذا النتن. نتن عصبية النسب. وماتت هذه النعرة. نعرة الجنس، واختفت تلك اللوثة. لوثة القوم، واستروح البشر أرج الآفاق العليا، بعيدا عن نتن اللحم والدم، ولوثة الطين والأرض. منذ ذلك اليوم لم يعد وطن المسلم هو الأرض، إنما عاد وطنه هو "دار الإسلام "الدار التي تسيطر عليها عقيدته وتحكم فيها شريعة الله وحدها، الدار التي يأوي إليها ويدافع عنها، ويستشهد لحمايتها ومد رقعتها. وهي "دار الإسلام "لكل من يدين بالإسلام عقيدة ويرتضي شريعته شريعة، وكذلك لكل من يرتضي شريعة الإسلام نظاما - ولو لم يكن مسلما - كأصحاب الديانات الكتابية

الذين يعيشون في "دار الإسلام ". والأرض التي لا يهيمن فيها الإسلام ولا تحكم فيها شريعته هي "دار الحرب "بالقياس إلى المسلم، وإلى الذي المعاهد كذلك. يحاربها المسلم ولو كان فيها مولده، وفيها قرابته من النسب وصهره، وفيها أمواله ومنافعه.

وكذلك حارب محمد - صلى الله عليه وسلم - مكة وهي مسقط رأسه، وفيها عشيرته وأهله، وفيها داره ودور صحابته وأموالهم التي تركوها. فلم تصبح دار إسلام له ولأمته إلا حين دانت للإسلام وطبقت فيها شريعته.

هذا هو الإسلام. هذا هو وحده. فالإسلام ليس كلمة تقال باللسان، ولا ميلادا في أرض عليها لافتة إسلامية وعنوان إسلامي. ولا وراثة مولد في بيت أبواه مسلمان.

(فلا وربك لا يُؤمِنُون حتى يُحكِّمُوك فِيما شجر بيْنهُمْ ثُم لا يجِدُوا فِي أنْفُسِهِمْ حرجا مِما قضيْت ويُسلمُوا تسْليما). [النساء: 65]

هذا هو وحده الإسلام، وهذه هي وحدها دار الإسلام. لا الأرض ولا الجنس، ولا النسب والا الصهر، ولا القبيلة، ولا العشيرة.

لقد أطلق الإسلام البشر من اللصوق بالطين ليتطلعوا إلى السماء، وأطلقهم من قيد الدم. قيد البهيمة. ليرتفعوا في عليين.

وطن المسلم الذي يحن إليه ويدافع عنه ليس قطعة أرض، وجنسية المسلم التي يعرف بها ليست جنسية حكم، وعشيرة المسلم التي يأوي إليها ويدفع عنها ليست قرابة دم، وراية المسلم التي يعتز بها ويستشهد تحتها ليست راية قوم، وانتصار المسلم الذي يهفوا إليه ويشكر الله عليه ليس غلبة جيش. إنما هو كما قال الله عنه:

(إذا جاء نصْرُ اللهِ والْفتْحُ، ورأيْت الناس يدْخُلُون فِي دِينِ اللهِ أفْواجا، فسبحْ بِحمْدِ ربك واسْتغْفِرْهُ إِنهُ كان توابا).. [سورة النصر]

إنه النصر تحت راية العقيدة دون سائر الرايات. والجهاد لنصرة دين الله وشريعته لا لأي هدف من الأهداف، والذياد عن "دار الإسلام "بشروطها تلك لا أية دار، والتجرد بعد هذا كله لله، لا لمغنم ولا لسمعة، ولا حمية لأرض أو قوم، أو ذود عن أهل أو ولد، إلا لحمايتهم من الفتنة عن دين الله:

عن أبي موسى رضي الله عنه قال: سئل رسول الله - صلى الله عليه وسلم - عن الرجل يقاتل شجاعة ويقاتل حمية ويقاتل رياء، أي ذلك في سبيل الله؟ فقال: "من قاتل لتكون كلمة الله هي العليا فهو في سبيل الله "..

وفي هذا وحده تكون الشهادة لا في أية حرب لأي هدف غير هذا الهدف الواحد. لله.

وكل أرض تحارب المسلم في عقيدته، وتصده عن دينه، وتعطل عمل شريعته، فهي "دار حرب "ولو كان فيها أهله وعشيرته وقومه وماله وتجارته. وكل أرض تقوم فيها عقيدته وتعمل فيها شريعته، فهي "دار إسلام "ولو لم يكن فيها أهل ولا عشيرة، ولا قوم ولا تجارة.

الوطن: دار تحكمها عقيدة ومنهاج حياة وشريعة من الله. هذا هو معنى الوطن اللائق "بالإنسان". والجنسية: عقيدة ومنهاج حياة. وهذه هي الآصرة اللائقة بالآدميين.

إن عصبية العشيرة والقبيلة والقوم والجنس واللون والأرض عصبية صغيرة متخلفة. عصبية جاهلية عرفتها البشرية في فترات انحطاطها الروحي، وسماها رسول الله - صلى الله عليه وسلم - "منتنة" بهذا الوصف الذي يفوح منه التقزز والاشمئزاز.

ولما ادعى اليهود أنهم شعب الله المختار بجنسهم وقومهم رد الله عليهم هذه الدعوى، ورد ميزان القيم إلى الإيمان وحده على توالي الأجيال، وتغاير الأقوام والأجناس والأوطان:

(وقالُوا كُونُوا هُودا أو نصارى تهْتدُوا قُلْ بلْ مِلة إبْراهِيم حنِيفا وما كان مِن المُشْركِين، قُولُوا آمنا بِاللهِ وما أُنْزِل إلينا وما أُنْزِل إلى إبْراهِيم وإسْماعِيل وإسْحاق ويعْقُوب والأسْباطِ وما أُوتِي مُوسى وعِيسى وما أُوتِي النبِيون مِنْ ربهِمْ لا نُفرقُ بيْن أحدٍ مِنْهُمْ ونحْنُ له مُسْلِمُون، فإِنْ آمنُوا بِمِثْلِ ما آمنْتُمْ بِهِ فقدِ اهْتدوْا وإنْ تولوْا فإِنما هُمْ فِي شِقاقٍ فسيكْفِيكهُمُ اللهُ وهُو السمِيعُ الْعلِيمُ، صِبْغة اللهِ ومنْ أحْسنُ مِن اللهِ صِبْغة ونحْنُ له عابِدُون).. [البقرة: 135 - 138]

فأما شعب الله المختار حقا فهو الأمة المسلمة التي تستظل براية الله على اختلاف ما بينها من الأجناس والأقوام والألوان والأوطان:

(كُنْتُمْ خيْر أمةٍ أُخْرِجتْ لِلناسِ تأْمُرُون بِالْمعْرُوفِ وتنْهوْن عنِ الْمُنْكرِ وتُؤْمِنُون بِاللهِ).. [آل عمران: 110]

الأمة التي يكون من الرعيل الأول فيها أبو بكر العربي، وبلال الحبشي، وصهيب الرومي، وسلمان الفارسي، وإخوانهم الكرام. والتي تتوالى أجيالها على هذا النسق الرائع. الجنسية فيها العقيدة، والوطن فيها هو دار الإسلام، والحاكم فيها هو الله، والدستور فيها هو القرآن.

هذا التصور الرفيع للدار وللجنسية وللقرابة هو الذي ينبغي أن يسيطر على قلوب أصحاب الدعوة إلى الله، والذي ينبغي أن يكون من الوضوح بحيث لا تختلط به أوشاب التصورات الجاهلية الدخيلة، ولا تتسرب إليه صور الشرك الخفية: الشرك بالأرض، والشرك بالجنس، والشرك بالقوم، والشرك بالنسب، والشرك بالمنافع الصغيرة القريبة، تلك التي يجمعها الله سبحانه في آية واحدة فيضعها في كفة، ويضع الإيمان ومقتضياته في كفة أخرى، ويدع للناس الخيار:

(قُلْ إنْ كان آباؤُكُمْ وأبْناؤُكُمْ وإخْوانُكُمْ وأزْواجُكُمْ وعشِيرتُكُمْ وأمْوالٌ اقْترفْتُمُوها وتِجارةٌ تخْشوْن كسادها ومساكِنُ ترْضوْنها أحب إليكُمْ مِن اللهِ ورسُولِهِ وجِهادٍ فِي سبِيلِهِ فتربصُوا حتى يأْتِي اللهُ بِأمْرِهِ واللهُ لا يهْدِي الْقوْم الْفاسِقِين).. [التوبة: 24]

كذلك لا ينبغي أن تقوم في نفوس أصحاب الدعوة إلى الله تلك الشكوك السطحية في حقيقة الجاهلية وحقيقة الإسلام، وفي صفة دار الحرب ودار الإسلام. فمن هنا يؤتى الكثير منهم في تصوراته ويقينه. إنه لا إسلام في أرض لا يحكمها الإسلام، ولا تقوم فيها

شريعته، ولا دار إسلام إلا التي يهيمن عليها الإسلام بمنهجه وقانونه، وليس وراء الإيمان إلا الكفر، وليس دون الإسلام إلا الجاهلية. وليس بعد الحق إلا الضلال.

نقْلةٌ بعِيدة

هناك حقيقة أولية، ينبغي أن تكون واضحة في نفوسنا تماما ونحن نقدم الإسلام للناس: الذين يؤمنون به والذين لا يؤمنون به على السواء. هذه الحقيقة تنبثق من طبيعة الإسلام ذاته، وتنبع من تاريخه.

إن الإسلام تصور مستقل للوجود والحياة، تصور كامل ذو خصائص متميزة، ومن ثم ينبثق منه منهج ذاتي مستقل للحياة كلها، بكل مقوماتها وارتباطاتها، ويقوم عليه نظام ذو خصائص معينة.

هذا التصور يخالف مخالفة أساسية سائر التصورات الجاهلية قديما وحديثا. وقد يلتقي مع هذه التصورات في جزئيات عرضية جانبية، ولكن الأصول التي تنبثق منها هذه الجزئيات مختلفة عن سائر ما عرفته البشرية من نظائرها.

ووظيفة الإسلام الأولى هي أن ينشئ حياة إنسانية توافق هذا التصور، وتمثله في صورة واقعية، وأن يقيم في الأرض نظاما يتبع المنهج الرباني الذي اختاره الله، وهو يخرج هذه الأمة المسلمة لتمثله وتقوم عليه، وهو - سبحانه - يقول:

(كُنْتُمْ خيْرَ أُمةٍ أُخْرِجتْ لِلناسِ تأْمُرُون بِالْمعْرُوفِ وتنْهوْن عنِ الْمُنْكرِ وتُؤْمِنُون بِاللهِ).. [آل عمران: 110]

ويقول في صفة هذه الأمة:

(الذِين إِنْ مكناهُمْ فِي الْأرْضِ أقامُوا الصلاة وآتوُا الزكاة وأمرُوا بِالْمعْرُوفِ ونهوْا عنِ الْمُنْكرِ).. [الحج: 41]

وليست وظيفة الإسلام إذن أن يصطلح مع التصورات الجاهلية السائدة في الأرض، ولا الأوضاع الجاهلية القائمة في كل مكان. لم تكن هذه وظيفته يوم جاء، ولن تكون هذه وظيفته اليوم ولا في المستقبل. فالجاهلية هي الجاهلية، الجاهلية هي الانحراف عن العبودية لله وحده وعن المنهج الإلهي في الحياة، واستنباط النظم والشرائع والقوانين والعادات والتقاليد والقيم والموازين من مصدر آخر غير المصدر الإلهي. الإسلام وهو الإسلام، ووظيفته هي نقل الناس من الجاهلية إلى الإسلام.

الجاهلية هي عبودية الناس للناس: بتشريع بعض الناس للناس ما لم يأذن به الله، كائنة ما كانت الصورة التي يتم بها هذا التشريع..

والإسلام هو عبودية الناس لله وحده بتلقيهم منه وحده تصوراتهم وعقائدهم وشرائعهم وقوانينهم وقيمهم وموازينهم والتحرر من عبودية العبيد.

هذه الحقيقة المنبثقة من طبيعة الإسلام، وطبيعة دوره في الأرض، هي التي يجب أن نقدم بها الإسلام للناس: الذين يؤمنون به والذين لا يؤمنون به على السواء.

إن الإسلام لا يقبل أنصاف الحلول مع الجاهلية. لا من ناحية التصور، ولا من ناحية الأوضاع المنبثقة من هذا التصور. فإما إسلام وإما جاهلية. وليس هنالك وضع آخر نصفه إسلام ونصفه جاهلية، يقبله الإسلام ويرضاه. فنظرة الإسلام واضحة في أن الحق واحد لا يتعدد، وأن ما عدا هذا الحق فهو الضلال. وهما غير قابلين للتلبس والامتزاج. وأنه إما حكم الله وإما حكم الجاهلية، وإما شريعة الله، وإما الهوى. والآيات القرآنية في هذا المعنى متواترة كثيرة:

(وأنِ احْكُمْ بيْنهُمْ بِما أنْزَل اللهُ ولا تتَّبِعْ أهْواءهُمْ واحْذرْهُمْ أنْ يفْتِنُوك عنْ بعْضِ ما أنْزَل اللهُ إِليْك). [المائدة: 49]

(فلِذلِك فادْعُ واستقِمْ كما أُمِرْت ولا تتَّبِعْ أهْواءهُمْ). [الشورى: 15]

(فإِنْ لمْ يسْتجِيبُوا لك فاعْلمْ أنما يتَّبعُون أهْواءهُمْ ومنْ أضلُّ مِمنِ اتبع هواهُ بِغيْرِ هُدى مِن اللهِ إِن الله لا يهْدِي القوْم الظالِمِين). [القصص: 50]

(ثُم جعلْناك على شرِيعةٍ مِن الأمْرِ فاتَّبِعْها ولا تتَّبِعْ أهْواء الذِين لا يعْلمُون، إِنهُمْ لنْ يُغْنُوا عنْك مِن اللهِ شيْئًا وإِن الظالِمِين بعْضُهُمْ أوْلِياءُ بعْضٍ والله ولِيُّ المُتقِين). [الجاثية: 18-19]

(أفحُكْم الجاهِلِيةِ يبْغُون ومنْ أحْسنُ مِن اللهِ حُكْمًا لِقوْمٍ يُوقِنُون). [المائدة: 50]

فهما أمران لا ثالث لهما. إما الاستجابة لله والرسول، وإما اتباع الهوى. إما حكم الجاهلية. إما الحكم بما أنزل الله كله وإما الفتنة عما أنزل الله. وليس بعد هذا التوكيد الصريح الجازم من الله سبحانه مجال للجدال أو للمحال.

وظيفة الإسلام إذن هي إقصاء الجاهلية من قيادة البشرية، وتولي هذه القيادة على منهجه الخاص، المستقل الملامح، الأصيل الخصائص. يريد بهذه القيادة الرشيدة الخير للبشرية واليسر. الخير الذي ينشأ من رد البشرية إلى خالقها، واليسر الذي ينشأ من التنسيق بين حركة البشرية، وتولي هذه القيادة منهجه الخاص، المستقل، ترتفع إلى المستوى الكريم الذي أراده الله لها، وتخلص من حكم الهوى. أو كما قال ربعي بن عامر حين سأله رستم قائد الفرس: ما الذي جاء بكم؟ فكان جوابه: "الله ابتعثنا لنخرج من شاء من عبادة العباد إلى عبادة الله وحده، ومن ضيق الدنيا إلى سعة الدنيا والآخرة، ومن جور الأديان إلى عدل الإسلام ".

لم يجيء الإسلام إذن ليربت على شهوات الناس الممثلة في تصوراتهم وأنظمتهم وأوضاعهم وعاداتهم وتقاليدهم. سواء منها ما عاصر مجيء الإسلام، أو ما تخوض البشرية فيه الآن، في الشرق أو في الغرب سواء. إنما جاء هذا كله إلغاء، وينسخه نسخا، ويقيم الحياة البشرية على أسسه الخاصة. جاء لينشئ الحياة إنشاء. لينشئ حياة تنبثق منه انبثاقا، وترتبط بمحوره ارتباطا. وقد تشابه جزئيات منه في الحياة التي يعيشها الناس في الجاهلية. ولكنها ليست هي، وليست منها. إنما هي مجرد مصادفة هذا التشابه الظاهري الجانبي في الفروع. أما أصل الشجرة فهو مختلف تماما. تلك شجرة تطلعها حكمة الله، وهذه شجرة تطلعها أهواء البشر:

(وَالْبَلَدُ الطَّيِّبُ يَخْرُجُ نَبَاتُهُ بِإِذْنِ رَبِّهِ وَالَّذِي خَبُثَ لَا يَخْرُجُ إِلَّا نَكِدًا). [الأعراف:
[58

وهذه الجاهلية خبثت قديما وخبثت حديثا. يختلف خبثها في مظهره وشكله، ولكنه
واحد في مغرسه وأصله. إنه هوى البشر الجهال المغرضين، الذين لا يملكون التخلص من
جهلهم وغرضهم، ومصلحة أفراد منهم أو طبقات أو أمم أو أجناس يغلبونها على العدل
والحق والخير. حتى تجيء شريعة الله فتنسخ هذاكله، وتشرع للناس جميعا تشريعا لا يشوبه
جهل البشر، ولا يلوثه هواهم، ولا تميل به مصلحة فريق منهم.

ولأن هذا هو الفارق الأصيل بين طبيعة منهج الله ومناهج الناس، فإنه يستحيل
الالتقاء بينهما في نظام واحد، ويستحيل التوفيق بينهما في وضع واحد. ويستحيل تلفيق
منهج نصفه من هنا ونصفه من هناك. وكما أن الله لا يغفر أن يشرك به. فكذلك هو لا يقبل
منهجا مع منهجه. هذه كتلك سواء بسواء. لأن هذه هي تلك على وجه اليقين.

هذه الحقيقة ينبغي أن تكون من القوة والوضوح في نفوسنا ونحن نقدم الإسلام
للناس بحيث لا نتلجلج في الإدلاء بها ولا نتلعثم، ولا ندع الناس في شك منها، ولا نتركهم
حتى يستيقنوا أن الإسلام حين يفيئون إليه سيبدل حياتهم تبديلا. سيبدل تصوراتهم عن
الحياة كلها. كما سيبدل أوضاعهم كذلك. سيبدلها ليعطيهم خيرا منها بما لا يقاس. سيبدلها
ليرفع تصوراتهم ويرفع أوضاعهم، ويجعلهم أقرب إلى المستوى الكريم اللائق بحياة الإنسان.
ولن يبقى لهم شيئا من أوضاع الجاهلية الهابطة التي هم فيها، اللهم إلا الجزئيات التي
يتصادف أن يكون لها من جزئيات النظام الإسلامي شبيه. وحتى هذه لن تكون هي بعينها،
لأنها ستكون مشدودة إلى أصل كبير يختلف اختلافا بينا عن الأصل الذي هم مشدودون
إليه الآن: أصل الجاهلية النكد الخبيث. وهو في الوقت ذاته لن يسلبهم شيئا من المعرفة
"العلمية البحتة "بل سيدفعها قوية إلى الأمام.

يجب ألا ندع الناس حتى يدركوا أن الإسلام ليس هو أي مذهب من المذاهب
الاجتماعية الوضعية، كما أنه ليس أي نظام من أنظمة الحكم الوضعية. بشتى أسمائها
وشياتها وراياتها جميعا. وإنما هو الإسلام فقط. الإسلام بشخصيته المستقلة وتصوره
المستقل، وأوضاعه المستقلة. الإسلام الذي يحقق للبشرية خيرا مما تحلم به كله من وراء
هذه الأوضاع. الإسلام الرفيع النظيف الجميل المتناسق الصادر مباشرة من الله العلي
الكبير.

وحين ندرك حقيقة الإسلام على هذا النحو، فإن هذا الإدراك بطبيعته سيجعلنا
نخاطب الناس ونحن نقدم لهم الإسلام، في ثقة وقوة، وفي عطف كذلك ورحمة. ثقة الذي
يستيقن أن ما معه هو الحق وأن ما عليه الناس هو الباطل. وعطف الذي يرى شقوة البشر،
وهو يعرف كيف يسعدهم. ورحمة الذي يرى ضلال الناس وهو يعرف أين الهدى الذي
ليس بعده هدى.

لن نتدسس إليهم بالإسلام تدسسا. ولن نربت على شهواتهم وتصوراتهم المنحرفة.
سنكون صرحاء معهم غاية الصراحة. هذه الجاهلية التي أنتم فيها نجس والله يريد أن
يطهركم. هذه الأوضاع التي أنتم فيها خبث، والله يريد أن يطيبكم. هذه الحياة التي تحيونها

دون، والله يريد أن يرفعكم. هذا الذي أنتم فيه شقوة وبؤس ونكد، والله يريد أن يخفف عنكم ويرحمكم ويسعدكم. والإسلام سيغير تصوراتكم وأوضاعكم وقيمكم، وسيرفعكم إلى حياة أخرى تنكرون معها هذه الحياة التي تعيشونها، وإلى أوضاع أخرى تحتقرون معها أوضاعكم في مشارق الأرض ومغاربها، وإلى قيم أخرى تشمئزون معها من قيمكم السائدة في الأرض جميعا. وإذا كنتم أنتم - لشقوتكم - لم تروا صورة واقعية للحياة الإسلامية، لأن أعداءكم - أعداء هذا الدين - يتكتلون للحيلولة دون قيام هذه الحياة، ودون تجسد هذه الصورة، فنحن قد رأيناها - والحمد لله ممثلة في ضمائرنا من خلال قرآننا وشريعتنا وتاريخنا وتصورنا المبدع للمستقبل الذي لا نشك في مجيئه.

هكذا ينبغي أن نخاطب الناس ونحن نقدم لهم الإسلام. لأن هذه هي الحقيقة، ولأن هذه هي الصورة التي خاطب الإسلام الناس بها أول مرة. سواء في الجزيرة العربية أم في فارس أم في الروم. أم في أي مكان خاطب الناس فيه.

نظر إليهم من عل، لأن هذه هي الحقيقة. وخاطبهم بلغة الحب والعطف لأنها حقيقة كذلك في طبيعته. وفاصلهم مفاصلة كاملة لا غموض فيها ولا تردد لأن هذه هي طريقته. ولم يقل لهم أبدا: إنه لن يمس حياتهم وأوضاعهم وتصوراتهم وقيمهم إلا بتعديلات طفيفة. أو أنه يشبه نظمهم وأوضاعهم التي ألفوها. كما يقول بعضنا اليوم للناس وهو يقدم إليهم الإسلام. مرة تحت عنوان: "ديمقراطية الإسلام ". ومرة تحت عنوان "اشتراكية الإسلام ". ومرة بأن الأوضاع الاقتصادية والسياسية والقانونية القائمة في عالمهم لا تحتاج من الإسلام إلا لتعديلات طفيفة.. إلى آخر هذا التدسس الناعم والتربيت على الشهوات.

كلا. إن الأمر مختلف جدا. والانتقال من هذه الجاهلية التي تعم وجه الأرض إلى الإسلام نقلة واسعة بعيدة، وصورة الحياة الإسلامية مغايرة تماما لصور الحياة الجاهلية قديما وحديثا. وهذه الشقوة التي تعانيها البشرية لن يرفعها عنها تغييرات طفيفة في جزئيات النظم والأوضاع. ولن ينجي البشر منها إلا تلك النقلة الواسعة البعيدة. النقلة من مناهج الخلق إلى منهج الخالق، ومن نظم البشر إلى نظام رب البشر، ومن أحكام العبيد إلى حكم رب العبيد.

هذه حقيقة. وحقيقة مثلها أن نجهر بها ونصدع، وألا ندع الناس في شك منها ولا لبس.

وقد يكره الناس هذا في أول الأمر، وقد يجفلون منه ويشفقون. ولكن الناس كذلك كرهوا مثل هذا وأشفقوا منه في أول العهد بالدعوة إلى الإسلام. أجفلوا وآذاهم أن يحقر محمد - صلى الله عليه وسلم - تصوراتهم، ويعيب آلهتهم، وينكر أوضاعهم، ويعتزل عاداتهم وتقاليدهم، ويتخذ لنفسه وللقلة المؤمنة معه أوضاعا وقيما وتقاليد غير أوضاع الجاهلية وقيمها وتقاليدها.

ثم ماذا؟ ثم فاؤوا إلى الحق الذي لم يعجبهم أول مرة، والذي أجفلوا منه:

(كَأَنَّهُمْ حُمُرٌ مُسْتَنْفِرَةٌ، فَرَّتْ مِنْ قَسْوَرَةٍ). [المدثر: 50 – 51]

والذي حاربوه ودافعوه بكل ما يملكون من قوة وحيلة، والذي عذبوا أهله عذابا شديدا وهم ضعاف في مكة، ثم قاتلوهم قتالا عنيدا وهم أقوياء في المدينة.

ولم تكن الدعوة في أول عهدها في وضع أقوى ولا أفضل منها الآن. كانت مجهولة مستنكرة من الجاهلية، وكانت محصورة في شعاب مكة، مطاردة من أصحاب الجاه والسلطان فيها، وكانت غريبة في زمانها في العالم كله. وكانت تحف بها امبراطوريات ضخمة عاتية تنكر كل مبادئها وأهدافها. ولكنها مع هذا كله كانت قوية، كما هي اليوم قوية، وكما هي غدا قوية. إن عناصر القوة الحقيقية كامنة في طبيعة هذه العقيدة ذاتها، ومن ثم فهي تملك أن تعمل في أسوأ الظروف وأشدها حرجا. إنها تكمن في الحق البسيط الوضاح الذي نقوم عليه. وفي تناسقها مع الفطرة التي لا تملك أن تقاوم سلطانها طويلا، وفي قدرتها على قيادة البشرية صعدا في طريق التقدم، في أية مرحلة كانت البشرية من التأخر أو التقدم الاقتصادي والاجتماعي والعلمي والعقلي. كما أنها تكمن في صراحتها هذه وهي تواجه الجاهلية بكل قواها المادية فلا تخرم حرفا واحدا من أصولها، ولا تربت على شهوات الجاهلية، ولا تتدسس إليها تدسسا. إنما تصدع بالحق صدعا مع إشعار الناس بأنها خير ورحمة وبركة.

والله الذي خلق البشر يعلم طبيعة تكوينهم ومداخل قلوبهم ويعلم كيف تستجيب حين تصدع بالحق صدعا. في صراحة وقوة. بلا تلعثم ولا وصوصة.

إن النفس البشرية فيها الاستعداد للانتقال الكامل من حياة إلى حياة. وذلك قد يكون أيسر عليها من التعديلات الجزئية في أحيان كثيرة. والانتقال الكامل من نظام حياة إلى نظام آخر أعلى منه وأكمل وأنظف، انتقال له ما يبرره في منطق النفس. ولكن ما الذي يبرر الانتقال من نظام الجاهلية إلى نظام الإسلام، إذا كان النظام الإسلامي لا يزيد إلا تغييرا طفيفا هنا، وتعديلا طفيفا هناك؟ إن البقاء على النظام المألوف أقرب إلى المنطق. لأنه على الأقل نظام قائم، قابل للإصلاح والتعديل، فلا ضرورة لطرحه، والانتقال إلى نظام غير قائم ولا مطبق، مادام أنه شبيه به في معظم خصائصه.

كذلك نجد بعض الذين يتحدثون عن الإسلام يقدمونه للناس كأنه منهم يحاولون هم دفع التهمة عنه. ومن بين ما يدفعون به أن الأنظمة الحاضرة تفعل كذا وكذا مما تعيب على الإسلام مثله، وأن الإسلام لم يصنع شيئا - في هذه الأمور - إلا ما تصنعه "الحضارات الحديثة "بعد ألف وأربعمئة عام.

وهان ذلك دفاعا. وساء ذلك دفاعا.

إن الإسلام لا يتخذ المبررات له من النظم الجاهلية والتصرفات النكدة التي نبعث منها. وهذه "الحضارات "التي تبهر الكثيرين وتهزم أرواحهم ليست سوى نظم جاهلية في صميمها. وهي نظم معيبة مهلهلة هابطة حين تقاس إلى الإسلام. ولا عبرة بأن حال أهلها بخير من حال السكان في ما يسمى الوطن الإسلامي أو "العالم الإسلامي ". فهؤلاء صاروا إلى هذا البؤس بتركهم للإسلام لا لأنهم مسلمون. وحجة الإسلام التي يدلى بها للناس: إنه خير

منها بما لا يقاس، وإنه جاء ليغيرها لا ليقرها، وليرفع البشرية عن وهدتها لا ليبارك تمرغها في هذا الوحل الذي يبدو في ثوب "الحضارة ".

فلا تبلغ بنا الهزيمة أن نتلمس للإسلام مشابهات في بعض الأنظمة القائمة، وفي بعض المذاهب القائمة، وفي بعض الأفكار القائمة. فنحن نرفض هذه الأنظمة في الشرق أو في الغرب سواء. إننا نرفضها كلها لأنها منحطة ومتخلفة بالقياس إلى ما يريد الإسلام أن يبلغ بالبشرية إليه.

وحين نخاطب الناس بهذه الحقيقة، ونقدم لهم القاعدة العقيدية للتصور الإسلامي الشامل، يكون لديهم في أعماق فطرتهم ما يبرر الانتقال من تصور إلى تصور، ومن وضع إلى وضع. ولكننا لا نخاطبهم بحجة مقنعة حين نقول لهم: تعالوا من نظام قائم فعلا إلى نظام آخر غير مطبق، لا يغير في نظامكم القائم إلا قليلا. وحجته إليكم أنكم تفعلون في هذا الأمر وذاك مثلما يفعل هو، ولا يكلفكم إلا تغيير القليل من عاداتكم وأوضاعكم وشهواتكم، وسيبقى لكم كل ما تحرصون عليه منها ولا يمسه مسا خفيفا.

هذا الذي يبدو سهلا في ظاهره، ليس مغريا في طبيعته، فضلا على أنه ليس هو الحقيقة. فالحقيقة أن الإسلام يبدل التصورات والمشاعر، كما يبدل النظم والأوضاع، كما يبدل الشرائع والقوانين تبديلا أساسيا لا يمت بصلة إلى قاعدة الحياة الجاهلية، التي تحياها البشرية. ويكفي أنه ينقلهم جملة وتفصيلا من عبادة العباد إلى عبادة الله وحده.

(فمنْ شاء فلْيُؤْمِنْ ومنْ شاء فلْيكُفُرْ).

(ومنْ كفر فإن الله غني عنِ الْعالمين).

والمسألة في حقيقتها هي مسألة كفر وإيمان، مسألة شرك وتوحيد، مسألة جاهلية وإسلام. وهذا ما ينبغي أن يكون واضحا. إن الناس ليسوا مسلمين - كما يدعون - وهم يحيون حياة الجاهلية. وإذا كان فيهم من يحب أن يخدع نفسه أو يخدع الآخرين، فيعتقد أن الإسلام يمكن أن يستقيم مع هذه الجاهلية فله ذلك. ولكن انخداعه أو خداعه لا يغير من حقيقة الواقع شيئا. ليس هذا إسلاما، وليس هؤلاء مسلمين. والدعوة اليوم إنما تقوم لترد هؤلاء الجاهلين إلى الإسلام، ولتجعل منهم مسلمين من جديد.

ونحن لا ندعو الناس إلى الإسلام لننال منهم أجرا. ولا نريد علوا في الأرض ولا فسادا. ولا نريد شيئا خاصا لأنفسنا إطلاقا، وحسابنا وأجرنا ليس على الناس. إنما نحن ندعو الناس إلى الإسلام لأننا نحبهم ونريد لهم الخير. لأن هذه هي طبيعة الداعية إلى الإسلام، وهذه هي دوافعه. ومن ثم يجب أن يعلموا منا حقيقة الإسلام، وحقيقة التكاليف التي سيطلبها إليهم، في مقابل الخير العميق الذي يحمله لهم. كما يجب أن يعرفوا رأينا في حقيقة ما هم عليه من الجاهلية. إنها الجاهلية وليست في شيء من الإسلام، إنها "الهوى" ما دام أنها ليست هي "الشريعة ". إنها "الضلال" ما دام أنها ليست هي الحق. فماذا بعد الحق إلا الضلال.

وليس في إسلامنا ما نخجل منه، وما نضطر للدفاع عنه، وليس فيه ما نتدسس به للناس تدسسا، أو ما نتلعثم في الجهر به على حقيقته. إن الهزيمة الروحية أمام الغرب وأمام الشرق وأمام أوضاع الجاهلية هنا وهناك هي التي تجعل بعض الناس. "المسلمين ". يتلمس للإسلام موافقات جزئية من النظم البشرية، أو يتلمس من أعمال "الحضارة "الجاهلية ما يسند به أعمال الإسلام وقضاءه في بعض الأمور.

إنه إذا كان هناك من يحتاج للدفاع والتبرير والاعتذار فليس هو الذي يقدم الإسلام للناس. وإنما هو ذاك الذي يحيا في هذه الجاهلية المهلهلة المليئة بالمتناقضات وبالنقائض والعيوب، ويريد أن يتلمس المبررات للجاهلية. وهؤلاء هم الذين يهاجمون الإسلام ويلجئون بعض محبيه الذين يجهلون حقيقته إلى الدفاع عنه، كأنه متهم مضطر للدفاع عن نفسه في قفص الاتهام.

بعض هؤلاء كانوا يواجهوننا - نحن القلائل المنتسبين إلى الإسلام - في أمريكا في السنوات التي قضيتها هناك - وكان بعضنا يتخذ موقف الدفاع والتبرير. وكنت على العكس أتخذ موقف المهاجم للجاهلية الغربية. سواء في معتقداتها الدينية المهلهلة. أو في أوضاعها الاجتماعية والاقتصادية والأخلاقية المؤذية. هذه التصورات عن الأقانيم وعن الخطيئة وعن الفداء، وهي لا تستقيم في عقل ولا ضمير. وهذه الرأسمالية باحتكارها ورباها وما فيها من بشاعة كالحة. وهذه الفردية الأثرة التي ينعدم معها التكافل إلا تحت مطارق القانون. وهذا التصور المادي التافه الجاف للحياة. وحرية البهائم التي يسمونها "حرية الاختلاط ". وسوق الرقيق التي يسمونها "حرية المرأة ". والسخف والحرج والتكلف المضاد لواقع الحياة في نظم الزواج والطلاق، والتفريق العنصري الحاد الخبيث. ثم. ما في الإسلام من منطق وسمو وإنسانية وبشاشة، وتطلع إلى آفاق تطلع البشرية دونها ولا تبلغها. ومن مواجهة الواقع في الوقت ذاته ومعالجته معالجة تقوم على قواعد الفطرة الإنسانية السليمة.

وكانت هذه حقائق نواجهها في واقع الحياة الغربية. وهي حقائق كانت تخجل أصاحبها حين تعرض في ضوء الإسلام. ولكن ناسا - يدعون الإسلام - ينهزمون أمام ذلك النتن الذي تعيش فيه الجاهلية، حتى ليتلمسون للإسلام مشابهات في هذا الركاب المضطرب البائس في الغرب. وفي تلك الشناعة المادية البشعة في الشرق أيضا.

ولست في حاجة بعد هذا إلى أن أقول: إننا نحن الذين نقدم الإسلام للناس، ليس لنا أن نجاري الجاهلية في شيء من تصوراتها، ولا في شيء من أوضاعها، ولا في شيء من تقاليدها. مهما يشتد ضغطها علينا.

إن وظيفتنا الأولى هي إحلال التصورات الإسلامية والتقاليد الإسلامية في مكان هذه الجاهلية. ولن يتحقق هذا بمجاراة الجاهلية والسير معها خطوات في أول الطريق، كما قد يخيل إلى البعض منا. إن هذا معناه إعلان الهزيمة منذ أول الطريق.

إن ضغط التصورات الاجتماعية السائدة، والتقاليد الاجتماعية الشائعة، ضغط ساحق عنيف، وبخاصة في دنيا المرأة. ولكن لا بد مما ليس منه بد. لا بد أن نثبت أولا، ولا

بد أن نستعلي ثانيا، ولا بد أن نُرى الجاهلية حقيقة الدرك الذي هي فيه بالقياس إلى الآفاق العليا المشرفة للحياة الإسلامية التي نريدها.

ولن يكون هذا بأن نجاري الجاهلية في بعض الخطوات، كما أنه لن يكون بأن نقاطعها الآن وننزوي عنها وننعزل. كلا، إنما هي المخالطة مع التميز، والأخذ والعطاء مع الترفع، والصدع بالحق في مودة، والاستعلاء بالإيمان في تواضع. والامتلاء بعد هذا كله بالحقيقة الواقعة. وهي أننا نعيش في وسط جاهلية، وأننا أهدى طريقا من هذه الجاهلية، وإنها نقلة بعيدة واسعة، هذه النقلة من الجاهلية إلى الإسلام، وإنها هوة فاصلة لا يقام فوقها معبر للالتقاء في منتصف الطريق، ولكن لينتقل عليه أهل الجاهلية إلى الإسلام، سواء كانوا ممن يعيشون فيما يسمى الوطن الإسلامي، ويزعمون أنهم مسلمون، أو كانوا يعيشون في غير الوطن "الإسلامي "، وليخرجوا من الظلمات إلى النور، ولينجوا من هذه الشقوة التي هم فيها، وينعموا بالخير الذي ذقناه نحن الذين عرفنا الإسلام وحاولنا أن نعيش به. وإلا فلنقل ما أمر الله سبحانه الرسول صلى الله عليه وسلم أن يقوله:

(لَكُمْ دِينُكُمْ وليَ دِينِ).. [الكافرون: 6]

استِعْلاءُ الإيمان

(ولا تَهِنُوا ولا تَحْزَنُوا وأنْتُمُ الْأَعْلَوْنَ إِنْ كُنْتُمْ مُؤْمِنِينَ). [آل عمران: 6]

أول ما يتبادر إلى الذهن من هذا التوجيه أنه ينصب على حالة الجهاد الممثلة في القتال. ولكن حقيقة هذا التوجيه ومداه أكبر وأبعد من هذه الحالة المفردة، بكل ملابساتها الكثيرة.

إنه يمثل الحالة الدائمة التي ينبغي أن يكون عليها شعور المؤمن وتصوره وتقديره للأشياء والأحداث والقيم والأشخاص سواء.

إنه يمثل حالة الاستعلاء التي يجب أن تستقر عليها نفس المؤمن إزاء كل شيء، وكل وضع، وكل قيمة، وكل أحد، والاستعلاء بالإيمان وقيمه على جميع القيم المنبثقة من أصل غير أصل الإيمان.

الاستعلاء على قوى الأرض الحائدة عن منهج الإيمان. وعلى قيم الأرض التي لم تنبثق من أصل الإيمان. وعلى تقاليد الأرض التي لم يصغها الإيمان، وعلى قوانين الأرض التي لم يشرعها الإيمان، وعلى أوضاع الأرض التي لم ينشئها الإيمان.

الاستعلاء. مع ضعف القوة، وقلة العدد، وفقر المال، كالاستعلاء مع القوة والكثرة والغنى على السواء.

الاستعلاء الذي لا يتهاوى أمام قوة باغية، ولا عرف اجتماعي ولا تشريع باطل، ولا وضع مقبول عند الناس ولا سند له من الإيمان.

وليست حالة التماسك والثبات في الجهاد إلا حالة واحدة من حالات الاستعلاء التي يشملها هذا التوجيه الإلهي العظيم.

والاستعلاء بالإيمان ليس مجرد عزمة مفردة، ولا نخوة دافعة، ولا حماسة فائرة، إنما هو الاستعلاء القائم على الحق الثابت المركوز في طبيعة الوجود. الحق الباقي وراء منطق القوة، وتصور البيئة، واصطلاح المجتمع، وتعارف الناس، لأنه موصول بالله الحي الذي لا يموت.

إن للمجتمع منطقه السائد وعرفه العام وضغطه الساحق ووزنه الثقيل. على من ليس يحتمي منه بركن ركين، وعلى من يواجهه بلا سند متين.. وللتصورات السائدة والأفكار الشائعة إيحاؤها الذي يصعب التخلص منه بغير الاستقرار على حقيقة تصغر في ظلها تلك التصورات والأفكار، والاستمداد من مصدر أعلى من مصدرها وأكبر وأقوى.

والذي يقف في وجه المجتمع، ومنطقه السائد، وعرفه العام، وقيمه واعتباراته، وأفكاره وتصوراته، وانحرافاته ونزواته. يشعر بالغربة كما يشعر بالوهن، ما لم يكن يستند إلى سند أقوى من الناس، وأثبت من الأرض، وأكرم من الحياة.

والله لا يترك المؤمن وحيدا يواجه الضغط، وينوء به الثقل، ويهده الوهن والحزن، ومن ثم يجيء هذا التوجيه:

(وَلَا تَهِنُوا وَلَا تَحْزَنُوا وَأَنْتُمُ الْأَعْلَوْنَ إِنْ كُنْتُمْ مُؤْمِنِينَ). [آل عمران: 139]

يجيء هذا التوجيه. ليواجه الوهن كما يواجه الحزن. هما الشعوران المباشران اللذان يساوران النفس في هذا المقام. يواجههما بالاستعلاء لا بمجرد الصبر والثبات، والاستعلاء الذي ينظر من عل إلى القوى الطاغية، والقيم السائدة، والتصورات الشائعة، والاعتبارات والأوضاع والتقاليد والعادات، والجماهير المتجمعة على الضلال.

إن المؤمن هو الأعلى. الأعلى هو سندا ومصدرا. فما تكون الأرض كلها؟ وما يكون الناس؟ وما تكون القيم السائدة في الأرض؟ والاعتبارات الشائعة عند الناس؟ وهو من الله يتلقى، وإلى الله يرجع، وعلى منهجه يسير؟

وهو الأعلى إدراكا وتصورا لحقيقة الوجود. فالإيمان بالله الواحد في هذه الصورة التي جاء بها الإسلام هو أكمل صورة للمعرفة بالحقيقة الكبرى. وحين تقاس هذه الصورة إلى ذلك الركام من التصورات والعقائد والمذاهب، سواء ما جاءت به الفلسفات الكبرى قديما وحديثا، وما انتهت إليه العقائد الوثنية والكتابية المحرفة، وما اعتفسته المذاهب المادية الكالحة. حين تقاس هذه الصورة المشرقة الواضحة الجميلة المتناسقة، إلى ذلك الركام وهذه التعسفات، تتجلى عظمة العقيدة الإسلامية كما لم تتجل قط. وما من شك ان الذين يعرفون هذه المعرفة هم الأعلون على كل من هناك [19].

وهو الأعلى تصورا للقيم والموازين التي توزن بها الحياة والأحداث والأشياء والأشخاص. فالعقيدة المنبثقة عن المعرفة بالله، بصفاته كما جاء بها الإسلام، ومن المعرفة بحقائق القيم في الوجود الكبير لا في ميدان الأرض الصغير. هذه العقيدة من شأنها أن تمنح المؤمن تصورا للقيم أعلى وأضبط من تلك الموازين المختلفة في أيدي البشر، الذين لا يدركون إلا ما تحت أقدامهم. ولا يثبتون على ميزان واحد في الجيل الواحد. بل في الأمة الواحدة. بل في النفس الواحدة من حين إلى حين.

وهو الأعلى ضميرا وشعورا، وخلقا وسلوكا. فإن عقيدته في الله ذي الأسماء الحسنى والصفات المثلى، هي بذاتها موحية بالرفعة والنظافة والطهارة والعفة والتقوى، والعمل الصالح والخلافة الراشدة. فضلا على إيحاء العقيدة عن الجزاء في الآخرة. الجزاء الذي تهون أمامه متاعب الدنيا وآلامها جميعا. ويطمئن إليه ضمير المؤمن، ولو خرج من الدنيا بغير نصيب.

وهو الأعلى شريعة ونظاما. وحين يراجع المؤمن كل ما عرفته البشرية قديما وحديثا، ويقيسه إلى شريعته ونظامه، فسيراه كله أشبه شيء بمحاولات الأطفال وخبط العميان، إلى جانب الشريعة الناضجة والنظام الكامل. وسينظر إلى البشرية الضالة من عل في عطف وإشفاق على بؤسها وشقوتها، ولا يجد في نفسه إلا الاستعلاء على الشقوة والضلال.

---

[19] يراجع فصل " تيه وركام " في كتاب: خصائص التصور الإسلامي ومقوماته.

وهكذا كان المسلمون الأوائل يقفون أمام المظاهر الجوفاء، والقوى المتنفجة، والاعتبارات التي كانت تعبد الناس في الجاهلية. والجاهلية ليست فترة من الزمان، إنما هي حالة من الحالات تتكرر كلما انحرف المجتمع عن نهج الإسلام، في الماضي والحاضر والمستقبل على السواء.

وهكذا وقف المغيرة ابن شعبة أمام صور الجاهلية وأوضاعها وقيمها وتصوراتها في معسكر رستم قائد الفرس المشهور:

"عن أبي عثمان النهدي قال: لما جاء المغيرة إلى القنطرة، فعبرها إلى أهل فارس أجلسوه، واستأذنوا رستم في إجازته، ولم يغيروا شيئا من شارتهم تقوية لتهاونهم، فأقبل المغيرة ابن شعبة والقوم في زيهم، عليهم التيجان والثياب المنسوجة بالذهب، وبسطهم على غلوة (والغلوة مسافة رمية سهم وتقدر بثلاثمائة أو أربعمائة خطوة) لا يصل إلى صاحبهم حتى يمشي عليها غلوة، وأقبل المغيرة وله أربع ضفائر يمشي حتى يجلس على سريره ووسادته، فوثبوا عليه فترتروه وأنزلوه ومغثوه [20]، فقال: كانت تبلغنا عنكم الأحلام، ولا أرى قوما أسفه منكم، إنا معشر العرب سواء لا يستعبد بعضنا بعضا، إلا أن يكون محاربا لصاحبه ؛ فظننت أنكم تواسون قومكم كما نتواسى. وكان أحسن من الذي صنعتم أن تخبروني أن بعضكم أرباب بعض، وأن هذا الأمر لا يستقيم فيكم، فلا آتكم، ولم آتكم ولكن دعوتموني. اليوم علمت أن أمركم مضمحل، وأنكم مغلوبون، وأن ملكا لا يقوم على هذه السيرة ولا على هذه العقول ".

كذلك وقف ربعي بن عامر مع رستم هذا وحاشيته قبل وقعة القادسية:

"أرسل سعد بن أبي وقاص قبل القادسية ربعي بن عامر رسولا إلى رستم، قائد الجيوش الفارسية وأميرهم، فدخل عليه وقد زينوا مجلسه بالنمارق والزرابي والحرير [21]، وأظهر اليواقيت واللآلئ الثمينة العظيمة، وعليه تاجه، وغير ذلك من الأمتعة الثمينة، وقد جلس على سرير من ذهب. ودخل ربعي بثياب صفيقة وترس وفرس قصيرة. ولم يزل راكبها حتى داس بها على طرف البساط ثم نزل وربطها ببعض تلك الوسائد. وأقبل وعليه سلاحه وبيضته على رأسه. فقالوا له: ضع سلاحك فقال: إني لم آتكم، وإنما جئتكم حين دعوتموني، فإن تركتموني هكذا وإلا رجعت. فقال رستم: ائذنوا له. فأقبل يتوكأ على رمحه فوق النمارق لخرق عامتها. فقال له رستم: ما جاء بكم ؟ فقال: الله ابتعثنا لنخرج من شاء من عبادة العباد إلى عبادة الله وحده، ومن ضيق الدنيا إلى سعة الدنيا والآخرة، ومن جور الأديان إلى عدل الإسلام.

وتتبدل الأحوال ويقف المسلم موقف المغلوب المجرد من القوة المادية، فلا يفارقه شعوره بأنه الأعلى. وينظر إلى غالبه من عل ما دام مؤمنا. ويستيقن أنها فترة وتمضي، وإن للإيمان كرة لا مفر منها. وهبها كانت القاضية فإنه لا يحني لها رأسا. إن الناس كلهم يموتون

---

[20] مغثوه: صرعوه.
[21] النمارق: الوسائد والحشايا للاتكاء. والزرابي: البسط المخملة.

أما هو فيستشهد. وهو يغادر هذه الأرض إلى الجنة، وغالبه يغادرها إلى النار. وشتان شتان. وهو يسمع نداء ربه الكريم:

(لا يَغُرَّنَّكَ تَقَلُّبُ الَّذِينَ كَفَرُوا فِي الْبِلادِ، مَتَاعٌ قَلِيلٌ ثُم مَأواهُمْ جهنمُ وبِئْس الْمِهادُ، لكِنِ الَّذِينَ اتَّقَوْا ربهُمْ لَهُمْ جناتٌ تجْري مِنْ تحتِها الأنْهارُ خالِدِينَ فِيها نُزُلًا مِنْ عِنْدِ اللهِ وما عِنْدَ اللهِ خيْرٌ لِلْأبْرارِ) ... [آل عمران: 196 - 198]

وتسود المجتمع عقائد وتصورات وقيم وأوضاع كلها مغايرة لعقيدته وتصوره وقيمه وموازينه، فلا يفارقه شعوره بأنه الأعلى، وبأن هؤلاء كلهم في الموقف الدون. وينظر إليهم من عل في كرامة واعتزاز، وفي رحمة كذلك وعطف، ورغبة في هدايتهم إلى الخير الذي معه، ورفعهم إلى الأفق الذي يعيش فيه.

ويضج الباطل ويصخب، ويرفع صوته وينفش ريشه، وتحيط به الهالات المصطنعة التي تغشي على الأبصار والبصائر، فلا ترى ما وراء الهالات من قبح شائه دميم، وفجر كالح لئيم. وينظر المؤمن من عل إلى الباطل المنتفش، وإلى الجموع المخدوعة، فلا يهن ولا يحزن، ولا ينقص إصراره على الحق الذي معه، وثباته على المنهج الذي يتبعه، ولا تضعف رغبته كذلك في هداية الضالين والمخدوعين.

ويغرق المجتمع في شهواته الهابطة، ويمضي مع نزواته الخليعة، ويلصق بالوحل والطين، حاسبا أنه يستمتع وينطلق من الأغلال والقيود. وتعز في مثل هذا المجتمع كل متعة بريئة وكل طيبة حلال، ولا يبقى إلا المشروع الآسن، وإلا الوحل والطين. وينظر المؤمن من عل إلى الغارقين في الوحل اللاصقين بالطين. وهو مفرد وحيد، فلا يهن ولا يحزن، ولا تراوده نفسه أن يخلع رداءه النظيف الطاهر، وينغمس في الحمأة، وهو الأعلى، وهو بمتعة الإيمان ولذة اليقين.

ويقف المؤمن قابضا على دينه كالقابض على الجمر في المجتمع الشارد عن الدين، وعن الفضيلة، وعن القيم العليا، وعن الاهتمامات النبيلة، وعن كل ما هو طاهر نظيف جميل. ويقف الآخرون هازئين بوقفته، ساخرين من تصوراته، ضاحكين من قيمه. فما يهن المؤمن وهو ينظر من عل إلى الساخرين والهازئين والضاحكين، وهو يقول كما قال واحد من الرهط الكرام الذين سبقوه في موكب الإيمان العريق الوضيء، في الطريق اللاحب الطويل. نوح عليه السلام.

(إنْ تسْخَرُوا مِنا فإنا نسْخَرُ مِنْكُمْ كما تسْخرُون).. [هود: 38]

وهو يرى نهاية الموكب الوضيء، ونهاية القافلة البائسة في قوله تعالى:

(إن الَّذِينَ أجْرمُوا كانُوا مِن الَّذِينَ آمنُوا يضْحكُون، وإذا مروا بِهمْ يتغامزُون، وإذا انْقلبُوا إلى أهْلِهمُ انْقلبُوا فكِهين، وإذا رأوْهُمْ قالُوا إن هؤُلاءِ لضالُون، وما أرْسِلُوا عليْهِمْ حافِظِين، فالْيوْم الَّذِينَ آمنُوا مِن الْكُفارِ يضْحكُون، على الأرائِكِ ينْظُرُون، هلْ ثُوب الْكُفارُ ما كانُوا يفْعلُون).؟ [المطففين: 29 - 36]

وقديما قص القرآن الكريم قول الكافرين للمؤمنين:

(وَإِذَا تُتْلَى عَلَيْهِمْ آيَاتُنَا بَيِّنَاتٍ قَالَ الَّذِينَ كَفَرُوا لِلَّذِينَ آمَنُوا أَيُّ الْفَرِيقَيْنِ خَيْرٌ مَقَامًا وَأَحْسَنُ نَدِيًّا). [مريم: 73]

أي الفريقين؟ الكبراء الذين لا يؤمنون بمحمد؟ أم الفقراء الذين يلتفون حوله؟ أي الفريقين؟ النضر بن الحارث، وعمرو بن هشام، والوليد بن المغيرة، وأبو سفيان بن حرب؟ أم بلال وعمار وصهيب وخباب؟ أفلو كان ما يدعو إليه محمد خيرا أفكان يكونون هم هؤلاء النفر، الذين لا سلطان لهم في قريش ولا خطر، وهم يجتمعون في بيت متواضع كدار الأرقم، ويكون معارضوه هم أولئك أصحاب الندوة الفخمة الضخمة، والمجد والجاه والسلطان؟.

إنه منطق الأرض، منطق المحجوبين عن الآفاق العليا في كل زمان ومكان. وإنها لحكمة الله أن تقف العقيدة مجردة من الزينة والطلاء عاطلة من عوامل الإغراء، لا قربى من حاكم، ولا اعتزاز بسلطان، ولا هتاف بلذة، ولا دغدغة لغريزة. وإنما هو الجهد والمشقة والجهاد والاستشهاد. ليقبل عليها من يقبل، وهو على يقين من نفسه أنه يريدها لذاتها خالصة لله من دون الناس، ومن دون ما تواضعوا عليه من قيم ومغريات، ولينصرف عنها من يبتغي المطامع والمنافع، ومن يشتهي الزينة والابهة، ومن يطلب المال والمتاع، ومن يقيم لاعتبارات الناس وزنا حين تخف في ميزان الله.

إن المؤمن لا يستمد قيمه وتصوراته وموازينه من الناس حتى يأسى على تقدير الناس، إنما يستمدها من رب الناس وهو حسبه وكافيه. إنه لا يستمدها من شهوات الخلق حتى يتأرجح مع شهوات الخلق، إنما يستمدها من ميزان الحق الثابت الذي لا يتأرجح ولا يميل. إنه لا يتلقاها من هذا العالم الفاني المحدود، وإنما تنبثق في ضميره من ينابيع الوجود. فأنى يجد في نفسه وهنا أو يجد في قلبه حزنا، وهو موصول برب الناس وميزان الحق وينابيع الوجود؟

إنه على الحق. فماذا بعد الحق إلا الضلال؟ وليكن للضلال سلطانه، وليكن له هيله وهيلمانه، ولتكن معه جموعه وجماهيره. إن هذا لا يغير من الحق شيئا، إنه على الحق وليس بعد الحق إلا الضلال، ولن يختار مؤمن الضلال على الحق - وهو مؤمن - ولن يعدل بالحق الضلال كائنة ما كانت الملابسات والأحوال.

(رَبَّنَا لَا تُزِغْ قُلُوبَنَا بَعْدَ إِذْ هَدَيْتَنَا وَهَبْ لَنَا مِنْ لَدُنْكَ رَحْمَةً إِنَّكَ أَنْتَ الْوَهَّابُ، رَبَّنَا إِنَّكَ جَامِعُ النَّاسِ لِيَوْمٍ لَا رَيْبَ فِيهِ إِنَّ اللَّهَ لَا يُخْلِفُ الْمِيعَادَ). [آل عمران: 8 - 9]

هذا هُو الطرِيْق

(وَالسَّماءِ ذاتِ الْبُرُوجِ، وَالْيَوْمِ الْمَوْعُودِ، وَشاهِدٍ وَمَشْهُودٍ، قُتِلَ أَصْحابُ الْأُخْدُودِ، النّارِ ذاتِ الْوَقُودِ، إِذْ هُمْ عَلَيْها قُعُودٌ، وَهُمْ عَلى ما يَفْعَلُونَ بِالْمُؤْمِنِينَ شُهُودٌ، وَما نَقَمُوا مِنْهُمْ إِلّا أَنْ يُؤْمِنُوا بِاللّهِ الْعَزِيزِ الْحَمِيدِ، الَّذِي لَهُ مُلْكُ السّماواتِ وَالْأَرْضِ وَاللّهُ عَلى كُلِّ شَيْءٍ شَهِيدٌ، إِنَّ الَّذِينَ فَتَنُوا الْمُؤْمِنِينَ وَالْمُؤْمِناتِ ثُمَّ لَمْ يَتُوبُوا فَلَهُمْ عَذابُ جَهَنَّمَ وَلَهُمْ عَذابُ الْحَرِيقِ، إِنَّ الَّذِينَ آمَنُوا وَعَمِلُوا الصّالِحاتِ لَهُمْ جَنّاتٌ تَجْرِي مِنْ تَحْتِهَا الْأَنْهارُ ذلِكَ الْفَوْزُ الْكَبِيرُ، إِنَّ بَطْشَ رَبِّكَ لَشَدِيدٌ، إِنَّهُ هُوَ يُبْدِئُ وَيُعِيدُ، وَهُوَ الْغَفُورُ الْوَدُودُ، ذُو الْعَرْشِ الْمَجِيدُ، فَعّالٌ لِما يُرِيدُ..)

إن قصة أصحاب الأخدود - كما وردت في سورة البروج - حقيقة بأن يتأملها المؤمنون الداعون إلى الله في كل أرض وفي كل جيل. فالقرآن بإيرادها في هذا الأسلوب مع مقدمتها والتعقيبات عليها، والتقريرات والتوجيهات المصاحبة لها. كان يخط بها خطوطا عميقة في تصور طبيعة الدعوة إلى الله، ودور البشر فيها، واحتمالاتها المتوقعة في مجالها الواسع - وهو أوسع رقعة من الأرض، وأبعد مدى من الحياة الدنيا - وكان يرسم للمؤمنين معالم الطريق، ويعد نفوسهم لتلقي أي من هذه الاحتمالات التي يجري بها القدر المرسوم، وفق الحكمة المكنونة في غيب الله المستور.

إنها قصة فئة آمنت بربها، واستعلنت حقيقة إيمانها. ثم تعرضت للفتنة من أعداء جبارين بطاشين مستهترين بحق "الإنسان" في حرية الاعتقاد بالحق والإيمان بالله العزيز الحميد، وبكرامة الإنسان عند الله عن أن يكون لعبة يتسلى بها الطغاة بآلام تعذيبها، ويتلهون بمنظرها في أثناء التعذيب بالحريق.

وقد ارتفع الإيمان بهذه القلوب على الفتنة، وانتصرت فيها العقيدة على الحياة، فلم ترضخ لتهديد الجبارين الطغاة، ولم تفتن عن دينها، وهي تحرق بالنار حتى تموت.

لقد تحررت هذه القلوب من عبوديتها للحياة، فلم يستذلها حب البقاء وهي تعاين الموت بهذه الطريقة البشعة، وانطلقت من قيود الأرض وجواذبها جميعا، وارتفعت على ذواتها بانتصار العقيدة على الحياة فيها.

وفي مقابل هذه القلوب المؤمنة الخيرة الرفيقة الكريمة كانت هناك جبلات جاحدة شريرة مجرمة لئيمة. وجلس أصحاب هذه الجبلات على النار. يشهدون كيف يتعذب المؤمنون ويتألمون. جلسوا يتلهون بمنظر الحياة تأكلها النار، والأناسي الكرام يتحولون وقودا وترابا. وكلما ألقي فتى فتاة، صبية أو عجوز، طفل أو شيخ، من المؤمنين الخيرين الكرام في النار، ارتفعت النشوة الخسيسة في نفوس الطغاة، وعربد السعار المجنون بالدماء والأشلاء.

هذا هو الحادث البشع الذي انتكست فيه جبلات الطغاة وارتكست في هذه الحمأة، فراحت تلتذ مشهد التعذيب المروع العنيف، بهذه الخساسة التي لم يرتكس فيها وحش قط، فالوحش يفترس ليقتات، لا ليلتذ آلام الفريسة في لؤم وخسة.

94

وهو ذاته الحادث الذي ارتفعت فيه أرواح المؤمنين وتحررت وانطلقت إلى ذلك الأوج السامي الرفيع، الذي تشرف به البشرية في جميع الأجيال والعصور.

في حساب الأرض يبدو أن الطغيان قد انتصر على الإيمان. وإن هذا الإيمان الذي بلغ الذروة العالية، في نفوس الفئة الخيرة الكريمة الثابتة المستعلية. لم يكن له وزن ولا حساب في المعركة التي دارت بين الإيمان والطغيان.

ولا تذكر الروايات التي وردت في هذا الحادث، كما لا تذكر النصوص القرآنية، أن الله قد أخذ أولئك الطغاة في الأرض بجريمتهم البشعة، كما أخذ قوم نوح وقوم هود وقوم صالح وقوم شعيب وقوم لوط. أو كما أخذ فرعون وجنوده أخذ عزيز مقتدر.

ففي حساب الأرض تبدو هذه الخاتمة اسيفة أليمة.

أفهكذا ينتهي الأمر، وتذهب الفئة المؤمنة التي ارتفعت إلى ذروة الإيمان؟ تذهب مع آلامها الفاجعة في الأخدود؟ بينما تذهب الفئة الباغية، التي ارتكست إلى هذه الحمأة، ناجية؟

حساب الأرض يحيك في الصدر شيء أمام هذه الخاتمة الأسيفة.

ولكن القرآن يعلم المؤمنين شيئا آخر، ويكشف لهم عن حقيقة أخرى، ويبصرهم بطبيعة القيم التي يزنون بها، وبمجال المعركة التي يخوضونها.

إن الحياة وسائر ما يلابسها من لذائذ وآلام، ومن متاع وحرمان. ليست هي القيمة الكبرى في الميزان. وليست هي السلعة التي تقرر حساب الربح والخسارة. والنصر ليس مقصورا على الغلبة الظاهرة. فهذه صورة واحدة من صور النصر الكثيرة.

إن القيمة الكبرى في ميزان الله هي قيمة العقيدة، وإن السلعة الرائجة في سوق الله هي سلعة الإيمان. وإن النصر في أرفع صوره هو انتصار الروح على المادة، وانتصار العقيدة على الألم، وانتصار الإيمان على الفتنة. وفي هذا الحادث انتصرت أرواح المؤمنين على الخوف والألم، وانتصرت على جواذب الأرض والحياة، وانتصرت على الفتنة انتصارا يشرف الجنس البشري كله في جميع الأعصار. وهذا هو الانتصار.

إن الناس جميعا يموتون، وتختلف الأسباب. ولكن الناس جميعا لا ينتصرون هذا الانتصار، ولا يرتفعون هذا الارتفاع، ولا يتحررون هذا التحرر، ولا ينطلقون هذا الانطلاق إلى هذه الآفاق. إنما هو اختيار الله وتكريمه لفئة كريمة من عباده لتشارك الناس في الموت، وتنفرد دون الناس في المجد، المجد في الملأ الأعلى، وفي دنيا الناس أيضا. إذا نحن وضعنا في الحساب نظرة الأجيال بعد الأجيال.

لقد كان في استطاعة المؤمنين أن ينجوا بحياتهم في مقابل الهزيمة لإيمانهم. ولكن كم كانوا يخسرون هم أنفسهم؟ وكم كانت البشرية كلها تخسر؟ كم كانوا يخسرون وهم يقتلون هذا المعنى الكبير، معنى زهادة الحياة بلا عقيدة، وبشاعتها بلا حرية، وانحطاطها حين يسيطر الطغاة على الأرواح بعد سيطرتهم على الأجساد؟

إنه معنى كريم جدا، ومعنى كبير جدا، هذا الذي ربحوه وهم بعد في الأرض، ربحوه وهم يجدون مس النار، فتحرق أجسادهم الفانية، وينتصر هذا المعنى الكريم الذي تزكيه النار.

ثم إن مجال المعركة ليس هو الأرض وحدها، وليس هو الحياة الدنيا وحدها. وشهود المعركة ليسوا هم الناس في جيل من الأجيال. إن الملأ الأعلى يشارك في أحداث الأرض ويشهدها ويشهد عليها، ويزنها بميزان غير ميزان الأرض في جيل من أجيالها، وغير ميزان الأرض في أجيالها جميعا. والملأ الأعلى يضم من الأرواح الكريمة أضعاف أضعاف ما تضم الأرض من الناس. وما من شك أن ثناء الملأ الأعلى وتكريمه أكبر وأرجح في أي ميزان من رأي أهل الأرض وتقديرهم على الإطلاق.

وبعد ذلك كله هناك الآخرة. وهي المجال الأصيل الذي يلحق به مجال الأرض، ولا ينفصل عنه، لا في الحقيقة الواقعة، ولا في حس المؤمن بهذه الحقيقة.

فالمعركة إذن لم تنته، وخاتمتها الحقيقية لم تجيء بعد، والحكم عليها بالجزء الذي عرض منها على الأرض حكم غير صحيح، لأنه حكم على الشطر الصغير منها والشطر الزهيد.

النظرة الأولى هي النظرة القصيرة المدى الضيقة المجال التي تعن للإنسان العجول. والنظرة الثانية الشاملة البعيدة المدى هي التي يروض القرآن المؤمنين عليها، لأنها تمثل الحقيقة التي يقوم عليها التصور الإيماني الصحيح.

ومن ثم وعد الله للمؤمنين جزاء على الإيمان والطاعة، والصبر على الابتلاء، والانتصار على فتن الحياة. هو طمأنينة القلب:

(الذِينَ آمنُوا وتطمئِن قُلُوبُهُم بِذِكرِ اللهِ ألا بِذِكرِ اللهِ تطْمئِن الْقُلُوبُ).. [الرعد: 28].

وهو الرضوان والود من الرحمن:

(إِن الذِينَ آمنُوا وعمِلُوا الصالِحاتِ سيجْعلُ لهُمُ الرحْمنُ وُدا) [مريم: 96].

وهو الذكر في الملأ الأعلى:

قال رسول الله - صلى الله عليه وسلم - إذا مات ولد العبد قال الله لملائكته: قبضتم ولد عبدي؟ فيقولون: نعم. فيقول: قبضتم ثمرة فؤاده؟ فيقولون: نعم. فيقول: ماذا قال عبدي؟ فيقولون: حمدك واسترجع. فيقول: ابنوا لعبدي بيتا في الجنة وسموه بيت الحمد ".. [أخرجه الترمذي].

وقال صلى الله عليه وسلم: يقول الله عز وجل: أنا عند ظن عبدي بي، وأنا معه حين يذكرني، فإذا ذكرني في نفسه ذكرته في نفسي، وإن ذكرني في ملأ ذكرته في ملأ خير منه. فإن اقترب إلي شبرا اقتربت إليه ذراعا، وإن اقترب إلي ذراعا اقتربت منه باعا، وإن أتاني مشيا أتيته هرولة ". [أخرجه الشيخان].

وهو اشتغال الملأ الأعلى بأمر المؤمنين في الأرض:

(الذِينَ يَحْمِلُونَ الْعَرْشَ وَمَنْ حَوْلَهُ يُسَبِّحُونَ بِحَمْدِ رَبِّهِمْ وَيُؤْمِنُونَ بِهِ وَيَسْتَغْفِرُونَ لِلَّذِينَ آمَنُوا رَبَّنَا وَسِعْتَ كُلَّ شَيْءٍ رَحْمَةً وَعِلْماً فَاغْفِرْ لِلَّذِينَ تَابُوا وَاتَّبَعُوا سَبِيلَكَ وَقِهِمْ عَذَابَ الْجَحِيمِ) [غافر: 7].

وهو الحياة عند الله للشهداء:

(وَلَا تَحْسَبَنَّ الَّذِينَ قُتِلُوا فِي سَبِيلِ اللهِ أَمْوَاتاً بَلْ أَحْيَاءٌ عِنْدَ رَبِّهِمْ يُرْزَقُونَ، فَرِحِينَ بِمَا آتَاهُمُ اللهُ مِنْ فَضْلِهِ وَيَسْتَبْشِرُونَ بِالَّذِينَ لَمْ يَلْحَقُوا بِهِمْ مِنْ خَلْفِهِمْ أَلَّا خَوْفٌ عَلَيْهِمْ وَلَا هُمْ يَحْزَنُونَ، يَسْتَبْشِرُونَ بِنِعْمَةٍ مِنَ اللهِ وَفَضْلٍ وَأَنَّ اللهَ لَا يُضِيعُ أَجْرَ الْمُؤْمِنِينَ) [آل عمران: 169 - 171].

كما كان وعده المتكرر بأخذ المكذبين والطغاة والمجرمين في الآخرة والإملاء لهم في الأرض والإمهال إلى حين. وإن كان أحيانا قد أخذ بعضهم في الدنيا. ولكن التركيز كله على الآخرة في الجزء الأخير:

(لَا يَغُرَّنَّكَ تَقَلُّبُ الَّذِينَ كَفَرُوا فِي الْبِلَادِ، مَتَاعٌ قَلِيلٌ ثُمَّ مَأْوَاهُمْ جَهَنَّمُ وَبِئْسَ الْمِهَادُ) [آل عمران: 196 - 197].

(وَلَا تَحْسَبَنَّ اللهَ غَافِلاً عَمَّا يَعْمَلُ الظَّالِمُونَ إِنَّمَا يُؤَخِّرُهُمْ لِيَوْمٍ تَشْخَصُ فِيهِ الْأَبْصَارُ، مُهْطِعِينَ مُقْنِعِي رُؤُوسِهِمْ لَا يَرْتَدُّ إِلَيْهِمْ طَرْفُهُمْ وَأَفْئِدَتُهُمْ هَوَاءٌ) [إبراهيم: 42 - 43].

(فَذَرْهُمْ يَخُوضُوا وَيَلْعَبُوا حَتَّى يُلَاقُوا يَوْمَهُمُ الَّذِي يُوعَدُونَ، يَوْمَ يَخْرُجُونَ مِنَ الْأَجْدَاثِ سِرَاعاً كَأَنَّهُمْ إِلَى نُصُبٍ يُوفِضُونَ، خَاشِعَةً أَبْصَارُهُمْ تَرْهَقُهُمْ ذِلَّةٌ ذَلِكَ الْيَوْمُ الَّذِي كَانُوا يُوعَدُونَ) [المعارج: 42 - 44].

وهكذا اتصلت حياة الناس بحياة الملأ الأعلى، واتصلت الدنيا بالآخرة، ولم تعد الأرض وحدها هي مجال المعركة بين الخير والشر، والحق والباطل، والإيمان والطغيان. ولم تعد الحياة الدنيا هي خاتمة المطاف، ولا موعد الفصل في هذا الصراع. كما أن الحياة وكل ما يتعلق بها من لذائذ وآلام ومتاع وحرمان، لم تعد هي القيمة العليا في الميزان.

انفسح المجال في المكان، وانفسح المجال في الزمان، وانفسح المجال في القيم والموازين، واتسعت آفاق النفس المؤمنة، وكبرت اهتماماتها، فصغرت الأرض وما عليها، والحياة الدنيا وما يتعلق بها، وكبر المؤمن بمقدار ما رأى وما عرف من الآفاق والحيوات، وكانت قصة أصحاب الأخدود في القمة في إنشاء هذا التصور الإيماني الواسع الشامل الكبير الكريم.

هناك إشعاع آخر تطلقه قصة أصحاب الأخدود وسورة البروج حول طبيعة الدعوة إلى الله، وموقف الداعية أمام كل احتمال.

لقد شهد تاريخ الدعوة إلى الله نماذج منوعة من نهايات في الأرض مختلفة للدعوات.

شهد مصارع قوم نوح، وقوم هود، وقوم شعيب، وقوم لوط، ونجاة الفئة المؤمنة القليلة العدد، مجرد النجاة. ولم يذكر القرآن للناجين دورا بعد ذلك في الأرض والحياة. وهذه النماذج تقرر أن الله سبحانه وتعالى يريد أحيانا أن يعجل للمكذبين الطغاة بقسط من العذاب في الدنيا، أما الجزاء الأوفى فهو مرصود لهم هناك.

وشهد تاريخ الدعوة مصرع فرعون وجنوده، ونجاة موسى وقومه، مع التمكين للقوم في الأرض فترة كانوا فيها أصلح ما كانوا في تاريخهم. وإن لم يرتقوا قط إلى الاستقامة الكاملة، وإلى إقامة دين الله في الأرض منهجا للحياة شاملا. وهذا نموذج غير النماذج الأولى.

وشهد تاريخ الدعوة كذلك مصرع المشركين الذين استعصوا على الهدى والإيمان بمحمد - صلى الله عليه وسلم - وانتصار المؤمنين انتصارا كاملا، مع انتصار العقيدة في نفوسهم انتصارا عجيبا. وتم للمرة الوحيدة في تاريخ البشرية أن أقيم منهج الله مهيمنا على الحياة في صورة لم تعرفها البشرية قط، من قبل ولا من بعد.

وشهد - كما رأينا - نموذج أصحاب الأخدود.

وشهد نماذج أخرى أقل ظهورا في سجل التاريخ الإيماني في القديم والحديث. وما يزال يشهد نماذج تتراوح بين هذه النهايات التي حفظها على مدار القرون.

ولم يكن بد من النموذج الذي يمثله حادث الأخدود، إلى جانب النماذج الأخرى. القريب منها والبعيد.

لم يكن بد من هذا النموذج الذي لا ينجو فيه المؤمنون، ولا يؤخذ فيه الكافرون. ذلك ليستقر في حس المؤمنين - أصحاب دعوة الله - أنهم قد يدعون إلى نهاية كهذه النهاية في طريقهم إلى الله. وأن ليس لهم من الأمر شيء، إنما أمرهم وأمر العقيدة إلى الله.

إن عليهم أن يؤدوا واجبهم، ثم يذهبوا، وواجبهم أن يختاروا الله، وأن يؤثروا العقيدة على الحياة، وأن يستعلوا بالإيمان على الفتنة وأن يصدقوا الله في العمل والنية. ثم يفعل الله بهم وبأعدائهم، كما يفعل بدعوته ودينه ما يشاء. وينتهي بهم إلى نهاية من تلك النهايات التي عرفها تاريخ الإيمان، أو إلى غيرها مما يعلمه هو وراءه.

إنهم أجراء عند الله. أينما وحيثما وكيفما أرادهم أن يعملوا، عملوا وقبضوا الأجر المعلوم. وليس لهم ولا عليهم أن تتجه الدعوة إلى أي مصير، فذلك شأن صاحب الأمر لا شأن الأجير.

وهم يقبضون الدفعة الأولى طمأنينة في القلب، ورفعة في الشعور، وجمالا في التصور، وانطلاقا من الأوهاق والجواذب، وتحررا من الخوف والقلق، في كل حال من الأحوال.

وهم يقبضون الدفعة الثانية ثناء في الملأ الأعلى وذكرا وكرامة، وهم بعد في هذه الأرض الصغيرة.

ثم هم يقبضون الدفعة الكبرى في الآخرة حسابا يسيرا ونعيما كبيرا.

ومع كل دفعة ما هو أكبر منها جميعا. رضوان الله، وانهم مختارون ليكونوا أداة لقدره وستارا لقدرته، يفعل بهم في الأرض ما يشاء.

وهكذا انتهت التربية القرآنية بالفئة المختارة من المسلمين في الصدر الأول إلى هذا التطور، الذي أطلقهم من أمر ذواتهم وشخوصهم. فأخرجوا أنفسهم من الأمر البتة، وعملوا أجراء عند صاحب الأمر ورضوا خيرة الله على أي وضع وعلى أي حال.

وكانت التربية النبوية تتمشى مع التوجيهات القرآنية، وتوجه القلوب والأنظار إلى الجنة، وإلى الصبر على الدور المختار حتى يأذن الله بما يشاء في الدنيا والآخرة سواء.

كان - صلى الله عليه وسلم - يرى عمارا وأمه وأباه - رضي الله عنهم - يعذبون العذاب الشديد في مكة، فما يزيد على أن يقول: "صبرا آل ياسر. موعدكم الجنة ".

وعن خباب بن الأرث - رضي الله عنه - قال: شكونا إلى رسول الله - صلى الله عليه وسلم - وهو متوسد بردة في ظل الكعبة، فقلنا: ألا تستنصر لنا؟ أو تدعو لنا؟ فقال: "قد كان من قبلكم يؤخذ الرجل فيحفر له في الأرض فيجعل فيها، ثم يؤتى بالمنشار فيوضع على رأسه فيجعل نصفين. ويمشط بأمشاط الحديد ما دون لحمه وعظمه. ما يبعده ذلك عن دينه. والله ليتممن الله تعالى هذا الأمر حتى يسير الراكب من صنعاء إلى حضرموت، فلا يخاف إلا الله، والذئب على غنمه، ولكنكم تستعجلون ". [أخرجه البخاري].

إن لله حكمة وراء كل وضع ووراء كل حال، ومدبر هذا الكون كله، المطلع على أوله وآخره، المنسق لأحداثه وروابطه. هو الذي يعرف الحكمة المكونة في غيبه المستور، الحكمة التي تتفق مع مشيئته في خط السير الطويل.

وفي بعض الأحيان يكشف لنا - بعد أجيال وقرون - عن حكمة حادث لم يكن معاصروه يدركون حكمته، ولعلهم كانوا يسألون لماذا؟ لماذا يا رب يقع هذا؟ وهذا السؤال نفسه هو الجهل الذي يتوقاه المؤمن. لأنه يعرف ابتداء أن هناك حكمة وراء كل قدر، ولأن سعة المجال في تصوره، وبعد المدى في الزمان والمكان والقيم والموازين تغنيه عن التفكير ابتداء في مثل هذا السؤال. فيسير مع دورة القدر في استسلام واطمئنان.

لقد كان القرآن ينشئ قلوبا يعدها لحمل الأمانة، وهذه القلوب كان يجب أن تكون من الصلابة والقوة والتجرد بحيث لا تتطلع - وهي تبذل كل شيء، وتحتمل كل شيء - إلى شيء في هذه الأرض، ولا تنظر إلا إلى الآخرة، ولا ترجو إلا رضوان الله، قلوبا مستعدة لقطع رحلة الأرض كلها في نصب وشقاء وحرمان وعذاب وتضحية حتى الموت. بلا جزاء في هذه الأرض قريب، ولوكان هذا الجزاء هو انتصار الدعوة، وغلبة الإسلام وظهور المسلمين، بل لوكان هذا الجزاء هو هلاك الظالمين بأخذهم أخذ عزيز مقتدركما فعل بالمكذبين الأولين.

حتى إذا وجدت هذه القلوب، التي تعلم أن ليس أمامها في رحلة الأرض إلا أن تعطي بلا مقابل - أي مقابل - وأن تنتظر الآخرة وحدها موعدا للفصل بين الحق والباطل. حتى إذا

وجدت هذه القلوب، وعلم الله منها صدق نيتها على ما بايعت وعاهدت، آتاها النصر في الأرض، وائتمنها عليه. لا لنفسها، ولكن لتقوم بأمانة المنهج الإلهي وهي أهل لأداء الأمانة منذ كانت لم توعد بشيء من المغنم في الدنيا تتقاضاه، ولم تتطلع إلى شئ من الغنم في الأرض تعطاه. وقد تجردت لله حقا يوم كانت لا تعلم لها جزاء إلا رضاه.

وكل الآيات التي ذكر فيها النصر، وذكر فيها المغانم، وذكر فيها أخذ المشركين في الأرض بأيدي المؤمنين نزلت في المدينة. بعد ذلك. وبعد أن أصبحت هذه الأمور خارج برنامج المؤمن وانتظاره وتطلعه. وجاء النصر ذاته لأن مشيئة الله اقتضت أن تكون لهذا المنهج واقعية في الحياة الإنسانية، تقررها في صورة عملية محددة تراها الأجيال. فلم يكن جزاء على التعب والنصب والتضحية والآلام، إنما كان قدرا من قدر الله تكمن وراءه حكمة نحاول رؤيتها الآن.

وهذه اللفتة جديرة بأن يتدبرها الدعاة إلى الله، في كل أرض وفي كل جيل. فهي كفيلة بأن تريهم معالم الطريق واضحة بلا غبش، وأن تثبت خطى الذين يريدون أن يقطعوا الطريق إلى نهايته، كيفما كانت هذه النهاية. ثم يكون قدر الله بدعوته وبهم ما يكون، فلا يتلفتون في أثناء الطريق الدامي المفروش بالجماجم والأشلاء، وبالعرق والدماء، إلى نصر أو غلبة، أو فيصل بين الحق والباطل في هذه الأرض. ولكن إذا كان الله يريد أن يصنع بهم شيئا من هذا لدعوته ولدينه فسيتم ما يريده الله. لا جزاء على الآلام والتضحيات. لا، فالأرض ليست دار جزاء. وإنما تحقيقا لقدر الله في أمر دعوته ومنهجه على أيدي ناس من عباده يختارهم ليمضي بهم من الأمر ما يشاء، وحسبهم هذا الاختيار الكريم، الذي تهون إلى جانبه وتصغر هذه الحياة، وكل ما يقع في رحلة الأرض من سراء أو ضراء.

هنالك حقيقة أخرى يشير إليها أحد التعقيبات القرآنية على قصة الأخدود في قوله تعالى:

(وَمَا نَقَمُوا مِنْهُمْ إِلَّا أَنْ يُؤْمِنُوا بِاللهِ الْعَزِيزِ الْحَمِيدِ).

حقيقة ينبغي أن يتأملها المؤمنون الداعون إلى الله في كل أرض وفي كل جيل.

إن المعركة بين المؤمنين وخصومهم هي في صميمها معركة عقيدة وليست شيئا آخر على الإطلاق. وإن خصومهم لا ينقمون منهم إلا الإيمان، ولا يسخطون منهم إلا العقيدة.

إنها ليست معركة سياسية ولا معركة اقتصادية، ولا معركة عنصرية. ولو كانت شيئا من هذا لسهل وقفها، وسهل حل إشكالها. ولكنها في صميمها معركة عقيدة - إما كفر وإما إيمان. إما جاهلية وإما إسلام.

ولقد كان كبار المشركين يعرضون على رسول الله - صلى الله عليه وسلم - المال والحكم والمتاع في مقابل شيء واحد، أن يدع معركة العقيدة وأن يدهن في هذا الأمر. ولو أجابهم - حاشاه - إلى شيء مما أرادوا ما بقيت بينهم وبينه معركة على الإطلاق.

إنها قضية عقيدة ومعركة عقيدة. وهذا ما يجب أن يستيقنه المؤمنون حيثما واجهوا عدوا لهم. فإنه لا يعاديهم لشيء إلا لهذه العقيدة "إلا أن يؤمنوا بالله العزيز الحميد" ويخلصوا له وحده الطاعة والخضوع.

وقد يحاول أعداء المؤمنين أن يرفعوا للمعركة راية غير راية العقيدة، راية اقتصادية أو سياسية أو عنصرية، كي يموهوا على المؤمنين حقيقة المعركة، ويطفئوا في أرواحهم شعلة العقيدة. فمن واجب المؤمنين ألا يُخدعوا، ومن واجبهم أن يدركوا أن هذا تمويه لغرض مبيت. وأن الذي يغير راية المعركة إنما يريد أن يخدعهم عن سلاح النصر الحقيقي فيها، النصر في أية صورة من الصور، سواء جاء في صورة الانطلاق الروحي كما وقع للمؤمنين في حادث الأخدود، أو في صورة الهيمنة - الناشئة من الانطلاق الروحي - كما حدث للجيل الأول من المسلمين.

ونحن نشهد نموذجا من تمويه الراية في محاولة الصليبية العالمية اليوم أن تخدعنا عن حقيقة المعركة، وأن تزور التاريخ، فتزعم لنا أن الحروب الصليبية كانت ستارا للاستعمار. كلا. إنما كان الاستعمار الذي جاء متأخرا هو الستار للروح الصليبية التي لم تعد قادرة على السفور كما كانت في القرون الوسطى. والتي تحطمت على صخرة العقيدة بقيادة مسلمين من شتى العناصر، وفيهم صلاح الدين الكردي، وتوران شاه المملوكي، العناصر التي نسيت قوميتها وذكرت عقيدتها فانتصرت تحت راية العقيدة.

(وما نقمُوا مِنْهُمْ إلا أنْ يُؤْمِنُوا بِاللهِ الْعَزِيزِ الْحمِيدِ).

وصدق الله العظيم، وكذب المموهون الخادعون.

معالم في الطريق

سيد قطب

www.ingramcontent.com/pod-product-compliance
Lightning Source LLC
Chambersburg PA
CBHW071956260326
41914CB00004B/821

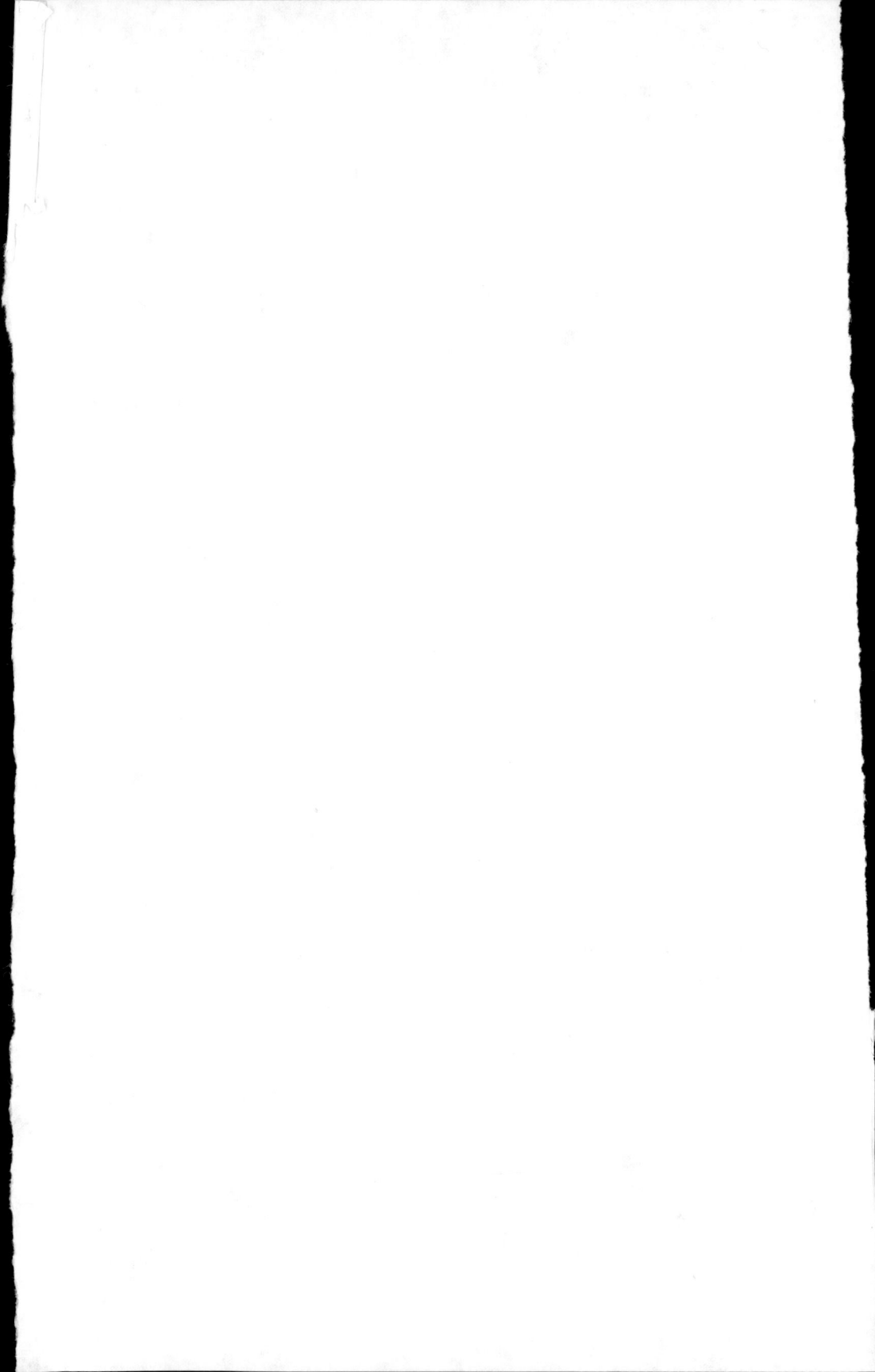